EARTH FROM ABOVE
LA TIERRA VISTA DESDE EL CIELO
LA TERRE VUE DU CIEL

Yann Arthus-Bertrand

NUESTRA TIERRA ES ARTE, Y EL FOTÓGRAFO ES SOLAMENTE EL TESTIGO DE ESTO.

La aceleración descontrolada de nuestra historia demográfica e industrial transforma radicalmente el paisaje de nuestro planeta.

Durante los últimos once años, he fotografiado la Tierra tratando de "mostrar" de manera simple y auténtica. Estas son las cualidades que prefiero en la fotografía. Durante estos miles de horas de vuelo, con mi cámara en las manos, es mucho lo que he recibido y me siento feliz de poder compartirlo con ustedes.

Esta visión del mundo no habría podido realizarse sin la ayuda de la UNESCO, de FUJIFILM, de CORBIS, de AIR FRANCE y de EUROCOPTER, copartícipes que se involucraron de manera particular en este proyecto.

Gracias por su confianza y por su amistad.

OUR EARTH IS ART, THE PHOTOGRAPHER IS ONLY A WITNESS.

The unbridled acceleration of our demographic and industrial history is radically changing the face of our planet.

For the past eleven years, I've been photographing the Earth and trying to "show" it in a simple and genuine manner, which are qualities I prefer in photography. During these thousands of hours I spent flying, camera in hand, I received a tremendous amount and it's my pleasure to share what I have learned with you.

This view of the world would not have been possible without the assistance of UNESCO, FUJIFILM, CORBIS, AIR FRANCE and EUROCOPTER, who all dedicated a great deal of effort to the project.

I thank them for their trust and friendship.

NOTRE TERRE EST ART, LE PHOTOGRAPHE EN EST SEULEMENT LE TÉMOIN.

L'accélération incontrôlée de notre histoire démographique et industrielle transforme radicalement le paysage de notre planète.

Pendant ces onze dernières années, j'ai photographié la Terre en essayant de « montrer » avec simplicité et authenticité, qualités que je préfère dans la photographie. Pendant ces milliers d'heures de vol, mon boîtier dans les mains, j'ai beaucoup reçu et suis heureux de vous faire partager cette vision du monde.

Ce travail n'aurait pas pu se faire sans l'aide de l'UNESCO, de FUJIFILM, de CORBIS, d'AIR FRANCE et d'EUROCOPTER, des partenaires qui se sont investis particulièrement dans ce projet.

Merci de leur confiance et de leur amitié.

Yann Arthus-Bertrand nos invita a viajar a través de las realidades del mundo. Sus fotografías aéreas reflejan la variedad de los medios naturales y de las expresiones de la vida, pero también la huella del hombre y los efectos nocivos que ha provocado en su ámbito natural. El presente trabajo constituye una "evaluación" del planeta en este inicio de milenio.

El conjunto indisoluble de las fotografías y de los textos que las acompañan y las complementan, nos invita a reflexionar sobre la evolución del planeta y sobre el futuro de sus habitantes.

Como fotógrafo testigo, Yann Arthus-Bertrand quiso dirigirse a la gran mayoría, a los ciudadanos de todos los países. Su proyecto enfatiza que, hoy más que nunca, los niveles y los modos actuales de consumo, de producción y de explotación de los recursos no son viables a largo plazo. Ilustra una etapa decisiva, en la que la alternativa que ofrece el desarrollo sustentable debe contribuir a provocar los cambios que permitirán "responder a las necesidades del presente sin comprometer la capacidad de las generaciones futuras de responder a las suyas". Los cambios, el compromiso efectivo sobre la vía del desarrollo sustentable, no dependen solamente de la voluntad de los gobiernos y de los poderosos de este mundo. Cada uno de nosotros, en forma individual, tiene un papel que desempeñar en el futuro del planeta, cada uno de nosotros tiene el poder y el deber de actuar y de movilizarse, masivamente, para influir en las personas responsables de tomar decisiones. Con estas imagenes, Yann Arthus-Bertrand nos ofrece los medios para tomar conciencia.

Fruto de un paciente trabajo de encuesta iniciado en 1990, que representa 3 000 horas de horas de vuelo en helicóptero y la visita a 85 países, estas fotografías, seleccionadas entre miles de tomas, deben su poder de emoción y de evocación a la mirada de Yann Arthus-Bertrand y a su preocupación por servir de testimonio para las generaciones futuras. Este trabajo no representa un fin en sí misma, sino una etapa importante en un proyecto destinado a continuar. Aún quedan decenas de países por recorrer, y gracias a las coordenadas geográficas de cada toma, otros fotógrafos podrán regresar a los mismos lugares y proseguir con este ambicioso proyecto.

Yann Arthus-Bertrand invites us to take a journey with him through the realities of the world. His aerial photographs reflect the variety of natural habitats and expressions of life, but also man's imprint and assault on his environment. This work constitutes a "state of the planet" at the beginning of this new millennium.

The indissociable collection of photographs and texts that accompany and complete them, invites each of us to think about the changes in the planet and the future of its inhabitants.

As a witness photographer, Yann Arthus-Bertrand wishes to address as many citizens of all countries as possible. This work underlines the fact that, more than ever, our present levels and styles of consumption, production and exploitation of resources are not viable over the long term. It illustrates a decisive stage at which the alternatives offered by sustainable development must help bring about changes that will make it possible to "answer the needs of the present without compromising the capacity of future generations to answer theirs." These changes, this efficient undertaking of a commitment to sustainable development, depend only on the wills of governments and those in power around the world. Each of us, individually, has a role to play in the future of the planet; each has the power and the duty to act and to rally, en masse, in order to influence the decision-makers. With these images, Yann Arthus-Bertrand offers us the way to such awareness.

Fruit of patient research work begun in 1990, representing 3,000 hours of flying-time by helicopter and 85 countries visited, these photographs, chosen from thousands of shots, owe their emotional and evocative power to Yann Arthus-Bertrand's eye and to his desire to be a witness for generations to come. This work is not an end in itself but an important stage in an ongoing project. There still remains several countries to visit, and thanks to the geographical coordinates of every shot, other photographers will be able to find the same sites and continue this ambitious undertaking.

Yann Arthus-Bertrand nous convie à un voyage à travers les réalités du monde. Ses photographies aériennes reflètent la variété des milieux naturels et des expressions de la vie, mais aussi l'empreinte de l'homme et les atteintes à son environnement. Ce travail constitue un « état des lieux » de la planète en ce début de millénaire.

L'ensemble indissociable des photographies et des textes qui les accompagnent et les complètent, invite chacun à réfléchir à l'évolution de la planète et au devenir de ses habitants.

Photographe témoin, Yann Arthus-Bertrand a souhaité s'adresser au plus grand nombre, aux citoyens de tous les pays. Ce travail souligne que, plus que jamais, les niveaux et modes actuels de consommation, de production et d'exploitation des ressources, ne sont pas viables à long terme. Elle illustre une étape décisive, où l'alternative qu'offre le développement durable doit aider à provoquer les changements qui permettront de « répondre aux besoins du présent sans compromettre la capacité des générations futures de répondre aux leurs ». Ces changements, cet engagement effectif dans la voie du développement durable, ne dépendent pas que des volontés des gouvernements et des puissants de ce monde. Chacun, individuellement, a un rôle à jouer pour l'avenir de la planète, chacun a le pouvoir et le devoir d'agir et de se mobiliser, en masse, pour influencer les décideurs. Par ces images, Yann Arthus-Bertrand nous offre les moyens de cette prise de conscience.

Fruit d'un patient travail d'enquête entamé en 1990, représentant 3000 heures de vol en hélicoptère et 85 pays visités, ces photographies, choisies parmi des milliers de prises de vues, doivent leur puissance d'émotion et d'évocation à l'œil de Yann Arthus-Bertrand et à son souci de témoigner pour les générations futures. Ce travail n'est pas une fin en soi mais une étape importante dans un projet appelé à se poursuivre. Il reste des dizaines de pays à parcourir, et grâce aux coordonnées géographiques de chaque prise de vue, d'autres photographes pourront retrouver les mêmes sites et prolonger cette ambitieuse entreprise.

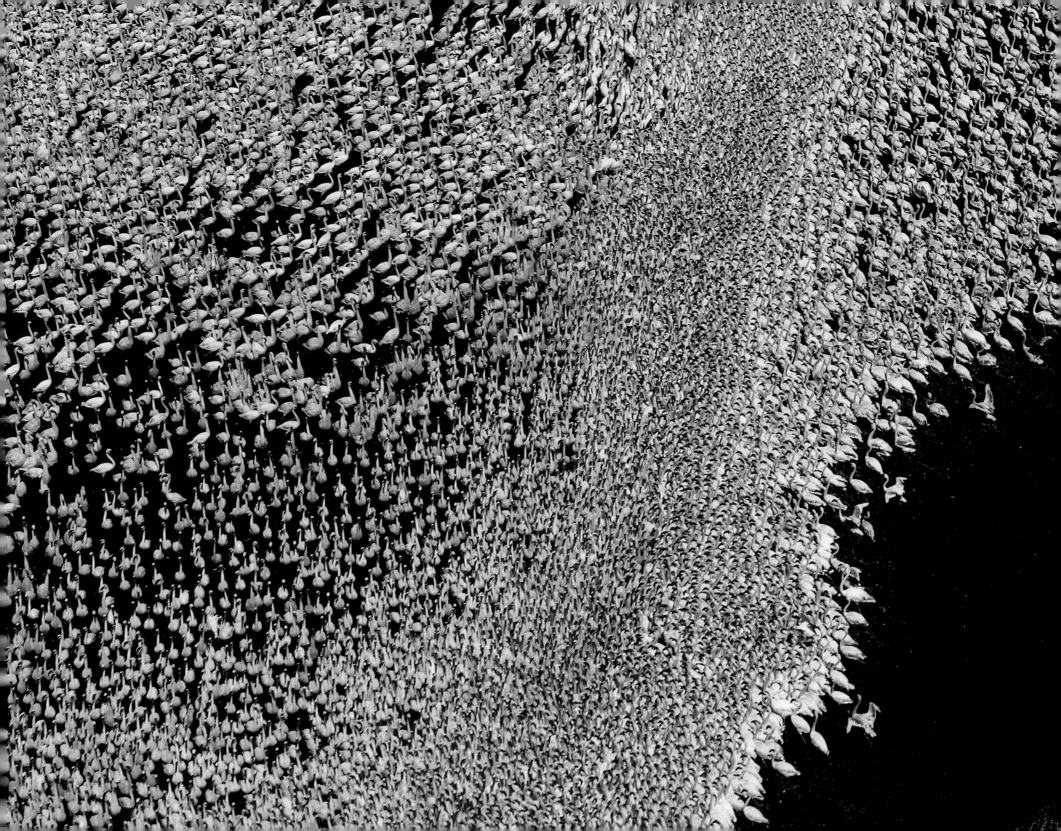

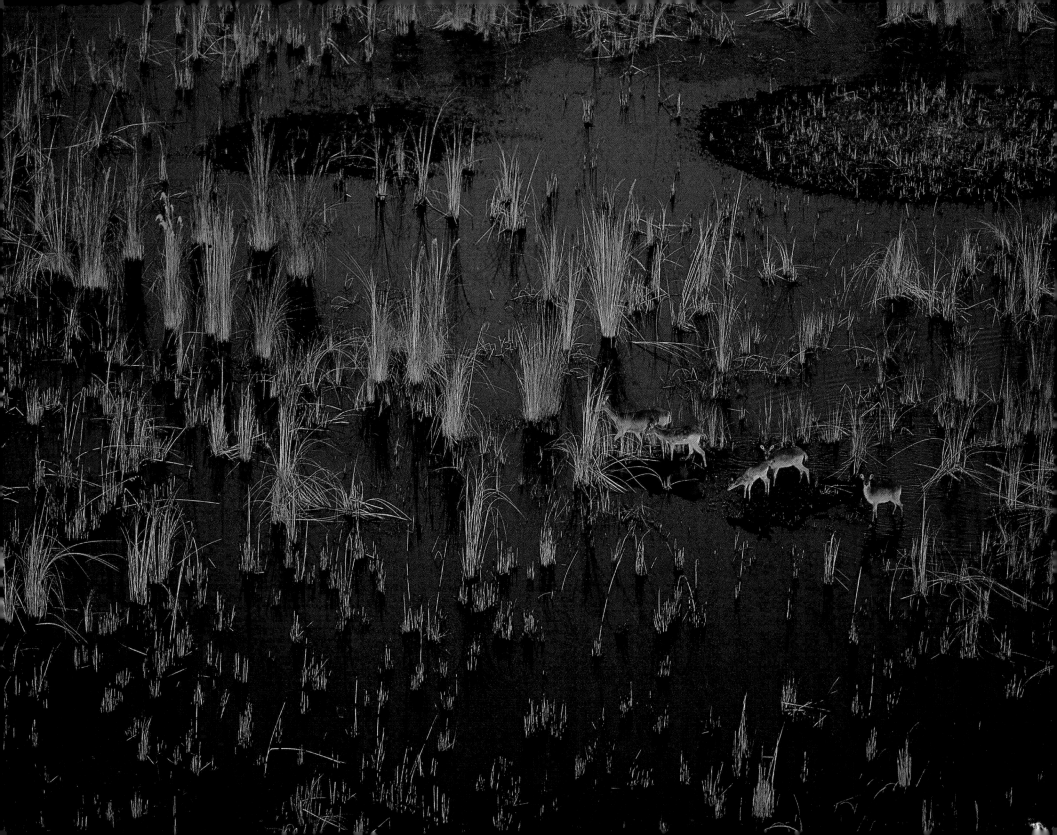

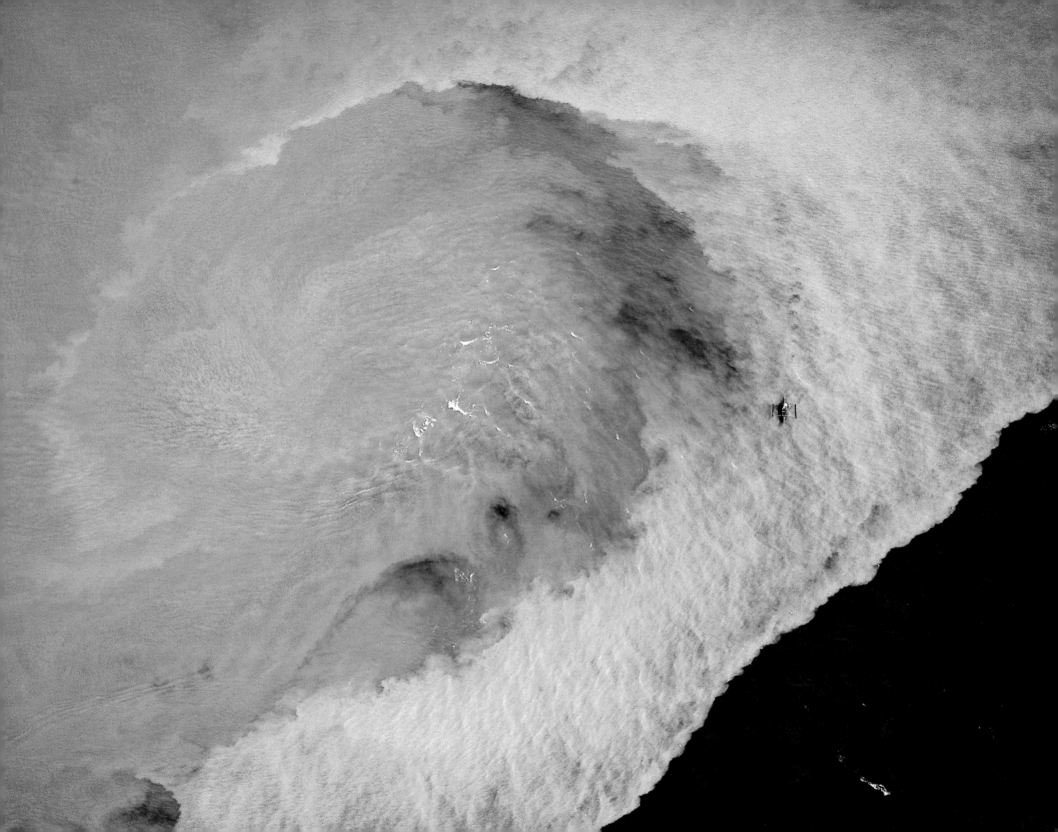

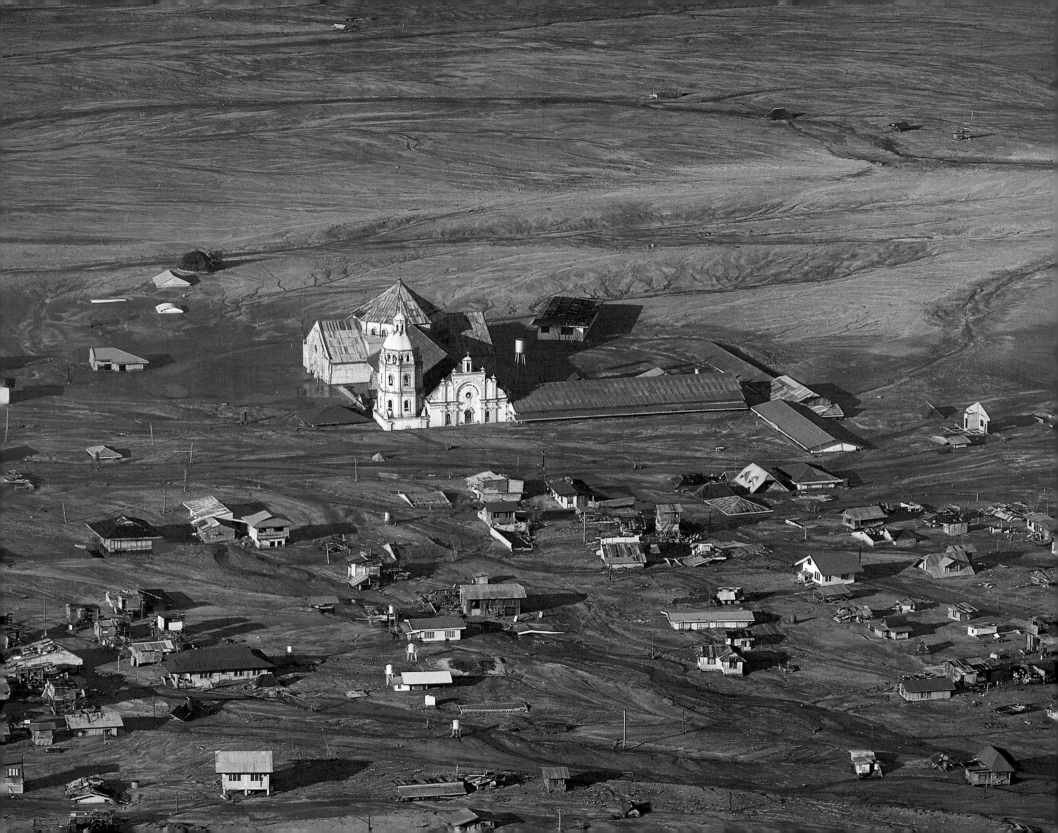

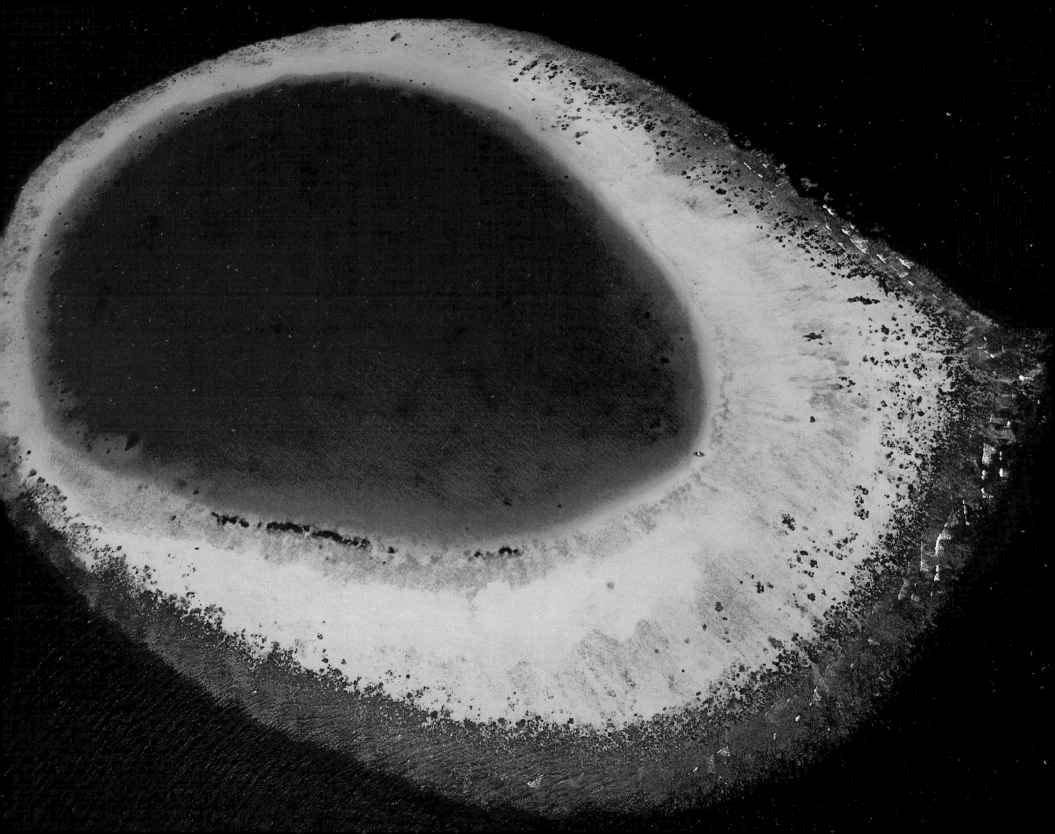

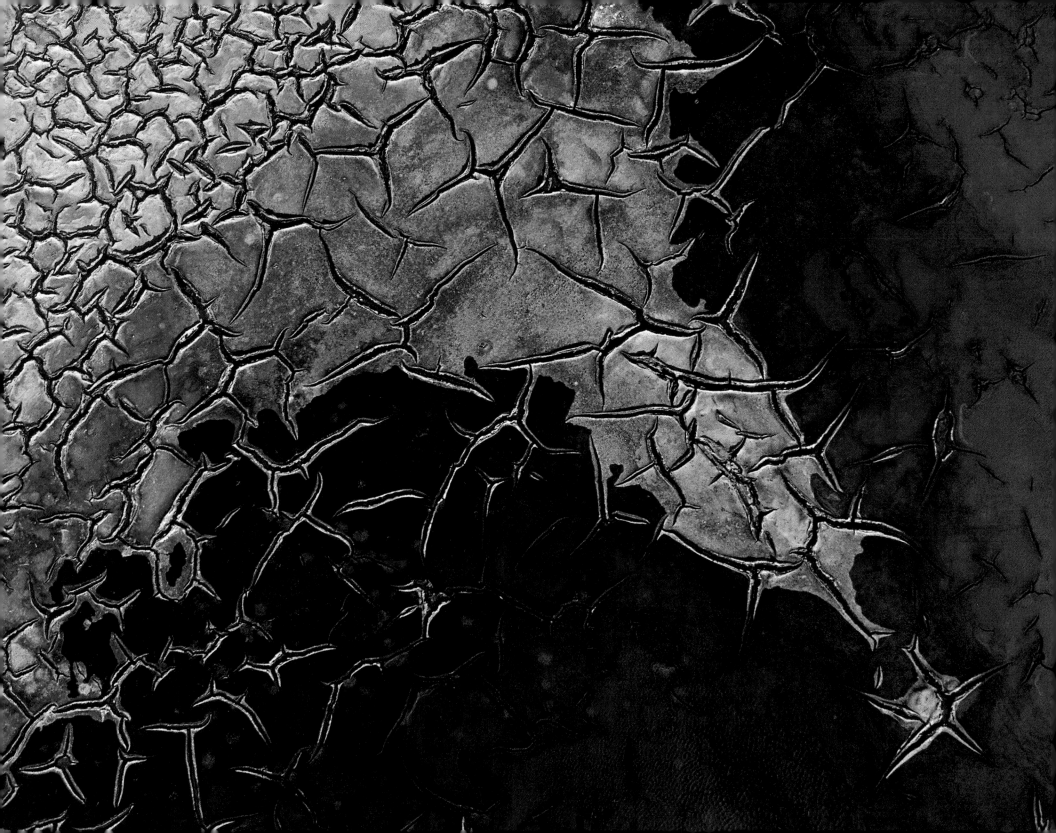

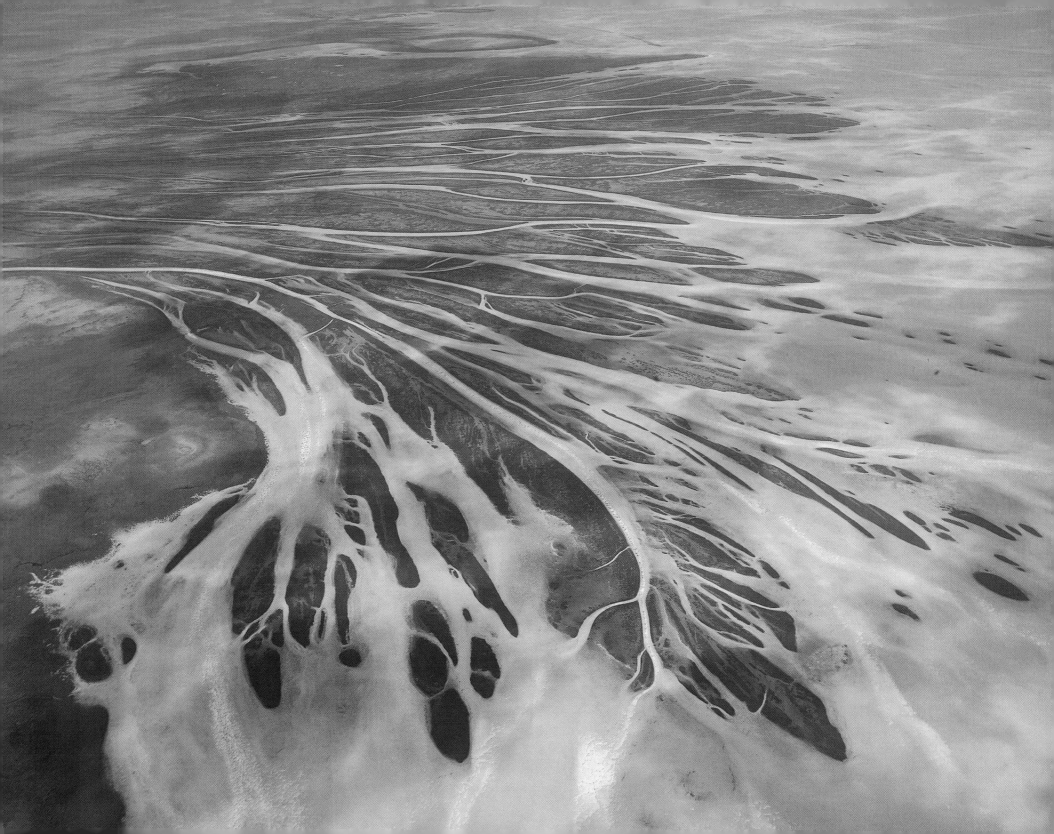

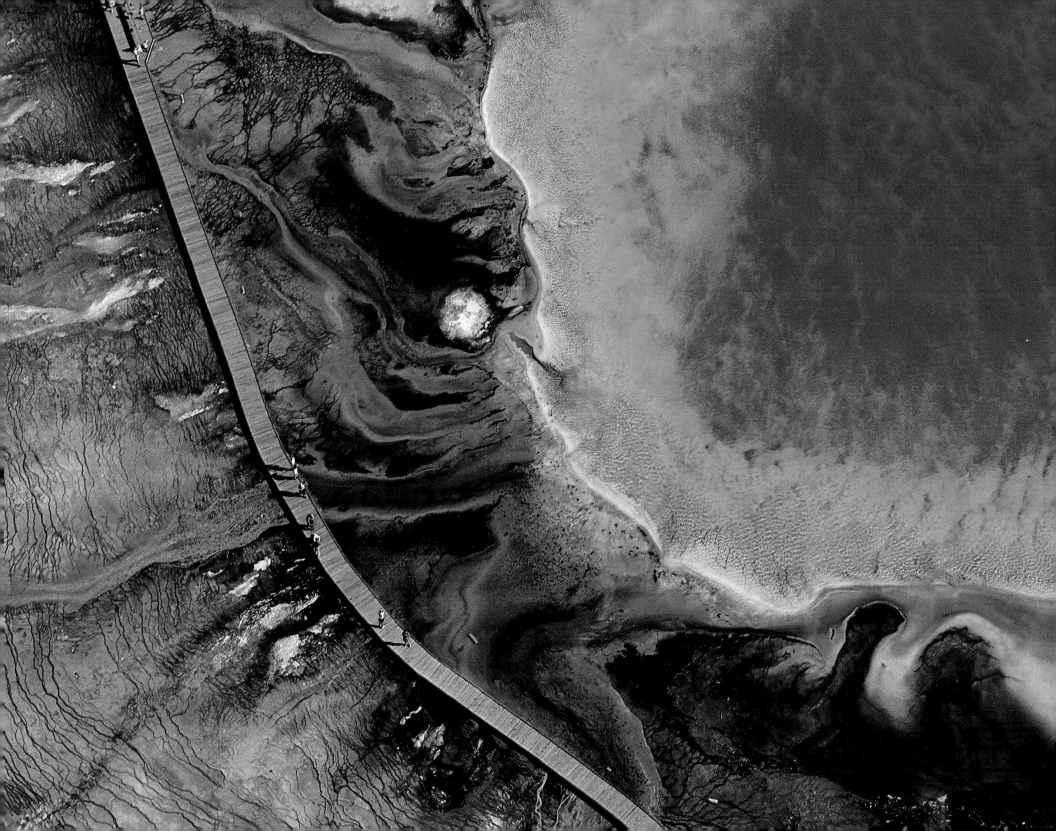

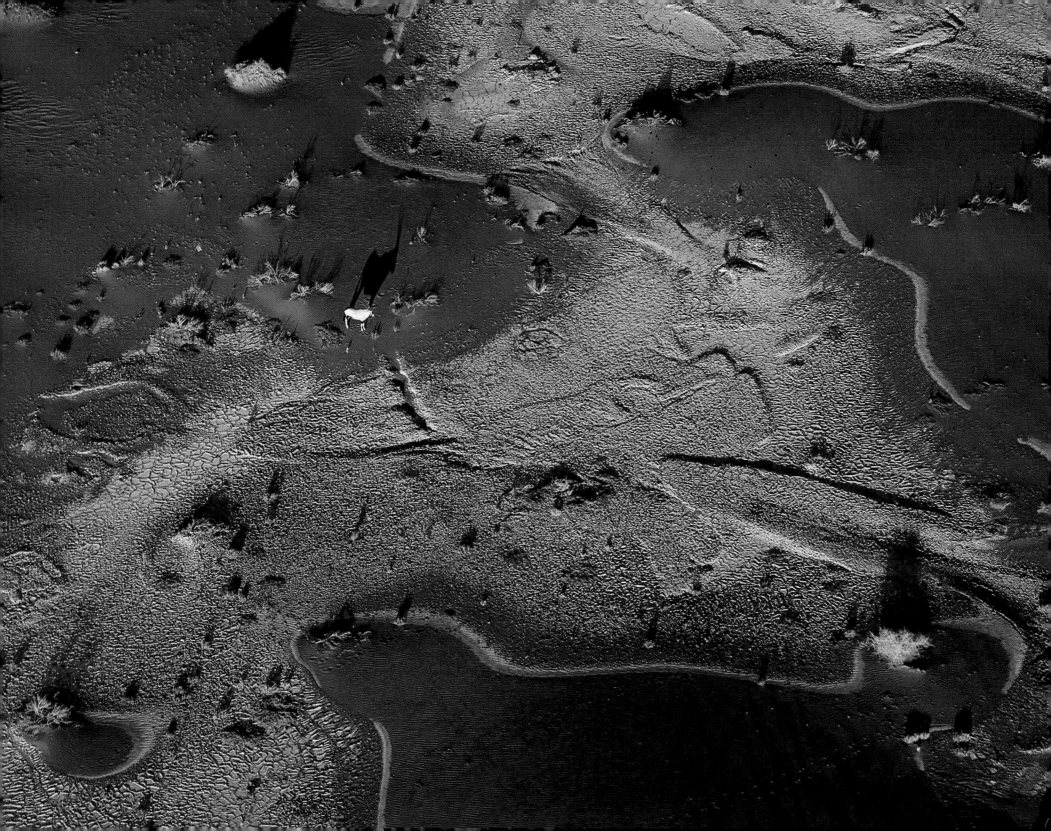

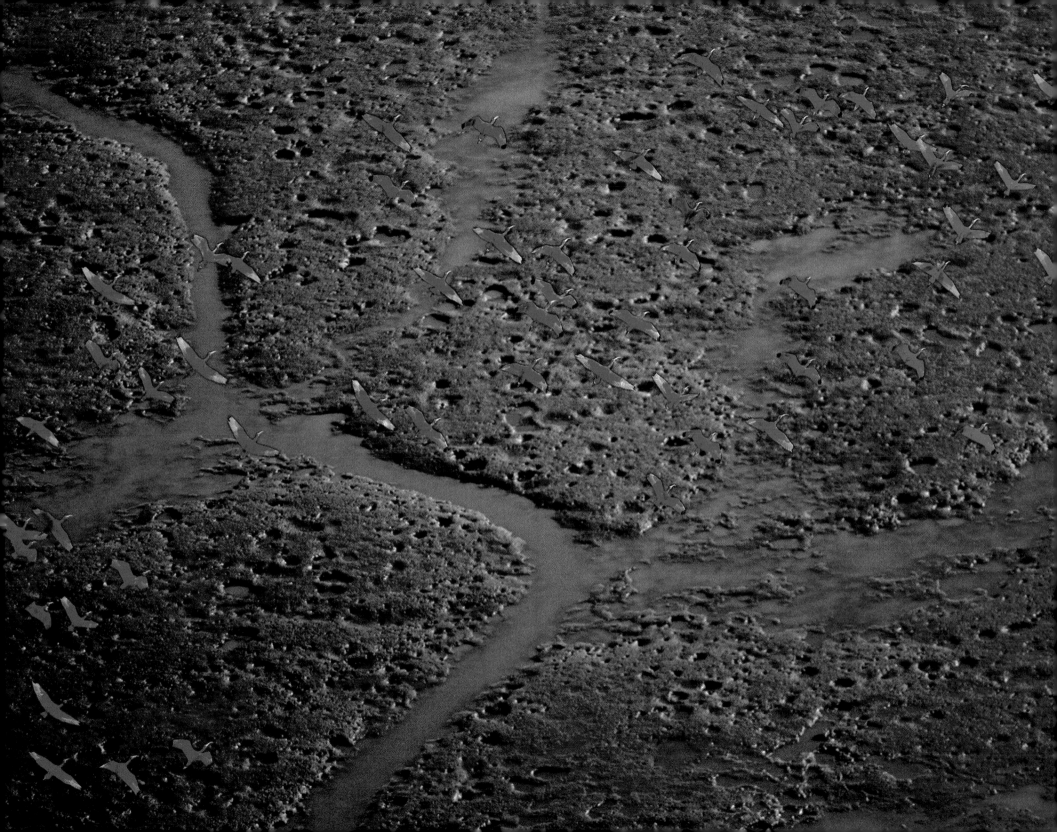

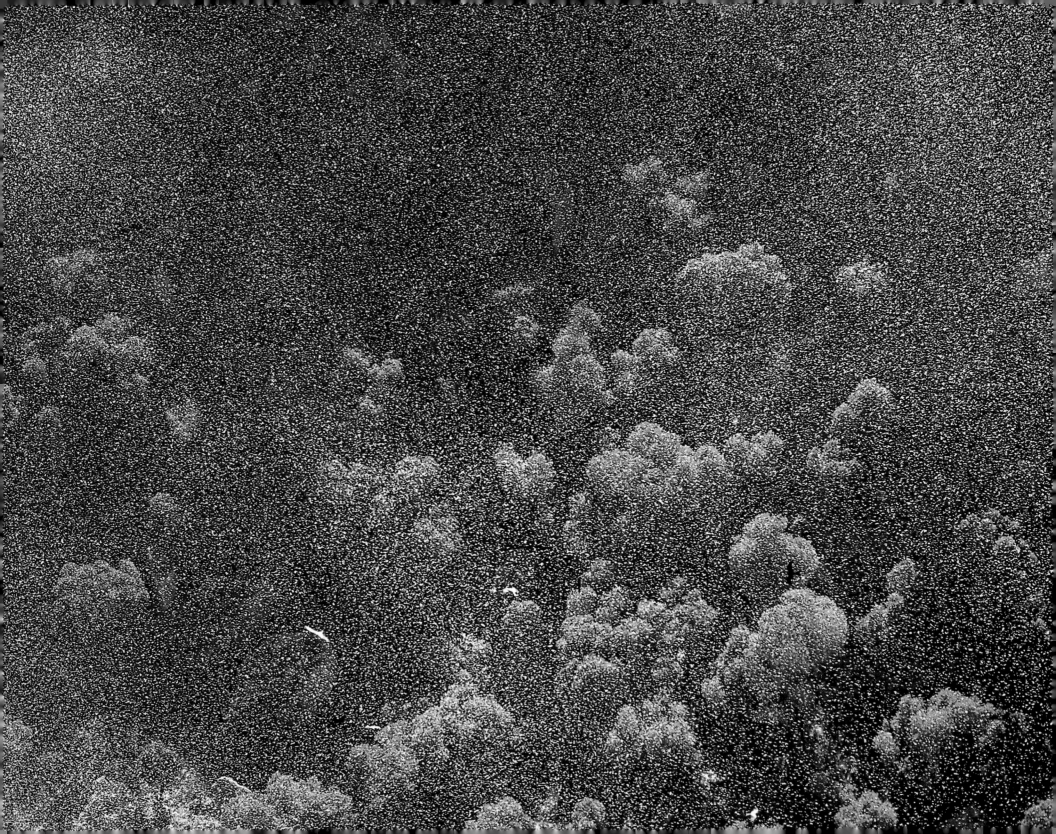

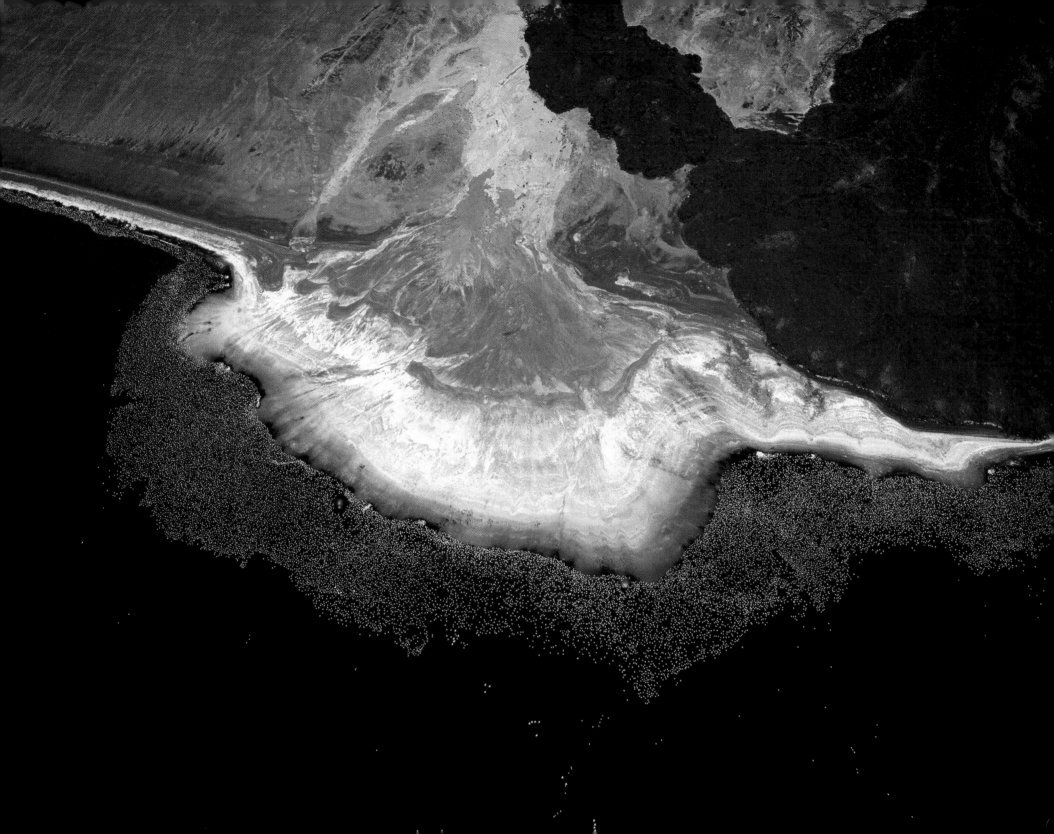

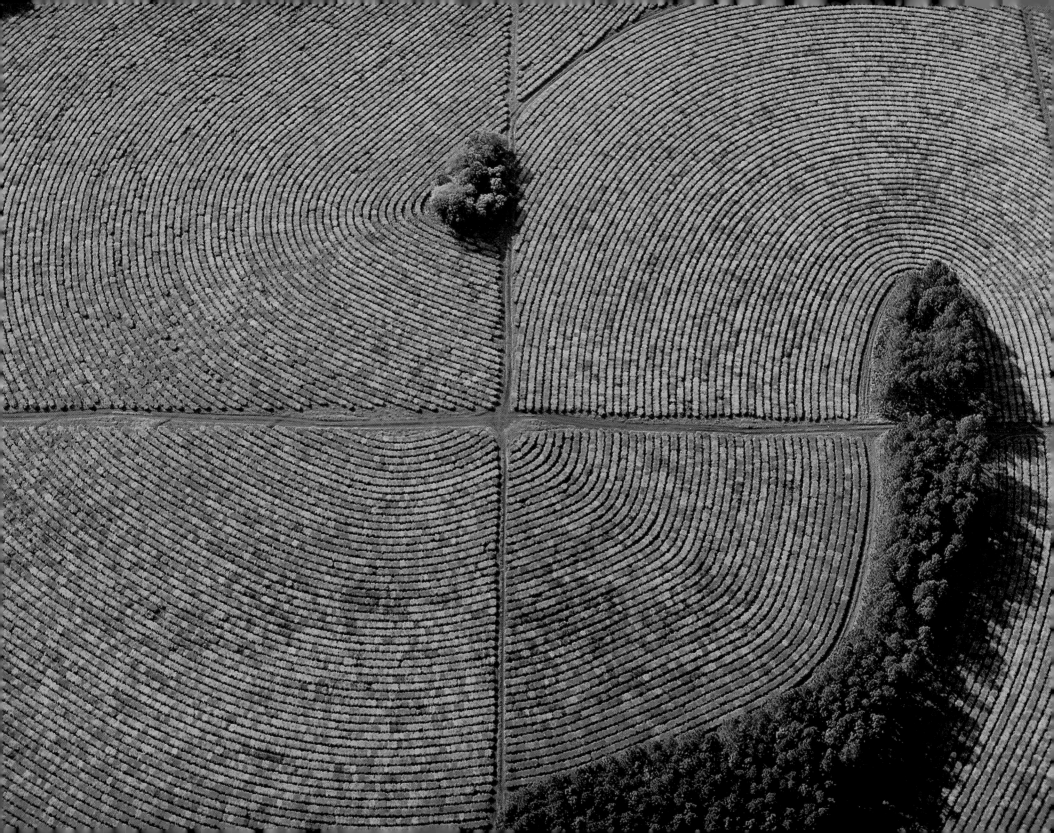

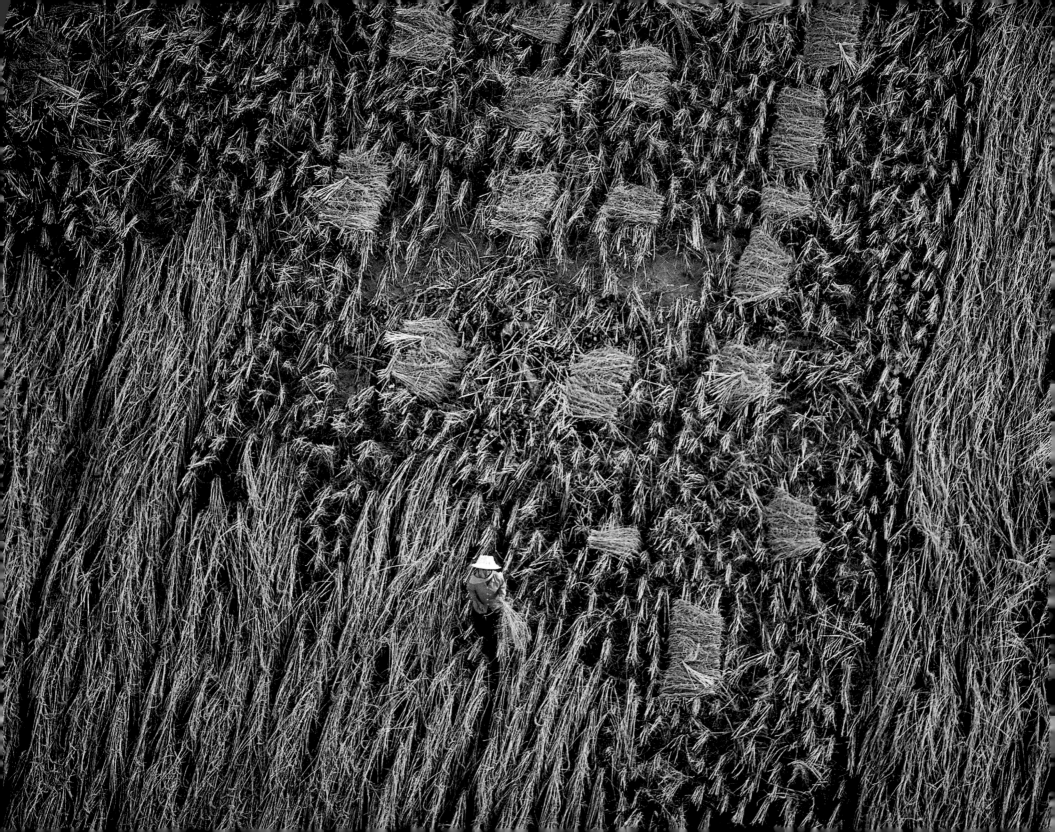

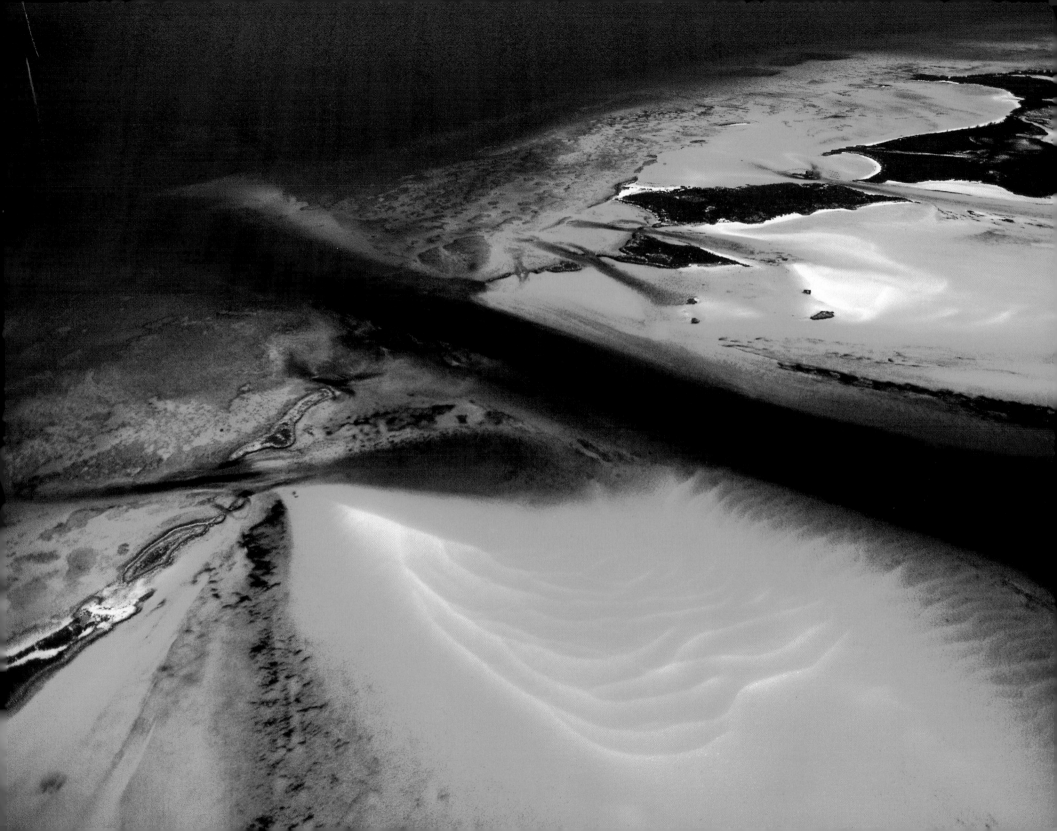

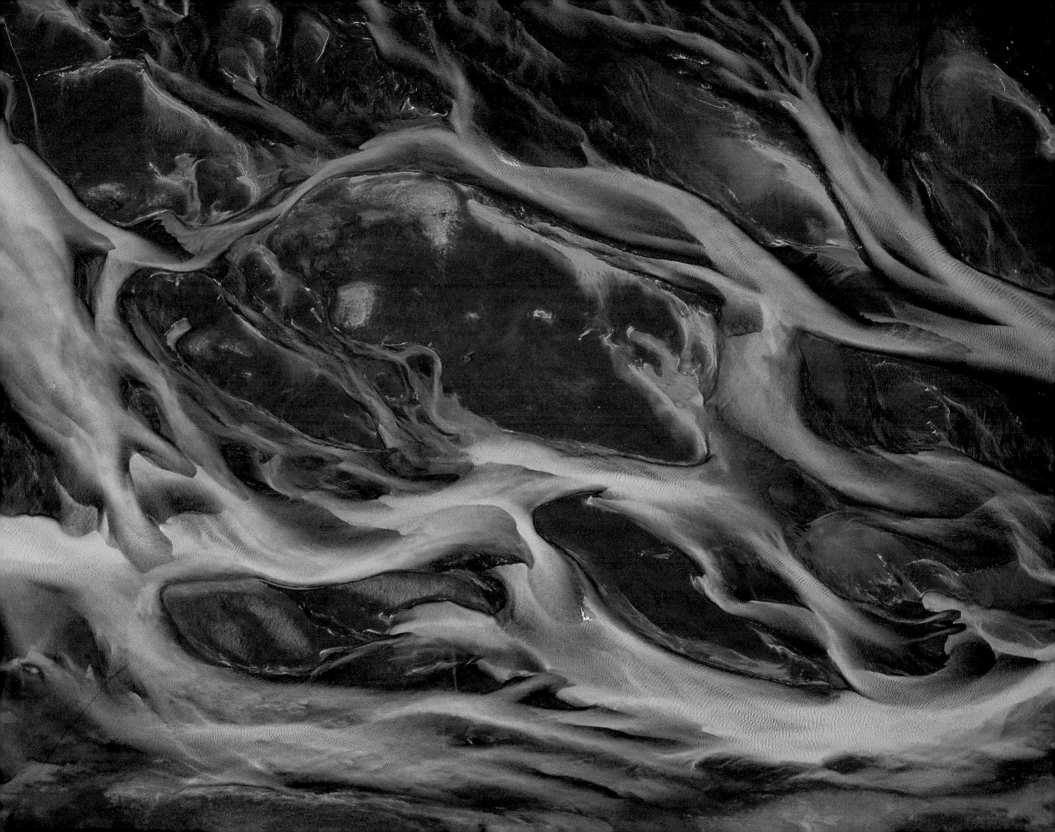

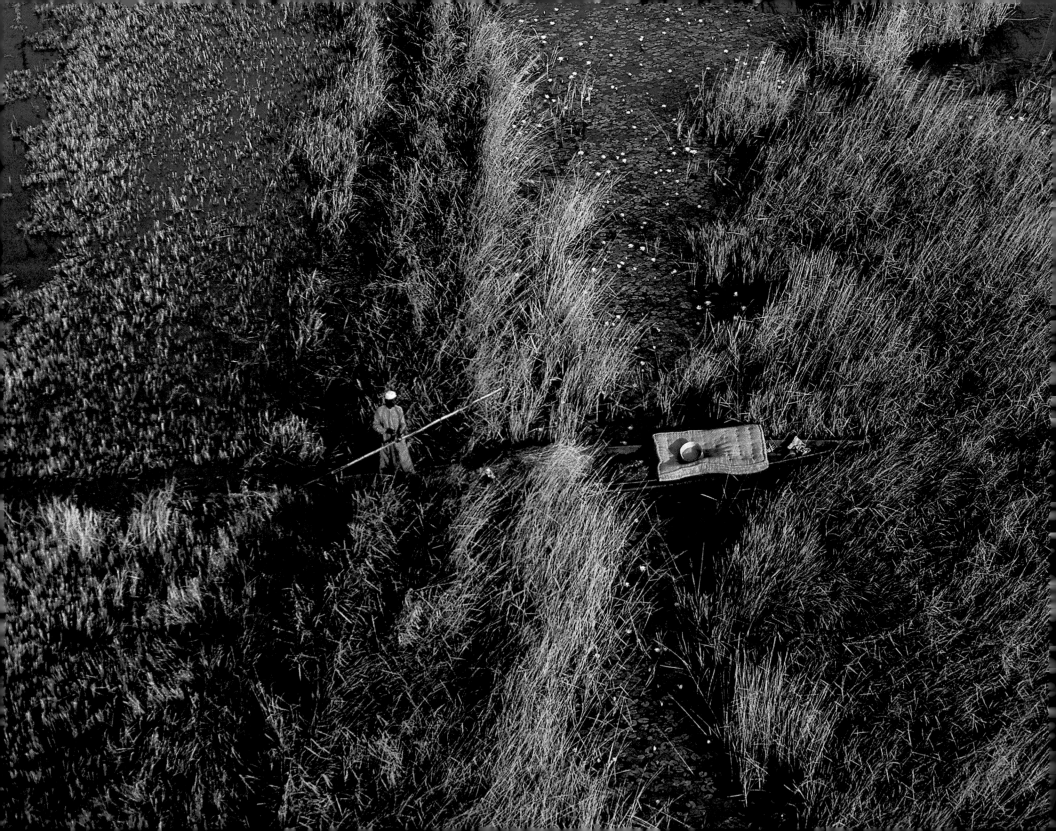

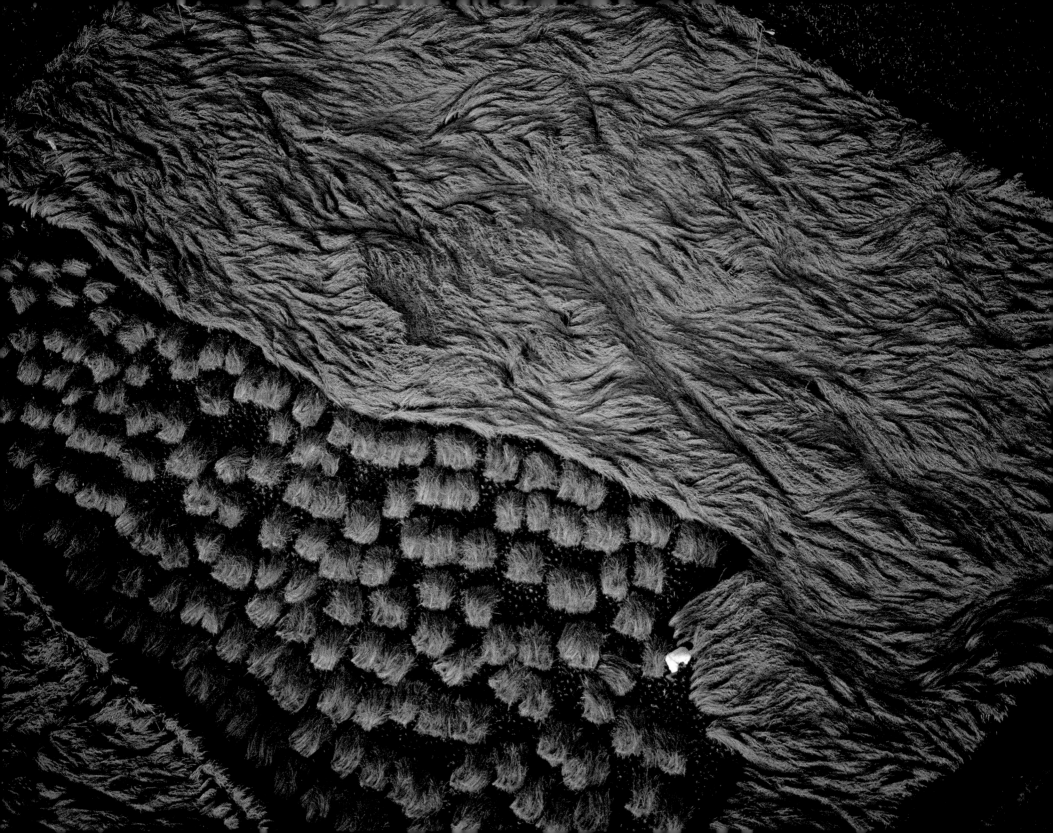

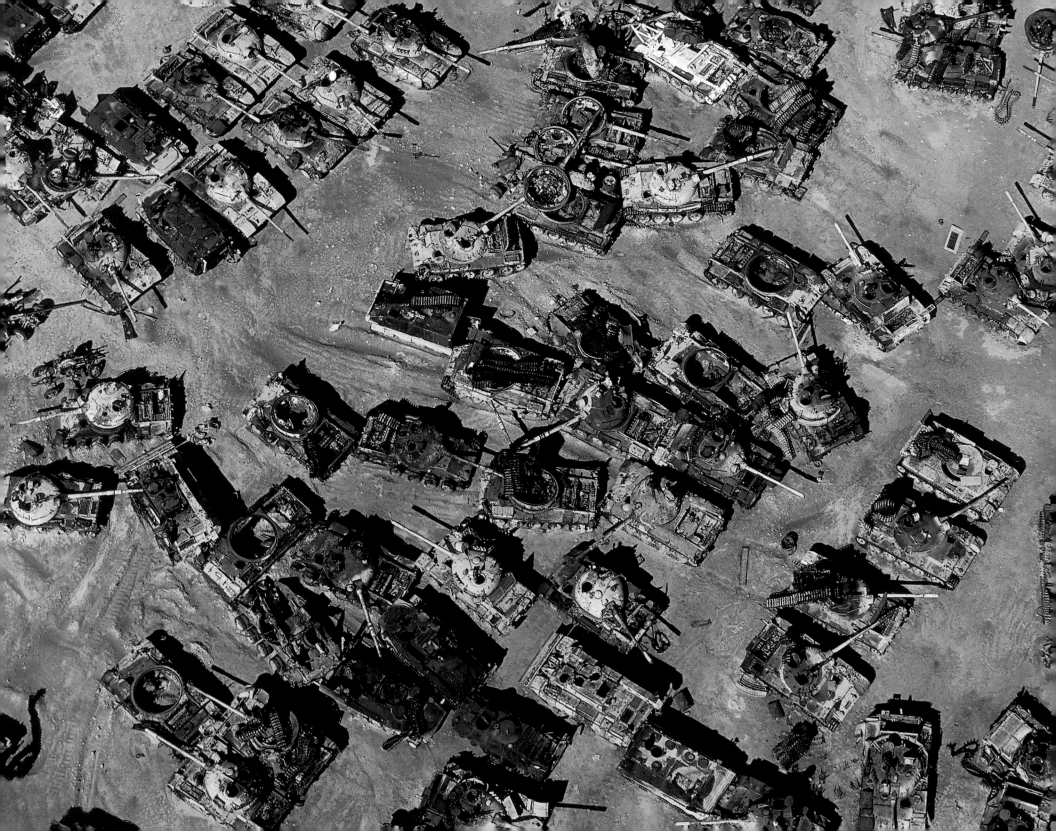

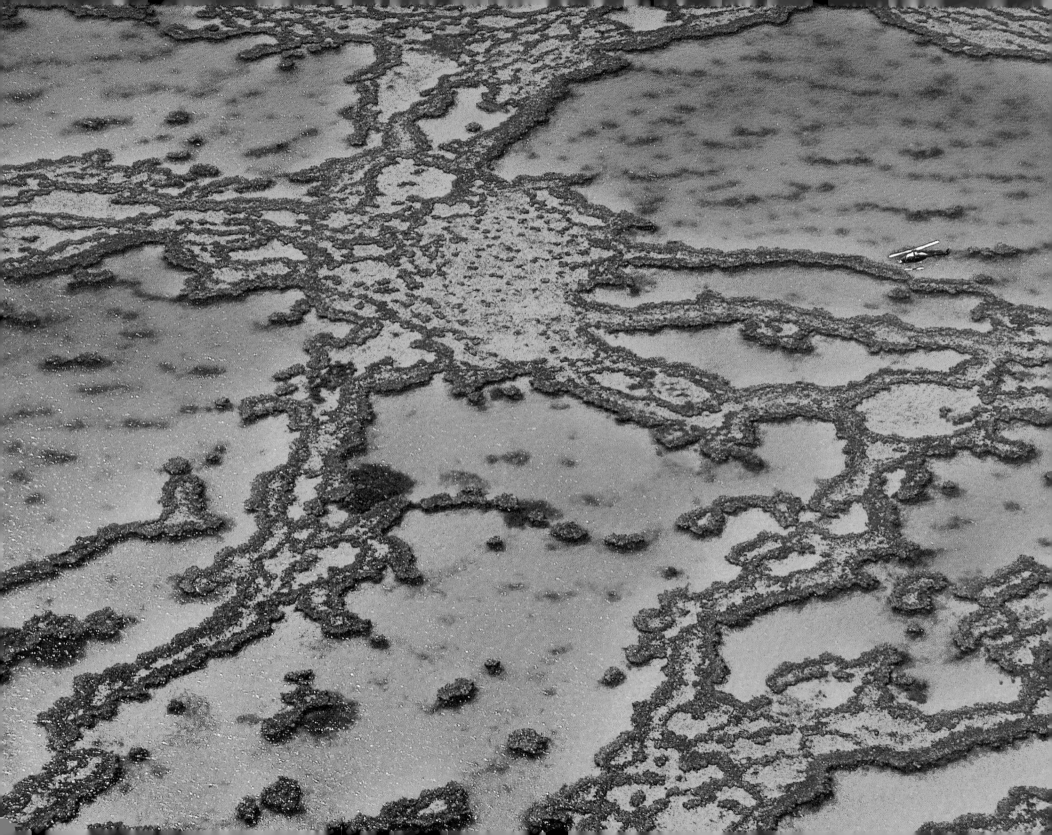

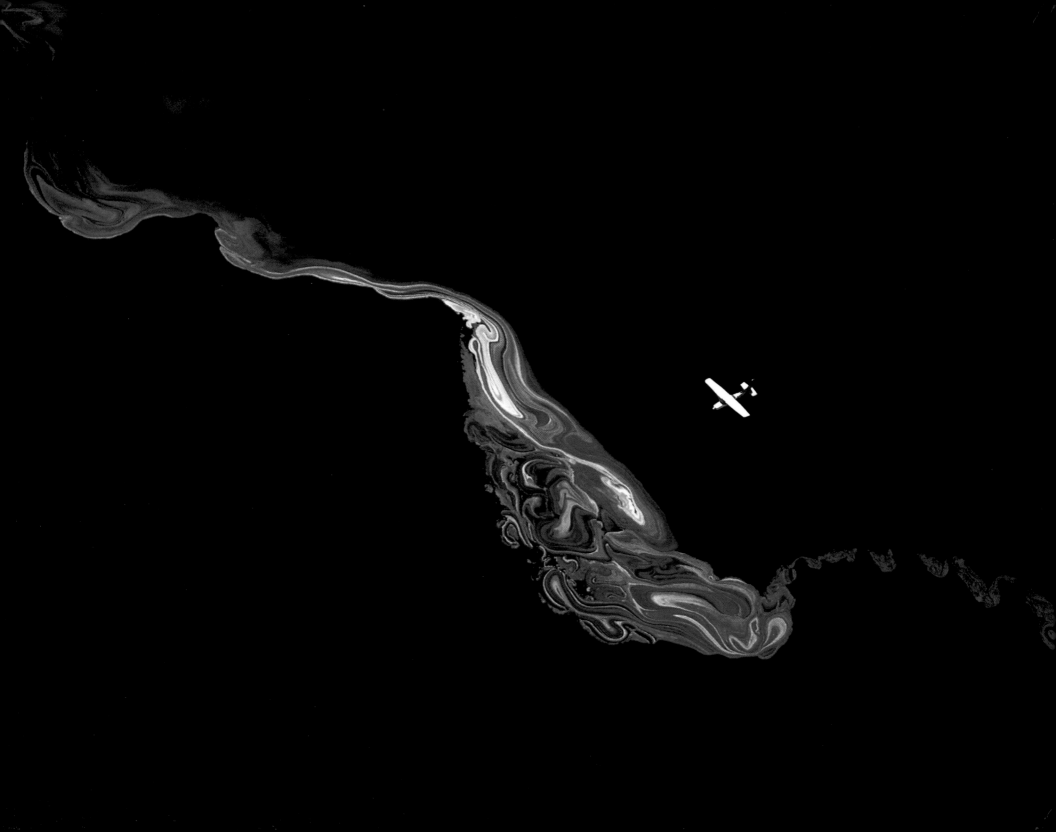

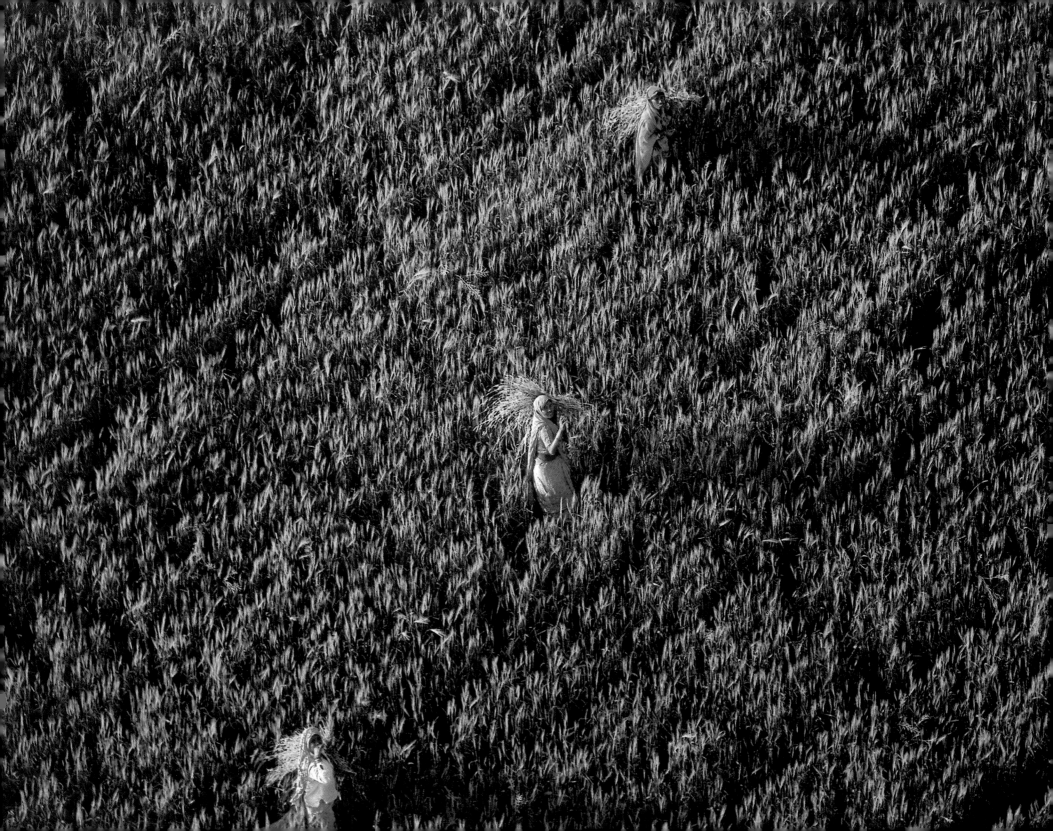

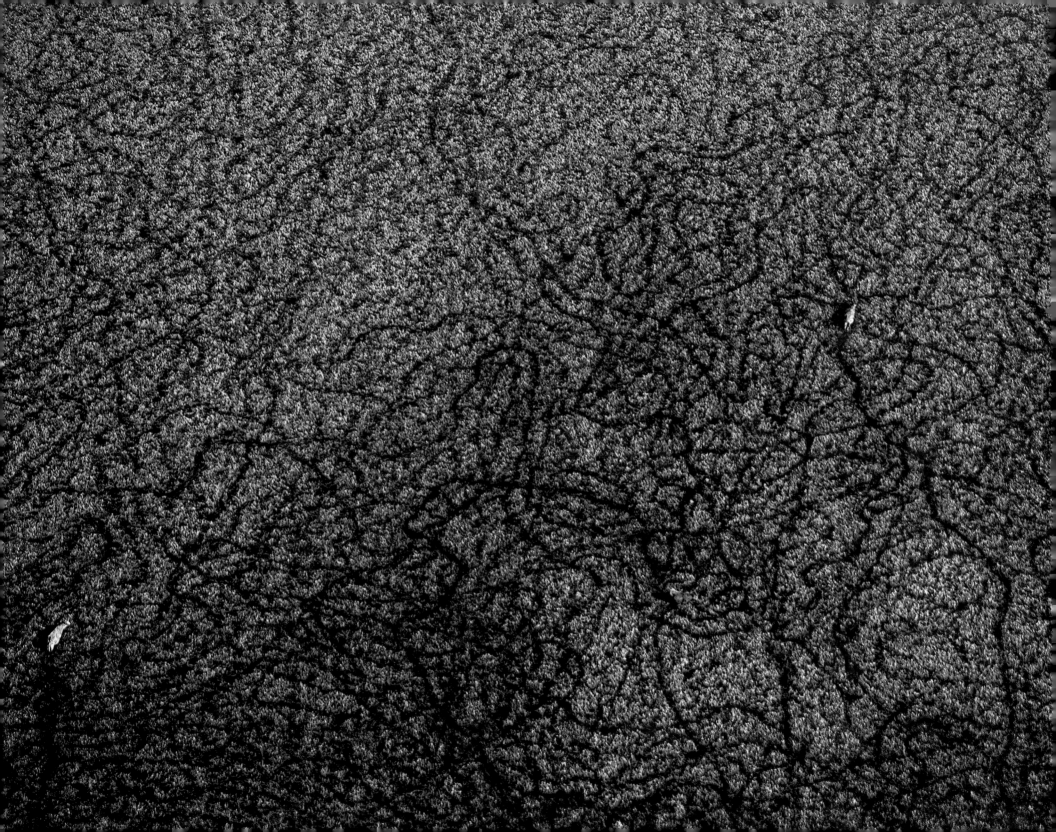

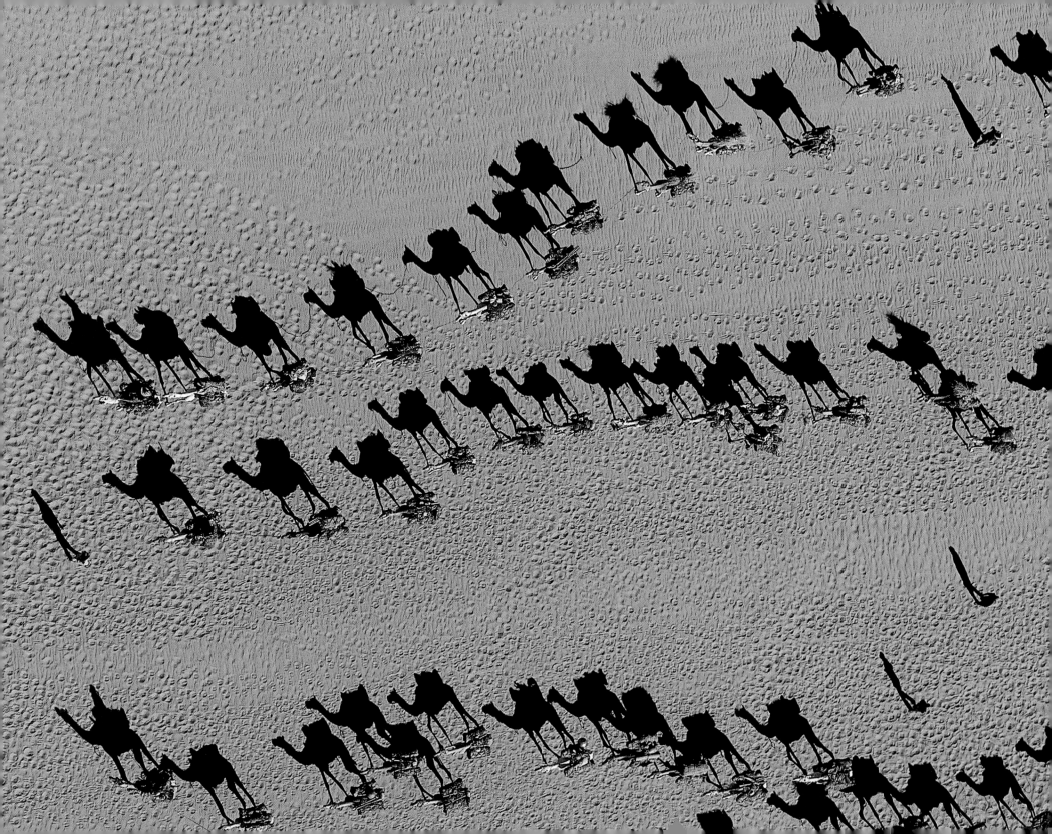

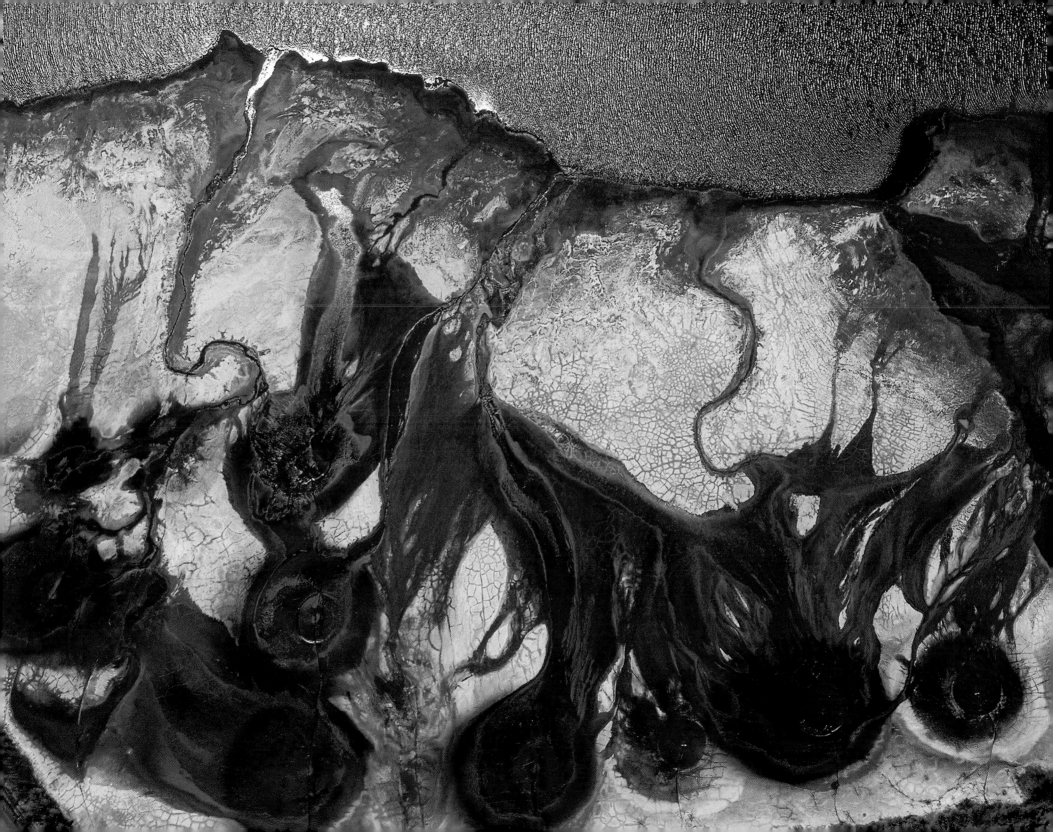

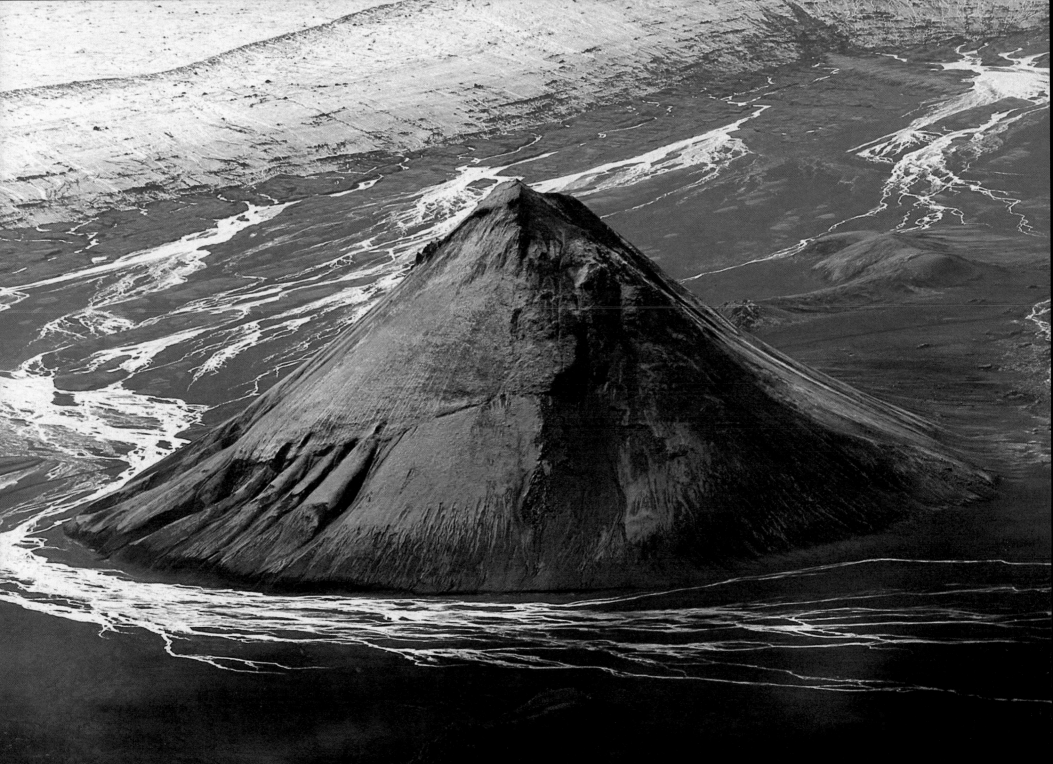

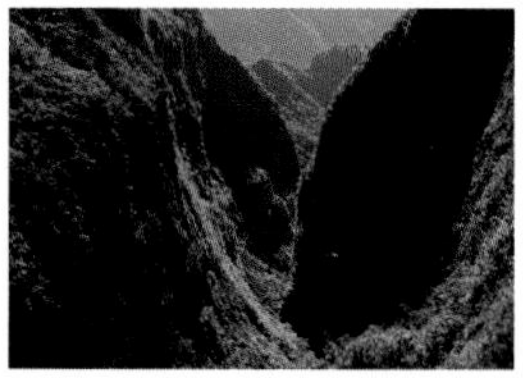

S 21°01' E 55°33'

GARGANTAS DEL BRAS DE CAVERNE, ISLA DE LA REUNIÓN, FRANCIA.

Numerosos gargantas comparables a las del río del Bras de Caverne, que cava su lecho en las fracturas volcánicas del circo de Salazie, dificultan el acceso a la parte central de la Isla de la Reunión. Algunos sitios no se exploraron sino tardíamente, como el hoyo de fuego, una barranca de 250 m visitada por primera vez en 1989. Preservada así de la influencia humana, la selva tropical, donde abundan brezos gigantes, helechos y líquenes, ha conservado su estado primario en los relieves volcánicos de la isla. En cambio, el bosque de altitud baja, convertido en zonas agrícolas o urbanas, desapareció. Más de treinta especies animales o vegetales, de las cuales una veintena son endémicas, se extinguieron en la isla desde hace 400 años. Dotadas de una gran diversidad biológica, los sistemas insulares están más expuestos generalmente al riesgo de extinción de especies que los continentes.

GORGES DU BRAS DE CAVERNE, RÉUNION ISLAND, FRANCE.

Numerous gorges, similar to those of the Bras de Caverne River, which hollows its bed out of the volcanic fractures of the Salazie Cirque, make any access to the central part of Réunion Island difficult. Some sites have never been explored until recently, such as Trou de Fer, a ravine 250 m deep that was visited for the first time in 1989. Preserved thus from human influence, the tropical forest, where gigantic heather, fern and lichen abound, has remained in its primeval state on the island's volcanic mountains. On the other hand, the low-altitude forest, converted into farming or urban zones, has disappeared. Over 30 animal or plant species, including about twenty endemic ones, have become extinct on the island in the last 400 years. Endowed with great biodiversity, island systems are generally more exposed to the risk of species extinction than continents.

GORGES DU BRAS DE CAVERNE, ÎLE DE LA RÉUNION, FRANCE.

De nombreuses gorges comparables à celles de la rivière du Bras de Caverne, qui creuse son lit dans les fractures volcaniques du cirque de Salazie, rendent difficile l'accès à la partie centrale de l'île de la Réunion. Certains sites n'ont été explorés que tardivement, comme le trou de fer, un ravin de 250 m visité pour la première fois en 1989. Ainsi préservée de l'emprise humaine, la forêt tropicale, où abondent bruyères géantes, fougères et lichens, a conservé son état primaire sur les reliefs volcaniques de l'île. En revanche, la forêt de basse altitude, convertie en zones agricoles ou urbaines, a disparu. Plus de 30 espèces animales ou végétales, dont une vingtaine endémiques, se sont éteintes dans l'île depuis 400 ans. Dotés d'une grande diversité biologique, les systèmes insulaires sont généralement plus exposés au risque d'extinction d'espèces que les continents.

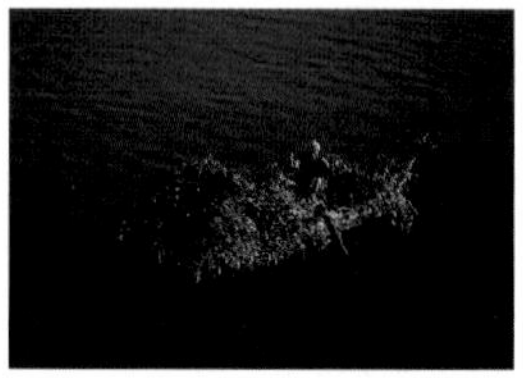

N 31°8' E 30°39'

BARCA SOBRE EL NILO, EGIPTO.

El Nilo, el segundo río más largo del mundo, atraviesa Sudán y Egipto a lo largo de 6 671 km. Es una vía de comunicación por la que circulan tanto lujosos hoteles flotantes para turistas como modestas embarcaciones que transportan principalmente cereales y forraje. Sin embargo, sigue siendo ante todo el principal recurso hídrico del país, ya que satisface el 90% del consumo de agua de los egipcios. Mientras que en años anteriores las crecidas del Nilo sólo garantizaban una disponibilidad de agua durante 3 ó 4 meses, con la construcción de la presa de Asuán en los años 1960 y la consiguiente regulación del caudal del río, se logró dotar al país de agua durante todo el año. Sin embargo, este ordenamiento genera problemas ecológicos importantes, ya que priva al río del limo que fertilizaba las tierras y compensaba la erosión marina del delta, que hoy en día retrocede entre 30 y 200 m por año.

BOAT ON THE NILE, EGYPT.

Second longest river in the world, the Nile flows through Sudan and Egypt, extending over 6,671 km (4,145 mi.). It is a thoroughfare traveled by luxurious floating hotels for tourists as well as humbler boats, mostly carrying fodder and cereals. Nevertheless it remains, above all, the country's principal water resource, providing 90% of the water consumed by Egyptians. Whereas, in the past, the yearly flooding of the Nile guaranteed water availability for only 3 or 4 months out of the year, the construction of the Aswan dam in the 60's has now made it possible for the country to be supplied with water all year round by regulating the river's flow. However, this system generates some major ecological problems since it deprives the river of the silt that used to fertilize the lands and compensated for the erosion by the sea of the delta, which recedes today at a rate of 30 to 200 m (100 to 650 ft) per year.

BARQUE SUR LE NIL, EGYPTE.

Deuxième plus long fleuve du monde, le Nil traverse le Soudan et l'Egypte sur 6 671 km. Il est une voie de communication sur laquelle circulent aussi bien de luxueux hôtels flottants pour touristes que de modestes embarcations transportant notamment fourrage et céréales. Pourtant, il reste avant tout la principale ressource hydrique du pays, couvrant 90 % de la consommation d'eau des Egyptiens. Alors qu'autrefois les crues annuelles du Nil ne garantissaient une disponibilité en eau que pendant 3 à 4 mois, la construction du barrage d'Assouan, dans les années 60, a permis en régulant le débit du fleuve, d'alimenter le pays en eau toute l'année. Cet aménagement engendre cependant des problèmes écologiques importants, puisqu'il prive le fleuve du limon qui fertilisait les terres et compensait l'érosion marine du delta dont le recul varie aujourd'hui de 30 à 200 m par an.

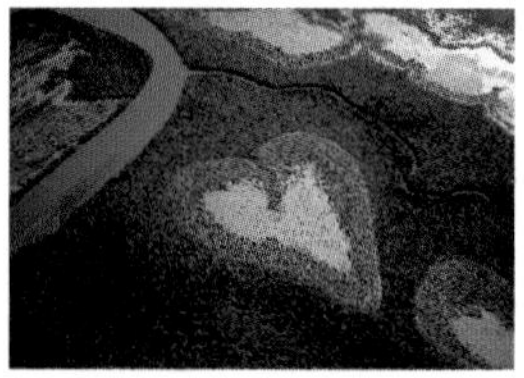

S 20°57' E 164°41'

CORAZÓN DE VOH, NUEVA CALEDONIA, FRANCIA.

El manglar es una formación arbolada anfibia, característica de los litorales tropicales y subtropicales, que crece en suelos salados y cenagosos expuestos a las alternancias de mareas. Constituido por diversas plantas halofitas (capaces de vivir en suelos salados), entre las cuales predominan los mangles, el manglar está presente en cuatro continentes y cubre una superficie total de 170 000 km², lo que equivale a cerca del 25% de las zonas costeras del mundo. Nueva Caledonia, conjunto de islas del Pacífico con una superficie de 18 575 km², cuenta con 200 km² de un manglar relativamente bajo (de 8 a 10 m) pero muy denso, localizado principalmente en la costa oeste de la isla más importante, Grande-Terre. En algunos lugares, tierra adentro, ahí donde el agua marina sólo penetra con las grandes mareas, la vegetación cede su lugar a extensiones desnudas y excesivamente saladas, que llaman tannes; así sucedió cerca de la ciudad de Voh, donde la naturaleza, dibujó un claro en forma de corazón. Muy rico en biodiversidad, el manglar es un hábitat frágil, que sufre la presión de diversas actividades humanas: sobreexplotación de los recursos naturales, desecación de los medios, expansión agrícola, urbanización del litoral, contaminación...

HEART IN VOH, NEW CALEDONIA, FRANCE.

The mangrove swamp is a formation of amphibian trees, characteristic of tropical and subtropical coastlines, that develops in salty, muddy soils exposed to the movements of shifting tides. Made up of various types of halophyte plants (i.e. those able to live on salty soil), predominantly mangrove trees, this swamp is found on four continents, covering a total surface of 170,000 sq. km., or close to 25% of the world's coastal zones. New Caledonia, a group of islands in the Pacific covering an area of 18,575 sq. km., contains 200 sq. km. of fairly low (8 to 10 m) but very dense mangrove swamp, mainly on the west coast of the largest island, Grande-Terre (New Caledonia Island). In certain places inland, where the sea water only penetrates during high tide, the vegetation gives way to bare, excessively salty spaces called "tannes"; this is the case near the city of Voh, where there is a clearing drawn by nature in the shape of a heart. Rich in biodiversity, mangrove swamp is a fragile habitat, subject to the pressure of various human activities: overexploitation of natural resources, drainage of surrounding areas, agricultural expansion, urbanization of the coast, pollution...

CŒUR DE VOH, NOUVELLE-CALÉDONIE, FRANCE.

La mangrove est une formation arborée amphibie caractéristique des littoraux tropicaux et subtropicaux, qui se développe sur les sols salés et vaseux exposés aux alternances de marées. Constituée de diverses plantes halophytes (capables de vivre sur les sols salés), avec une prédominance de palétuviers, elle est présente sur quatre continents, couvrant une superficie totale de 170 000 km², soit près de 25 % des zones côtières du monde. La Nouvelle-Calédonie, ensemble d'îles du Pacifique qui couvre 18 575 km², compte 200 km² d'une mangrove assez basse (8 à 10 m) mais très dense, principalement sur la côte ouest de l'île la plus importante, Grande-Terre. À certains endroits, à l'intérieur des terres, là où l'eau marine ne pénètre qu'au moment des grandes marées, la végétation cède la place à des étendues nues et sursalées, qui sont appelées tannes ; c'est le cas à proximité de la ville de Voh, où la nature a dessiné cette clairière en forme de cœur. Riche en diversité biologique, la mangrove est un habitat fragile, qui subit la pression de diverses activités humaines : surexploitation des ressources naturelles, assèchement des milieux, expansion agricole, urbanisation du littoral, pollution...

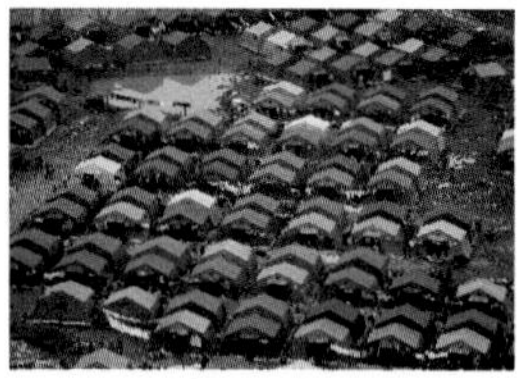

N 42°08' E 20°22'

CAMPO DE REFUGIADOS, AL NOROESTE DE KUKES, CERCA DE TIRANA, ALBANIA.

En Kosovo, provincia de Serbia cuya población está constituida en un 90% por albanos, la política discriminatoria de las autoridades de Belgrado ha generado fuertes tensiones. A finales de marzo de 1999, las potencias occidentales iniciaron una operación militar contra Serbia y la sometieron a intensos bombardeos. La policía y el ejército serbios provocaron y organizaron el éxodo de cientos de miles de kosovares. Acogidos ante esta urgencia por los países vecinos (Albania y Macedonia principalmente), los refugiados (cerca de un millón), quedaron instalados en campamentos de lona, como aquí en el noroeste de Kukes, en Albania.Desde 50 años, 50 millones de personas en el mundo han sido víctimas de desplazamientos forzados, y la década de 1990 ha asistido a una multiplicación de las guerras civiles, acompañadas de los más importantes movimientos de población desde 1945. La respuesta angloamericana, cómo consecuencia a los atentados ocurridos en los Estados-Unidos el 11 de septiembre del 2001, ha propiciado una situación de por sí difícil para la población afghana, aumentando la huida masiva de civiles hacía Iran y Pakistan, vecinos forzados a cerrar sus fronteras. Cada país se esfuerza por asegurar hogar, provisiones, y seguridad a 2 millónes de refugiados Afghanos.

REFUGEE CAMP NORTHWEST OF KUKES, CLOSE TO TIRANA, ALBANIA.

In Kosovo, a province of Serbia with a 90% Albanian population, the discriminatory policy of Belgrade authorities has created very strong tensions. At the end of March 1999, western powers launched a military operation against Serbia, submitting it to intensive bombardment. The Serbian police and army instigated and organized the exodus of hundreds of thousands of Kosovars. Several bordering countries suddenly had to welcome close to a million refugees who were housed in canvas camps, mostly in Albania, as portrayed here, as well as in Macedonia. Since 1950, about 50 million persons have been victims of forced displacements throughout the world, and the 1990's witnessed an increase in the number of civil wars, accompanied by the greatest migrations since 1945. The anglo-american counter-attack in Afghanistan following the September 11th attacks in the United States, has exacerbated an already difficult situation for the Afghan population by increasing the flow of civilians escaping to neighbouring Iran and Pakistan, who have been forced to close their borders. Each country is already striving to provide housing, supplies and safety to 2 million Afghan refugees.

CAMP DE RÉFUGIÉS AU NORD-OUEST DE KUKÉS, PRÈS DE TIRANA, ALBANIE.

Au Kosovo, province de Serbie peuplée à 90 % d'Albanais, la politique discriminatoire des autorités de Belgrade a engendré de très fortes tensions. Fin mars 1999, les puissances occidentales ont engagé une opération militaire contre la Serbie, la soumettant à des bombardements intensifs. La police et l'armée serbes ont provoqué et organisé l'exode de centaines de milliers de Kosovars. Accueillis dans l'urgence par les pays riverains, près d'un million de réfugiés ont été installés dans des campements de toile, essentiellement en Albanie, comme ici, et en Macédoine. Depuis 50 ans, on comptabilise plus de 50 millions de victimes de déplacements forcés dans le monde, et la décennie 1990 a vu une multiplication des guerres civiles accompagnées des plus importants mouvements de population depuis 1945. La riposte anglo-américaine aux attentats perpétrés aux Etats-Unis le 11 septembre 2001 a ainsi exacerbé une situation déjà difficile pour la population Afghane, accélérant la fuite massive des civils vers l'Iran et le Pakistan voisins, contraints de fermer leurs frontières. Chaque pays s'efforce déjà d'assurer logement, ravitaillement et sécurité à 2 millions de réfugiés Afghans.

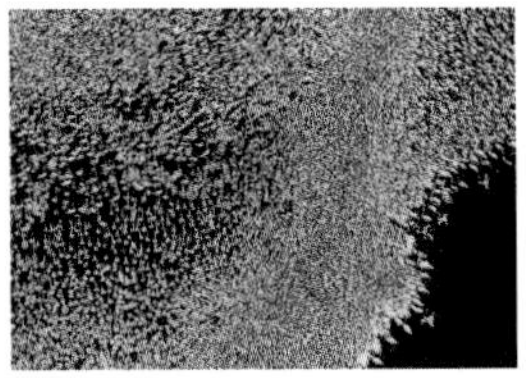

S 0°17' E 36°04'

FLAMENCOS EN EL LAGO NAKURU, KENIA.

Con una superficie de 62 km^2, el lago Nakuru cubre un tercio del parque nacional del mismo nombre, creado en 1968, y acoge a cerca de 370 especies de aves. Entre ellas, los flamencos enanos (Phoeniconaias minor) y los flamencos (Phoenicopterus ruber), de los que se han contado hasta 1.4 millones en el lugar, son quizás los más numerosos. Como el resto de los lagos alcalinos diseminados a lo largo del Rift-Valley, el hecho de estar ubicados en un sustrato rocoso volcánico, de tener una corriente débil, una intensa evaporación y una profundidad promedio de un metro, le confieren un fuerte contenido de sosa. Estas aguas salobres favorecen la proliferación de algas azul-verdoso, de microorganismos y de pequeños crustáceos, que constituyen el alimento principal de los flamencos. Sin embargo, el uso de productos químicos en los cultivos vecinos y las aguas usadas de la ciudad cercana de Nakuru han contaminado poco a poco las aguas del lago. Desde 1990, el lago Nakuru forma parte de las zonas húmedas de importancia internacional registradas de acuerdo a lo estipulado en el Convenio de Ramsar.

ROSE-COLORED FLAMINGOS ON LAKE NAKURU, KENYA.

With a surface area of 62 sq. km. (24 sq. mi.), Lake Nakuru covers one-third of the national park bearing the same name, which was created in 1968, and receives close to 370 species of birds. Among these, the lesser flamingos (Phoeniconaias minor) and the rose-colored or greater flamingos (Phoenicopterus ruber), 1.4 million of which have been counted on this site, are probably the most numerous. As in the case of other alkali lakes scattered along the Rift valley, its location on a rocky volcanic substratum, its low out-flow, its high rate of evaporation and its average depth of one meter, endow it with a high content of sodium carbonate. These briny waters encourage the proliferation of blue-green algae, microorganisms and small crustaceans, which form the basis of the flamingos' diet. However, chemicals used on bordering farmlands and wastewater from the nearby city of Nakuru have gradually polluted the lake's waters. In 1990, Lake Nakuru has been designated as a wetland of international importance according to the Ramsar convention.

FLAMANTS ROSES SUR LE LAC NAKURU, KENYA.

D'une superficie de 62 km^2, le lac Nakuru couvre un tiers du parc national du même nom créé en 1968, et accueille près de 370 espèces d'oiseaux. Parmi elles, les petits flamants (Phoeniconaias minor) et les flamants roses (Phoenicopterus ruber) , dont on a recensé jusqu'à 1,4 millions sur le site, sont sans doute les plus nombreux. Comme les autres lacs alcalins disséminés le long de la vallée du Rift, sa situation sur un substrat rocheux volcanique, son faible écoulement, son évaporation intense et sa profondeur moyenne d'un mètre lui confèrent une forte teneur en soude. Ces eaux saumâtres favorisent la prolifération d'algues bleu-vert, de micro-organismes et de petits crustacés qui constituent l'essentiel de l'alimentation des flamants. Cependant, les produits chimiques utilisés dans les cultures riveraines et les eaux usées de la proche ville de Nakuru ont peu à peu pollué les eaux du lac. Depuis 1990, le lac Nakuru fait partie des zones humides d'importance internationale recensées au titre de la convention de Ramsar.

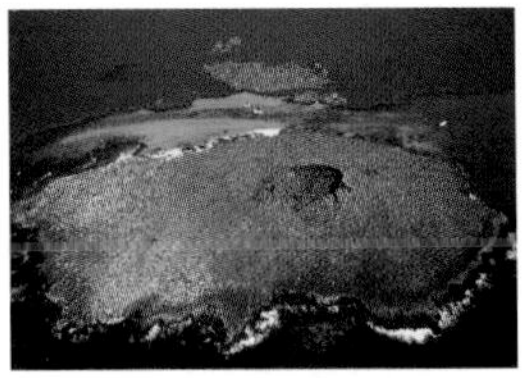

S 00° 22'35 W 90°35'35

VOLCÁN EN LA COSTA OESTE DE LA ISLA DE SAN SALVADOR, GRUPO DE ISLAS DEL SOMBRERO CHINO, ARCHIPIÉLAGO DE LAS GALÁPAGOS, ECUADOR.

Emergidas de las mareas del Océano Pacífico hace de 3 a 5 millones de años, las 19 islas de origen volcánico que forman el archipiélago de las Galápagos presentan, a pesar de su aspecto lunar, una riqueza biológica excepcional. Albergan principalmente a la colonia más grande de iguanas marinas del mundo y a la tortuga gigante, o "Galápago", que dio nombre al archipiélago. Si quienes llegan a estos lugares con sus barcos se sienten hechizados, Darwin, por su parte, encontró la inspiración para su teoría de la evolución de las especies. Reconocer a las islas Galápagos como Parque Nacional en 1959, e inscribirlas en la Lista del Patrimonio Mundial de la UNESCO en 1978, no evitaron que el crecimiento demográfico, la introducción de especies exóticas y la escalada del turismo (a pesar de estar fuertemente reglamentado desde 1998) pusieran en peligro este laboratorio natural de la evolución. El archipiélago se salvó milagrosamente de las casi 600 toneladas de fuel-oil que se derramaron durante el naufragio del petrolero Jessica, en enero de 2001, pero otras riberas no corrieron con tan buena suerte.

VOLCANO ON THE WEST COAST OF SAN SALVADOR (ALSO JAMES OR SANTIAGO) ISLAND, IN A GROUP OF ISLANDS CONTAINING THE SOMBRERO CHINO, GALÁPAGOS ARCHIPELAGO, ECUADOR.

Having emerged from the waves of the Pacific Ocean 3 to 5 million years ago, the 19 islands of volcanic origin that make up the Galápagos archipelago, in spite of their moonscapes, exhibit exceptional biological wealth. They harbor in particular the richest colony of marine iguanas in the world and the giant tortoise, or "galápago" in Spanish, which gave the archipelago its name. While visitors taken by boat to these places are enthralled by their natural enchantment, Darwin on the other hand found inspiration here for his theory of evolution. Recognition of the Galápagos Islands as a National Park in 1959 and their inclusion on the UNESCO World Heritage List in 1978 have not prevented population growth, the introduction of exotic species, and the rapid rise in tourism (strictly controlled however since 1998) from endangering this natural laboratory of evolution. The archipelago was miraculously spared from the 600 metric tons (660 tons) or so of fuel oil that leaked from the wreck of the oil tanker Jessica in January of 2001, whilst other shores were not so fortunate.

VOLCAN SUR LA CÔTE OUEST DE L'ÎLE DE SAN SALVADOR, GROUPE D'ÎLES DU CHAPEAU CHINOIS, ARCHIPEL DES GALÁPAGOS, ÉQUATEUR.

Emergées des flots de l'océan Pacifique il y a 3 à 5 millions d'années, les 19 îles d'origine volcanique qui constituent l'archipel des Galápagos présentent, en dépit de leur aspect lunaire, une exceptionnelle richesse biologique. Elles abritent notamment la plus riche colonie d'iguanes marins du monde et la tortue géante, ou « Galápago », qui a donné son nom à l'archipel. Si l'enchantement gagne ceux que leur bateau conduit dans ces lieux, Darwin, lui, s'en inspira pour sa théorie de l'évolution des espèces. La reconnaissance des îles Galápagos comme Parc National en 1959, et leur inscription sur la Liste du patrimoine mondial de l'Unesco en 1978, n'ont pas empêché l'accroissement démographique, l'introduction d'espèces exotiques et l'envolée du tourisme (pourtant sévèrement réglementé depuis 1998) de mettre en péril ce laboratoire naturel de l'évolution. L'archipel a été miraculeusement épargné par les quelque 600 tonnes de fioul échappées du naufrage du pétrolier Jessica, en janvier 2001, mais d'autres rivages n'ont pas eu cette chance.

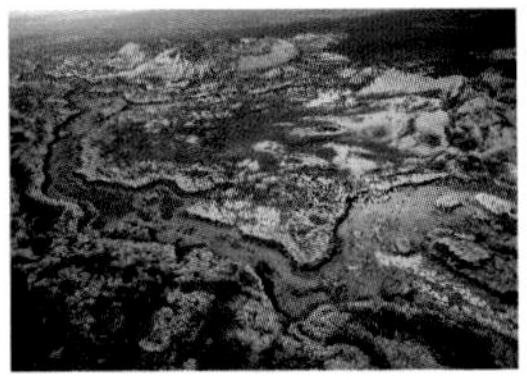

N 64°04' W 18°15'

CADENA DE VOLCANES DE LAKAGIGAR, ISLANDIA.

La región de Lakagigar, en el sur de Islandia, lleva aún las marcas de una de las erupciones volcánicas más violentas de todos los tiempos. En 1783, dos fisuras eruptivas con una longitud total de 25 km se abrieron a un lado y otro del volcán Laki, vomitando 12 km de lava, que cubrieron 565 km del territorio. Una nube de gas carbónico, de anhídrido sulfuroso y de cenizas se extiende en el conjunto de la isla y contamina pastizales y aguas superficiales. Murieron las tres cuartas partes del ganado y, después de una nueva erupción, en 1 785, una terrible hambruna diezmó a un cuatro de la población (más de 10 000 personas). Coronadas con 115 cráteres volcánicos, hoy en día las fisuras del Lakagigar están cerradas y las corrientes de lava recubiertas con un espeso tapete de musgo. Con más de 200 volcanes activos, Islandia ha producido ella sola un tercio de las emanaciones mundiales de lava durante los últimos 500 años.

LAKAGIGAR VOLCANIC MOUNTAIN CHAIN, ICELAND.

The Lakagigar region, in the southern part of Iceland, still bears the marks of one of the most violent volcanic eruptions in historic times. In 1783, two eruptive fissures measuring a total of 25 km opened up in various places on the Laki volcano, spewing out 12 cu. km. of lava that covered an area of 565 sq. km. (218 sq. mi.). A cloud of carbon dioxide, sulfuric anhydride and ash spread over the entire island and contaminated grazing lands and surface waters. Three-quarters of the livestock were wiped out and following a fresh eruption in 1785, a terrifying famine decimated a quarter of the population (over 10,000 people). Topped by a crown of 115 volcanic craters, the Lakagigar fissures have closed over today and the lava flows are covered in a thick carpet of moss. Iceland, with more than 200 active volcanoes, has produced one-third of the world's lava ejections alone over the past 500 years.

CHAÎNE DE VOLCANS DE LAKAGIGAR, ISLANDE.

La région de Lakagigar, au sud de l'Islande, porte encore les stigmates d'une des plus violentes éruptions volcaniques des temps historiques. En 1783, deux fissures éruptives d'une longueur totale de 25 km s'ouvrent de part et d'autre du volcan Laki, vomissant 12 km^3 de lave qui recouvrent 565 km^2 du territoire. Un nuage de gaz carbonique, d'anhydride sulfureux et de cendres s'étend sur l'ensemble de l'île et contamine pâturages et eaux de surface. Les trois quarts du bétail sont anéantis et, au terme d'une nouvelle éruption, en 1785, une terrible famine décime un quart de la population (plus de 10 000 personnes). Couronnées par 115 cratères volcaniques, les fissures du Lakagigar sont aujourd'hui refermées et les coulées de laves recouvertes d'un épais tapis de mousse. Avec plus de 200 volcans actifs, l'Islande a produit à elle seule au cours des 500 dernières années le tiers des émanations de lave du monde.

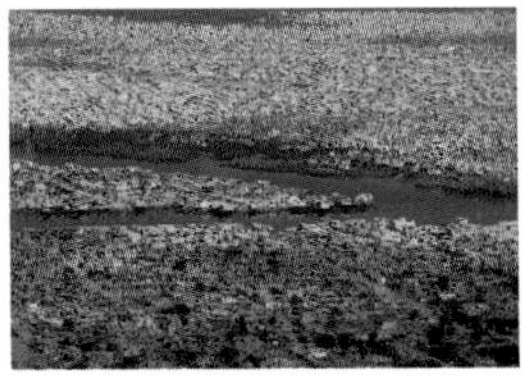

S 2°37' W 79°54'

SUBURBIO DE GUAYAQUIL, GUAYAS, ECUADOR.

Con 2 millones de habitantes, Guayaquil, en Ecuador, tiene una población un tercio mayor que Quito, la capital (1.56 millones de habitantes). La prosperidad de este gran centro portuario industrial y comercial, que controla el 50% de las exportaciones y el 90% de las importaciones del país, ha atraído a un número creciente de emigrantes, llegados de las zonas rurales vecinas. Una quinta parte de la población de Guayaquil vive actualmente en suburbios cuyas casas construidas sobre pilotes están instaladas en zonas pantanosas. Estos barrios pobres, donde el suelo está artificialmente constituido de desechos acumulados por las mareas, no disponen de ninguna infraestructura sanitaria y tienen preocupantes problemas de salubridad. Durante las últimas décadas, la población de América Latina a tenido el mayor índice de urbanización del mundo (pasó de 41% al 77% de población urbana entre 1950 y 1999). En el conjunto de los continentes, 1 millón de personas se suman cada semana a la población urbana, que alcanza el 47% en el año 2000.

SHANTY-TOWN IN GUAYAQUIL, GUAYAS, ECUADOR.

With 2 million inhabitants, Guayaquil, Ecuador, has one-third more population than Quito, the capital city (1.56 million inhabitants). The prosperity of this large port and industrial and commercial center, which controls 50% of the country's exports and 90% of its imports, has attracted an increasing number of migrants from the neighboring countryside. One-fifth of the population of Guayaquil lives today in shanty-towns whose houses, on poles, are built in the swampy areas. These poor districts, where the ground is made artificially of flotsam and jetsam, have no infrastructure for sanitation and are suffering from alarming health problems. Over the past few decades, the Latin American population has experienced the highest rate of urbanization in the world (with city-dwellers increasing from 41% to 77% of the population between 1950 and 1999). On all continents together, 1 million people are added every week to the urban population, which reached 47% in 2000.

BIDONVILLE DE GUAYAQUIL, GUAYAS, ÉQUATEUR.

Avec 2 millions d'habitants, Guayaquil, en Équateur, est d'un tiers plus peuplée que Quito, la capitale (1,56 million d'habitants). La prospérité de ce grand centre portuaire industriel et commercial, qui contrôle 50 % des exportations et 90 % des importations du pays, a attiré un nombre croissant de migrants venus des campagnes voisines. Un cinquième de la population de Guayaquil vit aujourd'hui dans des bidonvilles dont les maisons sur pilotis sont installées sur des zones marécageuses. Ces quartiers pauvres, où le sol est artificiellement constitué de déchets accumulés par les marées, ne disposent d'aucune infrastructure sanitaire et connaissent d'inquiétants problèmes de salubrité. Au cours des dernières décennies, la population d'Amérique latine a connu le plus fort taux d'urbanisation du monde (passant de 41 % à 77 % de citadins entre 1950 et 1999). Sur l'ensemble des continents, 1 million de personnes s'ajoutent chaque semaine à la population urbaine, qui atteint 47 % en 2000.

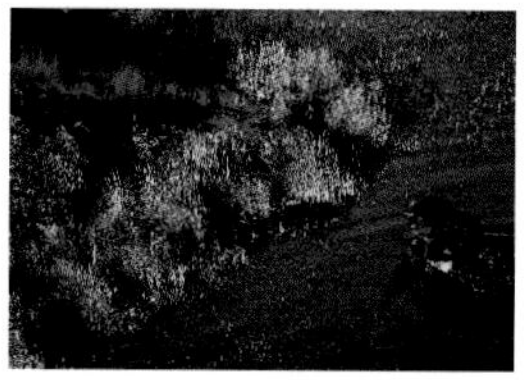

S 19°26' E 23°03'

ELEFANTES EN EL DELTA DEL OKAVANGO, BOTSWANA.

El delta del Okavango, amplia zona húmeda en el corazón de Botswana, alberga a una fauna rica y variada, en particular varias decenas de miles de elefantes. Víctima de una cacería intensa por su marfil, el elefante africano (Loxodonta africana), el mayor de los mamíferos terrestres, estuvo a punto de desaparecer. Entre 1945 y finales de los años 80, el número de elefantes del continente pasó efectivamente de 2.5 millones a menos de 500 000. Ante esta dramática disminución, se decidió la total prohibición del comercio internacional de marfil en 1989, en el marco del CITES (Convenio internacional de especies en peligro de extinción). Sin embargo, Botswana, Namibia y Zimbabwe, donde las poblaciones de elefantes ahora se encuentran en aumento, expresaron desde 1997 su deseo de retomar en forma parcial el comercio del marfil, a pesar de las posibles consecuencias en una especie que sigue estando en peligro de extinción en todo el continente. En 1999, se autorizó la venta excepcional de una reserva de 50 toneladas de marfil (que representa 5 446 colmillos) con destino a Japón, por un monto de 5 millones de dólares, que posteriormente fueron invertidos en programas de conservación y de gestión participativa de elefantes por las comunidades locales de los tres paises referidos.

ELEPHANTS IN THE OKAVANGO DELTA, BOTSWANA.

The Okavango delta, an immense wetland in the heart of Botswana, harbors a rich and varied fauna, and in particular several tens of thousands of elephants. Heavily hunted for its ivory, the African elephant (Loxodonta africana), largest of all terrestrial mammals, almost disappeared. Between 1945 and the late 1980's, the number of elephants on the continent dropped indeed from 2.5 million to less than 500,000. In reaction to this dramatic decline, a total ban on international ivory trade was declared in 1989 as part of the CITES (Convention on International Trade in Endangered Species). However, since 1997, Botswana, Namibia and Zimbabwe, where elephant populations have been on the increase, have expressed their wish for a partial resumption of the ivory trade, in spite of the possible consequences for a species that is still endangered on a continental scale. A one-off sale of a 50 metric ton (50 tons) stock of ivory (representing 5,446 tusks), purchased by Japan for approximately $5 million (US), was authorized in 1999. All of these funds have been channeled to elephant conservation and community-based management programs in the three concerned countries.

ÉLÉPHANTS DANS LE DELTA DE L'OKAVANGO, BOTSWANA.

Le delta de l'Okavango, vaste zone humide au cœur du Botswana, abrite une faune riche et diversifiée, en particulier plusieurs dizaines de milliers d'éléphants. Intensément chassé pour son ivoire, l'éléphant d'Afrique (Loxodonta africana), le plus gros des mammifères terrestres, a bien failli disparaître. Entre 1945 et la fin des années 1980, le nombre d'éléphants du continent est en effet passé de 2,5 millions à moins de 500 000. Face à ce déclin dramatique, l'interdiction totale du commerce international de l'ivoire fut décidée en 1989 dans le cadre de la CITES (Convention sur le commerce international des espèces de faune et de flore sauvage menacées d'extinction). Le Botswana, la Namibie et le Zimbabwe, où les populations d'éléphants sont désormais en augmentation, ont cependant exprimé dès 1997 leur souhait d'une reprise partielle du commerce de l'ivoire, malgré les conséquences possibles sur une espèce toujours menacée à l'échelle du continent. La vente exceptionnelle d'un stock de 50 tonnes d'ivoire (représentant 5446 défenses) à destination du Japon fut autorisée en 1999, pour un montant de 5 millions de dollars, investis ensuite dans des programmes de conservation et de gestion participative des éléphants par les communautés locales des trois pays concernés.

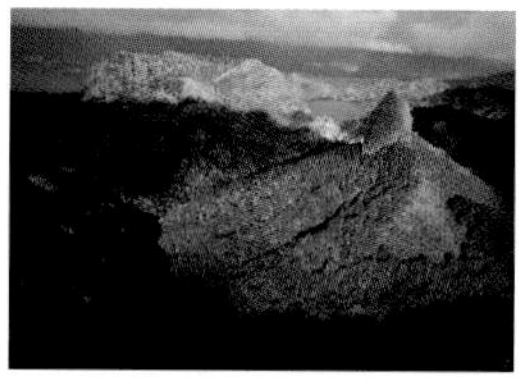

S 40°40' W 71°16'

HAYAS SOBRE LOS MONTES TRAFUL, PROVINCIA DE NEUQUÉN, ARGENTINA.

En el corazón del parque nacional Nahuel Huapi, en el suroeste de la provincia de Neuquén, en Argentina, un gran número de lagos de altura (700 m en promedio) con aguas de un azul intenso y de origen glaciar, bañan las faldas de los montes y de los picos rocosos de la Cordillera de los Andes. La humedad del clima de esta región favorece el desarrollo de hayas (variedades *Nothofagus pumilio* y *antartica*) que han colonizado los flancos de las montañas, alegrándolas con arrebolados colores durante el otoño. Más al sur, a medida que la altura disminuye sensiblemente, los bosques de hayas van escaseando progresivamente, dando paso a la estepa de la Patagonia. La parte de la Cordillera de los Andes, localizada entre Argentina y Chile constituye, con una extensión de cerca de 5 000 km, la mayor frontera natural terrestre del planeta, y comprende la cima del Aconcagua, que desde sus 6 960 m, domina todo el continente sudamericano.

BEECH TREES ON THE TRAFUL MOUNTAINS, NEUQUÉN PROVINCE, ARGENTINA.

In the heart of Nahuel Huapí National Park, in the southwest part of Neuquén province, Argentina, many high-altitude lakes (700 m (2,300 ft) on average) with intense blue colored waters of glacial origin, lie amidst the mountains and rocky peaks of the Cordillera de los Andes. The dampness of the climate in this region encourages the development of beech trees (*Nothofagus pumilio* and *Antartica* varieties) that have populated the mountainsides, brightening them with flaming colors in the fall. Farther south, where the altitude is appreciably lower, the beech forests thin out bit-by-bit, giving way to the Patagonian Steppe. The part of the Cordillera de los Andes situated between Argentina and Chile, approximately 5,000 km (3,100 mi.) long, forms the planet's longest natural terrestrial border, and includes Aconcagua Peak, which, at an altitude of 6960 m (22,840 ft), dominates the entire South American continent.

HÊTRES SUR LES MONTS TRAFUL, PROVINCE DU NEUQUÉN, ARGENTINE.

Au cœur du parc national de Nahuel Huapi, dans le sud-ouest de la province du Neuquén, en Argentine, de nombreux lacs d'altitude (700 m en moyenne) aux eaux d'un bleu intense, d'origine glaciaire, baignent les pieds des monts et des pics rocheux de la cordillère des Andes. L'humidité du climat de cette région favorise le développement de hêtres (variétés *Nothofagus pumilio* et *antartica)* qui ont colonisé les flancs des montagnes, les égayant de couleurs flamboyantes en automne. Plus au sud, alors que l'altitude décroît sensiblement, les forêts de hêtres s'éclaircissent progressivement, cédant la place à la steppe de Patagonie. La partie de la cordillère des Andes située entre l'Argentine et le Chili constitue, avec une longueur d'environ 5 000 km, la plus longue frontière naturelle terrestre de la planète, et comprend le sommet Aconcagua, qui domine, de ses 6960 m, tout le continent sud-américain.

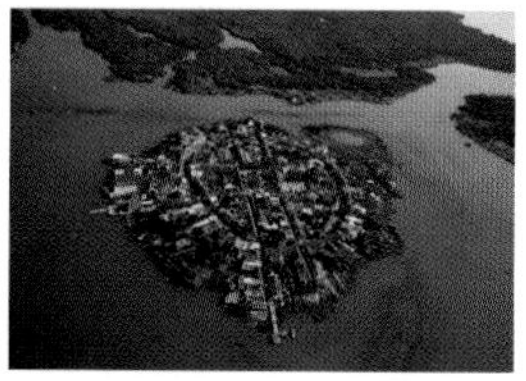

N 21°54' W 105°28'

MEXCALTITLÁN, NAYARIT, MÉXICO.

En la costa del Pacífico al noroeste de México, en la ribera del Estado de Nayarit, el pueblo de Mexcaltitlán, aislado en un promontorio de arena de 400 m de largo, emerge de los meandros pantanosos de una vasta laguna costera. Hacia el final de la temporada de lluvias, en septiembre, las aguas de la laguna inundan las callejuelas del pueblo, obligando a los habitantes a circular en canoas, y dan al conjunto el aspecto de una "Venecia mexicana". Algunos historiadores ven en este pueblo de pescadores la mítica Aztlán, de donde serían originarios los Aztecas. Mitad terrestre, mitad acuática, Mexcaltitlán es imagen del rico patrimonio cultural que lo rodea: un almocárabe de canales que se hilvanan en el manglar, donde más de 300 especies de aves se han identificado. En la escala del territorio, la diversidad biológica es una de las más altas del planeta: en solamente el 1.4% de las tierras emergidas, México es el primer país del mundo en cuanto al número de especies de mamíferos (450), y alberga, para cada categoría animal y vegetal, el 10% de las especies conocidas.

MEXCALTITLAN, NAYARIT, MEXICO.

The village of Mexcaltitlan, isolated on a promontory of sand 400 m (130 ft.) long, emerges from the swampy meanders of an immense inland lagoon on the shore of the state of Nayarit, Pacific coast of northwestern Mexico. Towards the end of the rainy season in September, the lagoon waters flood the village lanes, forcing inhabitants to travel by canoe, and giving the whole area the appearance of a "Mexican Venice". Some historians see in this fishing village the mythical island of Aztlan, where the Aztecs supposedly originated from. Half-terrestrial and half-aquatic, Mexcaltitlan reflects the rich natural heritage that surrounds it: an interlaced design of channels threading their way through the mangrove swamp, where more than 300 species of birds have been identified. On a territorial level, its biodiversity is one of the greatest on the planet: Mexico represents 1.4% of all emerged land, and is the leading country in the number of mammal species (450), harboring 10% of all known species in every animal and plant category.

MEXCALTITÁN, NAYARIT, MEXIQUE.

Sur la côte Pacifique au nord-ouest du Mexique, sur le rivage de l'Etat du Nayarit, le village de Mexcaltitán, isolé sur un promontoire de sable de 400 m de long, émerge des méandres marécageux d'une vaste lagune côtière. Vers la fin de la saison des pluies, en septembre, les eaux de la lagune inondent les ruelles du village, contraignant les habitants à circuler en canoë, et donnent à l'ensemble des airs de « Venise mexicaine ». Certains historiens voient en ce village de pêcheurs la mythique île d'Aztlán, d'où seraient originaires les Aztèques. Mi-terrestre mi-aquatique, Mexcaltitán est à l'image du riche patrimoine naturel qui l'entoure : un entrelacs de canaux se faufilant dans la mangrove, où plus de 300 espèces d'oiseaux ont été identifiées. À l'échelle du territoire, la diversité biologique est l'une des plus élevées de la planète : sur seulement 1,4 % des terres émergées, le Mexique est le premier pays au monde pour le nombre d'espèces de mammifères (450), et abrite, pour chaque catégorie animale et végétale, 10 % des espèces connues.

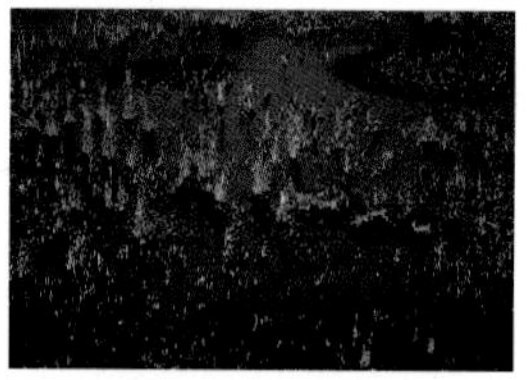

S 18°45' E 22°45'

COBES LECHWE EN EL DELTA DEL OKAVANGO, BOTSWANA.

Abundantes en el delta del Okavango, en Botswana, los cobes lechwe son antílopes característicos de los medios pantanosos; esta especie vive sobre todo en el agua y encuentra en los islotes con vegetación su alimento, así como una protección frente a los depredadores. El delta del Okavango alberga 40 especies de grandes mamíferos, 400 de aves, 95 de reptiles y anfibios, 70 de peces y 1 060 de vegetales. Hace dos millones de años, el Río Okavango se unió con el Limpopo para desembocar en el Océano Índico, pero las fallas creadas por una intensa actividad tectónica lo desviaron de su recorrido inicial haciéndolo detener su recorrido en un vasto delta de 15 000 km² en la entrada del Desierto de Kalahari. Desde 1966, el delta del Okavango fue designado como miembro del Convenio de Ramsar, relativa a las zonas húmedas de importancia internacional, que comprende 1075 sitios en el mundo donde se busca conservar de manera sustentable las actividades sociales y económicas con el mantenimiento de los equilibrios naturales.

COBES LECHWE IN THE OKAVANGO DELTA, BOTSWANA.

Cobes lechwes are antelopes characteristic of marshy environments. They are abundant in the Okavango Delta, live especially in water and find their food, as well as protection from predators, on the islets of vegetation. The Okavango Delta harbors 40 species of large mammals, 400 species of birds, 95 species of reptiles and amphibians, 70 species of fish and 1,060 species of plants. Two million years ago, the Okavango River joined the Limpopo to empty into the Indian Ocean, but faults created by intense tectonic activity deviated it from its initial course, which now ends in a huge 15,000 sq. km.-wide interior delta at the entrance of the Kalahari Desert. Since 1996, the Okavango Delta has been designated as a wetland of international importance according to the Ramsar Convention, which benefits 1,075 sites in the world and attempts to reconcile social and economic activities in a sustainable way while preserving a natural harmony.

COBES LECHWE DANS LE DELTA DE L'OKAVANGO, BOTSWANA.

Abondants dans le delta de l'Okavango, au Botswana, les cobes lechwe sont des antilopes caractéristiques des milieux marécageux ; cette espèce vit surtout dans l'eau et trouve dans les îlots de végétation sa nourriture ainsi qu'une protection face aux prédateurs. Le delta de l'Okavango abrite 40 espèces de grands mammifères, 400 d'oiseaux, 95 de reptiles et amphibiens, 70 de poissons et 1 060 de végétaux. Il y a deux millions d'années, la rivière Okavango rejoignait le fleuve Limpopo pour se jeter dans l'océan Indien, mais les failles créées par une intense activité tectonique l'ont déviée de son parcours initial, lui faisant achever sa course en un vaste delta de 15 000 km² à l'entrée du désert du Kalahari. Depuis 1996, le delta de l'Okavango est désigné au titre de la convention de Ramsar, relative aux zones humides d'importance internationale, concernant 1075 sites dans le monde, où l'on cherche à concilier durablement les activités sociales et économiques avec le maintien des équilibres naturels.

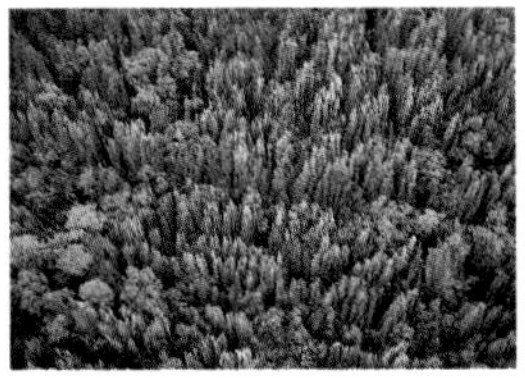

S 18°47' E 45°03'

TSINGY DE BEHAMARA, REGIÓN DE MAJUNGA, MADAGASCAR.

Con una superficie de 587 000 km², Madagascar es la cuarta isla más grande del mundo. Al oeste, en la parte más árida, se encuentra el extraño bosque mineral de los Tsingy de Behamara. Esta formación geológica, llamada carst, es el resultado de la erosión, de la acidez de las lluvias que disolvieron poco a poco la roca de la planicie calcárea y modelado las aristas cortantes de entre veinte y treinta metros de altura. La penetración del hombre en este medio cerrado no es nada fácil, de ahí su nombre, tsingy, que en lengua malagache significa "caminar de puntas". El lugar, clasificado como reserva natural integral desde 1927 e inscrito en la Lista del Patrimonio Mundial de la UNESCO en 1990, alberga una vegetación y una fauna características, a imagen de la diversidad de las especies presentes en toda la isla. En efecto, separada del continente africano hace más de 100 millones de años, la "Gran Isla" ha visto evolucionar su vegetación y su fauna en forma totalmente autónoma; así pues, es uno de los ejemplos más extraordinarios de endemismo (carácter de una especie viviente confinada a una zona particular) del medio insular: más del 80% de las casi 12 000 especies vegetales y casi 1 200 especies animales registradas en la isla no se han desarrollado en ninguna otra parte del mundo. Sin embargo, cerca de 300 especies de Madagascar podrían estar en vías de extinción.

TSINGY DE BEMARAHA, NEAR MAJUNGA, MADAGASCAR.

With a surface area of 587,000 sq. km. (226,600 sq.mi.), Madagascar is the fourth largest island in the world. In its western, most arid part, the strange mineral forest named Tsingy de Bemaraha is found. This geological formation, known as "karst", results from erosion : acid rains have slowly dissolved the chalky plateau's stone and chiseled these jagged ridges twenty to thirty meters high. Exploring this closed environment is rather difficult, hence its name "tsingy", meaning "to walk on tip-toes" in the Malagasy language. This site, classified as an entire natural reserve since 1927 and inscribed on the UNESCO World Heritage List in 1990, harbors a vegetation and wildlife as diverse as the species found on the rest of the island. Indeed, the "Grande Ile" saw its vegetation and wildlife evolve in a completely autonomous way since its separation from the African continent over 100 million years ago. It is one of the most remarkable examples of endemism (a characteristic of a living species confined to a particular area) found within island environments : over 80% of the 12,000 or so plant species and nearly 1,200 animal species catalogued on the island have not developed anywhere else. However, nearly 300 species on Madagascar are believed to be endangered.

TSINGY DE BEMAHARA, RÉGION DE MAJUNGA, MADAGASCAR.

Avec une superficie de 587 000 km², Madagascar est la quatrième plus importante île du monde. À l'ouest, dans la partie la plus aride, se trouve l'étrange forêt minérale des Tsingy de Bemahara. Cette formation géologique, appelée karst, est le résultat de l'érosion, l'acidité des pluies ayant peu à peu dissous la pierre du plateau calcaire et ciselé ces arêtes tranchantes de vingt à trente mètres de haut. La pénétration de l'homme dans ce milieu fermé se révèle peu aisée, d'où son nom, tsingy signifiant en langue malgache « marcher sur la pointe des pieds ». Le site, classé en réserve naturelle intégrale dès 1927 et inscrit sur la Liste du patrimoine mondial de l'Unesco en 1990, abrite une végétation et une faune caractéristiques, à l'image de la diversité des espèces présentes sur l'ensemble de l'île. En effet, détachée du continent africain il y a plus de 100 millions d'années, la « Grande Ile » a vu sa végétation et sa faune évoluer de manière totalement autonome ; elle est ainsi l'un des plus formidables exemples d'endémisme (caractère d'une espèce vivante confinée dans une aire particulière) des milieux insulaires : plus de 80 % des quelque 12 000 espèces végétales et presque 1 200 espèces animales répertoriées dans l'île ne se sont développées nulle part ailleurs. Près de 300 espèces de Madagascar seraient cependant menacées d'extinction.

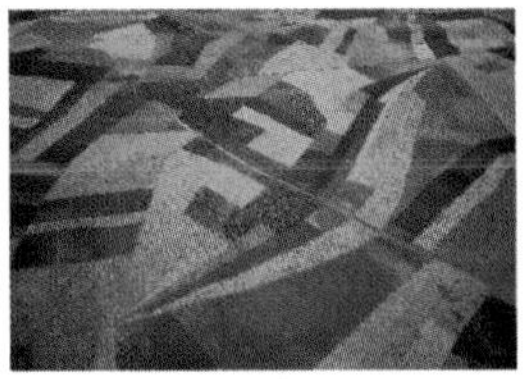

N 32°33' W 6°36'

PAISAJE AGRÍCOLA ENTRE LA PRESA AL MASSIRA Y RABAT, MARRUECOS.

Preocupado por mejorar su producción agrícola, Marruecos fomenta el desarrollo, en amplias zonas de explotación, de una agricultura moderna esencialmente orientada hacia la producción intensiva de cereales (trigo, cebada, maíz). Como el país no cuenta con una pluviosidad suficiente en todo su territorio, recurrir a la irrigación es a menudo indispensable. Con una riqueza mayor de cursos de agua que el resto de los países del Maghreb, Marruecos emprendió desde hace tiempo la construcción de grandes presas, que permiten proveer de agua importantes perímetros cultivados, que pueden alcanzar los 1 000 km². La superficie de las tierras irrigadas de Marruecos representa cerca de 800 000 hectáreas, o sea más del 11% del territorio. La construcción de nuevas presas, como la de Mjaàra, la más grande del país, debería permitir aumentar aún más estas superficies.

AGRICULTURAL LANDSCAPE BETWEEN THE AL MASSIRA DAM AND RABAT, MOROCCO.

Anxious to improve its agricultural yields, Morocco is encouraging the development of modern farming, essentially oriented toward intensive production of cereals (wheat, barley, corn...), over huge areas of exploitation. As the country does not have sufficient rainfall over all of its territory, it often proves essential to use irrigation. Morocco, richer in waterways than other Maghreban countries, has long been involved in the construction of large dams that make it possible to supply water to large farmed areas covering up to 1,000 sq. km. (400 sq. mi.). The surface area of irrigated lands in Morocco represents close to 800,000 hectares (2,000,000 acres), or over 11% of its territory; the construction of new dams such as the Mjaara, the largest in the country, should make it possible to extend these areas even more.

PAYSAGE AGRICOLE ENTRE LE BARRAGE AL MASSIRA ET RABAT, MAROC.

Soucieux d'améliorer ses rendements agricoles, le Maroc encourage le développement, sur de vastes zones d'exploitation, d'une agriculture moderne essentiellement orientée vers la production intensive de céréales (blé, orge, maïs...). Le pays ne bénéficiant pas d'une pluviosité suffisante sur la totalité de son territoire, le recours à l'irrigation s'avère souvent indispensable. Plus riche en cours d'eau que les autres pays du Maghreb, le Maroc s'est depuis longtemps engagé dans la construction de grands barrages qui permettent de pourvoir en eau d'importants périmètres cultivés pouvant atteindre 1 000 km². La superficie des terres irriguées du Maroc représente près de 800 000 hectares, soit plus de 11 % du territoire ; la construction de nouveaux barrages, tel celui de Mjaàra, le plus grand du pays, devrait permettre d'augmenter encore ces surfaces.

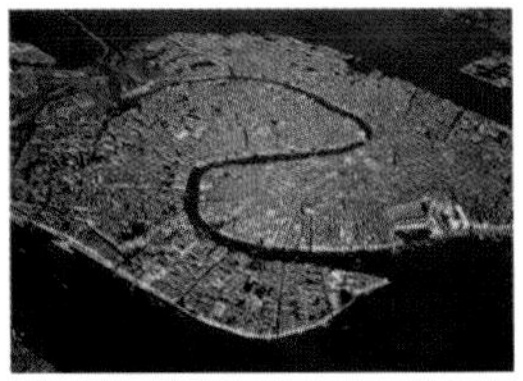

N 45° 35' E 12° 34'

VISTA GENERAL DE VENECIA, ITALIA.

Venecia no es una isla, sino un archipiélago constituido por 118 islas, separadas por 200 canales montados por una sucesión de más de 400 puentes. El Gran Canal, "la calle más hermosa del mundo" según Commynes, cronista francés del siglo XV, es su principal arteria. En sus riberas, los miembros de la aristocracia veneciana edificaron los palacios más hermosos de la época medieval y del Renacimiento, así como las principales iglesias de la ciudad. Semejantes construcciones, así como el resto de los principales puntos de referencia de la ciudad como la Plaza de San Marcos, el Palacio Ducale, o el Teatro La Fenice (por citar sólo algunos), simbolizan el destino excepcional de la Serenísima, relacionada ante todo con el dominio del mar; porque, desde el año mil, Venecia trata de imponer su poderío marítimo, en el plano comercial y político, primero en el Mar Adriático y después en todo el Mediterráneo y hasta los confines del Mar Negro, con la instalación de establecimientos comerciales. Las potencias marítimas dominaron al mundo hasta el siglo XVII : Atenas, Roma, Génova, Venecia, los Países Bajos e Inglaterra, después las potencias continentales ganaron la batalla. Se cree que el siglo XXI asistirá al regreso de las potencias marítimas, Europa, Estados Unidos y Japón, tanto por razones comerciales como por la ubicación de las poblaciones en las cercanías de los mares y de los océanos.

GENERAL VIEW OF VENICE, ITALY.

Venice is not an island, but an archipelago of 118 islands separated by 200 canals spanned by over 400 bridges. The Grand Canal, the "most beautiful street in the world" according to Commynes, a French chronicler of the 15th century, constitutes its main artery; on its banks, members of Venetian aristocracy built the most beautiful palaces of the Middle Ages and Renaissance as well as the city's main churches. Such constructions, as well as the city's other main landmarks, namely Saint Mark's Square, the Doges' Palace or La Fenice theater (to mention only a few), symbolize the exceptional destiny of the Serenissima, connected above all to its command of the seas: from the year 1,000 on, Venice tried to impose its sea power on commercial and political levels, throughout the Adriatic, the Mediterranean and as far as the confines of the Black Sea, by establishing commercial outposts. Naval powers dominated the world until the 17th century: Athens, Rome, Genoa, Venice, the Netherlands and England, and then the continental powers won over. It is believed that the 21st century will witness a return to great sea powers for trading reasons, i.e. Europe, the United States and Japan, and also due to populations being located close to seas and oceans.

VUE GÉNÉRALE DE VENISE, ITALIE.

Venise n'est pas une île, mais un archipel de 118 îles, séparées par 200 canaux qu'enjambent plus de 400 ponts. Le Grand Canal, « plus belle rue du monde » d'après Commynes, chroniqueur français du XVe siècle, en constitue la principale artère ; sur ses rives, ont été édifiés les plus beaux palais de l'époque médiévale et de la Renaissance par les membres de l'aristocratie vénitienne ainsi que les principales églises de la ville. De telles constructions, comme d'ailleurs les autres principaux points de repère de la ville que sont la place Saint Marc, le Palais des Doges ou encore le théâtre de la Fenice (pour n'en citer que quelques uns), symbolisent le destin exceptionnel de la Sérénissime, lié avant tout à la maîtrise de la mer ; car dès l'an mil, Venise tente d'imposer sa puissance maritime, sur les plans commercial et politique, dans l'Adriatique puis dans l'ensemble de la Méditerranée et jusqu'aux confins de la mer Noire, par l'établissement de comptoirs commerciaux. Les puissances maritimes ont dominé le monde jusqu'au XVIIe siècle : Athènes, Rome, Gênes, Venise, les Pays-Bas et l'Angleterre, puis les puissances continentales l'ont emporté. On pense que le XXIe siècle verra le retour des grandes puissances maritimes, Europe, Etats-Unis et Japon, tant pour des raisons de commerce que pour la localisation des populations au voisinage des mers et des océans.

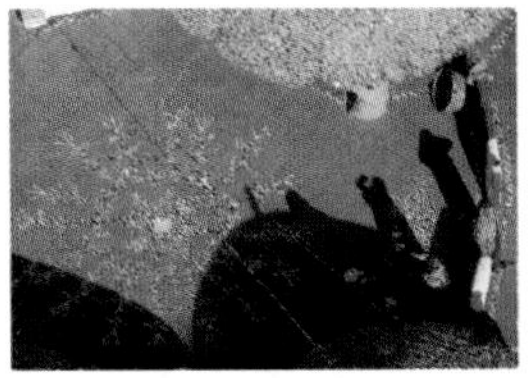

N 26°21' E 72°45'

DIBUJO EN EL PATIO DE UNA CASA DE PUEBLO AL OESTE DE JODHPUR, RAJASTHAN, INDIA.

En el Estado de Rajasthan, en la India, los muros y los patios de las casas a menudo están adornadas con motivos decorativos realizados en cal o en otras substancias de origen mineral. Con una antigüedad de casi 5 000 años, esta tradición está más particularmente arraigada en las zonas rurales. Existen dos tipos de dibujos: las figuras geométricas se llaman mandana y las representaciones de personajes o de animales se llaman thapa. Elaborados por mujeres, los dibujos se renuevan para cada una de las fiestas, en los muros y los pisos enlucidos con una mezcla de lodo y de estiércol de vaca. Al personalizar cada hogar, tienen, además de su carácter meramente estético, una importante función social: son el testimonio de la prosperidad de los habitantes del lugar y traen, dicen, alegría y felicidad. Solamente los hogares en duelo se abstienen de decorar de esta forma su casa durante todo el año que sigue al deceso.

DRAWING IN THE COURTYARD OF A VILLAGE HOUSE IN THE WESTERN PART OF JODHPUR, RAJASTHAN, INDIA.

In Rajasthan, India, walls and courtyards of houses are often adorned with decorative motifs generally done in lime or other substances of mineral origin. Nearly 5,000 years old, this tradition is more firmly established in rural areas. There are two types of drawings: the geometric figures are called mandana and the representations of persons or animals, thapa. Drawn by women, they are replaced for every feast on walls and floors freshly roughcast with a mixture of mud and cowdung. Giving a personal touch to every home, they have, besides their merely aesthetic character, an important social function: they testify to the prosperity of the inhabitants of that place and are said to bring good fortune and happiness. Only homes in mourning abstain from decorating their house in this fashion for a whole year following a death.

DESSIN DANS LA COUR D'UNE MAISON VILLAGEOISE À L'OUEST DE JODHPUR, RAJASTHAN, INDE.

Dans l'État du Rajasthan, en Inde, les murs et les cours des maisons sont souvent ornés de motifs décoratifs généralement réalisés à la chaux ou au moyen d'autres substances d'origine minérale. Vieille de près de 5 000 ans, cette tradition est plus particulièrement ancrée dans les milieux ruraux. Les dessins réalisés sont de deux types : on appelle mandana les figures géométriques et thapa les représentations de personnages ou d'animaux. Exécutés par les femmes, ils sont renouvelés lors de chaque fête sur des murs et des sols recrépis d'un mélange de boue et de bouse de vache. Personnalisant chaque demeure, ils ont, outre leur caractère purement esthétique, une importante fonction sociale : ils témoignent de la prospérité des habitants du lieu et apportent, dit-on, bonheur et félicité. Seuls les foyers endeuillés s'abstiennent de décorer ainsi leur maison durant toute l'année suivant un décès.

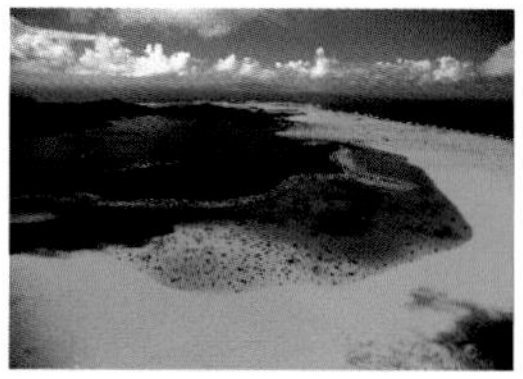

S 16°30' W 151°44'

BORA BORA, POLINESIA FRANCESA, FRANCIA.

El Archipiélago de las Îles Sous le Vent, en la Polinesia francesa, territorio de ultramar desde 1946, alberga a esta isla de 38 km^2 cuyo nombre significa "la que nació primero". Está constituida por la parte emergente del cráter de un viejo volcán, con una antigüedad de 7 millones de años, rodeada de un arrecife-barrera de coral. En este último se desarrollaron motus, islotes coralífero recubiertos de una vegetación constituida casi exclusivamente de cocoteros. La única salida de la laguna al mar es el paso de Teavanui, lo suficientemente profunda para permitir la entrada de cargueros y de navíos de guerra. Por lo demás, la isla fue utilizada como base militar por los norteamericanos de 1942 a 1946 y fue, hasta que se construyó el aeropuerto de Tahití, una de las únicas islas de la región en que disponían de una pista de aviación. Como en la mayoría de las regiones coralíferas, que representan casi 18 millones de km^2 en el mundo, las aguas de Bora-Bora contienen una enorme biodiversidad; se cuentan más de 300 especies diferentes de peces. Las principales actividades de la isla son la pesca y el turismo.

BORA BORA, FRENCH POLYNESIA, FRANCE.

The Leeward Islands (or Iles-sous-le-vent archipelago) in French Polynesia - an overseas territory since 1946 - include this 38 sq. km (15 sq. mi.) island, whose name means "the first born". It is made up of the emerged part of a 7 million years old volcano crater, surrounded by a barrier reef, where motus have developed - coral islets covered with vegetation consisting almost exclusively of coconut trees. The only opening of the lagoon to the ocean is the Teavanui channel, which is deep enough to permit freighters and warships to enter. The island was also used as a military basis by Americans from 1942 to 1946 and was, until the construction of the Tahiti airport, one of the only ones in the region to possess a landing strip. As in most coral regions, which represent close to 18 million sq. km. (7 million sq. mi.) around the world, the waters of Bora-Bora have great biodiversity; more than 300 different species of fish can be counted there. The island's main activities are fishing and tourism.

BORA BORA, POLYNÉSIE FRANÇAISE, FRANCE.

L'Archipel des Iles Sous le Vent, en Polynésie française, Territoire d'outre-mer depuis 1946, abrite cette île de 38 km^2 dont le nom signifie « la première née ». Elle est constituée de la partie émergée du cratère d'un ancien volcan, vieux de 7 millions d'années, entourée d'un récif-barrière de corail. Sur ce dernier se sont développés des motus, îlots coralliens couverts d'une végétation constituée presque exclusivement de cocotiers. La seule ouverture du lagon sur l'océan est la passe de Teavanui, suffisamment profonde pour permettre l'entrée des cargos et navires de guerre. L'île a d'ailleurs été utilisée comme base militaire par les Américains de 1942 à 1946 et fut, jusqu'à la construction de l'aéroport de Tahiti, l'une des seules de la région à disposer d'une piste d'aviation. Comme dans la plupart des régions coralliennes qui représentent près de 18 millions de km^2 dans le monde, les eaux de Bora Bora comportent une grande diversité biologique ; on y dénombre plus de 300 espèces différentes de poissons. Les activités principales de l'île sont la pêche et le tourisme.

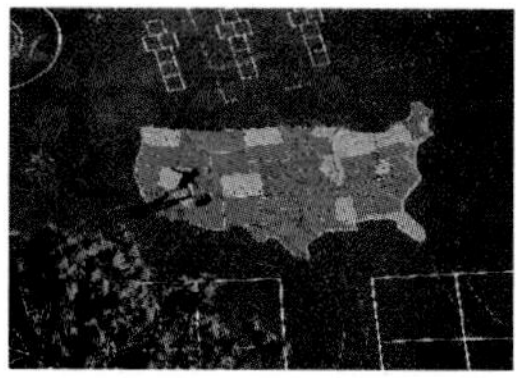

N 33°50' W 118°20'

JOVEN DEPORTISTA EN LA ESCUELA PRIMARIA TORRANCE CORNESTONE EN LOS ANGELES, CALIFORNIA, ESTADOS UNIDOS.

A imagen de este alumno que practica baloncesto en el patio de su escuela en Los Angeles, en California, el deporte forma parte integrante del sistema educativo norteamericano. Al ser un criterio importante para la admisión en las universidades, las capacidades deportivas permiten a menudo obtener una beca de estudios. En los Estados Unidos, donde la escuela es obligatoria de los 6 a los 16 años, 5.4% de la población llega al nivel universitario, lo que es una de las proporciones más elevadas del mundo. Pero en el seno de la humanidad, siguen existiendo muchos contrastes en el acceso a la educación. En África, la enseñanza secundaria solo beneficia al 5% de los niños, y el objetivo compartido a nivel internacional de volver universal la enseñanza primaria está aún lejos de poder alcanzarse: 110 millones de niños (1 de cada 5) no van a la escuela en los países en vías de desarrollo. Al comenzar este tercer milenio, uno de cada cinco adultos no sabe leer ni escribir: en estos casi 900 millones de adultos analfabetos, el 98% se encuentra en los países en vías de desarrollo, y dos tercios son mujeres.

YOUNG SPORTSMAN AT TORRANCE CORNESTONE ELEMENTARY SCHOOL, LOS ANGELES, CALIFORNIA, UNITED STATES.

This pupil training to play basketball in his Los Angeles, California, schoolyard, is an example of how sports activities form an integral part of the American educational system. An important criterion for admission to universities, sports abilities often enable students to obtain scholarships. In the United States, where school is obligatory from 6 to 16 years of age, 5.4% of the population reach the university level, one of the highest proportions in the world. But access to education continues to be widely divergent for humankind. Only 5% of African children benefit from secondary school teaching, and the internationally shared goal of making primary school teaching universal is still far from being reached: 110 million children (1 out of 5) do not attend school in developing countries. At this beginning of the third millennium, one adult out of five can neither read nor write: out of these approximately 900 million illiterate adults, 98% live in developing countries, and two-thirds of them are women.

JEUNE SPORTIF DE L'ÉCOLE ÉLÉMENTAIRE TORRANCE CORNESTONE À LOS ANGELES, CALIFORNIE, ÉTATS-UNIS.

À l'image de cet élève qui s'entraîne à jouer au basket dans la cour de son école de Los Angeles, en Californie, le sport fait partie intégrante du système éducatif nord-américain. Important critère d'admission dans les universités, les capacités sportives permettent souvent d'obtenir des bourses d'études. Aux États-Unis, où l'école est obligatoire de 6 à 16 ans, 5,4 % de la population parvient au niveau universitaire, ce qui est l'une des plus fortes proportions du monde. Mais l'accès à l'éducation demeure très contrasté au sein de l'humanité. L'enseignement secondaire ne profite, en Afrique, qu'à 5 % des enfants, et l'objectif partagé au niveau international de rendre universel l'enseignement primaire est encore loin d'être atteint : 110 millions d'enfants (1 sur 5) ne fréquentent pas l'école dans les pays en développement. En ce début de troisième millénaire, un adulte sur cinq ne sait ni lire ni écrire : sur ces quelque 900 millions d'adultes illettrés, 98 % se trouvent dans les pays en développement, et les deux-tiers sont des femmes.

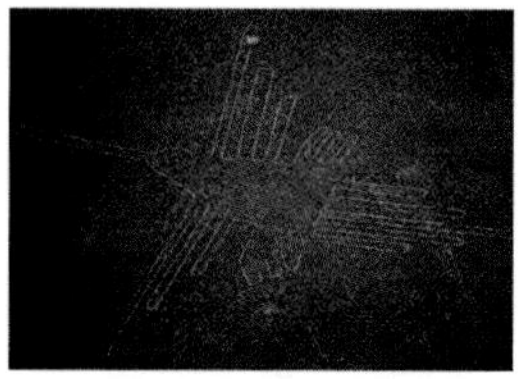

S 14°41' W 75°08'

DIBUJO DE UN COLIBRÍ EN NAZCA, PERÚ.

Hace dos mil años, el pueblo de Nazca cavó surcos en el suelo desértico de la pampa peruana, dibujando impresionantes figuras geométricas y representaciones estilizadas de plantas o de animales. Este colibrí, de casi 98 m, forma parte de las 18 siluetas de aves de este lugar inscrito en la Lista del Patrimonio Mundial de la UNESCO en 1994. Fue gracias al apasionado trabajo de la matemática alemana Maria Reiche, quien, de 1945 hasta su muerte en 1998, se dedicó a la actualización, al mantenimiento y al estudio de estos trazos, en donde todavía podemos admirar lo que probablemente era un calendario astronómico. Hoy en día, el sitio de Nazca está amenazado por los huaqueros, saqueadores de tumbas precolombinas, así como por el flujo turístico, la erosión y la contaminación industrial.

DRAWING OF A HUMMINGBIRD AT NAZCA, PERU.

Two thousand years ago, the Nazca people dug grooves in the desert soil of the Peruvian pampa, describing impressive geometric figures and stylized representations of plants or animals. This hummingbird, nearly 98 m (322 ft.) in length, forms part of the 18 outlines of birds on this site, inscribed on the UNESCO World Heritage List in 1994. Thanks to the unflagging work of the German mathematician Maria Reiche, who, from 1945 until her death in 1998, devoted herself to unveiling, caring after and studying these lines, we can still admire what was probably an astronomical calendar. The Nazca site is threatened today by huaqueros, or pillagers of pre-Columbian tombs, as well as by crowds of tourists, erosion and industrial pollution.

DESSIN DE COLIBRI À NAZCA, PÉROU.

Il y a deux mille ans, le peuple Nazca a creusé des sillons dans le sol désertique de la pampa péruvienne, dessinant d'impressionnantes figures géométriques et représentations stylisées de plantes ou d'animaux. Ce colibri de près de 98 m fait partie des 18 silhouettes d'oiseaux de ce site inscrit sur la Liste du patrimoine mondial de l'Unesco en 1994. C'est grâce au travail acharné de la mathématicienne allemande Maria Reiche, qui, de 1945 jusqu'à sa mort en 1998, s'est consacrée à la mise au jour, à l'entretien et à l'étude de ces tracés, que l'on peut encore admirer ce qui était probablement un calendrier astronomique. Le site de Nazca est aujourd'hui menacé par les huaqueros, pilleurs de tombes précolombiennes, ainsi que par l'afflux touristique, l'érosion et la pollution industrielle.

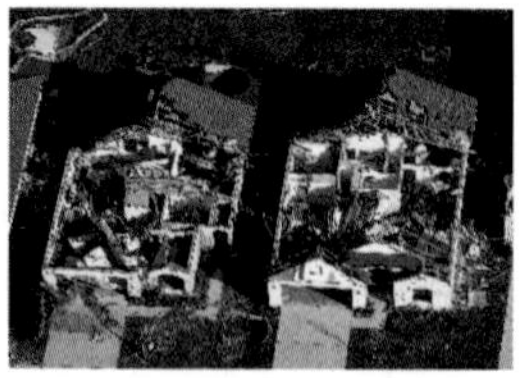

N 28°17' W 81°24'

DAÑOS PROVOCADOS POR UN TORNADO EN EL CONDADO DE OSCEOLA, FLORIDA, ESTADOS UNIDOS.

El 22 de febrero de 1998, un tornado de categoría 4 (vientos de 300 a 400 km/h) culminó su carrera en el condado de Osceola, después de devastar otros tres condados del centro de Florida. Llevándose en su torbellino varios cientos de casas, mató a 38 personas e hirió a 250. Este tipo de tornados violentos, muy raros en Florida, está generalmente relacionado con el fenómeno climatológico de El Niño que, cada cinco años aproximadamente, provoca fuertes perturbaciones en todo el globo. Así pues, el periodo comprendido entre abril de 1997 y junio de 1998, estuvo marcado por un gran número de catástrofes: tornados en Estados Unidos, ciclones en México y en Tahití, sequías en Indonesia y en el Amazonas, lluvias torrenciales en Somalia y en Kenia. Durante esos 15 meses, El Niño podría haber provocado la desaparición de más de 20 000 personas en todo el mundo. Más frecuentes y más devastadoras que antes, las catástrofes naturales habrían provocado, durante la última década, pérdidas ocho veces mayores que en los años 60.

DAMAGES FROM A TORNADO IN OSCEOLA COUNTY, FLORIDA, UNITED STATES.

On February 22nd, 1998, an F4 tornado (winds from 300 to 400 km per hr (190 to 250 mph)) reached the end of its path in Osceola County, after devastating three other counties in central Florida. Carrying away hundreds of dwellings in its vortex, it killed 38 people and injured 250. This type of violent tornado, fairly rare in Florida, is usually associated with the climatic phenomenon El Niño, which causes strong disturbances around the globe approximately every five years. Thus the period from April 1997, to June 1998, was marked by a number of disasters: tornados in the United States, cyclones in Mexico and Tahiti, drought in Indonesia and Amazonia, and torrential rains in Somalia and Kenya. During these 15 months, El Niño is said to have led to the death of over 20,000 people around the world. More frequent and more devastating now than ever before, natural catastrophes during the last decade are believed to have caused losses eight times greater than those suffered in the 60's.

DÉGÂTS D'UNE TORNADE DANS LE COMTÉ D'OSCEOLA, FLORIDE, ÉTATS-UNIS.

Le 22 février 1998, une tornade de force 4 (vents de 300 à 400 km/h) a terminé sa course dans le comté d'Osceola, après avoir dévasté trois autres comtés du centre de la Floride. Emportant dans son tourbillon plusieurs centaines d'habitations, elle a tué 38 personnes et en a blessé 250. Ce type de tornade violente, assez rare en Floride, est généralement lié au phénomène climatique El Niño qui, tous les cinq ans environ, provoque de fortes perturbations sur l'ensemble du globe. Ainsi la période d'avril 1997 à juin 1998 a été marquée par nombre de catastrophes : tornades aux États-Unis, cyclones au Mexique et à Tahiti, sécheresse en Indonésie et en Amazonie, pluies diluviennes en Somalie et au Kenya. Durant ces 15 mois, El Niño aurait été à l'origine de la disparition de plus de 20 000 personnes dans le monde. Plus fréquentes et plus dévastatrices qu'auparavant, les catastrophes naturelles auraient provoqué, au cours de la dernière décennie, des pertes huit fois plus importantes que dans les années 60.

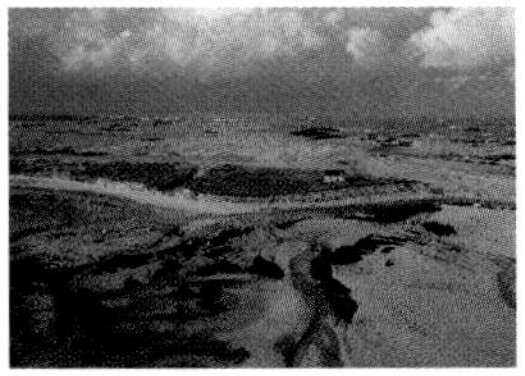

N 48°39' W 4°13'

CASA EN KEREMMA EN LA CALETA DE KERNIC CON MAREA BAJA, FINISTERRE, FRANCIA.

En el litoral de la Mancha, en Bretaña, la estrecha lengua de sedimentos graníticos, sobre la que se construyó esta casa en 1953, prolonga las dunas de Keremma y cierra casi por completo la caleta de Kernic, dejando un paso estrecho a los barcos para entrar a la bahía. Poniendo al descubierto amplias extensiones de arena cuando hay marea baja, y envolviendo de agua esta delgada espiga de dunas cuando hay marea alta, el vaivén cotidiano de estas mareas (con una amplitud de cerca de 8m) y las violentas corrientes marinas han erosionado poco a poco el frágil apoyo de esta aislada construcción. La casa, que en 1983 se encontraba a 45 metros del mar, solo se encontraba a 2 metros del vacío en 1999. Desapareció del paisaje en marzo de 2000, porque el inexorable deslizamiento de la duna obligó a su propietario a demolerla antes de que ésta se derrumbara. Algunos ordenamientos realizados por el Conservatorio del Litoral intentan proteger las dunas de Keremma de la acción erosiva de las olas. Las mareas, variaciones diarias del nivel del mar que resultan de las atracciones lunar y solar, afectan al conjunto de los mares del globo, con amplitudes que varían desde algunos centímetros sobre todo en el Mediterráneo, hasta más de 16 m (Bahía de Fundy, Canadá) en el Atlántico.

HOUSE OF KEREMMA IN KERNIC COVE AT LOW TIDE, FINISTÈRE, FRANCE.

On the coast of the English Channel, in Brittany, the narrow strip of granite deposits on which this house was constructed in 1953 is an extension of the Keremma dunes, and practically encloses Kernic cove, leaving only a narrow channel for boats to enter the bay. Uncovering large stretches of sand at low tide and surrounding this narrow, duny spit with water at high tide, the daily rise and fall of the tides (a difference of about 8 m) and the violent ocean currents have gradually eroded the fragile base of this isolated dwelling. The house, which was at a distance of 45 meters from the sea in 1983, stood only 2 meters (6 ft.) from the edge in 1999. It vanished from the landscape in March of 2000 : the inexorable crumbling of the dune forced the owner to have it demolished and removed before it collapsed. Work is being done by the Conservatoire du Littoral (Conservatoire of coasts) in an attempt to protect the Keremma dunes from the erosive effect of the waves. Tides are daily variations in sea level resulting from the attraction of the moon and the sun. They affect all the earth's seas with various amplitudes : several centimeters for the Mediterranean to more than 16 m (Bay of Fundy, Canada) for the Atlantic.

MAISON DE KEREMMA DE L'ANSE DE KERNIC À MARÉE BASSE, FINISTÈRE, FRANCE.

Sur le littoral de la Manche, en Bretagne, l'étroite langue de sédiments granitiques, sur laquelle cette maison a été construite en 1953, prolonge les dunes de Keremma et ferme presque entièrement l'anse de Kernic, laissant aux bateaux une passe étroite pour pénétrer dans la baie. Découvrant de vastes étendues sableuses à marée basse, encerclant d'eau cette mince flèche dunaire à marée haute, le va-et-vient quotidien des marées (environ 8 m d'amplitude) et les violents courants marins ont peu à peu érodé le fragile support de cette habitation isolée. La maison, qui se trouvait en 1983 à 45 mètres de la mer, n'était plus qu'à 2 mètres du vide en 1999. Elle disparut du paysage en mars 2000, l'inexorable affaissement de la dune ayant contraint le propriétaire à la faire démolir avant qu'elle ne s'effondre. Des aménagements réalisés par le Conservatoire du littoral tentent de protéger les dunes de Keremma contre l'action érosive des vagues. Les marées, variations journalières du niveau de la mer qui résultent des attractions lunaire et solaire, touchent l'ensemble des mers du globe avec des amplitudes variant de quelques centimètres, notamment pour la Méditerranée, à plus de 16 m (baie de Fundy, Canada) pour l'Atlantique.

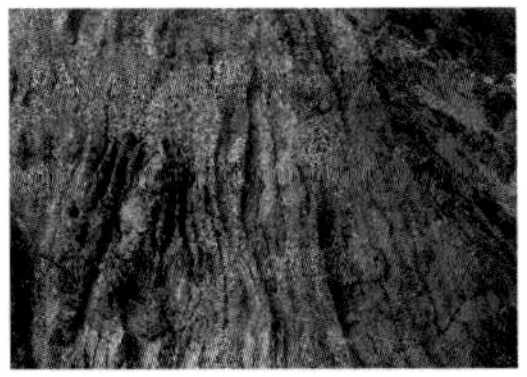

N 7°04' E 125°36'

EXPLOTACIÓN AURÍFERA CERCA DE DAVAO, ISLA DE MINDANAO, FILIPINAS.

Instalados en los lugares donde se explotan filones auríferos en la isla de Mindanao, los buscadores de oro filipinos ocupan precarios albergues hechos con ramas y lonas colgadas de los flancos de las montañas. Sus vertientes, a las que excavan sin descanso, se han debilitado por la red de galerías que a menudo se desploman por las torrenciales lluvias de los monzones, provocando la muerte de decenas de mineros. A menudo extraído con herramientas rudimentarias, como martillos o cinceles, el metal precioso se estaría sacando de aquí a razón de 40 kg por día. Desde la prehistoria, 150 000 toneladas de oro podrían haberse extraído de la totalidad del globo, del cual un tercio se utiliza para la fabricación de objetos, un tercio es atesorado por los estados y el resto se pierde sobre todo por desgaste. Hoy en día, se extraen anualmente casi 2 500 toneladas en el mundo, principalmente en África del Sur (20%), en los Estados Unidos (15%) y en Australia (13%).

GOLD MINING NEAR DAVAO, ON THE ISLAND OF MINDANAO, PHILIPPINES.

Established on exploitation sites of gold-bearing veins on the island of Mindanao, Filipino gold-seekers live in precarious shelters of branches and canvas clinging to the mountainsides. The slopes, undergoing relentless digging, are being weakened by the network of galleries, which frequently collapse under the torrential rains of the monsoons, causing the death of dozens of miners. Often extracted with rudimentary tools such as hammers or chisels, the precious metal is purportedly being removed from here at a rate of 40 kg (88 lb) per day. Since prehistoric times, 150,000 metric tons (165,000 tons) of gold are calculated to have been exploited around the globe, a third of it being used for manufacturing objects, a third hoarded by different states, and the rest lost, mostly through erosion. At the present time, nearly 2,500 metric tons (2,750 tons) are extracted every year throughout the world, mainly in South Africa (20%), the United States (15%) and Australia (13%).

EXPLOITATION AURIFÈRE PRÈS DE DAVAO, ÎLE DE MINDANAO, PHILIPPINES.

Installés sur les sites d'exploitation des filons aurifères de l'île de Mindanao, les chercheurs d'or philippins occupent des abris précaires de branchages et de bâches accrochés aux flancs des montagnes. Creusés sans répit, les versants sont fragilisés par le réseau de galeries qui s'effondrent fréquemment sous les pluies torrentielles des moussons, causant la mort de dizaines de mineurs. Souvent extrait au moyen d'un outillage rudimentaire, tel que marteaux ou ciseaux, le métal précieux serait ici prélevé à raison de 40 kg par jour. Depuis la préhistoire, 150 000 tonnes d'or auraient été exploitées sur l'ensemble du globe, un tiers étant utilisé pour la fabrication d'objets, un tiers thésaurisé par les états, et le reste perdu notamment par usure. Actuellement, près de 2 500 tonnes sont extraites chaque année dans le monde, principalement en Afrique du Sud (20 %), aux Etats-Unis (15 %) et en Australie (13 %).

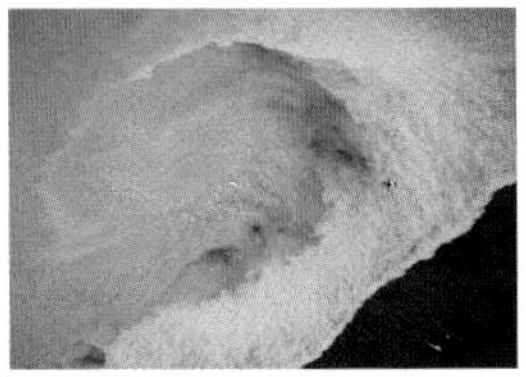

N 6°52' E 126°3'

DESECHOS DE UNA MINA DE ORO EN EL LITORAL DE LA ISLA DE MINDANAO, FILIPINAS.

La explotación de los yacimientos auríferos de la isla de Mindanao, al sur de las Filipinas, constituye una aportación económica sustancial para el país, que en los últimos años ha producido en promedio 8 toneladas de oro al año. Sin embargo, los desechos y los sedimentos que provienen de las operaciones de lavado y de selección del metal precioso se vierten diariamente en los ríos y en el mar. Estos desechos, llamados blancartes, vuelven opacas las aguas y amenazan a la fauna y a la flora marinas, tanto en el litoral como en alta mar, sobre todo a los pólipos coralíferos cuya sobrevivencia depende en gran parte de la luz. Por otra parte, productos químicos, como el mercurio y el ácido clorhídrico que se utilizan para limpiar y refinar las partículas de oro, también son vertidos en las aguas, y por su toxicidad amplifican los efectos de esta contaminación marina. Los daños provocados por las actividades mineras también afectaron al río húngaro Tisza, en enero de 2000, contaminado con cianuro (empleado en el proceso de extracción) que escapó de una mina de oro rumana.

GOLDMINE WASTES ON THE COAST OF THE ISLAND OF MINDANAO, PHILIPPINES.

The working of goldfields on the island of Mindanao, in the southern Philippines, constitutes a substantial economic contribution for the country, which has produced 8 metric tons of gold per year on average over these last few years. However, the wastes and sediments produced by washing and sorting the precious metal are poured daily into the rivers and the sea. These wastes, called "dump", make the waters opaque and are dangerous to marine fauna and flora, both along the coastline and further out at sea, and in particular to the coral polyps, whose survival depends largely on the presence of light. In addition, chemicals such as mercury and hydrochloric acid, used for cleaning and refining gold particles, are also discharged into the waters, increasing the effects of this marine pollution with their toxicity. Damages due to mining activities have also affected the Hungarian river, the Tisza, contaminated in January of 2000 with cyanide (used in the extraction process) that had escaped from a Romanian goldmine.

REJETS DE MINE D'OR SUR LE LITTORAL DE L'ÎLE DE MINDANAO, PHILIPPINES.

L'exploitation des gisements aurifères de l'île de Mindanao, au sud des Philippines, constitue un apport économique substantiel pour le pays, qui ces dernières années a produit en moyenne 8 tonnes d'or par an. Cependant, les déchets et sédiments issus des opérations de lavage et triage du métal précieux sont quotidiennement déversés dans les rivières et dans la mer. Ces rejets, appelés haldes, opacifient les eaux et mettent en péril la faune et la flore marines, tant sur le littoral que plus au large, en particulier les polypes coralliens dont la survie dépend en grande partie de la lumière. Par ailleurs, des produits chimiques, comme le mercure et l'acide chlorhydrique utilisés pour le nettoyage et le raffinage des particules d'or, sont également rejetés dans les eaux, amplifiant par leur toxicité les effets de cette pollution marine. Les dégâts dus aux activités minières ont également frappé la rivière hongroise Tisza, en janvier 2000, contaminée par du cyanure (utilisé dans le processus d'extraction) échappé d'une mine d'or roumaine.

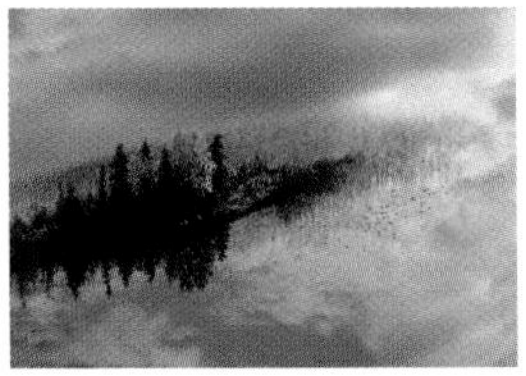

N 60°46' W 150°12'

ISLOTE BOSCOSO EN UN LAGO DE LA PENÍNSULA DE KENAI, ALASKA, ESTADOS UNIDOS.

En Alaska, el estado norteamericano más grande, con 1.5 millones de km² (o sea 1/5 de los Estados Unidos), la península de Kenai, en la costa meridional está protegida, a diferencia de la mayor parte del territorio, del permafrost (congelación permanente del suelo) gracias a un clima oceánico templado. Presenta paisajes de bosques y lagos, donde las aguas claras reflejan el cielo antes de que el invierno las convierta en hielo. Con una gran población de peces, en estos lagos abundan las truchas arcoiris y los lucios nórdicos, pero sobre todo los salmones que remontan las corrientes de agua de la península en verano y hacen las delicias de los osos negros y de los grislis de la región. Estos salmones también son objeto de una pesca deportiva y comercial; cada año se capturan 10 millones de salmones y abastecen las industrias de envasado de Alaska, que proporcionan la mitad de las conservas de salmón en el mundo.

WOODED ISLET ON A LAKE ON THE KENAI PENINSULA, ALASKA, UNITED STATES.

In Alaska, the largest American state, which occupies 1.5 million sq. km. (580,000 sq. mi.) - or one-fifth of the area of the United States, the Kenai Peninsula on the southern coast is, unlike most of the rest of the Alaskan territory, protected from permafrost (perennial freezing of the ground) by a moderate ocean climate. It exhibits landscapes of forests and lakes whose transparent waters reflect the sky before winter transforms them into ice. Full of fish, these lakes abound with rainbow trout and northern pike, and especially salmon that swim up-river through the peninsula in the summer, to the delight of black bears and grizzlies in the region. These salmon are also the target of sport and commercial fishing; 10 million are caught every year and supply the Alaskan packaging industries, which provide salmon for half the canneries in the world.

ILOT BOISÉ SUR UN LAC DE LA PÉNINSULE DE KENAÏ, ALASKA, ÉTATS-UNIS.

En Alaska, plus grand état américain avec 1,5 millions de km² (soit 1/5ᵉ des États-Unis), la péninsule de Kenaï, sur la côte méridionale est, contrairement à la majeure partie du territoire, préservée du permafrost (gel permanent du sol) par un climat océanique tempéré. Elle présente des paysages de forêts et de lacs dont les eaux claires reflètent le ciel avant que l'hiver ne les transforme en glace. Très poissonneux, ces lacs foisonnent de truites arc-en-ciel et de brochets nordiques, mais surtout de saumons qui remontent les cours d'eau de la péninsule en été et font le bonheur des ours noirs et des grizzlys de la région. Ces saumons font également l'objet d'une pêche sportive et commerciale ; 10 millions d'entre eux sont capturés chaque année et alimentent les industries de conditionnement de l'Alaska, qui fournissent pour moitié les conserveries de saumon du monde.

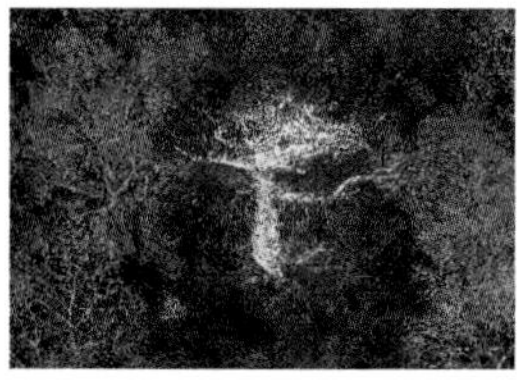

N 5°06' W 6°34'

CENIZAS DE UN ÁRBOL CERCA DE LOS MONTES GOROWI KONGOLI, BOUNA, COSTA DE MARFIL.

Al noreste de la Costa de Marfil, en una región cubierta por sabanas arbustivas y bosques claros, este árbol, derribado por el viento o por un rayo, se consumió lentamente después del paso de un incendio de sabana. Este tipo de incendios, muy frecuentes en el África del Oeste, pueden abarcar hasta un 30% de la sabana cada año. Aunque a veces tienen un origen natural, la mayoría son provocados por las técnicas tradicionelles agrícolas, de pastoreo y cinegéticas, de los pueblos de las sabanas :el paso del fuego proporciona a los suelos un fertilizante natural de origen orgánico (las cenizas) y contribuye a la rápida regeneración de los vegetales; al eliminar las hierbas altas, facilita el acercamiento y el ojeo de la caza. Desafortunadamente, la mayoría de los incendios de sabana se hace tardíamente durante la estación seca y se vuelven incontrolables con lo que destruyen poco a poco el estrato arbolado y aceleran el proceso de erosión. Esta amenaza es tanto más preocupante en Costa de Marfil cuanto que el país presenta, con 3.1% de bosques destruidos cada año, el índice más elevado de deforestación de África. Cerca del 90% de la madera extraída en África Occidental se consume en forma de leña y de carbón: por lo menos el 90% de la población dependen de ella para sus necesidades de combustible. En el mundo, la madera sigue siendo la principal fuente de energía para dos mil millones de personas que no tienen acceso a otras fuentes, como la electricidad.

ASHES OF A TREE CLOSE TO THE GOROWI KONGOLI MOUNTAINS, BOUNA, CÔTE-D'IVOIRE.

In northeastern Côte-d'Ivoire, in a region covered in shrubby savannas and sparse forests, this tree, felled by wind or lightning, is slowly being consumed after a bush fire passed. These fires, which are very frequent in West Africa, can cover up to 30% of the entire bush every year. Sometimes of natural origin, they are usually produced by the traditional farming, shepherding and hunting techniques of the savanna peoples: the passing fire provides soils with a natural fertilizer of organic origin (ashes) and contributes to the fast regeneration of plants; by eliminating the tall grass, it makes it easier to approach and chase game. Most bush fires unfortunately start late in the dry season and get out of control, gradually destroying the tree stratum and accelerating the erosion process. This threat is all the more alarming in Côte-d'Ivoire as this country exhibits the highest rate of deforestation in Africa, with 3.1% of its forest destroyed every year. Nearly 90% of the wood exploited in West Africa is consumed in the form of firewood and charcoal: at least 90% of the population depends on it for their fuel needs. Throughout the world, wood is still the main source of energy for two billion people who have no access to other sources, such as electricity.

CENDRES D'UN ARBRE PRÈS DES MONTS GOROWI KONGOLI, BOUNA, CÔTE-D'IVOIRE.

Au nord-est de la Côte-d'Ivoire, dans une région couverte de savanes arbustives et de forêts claires, cet arbre, abattu par le vent ou la foudre, s'est lentement consumé après le passage d'un feu de brousse. Ces feux, très fréquents en Afrique de l'Ouest, peuvent parcourir jusqu'à 30 % de l'ensemble de la brousse chaque année. Parfois d'origine naturelle, ils sont pour la plupart provoqués par les techniques traditionnelles agricoles, pastorales et cynégétiques, des peuples de savane : le passage du feu fournit aux sols un engrais naturel d'origine organique (les cendres) et contribue à la régénération rapide des végétaux ; en éliminant les hautes herbes, il facilite l'approche et le rabattage du gibier. La plupart des feux de brousse sont malheureusement déclenchés tardivement pendant la saison sèche et deviennent incontrôlables, détruisant peu à peu la strate arborée et accélérant le processus d'érosion. Cette menace est d'autant plus inquiétante en Côte-d'Ivoire que le pays présente, avec 3,1 % de forêt détruits chaque année, le plus fort taux de déforestation d'Afrique. Près de 90 % du bois exploité en Afrique occidentale sont consommés sous forme de bois de feu et de charbon de bois : au moins 90 % de la population en dépendent pour leurs besoins en combustible. Dans le monde, le bois demeure la première source d'énergie pour deux milliards de personnes ne disposant pas d'accès à d'autres sources comme l'électricité.

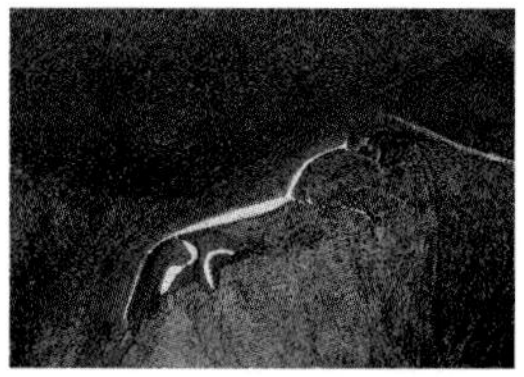

N 51°34' W 1°33'

CABALLO BLANCO DE UFFINGTON, OXFORDSHIRE, INGLATERRA.

La silueta de un caballo con una longitud de 111 m que probablemente realizaron los celtas de la Edad de Hierro, hacia el año 100 a.c., se encuentra grabada en la piedra caliza de una colina de la provincia de Oxfordshire, más abajo de las ruinas del castillo de Uffington. La tradición local ve en esta representación estilizada la imagen de un dragón, dibujado en honor a San Jorge quien, según cuenta la leyenda, habría destruido al monstruo en una colina cercana. Pero la hipótesis mas verosímil es que se trata de un grabado dedicado al culto de la diosa celta Epona, a la que por lo general se le representaba en forma de caballo. Existe un cierto numero de dibujos similares hechos en tiza, representaciones de hombres o de animales, que todavía pueden verse en Inglaterra y en Escandinavia, pero la mayoría fueron definitivamente borrados por la vegetación.

WHITE HORSE IN UFFINGTON, OXFORDSHIRE, ENGLAND.

Cut in the limestone of a hill in Oxfordshire, below the ruins of Uffington Castle, the silhouette of a horse measuring 111 m (364 ft) in length was probably made by Celts from the Iron Age, around the year 100 B. C. Local tradition sees in this stylized representation the image of a dragon, drawn in honor of Saint George, who, according to legend, vanquished the monster on a hill nearby. Nevertheless, the most likely hypothesis is that it is an engraving dedicated to the Celtic goddess, Epona, who was generally depicted with features of a horse. There still exists a number of similar chalk drawings representing men or animals in England and Scandinavia, but most have permanently been covered by vegetation.

CHEVAL BLANC D'UFFINGTON, OXFORDSHIRE, ANGLETERRE.

Gravée dans le calcaire d'une colline de la province de l'Oxfordshire, en contrebas des ruines du château d'Uffington, la silhouette d'un cheval, d'une longueur de 111 m, a probablement été réalisée par les Celtes de l'âge du fer, aux environs de l'an 100 av. J.-C. La tradition locale voit dans cette représentation stylisée l'image d'un dragon, dessiné en hommage à Saint-Georges qui, selon la légende, aurait terrassé le monstre sur une colline toute proche. Mais l'hypothèse la plus vraisemblable est celle d'une gravure dédiée au culte de la déesse celte Epona, qui était généralement représentée sous les traits d'un cheval. Il existe un certain nombre de dessins de craie similaires, représentations d'hommes ou d'animaux, encore visibles en Angleterre et en Scandinavie, mais la plupart ont été définitivement effacés par la végétation.

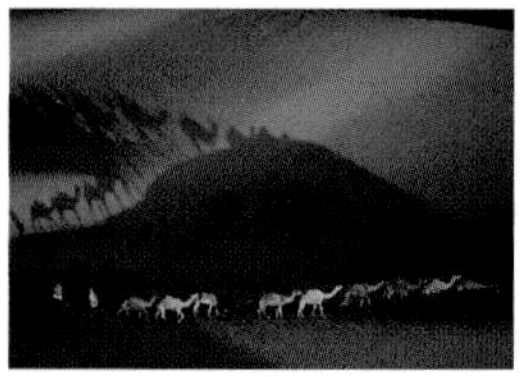

N 18°09' W 15°29'

CARAVANA DE DROMEDARIOS EN LOS ALREDEDORES DE NOUAKCHOTT, MAURITANIA.

En todos los países vecinos del Sahara, como Mauritania, el dromedario, perfectamente adaptado a la aridez del lugar, representa una parte importante del ganado nacional. Su domesticación, hace varios miles de años, permitió al hombre conquistar el desierto y posteriormente desarrollar rutas comerciales transaharianas. Verdadera "nave del desierto", este animal efectivamente solo consume de 10 a 20 kg de vegetales al día y puede permanecer sin beber agua los tres meses que dura la estación fresca. En cambio, durante el verano, solo puede aguantar algunos días sin beber, mientras que un hombre en las mismas condiciones moriría por deshidratación en 24 horas. La reserva de grasa que almacena en su única joroba interviene en su regulación térmica, lo que le permite soportar una alta temperatura en su cuerpo sin sudar para enfriarse. En Mauritania, los moros crían al dromedario por su leche y su carne, así como por su piel y su lana. A finales de los años 90, el ganado de dromedarios en el país podría haber sido de un millón de cabezas.

CARAVAN OF DROMEDARIES IN THE VICINITY OF NOUAKCHOTT, MAURITANIA.

In all countries bordering the Sahara, such as Mauritania, the dromedary, perfectly adapted to the aridness of the environment, represents a large part of the national livestock. Its domestication several thousand years ago enabled man to conquer the desert and then to develop trans-Sahara trade routes. A true "desert ship", this animal actually consumes only 10 to 20 kg (22 to 44 lb) of plants per day and can go without water during the three-month long cool season. On the other hand, it can only last a few days without drinking in the summer, whereas a man, under the same conditions, would die of dehydration in 24 hours. The fat reserves contained in its unique hump play a part in regulating its body heat, allowing the animal to withstand a warming of its body without sweating to cool off. In Mauritania, the Moors raise dromedaries for their milk and meat, as well as for their hides and wool. By the end of the 90's, the dromedary population in this country was estimated to be in the order of one million heads.

CARAVANE DE DROMADAIRES AUX ENVIRONS DE NOUAKCHOTT, MAURITANIE.

Dans tous les pays riverains du Sahara, comme la Mauritanie, le dromadaire, parfaitement adapté à l'aridité du milieu, représente une partie importante du cheptel national. Sa domestication, il y a plusieurs milliers d'années, a permis à l'homme de conquérir le désert puis de développer des routes commerciales transsahariennes. Véritable « vaisseau du désert », cet animal ne consomme en effet que 10 à 20 kg de végétaux par jour et peut se passer d'eau pendant les trois mois que dure la saison fraîche. En revanche, l'été, il ne peut tenir que quelques jours sans boire, quand un homme dans les mêmes conditions mourrait de déshydratation en 24 heures. La réserve de graisse contenue dans son unique bosse intervient dans sa régulation thermique, ce qui lui permet de supporter un échauffement de son corps sans transpirer pour se refroidir. En Mauritanie, les Maures élèvent le dromadaire pour son lait et sa viande, ainsi que pour son cuir et sa laine. À la fin des années 1990, le cheptel de dromadaires du pays serait de l'ordre d'un million de têtes.

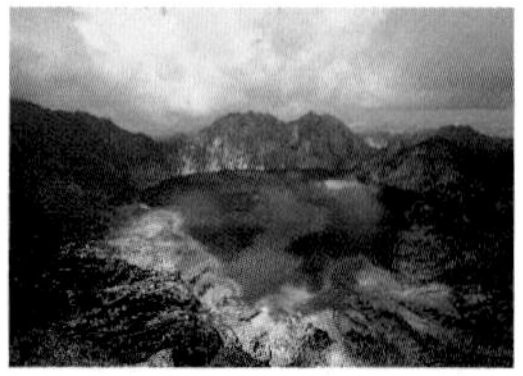

N 15°08' E 120°21'

EL PINATUBO, VOLCÁN AL NORTE DE MANILA, ISLA DE LUZÓN, FILIPINAS.

En 1991, la erupción del volcán Pinatubo, la más importante del siglo, inyectó a la atmósfera cerca de 30 millones de toneladas de sulfatos hasta alturas cercanas a los 25 km, y formaron un velo de aerosoles que hizo pasar temporalmente la radiación solar disponible para el planeta de 200 watts por metro cuadrado a 196 watts por metro cuadrado. Este episodio geológico provocó entre 1992 y 1993 una disminución de las temperaturas globales terrestres de varias décimas de grados. En el siglo XX, ya se habían apreciado las consecuencias de otras dos erupciones violentas, la del Monte Agung (Indonesia) en 1963 y la del Chichonal (México) en 1982. Sin embargo, los efectos atmosféricos y climáticos de tales sucesos son limitados en el tiempo y no deben hacer olvidar los riesgos de recalentamiento global de los climas terrestres relacionados con las actividades humanas, en particular la deforestación y el creciente consumo de combustibles fósiles, que ya se han cuadruplicado en cincuenta años. Durante el mismo periodo, la población mundial solo se duplicó.

THE PINATUBO, A VOLCANO NORTH OF MANILA, LUZON ISLAND, PHILIPPINES.

In 1991, the eruption of the Pinatubo volcano, the largest one of the century, hurled about 30 million metric tons (33 million tons) of sulfates into the atmosphere at altitudes of up to 25 km (15 mi.) or so, forming a cloud of aerosols that temporarily reduced the penetration of solar radiation available for the planet from 200 watts per sq. m. to 196 watts per sq. m. This geological episode caused a lowering of overall terrestrial temperatures by several tenths of a degree in 1992-1993. In the 20th century, the consequences of two other violent eruptions, those of Mount Agung (Indonesia) in 1963 and El Chichón (Mexico) in 1982, had already been observed. The atmospheric and climatic effects of such events are limited, however, in time and must not make us forget the risks of global warming of the earth's climates due to human activities, in particular to deforestation and the growing consumption of fossil fuels, which has already increased by a factor of four in fifty years. Over the same period, the world population merely doubled.

LE PINATUBO, VOLCAN AU NORD DE MANILLE, ÎLE DE LUZON, PHILIPPINES.

En 1991, l'éruption du volcan Pinatubo, la plus importante du siècle, a injecté dans l'atmosphère environ 30 millions de tonnes de sulfates jusqu'à des altitudes voisines de 25 km, formant un voile d'aérosols qui a fait passer temporairement le rayonnement solaire disponible pour la planète de 200 watts par mètre carré à 196 watts par mètre carré. Cet épisode géologique a entraîné en 1992-1993 un abaissement des températures globales terrestres de plusieurs dixièmes de degrés. Au XXe siècle, on avait déjà noté les conséquences de deux autres éruptions violentes, celles du mont Agung (Indonésie) en 1963 et d'El Chichón (Mexique) en 1982. Les effets atmosphériques et climatiques de tels événements sont toutefois limités dans le temps et ne doivent pas faire oublier les risques de réchauffement global des climats terrestres liés aux activités humaines, en particulier la déforestation et la consommation croissante de combustibles fossiles déjà multipliée par quatre en cinquante ans. Durant la même période, la population mondiale ne faisait que doubler.

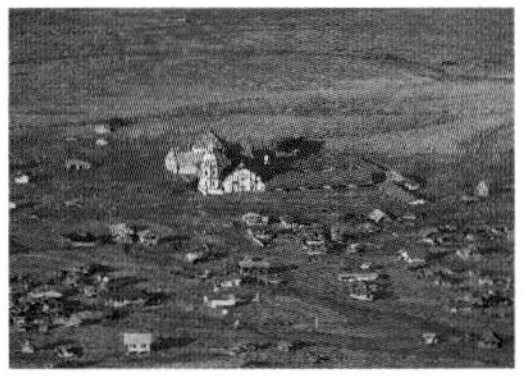

N 14°59' E 120°39'

PUEBLO DE BACOLOR BAJO UN DESLIZAMIENTO DE LODO, ISLA DE LUZÓN, FILIPINAS.

En 1991, el volcán Pinatubo, en la isla de Luzón en las Filipinas, entró en erupción después de casi seis siglos de permanecer dormido, y proyectó hasta un altura de 35 000 metros una nube de 18 millones de m³ de gas sulfuroso y de cenizas que eliminó cualquier tipo de vida en un radio de 14 km. En los días que siguieron, las lluvias torrenciales de un ciclón se mezclaron con las cenizas regadas a varios miles de km², y provocaron importantes deslizamientos de lodo, los lahares, que se tragaron a pueblos enteros. Incluso varios años después de la erupción, este fenómeno se sigue reproduciendo con cada tormenta tropical y nuevos pueblos, como Bacolor en 1995, son devastados por los lahares. Antes de la desastrosa erupción del 15 de junio de 1991, cerca de 60 000 personas pudieron ser evacuadas, y gracias a ello el balance se limitó a 875 muertos y a un millón de damnificados. Cerca de 600 millones de habitantes en nuestro planeta viven bajo la amenaza de los volcanes, y cada año mueren en promedio mas de 700 personas durante erupciones volcánicas. Este balance es sin embargo menor que el de otro tipo de catástrofes naturales.

VILLAGE OF BACOLOR UNDER A MUDSLIDE, LUZON ISLAND, PHILIPPINES.

In 1991, the Pinatubo volcano, on Luzon Island in the Philippines, erupted after having been dormant for nearly six centuries, ejecting to an altitude of 35,000 m a cloud of 18 million cu. m. (636 million cu. ft.) of sulfur-containing gas and ash that annihilated all life within a radius of 14 km. In the days following, torrential rains from a cyclone mingled with the ash scattered over several thousand sq. km., producing large mudslides, or lahars, that swallowed up whole villages. Even several years after the eruption, this phenomenon recurs with every tropical storm, and new villages, such as Bacolor in 1995, are devastated by lahars. Before the cataclysmic eruption of June 15, 1991, close to 60,000 people were successfully evacuated, limiting the final toll to 875 dead and a million disaster victims. Some 600 million inhabitants on our planet live under the threat of volcanoes and, every year, an average of more than 700 people are killed in volcanic eruptions. This toll is lower however than that of other types of natural disaster.

VILLAGE DE BACOLOR SOUS UNE COULÉE DE BOUE, ÎLE DE LUZON, PHILIPPINES.

En 1991, le volcan Pinatubo, sur l'île de Luçon aux Philippines, entre en éruption après près de six siècles de sommeil, projetant jusqu'à 35 000 m d'altitude un nuage de 18 millions de m³ de gaz sulfureux et de cendres qui anéantit toute vie dans un rayon de 14 km. Dans les jours qui suivent, les pluies diluviennes d'un cyclone se mêlent aux cendres éparpillées sur plusieurs milliers de km², provoquant d'importantes coulées de boues, les lahars, qui engloutissent des villages entiers. Même plusieurs années après l'éruption, ce phénomène se reproduit à chaque tempête tropicale et de nouveaux villages, comme Bacolor en 1995, sont dévastés par des lahars. Avant l'éruption cataclysmique du 15 juin 1991, près de 60 000 personnes ont pu être évacuées, limitant le bilan à 875 morts et un million de sinistrés. Quelque 600 millions d'habitants de notre planète vivent sous la menace de volcans et, chaque année, en moyenne, plus de 700 personnes sont tuées lors d'éruptions volcaniques. Ce bilan est cependant plus faible que celui des autres types de catastrophes naturelles.

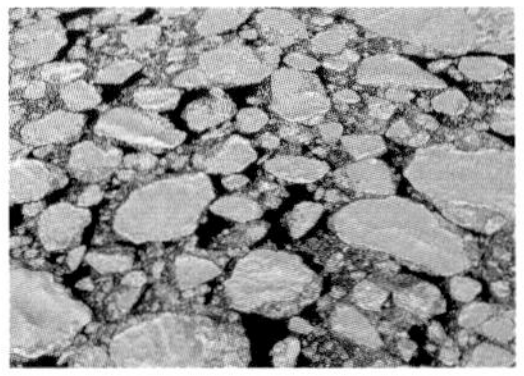

N 75°57' W 92°28'

PAISAJE HELADO, TERRITORIO NUNAVUT, CANADÁ.

A 200 km del círculo polar, el Nunavut representa 2 millones de km² de archipiélagos, de agua y de hielo, lo que equivale a 1/5 del Canadá. En invierno, mientras que las temperaturas pueden alcanzar mínimos de -37°C, la banquisa permanente del centro del Artico y la banquisa costera formada por la congelación de las aguas de los estuarios y de las bahías se juntan, y ofrecen un paisaje continuo de hielo sobre el que sólo pueden desplazarse perros de tiro y motonieves. En verano, el hielo se funde y se fractura bajo la acción de las corrientes marinas y de los vientos y crean plataformas que se deslizan, llamadas *pack*. Esta liberación de la temporada de las aguas permite que se vuelvan a abrir las rutas de migración de las ballenas y de otros mamíferos marinos, y la llegada de los cargueros de abastecimiento. Ocupado por mas de 20 000 inuits, que representan el 85% de la población local, el Nunavut, cuyo nombre significa "nuestra tierra" en la lengua de los inuits, el inuktitut, obtuvo su estatuto de territorio en abril de 1999. El pueblo inuit está presente en tres continentes en el conjunto de la zona ubicada mas allá del círculo polar ártico, a razón de 55 000 individuos en América del Norte (Alaska y Canadá), más de 42 000 en Groenlandia, y 2 000 en Siberia.

ICE LANDSCAPE, NUNAVUT TERRITORY, CANADA

With 60% of its area north of the Arctic Circle, Nunavut represents 2 million sq. km. of archipelagos, water and ice, and one-fifth the area of Canada. In winter, while temperatures can reach lows of -37°C (-35°F), the permanent ice cap of the central Arctic and the coastal ice, formed by the freezing of estuary and bay waters, are joined, offering a continuous landscape of ice negotiable by dogsled and snowmobile. In summer, the ice melts and breaks up under the effect of ocean currents and winds, creating drifting platforms called *pack ice*. This seasonal breaking-up of the waters permits the reopening of migration routes for whales and other marine mammals, and the arrival of supply ships. Inhabited by more than 20,000 Inuit, who represent 85% of the local population, Nunavut, whose name means "our earth" in the Inuit language, Inuktitut, attained the status of territory in April of 1999. The Inuit people are to be found on three continents in the entire area situated beyond the Arctic Circle, with a total of 55,000 individuals in North America (Alaska and Canada), over 42,000 in Greenland, and 2,000 in Siberia.

PAYSAGE DE GLACE, TERRITOIRE NUNAVUT, CANADA.

À 200 km du cercle polaire, le Nunavut représente 2 millions de km² d'archipels, d'eau et de glace, soit 1/5ᵉ du Canada. En hiver, alors que les températures peuvent atteindre des minima de -37 °C, la banquise permanente du centre de l'Arctique et la banquise côtière formée par le gel des eaux des estuaires et des baies se rejoignent, offrant un paysage continu de glace praticable par les attelages de chiens et les motoneiges. En été, la glace fond et se fracture sous l'action des courants marins et des vents, créant des plates-formes dérivantes appelées *pack*. Cette libération saisonnière des eaux permet la réouverture des routes de migration des baleines et autres mammifères marins, et l'arrivée des cargos de ravitaillement. Occupé par plus de 20 000 Inuits, qui représentent 85 % de la population locale, le Nunavut, dont le nom signifie « notre terre » dans la langue des Inuits, l'inuktitut, a accédé au statut de territoire en avril 1999. Le peuple inuit est présent sur trois continents dans l'ensemble de la zone située au-delà du cercle polaire arctique, à raison de 55 000 individus en Amérique du Nord (Alaska et Canada), plus de 42 000 au Groenland, et 2 000 en Sibérie.

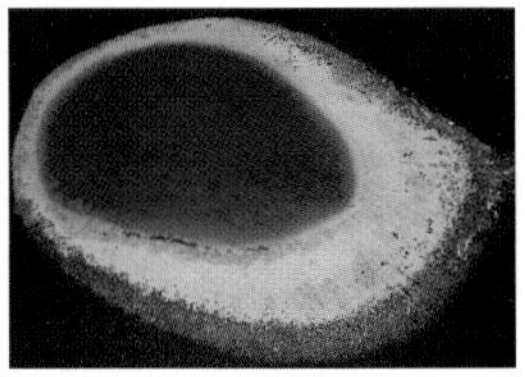

N 4°16' E 73°28'

EL OJO DE LAS MALDIVAS, ATOLÓN DE MALE NORD, MALDIVAS.

El ojo de las Maldivas es un faro, formación coralífera desarrollada en un soporte rocoso que se desplomó con el paso del tiempo, y sólo dejó aparecer un arrecife anular que rodea a una laguna poco profunda. Dado que la formación de corales requiere una temperatura del agua relativamente alta, los atolones se desarrollan principalmente en las regiones intertropicales. El archipiélago de las Maldivas, en el corazón de las aguas tibias (27°C) del Océano Índico, esta compuesto por 26 grandes atolones que reúnen 1190 islas o islotes, de los cuales los turistas habitan cerca de 300 ya sea de forma permanente, o bien por temporadas. Dado que es el país mas bajo del mundo con un punto culminante que no sobrepasa los 2.50 m, el archipiélago de las Maldivas sufrió los efectos devastadores de varios maremotos; sería el primer territorio tragado si el nivel de los océanos llegara a elevarse.

L'ŒIL DES MALDIVES, NORTH MALE ATOLL, MALDIVES.

L'Œil des Maldives is a faro, a coral formation growing on a rocky base that has crumbled with time, leaving only a ring-shaped reef surrounding a shallow lagoon. Since the coral formation requires a relatively high water temperature, atolls develop mostly in intertropical regions. The Maldive archipelago, in the heart of the warm water (27°C (80°F)) of the Indian Ocean, is composed of 26 large atolls grouping together 1190 islands or islets, close to 300 of which are permanently inhabited or visited seasonally by tourists. The country with the lowest altitude in the world, whose highest point does not exceed 2.50 m (8 ft), the Maldive archipelago has suffered the devastating effects of several tidal waves; it would be the first territory swallowed up if the ocean level ever rose.

L'ŒIL DES MALDIVES, ATOLL DE MALE NORD, MALDIVES.

L'Œil des Maldives est un faro, formation corallienne développée sur un support rocheux qui s'est affaissé au cours du temps, ne laissant apparaître qu'un récif annulaire entourant une lagune peu profonde. La formation de coraux nécessitant une température de l'eau relativement élevée, les atolls se développent principalement dans les régions intertropicales. L'archipel des Maldives, au cœur des eaux tièdes (27 °C) de l'océan Indien, est composé de 26 grands atolls regroupant 1190 îles ou îlots, dont près de 300 sont habités de façon permanente, ou saisonnière par des touristes. Pays le plus bas du monde avec un point culminant n'excédant pas 2,50 m, l'archipel des Maldives a subi les effets dévastateurs de plusieurs raz de marée ; il serait le premier territoire englouti si le niveau des océans venait à s'élever.

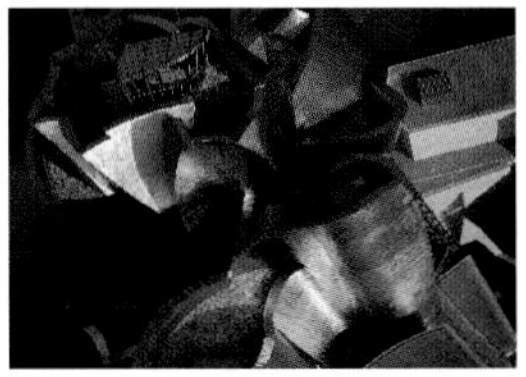

N 43°24' W 2°91'

MUSEO GUGGENHEIM DE BILBAO, PAÍS VASCO, ESPAÑA.

Inaugurado en 1997, tres años después de la colocación de la primera piedra, el museo Guggenheim de Bilbao se inscribe en el marco de un programa de reconversión urbanística de esta ciudad industrial. Con un costo de construcción de 100 millones de dólares, el edificio fue concebido a través de un programa informático que se utiliza en aeronáutica, por el arquitecto californiano Franck O. Gehry. Su estructura de vidrio, acero y piedra caliza, en parte recubierta de titanio, recuerda la tradición de construcción naval de la ciudad. Con una superficie total de 24 000 m², el museo ofrece 11 000 m² de espacio de exposición, repartidos en 19 salas, entre las que se encuentra una de las galerías más grande del mundo (130 m x 30 m). Al igual que todos los museos norteamericanos o europeos, administrados por la Fundación Salomón R. Guggenheim, celebre mecenas, el museo presenta obras de arte contemporáneo. En menos de un año, mas de 1 300 000 visitantes han venido a admirarlas, y este atractivo cultural le ha dado a la ciudad un nuevo aliento. Actualmente, se han enlistado más de 40 000 museos y colecciones públicas en el mundo.

GUGGENHEIM MUSEUM BILBAO, BASQUE COUNTRY, SPAIN.

Inaugurated in 1997, three years after the foundation stone was laid, the Guggenheim Museum Bilbao comes within the framework of a program of urban redevelopment of this industrial city. With a construction cost of $100 million (US), the building was conceived by California architect Frank O. Gehry, with the help of a computer program used in aeronautics. Its structure in glass, steel and limestone, partly covered in titanium, recalls the city's tradition of naval construction. The museum, with a total surface area of 24,000 sq. m. (350,400 sq. ft.), offers 11,000 sq. m. (160,600 sq. ft.) of exhibition space distributed through 19 rooms, including one of the largest galleries in the world (130 m x 30 m (425 ft x 98 ft)). As in the case of all American or European museums managed by the Solomon R. Guggenheim Foundation, of the famous multi-millionaire, the museum exhibits works of contemporary art. In less than one year, more than 1,300,000 visitors had come to admire them, and this cultural attraction has breathed new life into the city. At present, more than 40,000 museums and public collections are listed in the world.

MUSÉE GUGGENHEIM DE BILBAO, PAYS BASQUE, ESPAGNE.

Inauguré en 1997, trois ans après la pose de la première pierre, le musée Guggenheim de Bilbao s'inscrit dans le cadre d'un programme de reconversion urbanistique de cette ville industrielle. D'un coût de construction de 100 millions de dollars, le bâtiment a été conçu à l'aide d'un programme informatique utilisé dans l'aéronautique, par l'architecte californien Franck O. Gehry. Sa structure de verre, d'acier et de pierre calcaire, en partie couverte de titane, évoque la tradition de construction navale de la ville. D'une superficie totale de 24 000 m², le musée offre 11 000 m² d'espace d'exposition répartis en 19 salles, parmi lesquelles l'une des plus grandes galeries du monde (130 m x 30 m). Comme l'ensemble des musées américains ou européens gérés par la fondation Solomon R. Guggenheim, célèbre mécène, le musée présente des œuvres d'art contemporain. En moins d'un an, plus de 1 300 000 visiteurs sont venus les admirer, et cette attraction culturelle a redonné à la ville un nouveau souffle. Actuellement, plus de 40 000 musées et collections publiques ont été répertoriés dans le monde.

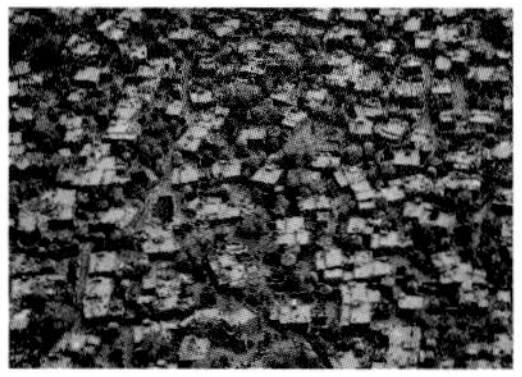

N 14°23' W 3°39'

PUEBLO DOGON CERCA DE BANDIAGARA, MALI.

Presentes desde hace más de cinco siglos en el noreste de Mali, los dogones, agricultores sedentarios, se refugiaron en las inmediaciones del acantilado de Bandiagara, cerca de Mopti, para escapar a la islamización. Sus pueblos están formados de un conjunto de terrenos concedidos, y cada uno, cerrado por un muro, alberga a una familia. Construidas con banco (mezcla de tierra, paja y cascarilla de arroz), las habitaciones de forma rectangular y sin ventanas, tienen un techo con bancales que se emplea para secar las cosechas. Cada concesión cuenta con varios graneros para mijo elevados sobre piedras, por lo general en forma cilíndrica y coronados con un techo cónico de paja, donde almacenan las reservas de granos. Los dogones, cuyo numero alcanzaría los 300 000, son conocidos tanto por la calidad de su artesanía como por sus prácticas animistas especificas. La riqueza de la cultura tradicional dogon ha empujado a la clasificación de los acantilados de Bandiagara en la Lista del Patrimonio Mundial de la UNESCO en 1989.

DOGON VILLAGE CLOSE TO BANDIAGARA, MALI.

The Dogon, sedentary farmers who have been in northeastern Mali for over five centuries, took refuge near the Bandiagara cliffs, close to Mopti, in order to escape from Islamization. Their villages are made up of a collection of plots enclosed by a surrounding wall, each of which shelter a family. Built in adobe (a mixture of earth, straw and rice ball), the dwellings, which are rectangular and windowless, have a terrace roof used to dry out their harvest. Each plot has several millet granaries raised on stones, usually cylindrical and capped with a conical straw roof, where grain reserves are stored. The Dogon, who are believed to number 300,000, are known both for the quality of their handicraft and for their specific animistic practices. The wealth of the traditional Dogon culture led to the classification of the Bandiagara cliffs on the UNESCO World Heritage List in 1989.

VILLAGE DOGON PRÈS DE BANDIAGARA, MALI.

Présents depuis plus de cinq siècles au nord-est du Mali, les Dogons, agriculteurs sédentaires, se sont réfugiés aux abords de la falaise de Bandiagara, près de Mopti, afin d'échapper à l'islamisation. Leurs villages sont constitués d'un ensemble de concessions dont chacune, fermée par un mur d'enceinte, abrite une famille. Construites en banco (mélange de terre, de paille et de balle de riz), les habitations, de forme rectangulaire et dépourvues de fenêtre, disposent d'un toit en terrasse utilisé pour faire sécher les récoltes. Chaque concession compte plusieurs greniers à mil hissés sur des pierres, généralement cylindriques et coiffés d'un toit conique en paille, où sont stockées les réserves de grain. Les Dogons, qui seraient au nombre de 300 000, sont connus tant pour la qualité de leur artisanat que pour leurs pratiques animistes spécifiques. La richesse de la culture traditionnelle Dogon a incité au classement des falaises de Bandiagara sur la Liste du patrimoine mondial de l'Unesco en 1989.

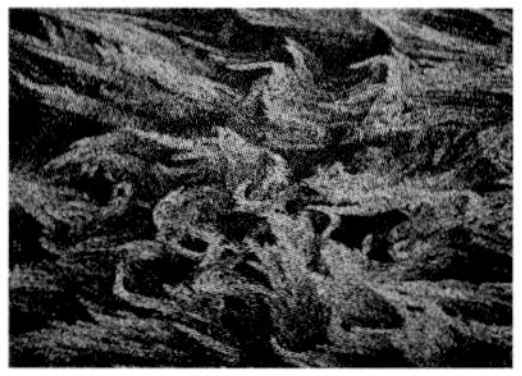

N 47°55' W 2°50'

ALGAS (ORIGINARIAS DE JAPÓN) EN EL GOLFO DE MORBIHAN, FRANCIA.

En los años 20, una epidemia diezmó a la *Crassostrea angulata*, la especie de ostra mas explotada en Francia. Una especie japonesa, la *Crassostrea gigas* fue introducida e, involuntariamente junto con ella, unas treinta especies animales y de algas, que viven hoy en día en las aguas de la Mancha y del Océano Atlántico. Es el caso del sargazo (*Sargassum miticum*), que tomó el lugar de las especies locales, como aquí en el Golfo de Morbihan. Se temió una proliferación galopante, pero esta especie, al mismo tiempo que se volvió abundante, parece haber encontrado su lugar en el ecosistema. Sin embargo, es objeto de una vigilancia particular. Bañada por el mar a lo largo de 2 730 km, Bretaña, donde el 70% del litoral esta en vías de urbanización, se ve favorecida por las acciones de protección de los espacios naturales relevantes por parte del Conservatoire du Littoral desde 1975 en el conjunto del paseo marítimo francés. En Bretaña, 5 239 ha, que corresponden a 78 emplazamientos, y a 161.5 km de ribera fueron adquiridos por el Conservatorio, que garantiza su rehabilitación y su estudio científico. De los 6 000 km de costas metropolitanas, 600 km están ya definitivamente protegidos.

ALGAE (ORIGINALLY FROM JAPAN) IN THE GULF OF MORBIHAN, FRANCE.

In the 1920's, an epidemic decimated the *Crassostrea angulata*, France's most exploited species of oyster at the time. A Japanese species, *Crassostrea gigas* was then introduced, along with, accidentally, about thirty animal species and algae that today inhabit the waters of the English Channel and the Atlantic Ocean. One of these was Sargassum (*Sargassum miticum*), which replaced the local species, as was the case here in the Gulf of Morbihan. A runaway proliferation was feared, but this species, though now abundant, seems to have found a place for itself in the ecosystem. It is still under careful surveillance however. Washed by the sea along a stretch of 2,730 km (1,700 mi.), Brittany, 70% of whose coastline is undergoing a process of urbanization, enjoys certain measures for protecting the remarkable natural spaces that have been implemented by the Conservatoire du Littoral since 1975 along the entire French seacoast. In Brittany, 5239 hectares, corresponding to 78 sites and 161.5 km (100 mi.) of shoreline, have been acquired by the Conservatoire, which ensures their restoration and scientific monitoring. Of the 6,000 km (3700 mi) of metropolitan coast, 600 km (370 mi) will now permanently be protected.

ALGUES (ORIGINAIRES DU JAPON) DANS LE GOLFE DU MORBIHAN, FRANCE.

Dans les années 20, une épidémie décima *Crassostrea angulata*, l'espèce d'huître la plus exploitée en France. Une espèce japonaise, *Crassostrea gigas* fut introduite et, involontairement avec elle, une trentaine d'espèces animales et d'algues qui vivent aujourd'hui dans les eaux de la Manche et de l'océan Atlantique. C'est le cas de la Sargasse (*Sargassum miticum*) qui a pris la place d'espèces locales, comme ici dans le golfe du Morbihan. On a craint une prolifération galopante, mais cette espèce, tout en étant devenue abondante, semble avoir trouvé sa place dans l'écosystème. Elle fait néanmoins l'objet d'une surveillance attentive. Baignée par la mer sur 2 730 km, la Bretagne, dont 70 % du littoral est en voie d'urbanisation, bénéficie des actions de protection des espaces naturels remarquables menées par le Conservatoire du Littoral depuis 1975 sur l'ensemble du bord de mer français. En Bretagne, 5239 ha, correspondant à 78 sites et 161,5 km de rivage, ont été acquis par le Conservatoire, qui en assure la réhabilitation et le suivi scientifique. Sur les 6000 km de côtes métropolitaines, 600 km sont désormais définitivement protégés.

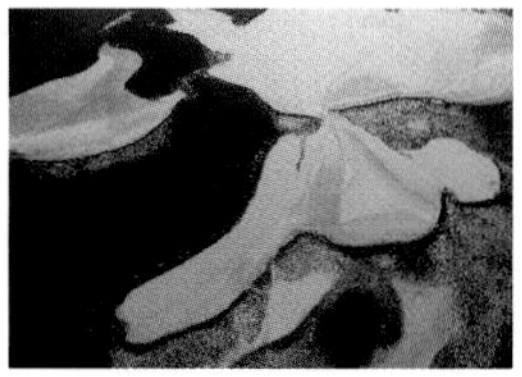

N 32°32' E 37°34'

PAISAJE ENTRE SAFAWI Y QASR BURQU, CERCA DE MAFRAQ, JORDANIA.

Favorecido por 500 a 600 mm de precipitaciones anuales, el Norte de Jordania presenta un paisaje de estepas donde se entremezclan la arena y la vegetación, como aquí entre Safawi y Qasr Burqu, contrariamente a lo que sucede en la mayor parte del país (80%), que es desértica y recibe menos de 100 mm de lluvia al año. En este territorio, casi enclavado de hecho, el principal recurso hídrico esta constituido por el Jordán, río que dio nombre al país. El uso de este curso de agua, que hace frontera con Israel y Cisjordania, al oeste, es un reto geopolítico regional. Los problemas de acceso a los recursos en agua se plantean en el conjunto de los países del Cercano y del Medio Oriente, en particular para aquellos que no controlan la integralidad del curso de un río, de su nacimiento a su desembocadura. Tales retos están relacionados sobre todo las aguas del Tigris y del Eufrates (Turquia, Siria, Irak) y las del Nilo (Sudán, Egipto). Actualmente, existen una decena de conflictos en el mundo relacionados con una guerra por el agua.

LANDSCAPE BETWEEN SAFAWI AND QASR BURQU, NEAR MAFRAQ, JORDAN.

Enjoying 500 to 600 mm (20 to 24 in.) of annual precipitation, northern Jordan exhibits a landscape of steppe where sand and vegetation intermingle - as seen here between Safawi and Qasr Burqu -, unlike the majority of the country (80%), which is desert, and receives less than 100 mm (4 in) of rain per year. In this territory, which is actually nearly landlocked, the principal water resource is the Jordan River, which gave the country its name. This river, which forms a border with Israel and Cis-Jordania to the west, is a regional, geopolitical bone of contention. Problems of access to water resources are faced by all countries in the Near and Middle East, in particular by those who do not control the entire length of a river, from source to mouth. Such bones of contention are especially the waters of the Tigris and Euphrates (Turkey, Syria, Iraq) and those of the Nile (Sudan, Egypt). At present, the conflicts in the world related to war over water number about ten.

PAYSAGE ENTRE SAFAWI ET QASR BURQU, PRÈS DE MAFRAQ, JORDANIE.

Bénéficiant de 500 à 600 mm de précipitations annuelles, le Nord de la Jordanie présente un paysage de steppes où sables et végétation s'entremêlent - comme ici entre Safawi et Qasr Burqu -, contrairement à la majorité du pays (80 %) qui est désertique, et reçoit moins de 100 mm de pluie par an. Dans ce territoire de fait presque enclavé, la principale ressource hydrique est constituée par le Jourdain, fleuve qui a donné son nom au pays. L'utilisation de ce cours d'eau, qui forme frontière avec Israël et la Cisjordanie, à l'ouest, est un enjeu géopolitique régional. Les problèmes d'accès aux ressources en eau se posent dans l'ensemble des pays du Proche et du Moyen-Orient, en particulier pour ceux qui ne contrôlent pas l'intégralité du cours d'un fleuve, de sa source à son embouchure. De tels enjeux concernent notamment les eaux du Tigre et de l'Euphrate (Turquie, Syrie, Irak) et celles du Nil (Soudan, Égypte). Actuellement, on dénombre une dizaine de conflits dans le monde liés à une guerre de l'eau.

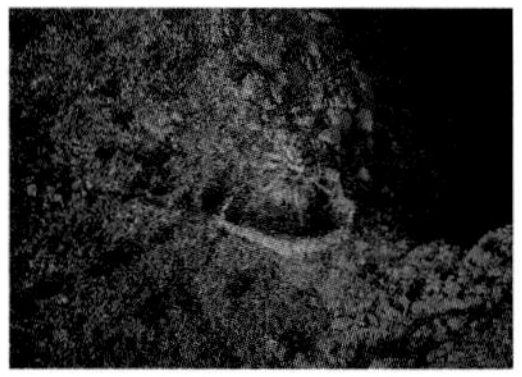

N 26°06' E 56°16'

PALMERAS EN LAS MONTAÑAS DE LA PENÍNSULA DE MUSANDAM, OMÁN.

Las montañas calcáreas que dominan al sultanato de Omán son de hecho fondos marinos que emergieron como resultado del contacto entre la península arábica y el fondo del océano durante importantes movimientos tectónicos. Aislada del resto del país en el extremo norte por una porción de los Emiratos Arabes Unidos, la península de Musandam se eleva sobre el estrecho de Ormuz, que une al Golfo Pérsico con el Golfo de Omán. En estas alturas desoladas, la vegetación es escasa, a menudo inexistente; y sin embargo es en esta topografía, que culmina a 2 000 metros sobre el nivel del mar, que los aldeanos Shihuh vienen a instalarse para hacer pastar su ganado después de la estación de lluvias. Alrededor de sus campos de altura o como aquí, rodeando estas palmeras de dátiles, los habitantes edificaron bardas de piedra. Además de servir como protección contra la voracidad de las cabras, este sistema permite recolectar el agua y detener la erosión atrapando el limo fértil, durante las violentas pero escasas lluvias que caen en invierno.

PALM TREES IN THE MOUNTAINS ON THE MUSANDAM PENINSULA, OMAN.

The limestone mountains that dominate the Sultanate of Oman are in fact seafloors that have emerged as a result of contact between Arabian Peninsula and the ocean floor during major tectonic movements. Isolated from the rest of the country to the extreme north by a portion of the United Arab Emirates, the Musandam Peninsula towers above the strait of Ormuz, which joins the Persian Gulf to the Gulf of Oman. Here on these desolate heights, vegetation is rare, and sometimes non-existent; yet these mountains, rising at their highest point to 2000 m (6500 ft) above sea level, are where the Shihuh villagers come to graze their livestock after the rainy season. Around their high-altitude fields or, as is the case here, surrounding these date palms, inhabitants have built stone walls. Besides being a protection against the voracity of the goats, this system enables water to be harvested and the erosion to be reduced by trapping the fertile silt during the violent but rare rains that fall in winter.

PALMIERS DANS LES MONTAGNES DE LA PÉNINSULE DE MUSANDAM, OMAN.

Les montagnes calcaires qui dominent le sultanat d'Oman sont en fait des fonds marins émergés résultant du contact entre la péninsule arabique et le plancher de l'océan lors d'importants mouvements tectoniques. Isolée du reste du pays à l'extrême nord, par une portion des Emirats Arabes Unis, la péninsule de Musandam se dresse au dessus du détroit d'Ormuz qui relie le Golfe Persique au Golfe d'Oman. Sur ces hauteurs désolées, la végétation est rare, parfois inexistante ; c'est pourtant dans ces reliefs, culminant à 2000 m au dessus du niveau de la mer, que les villageois Shihuh vont s'installer pour faire paître leur cheptel après la saison des pluies. Autour de leurs champs d'altitude ou comme ici, encerclant ces palmiers dattiers, les habitants ont édifié des murets de pierre. Outre une protection contre la voracité des chèvres, ce système permet de récolter l'eau et de limiter l'érosion en piégeant le limon fertile, lors des pluies violentes mais rares qui s'abattent en hiver.

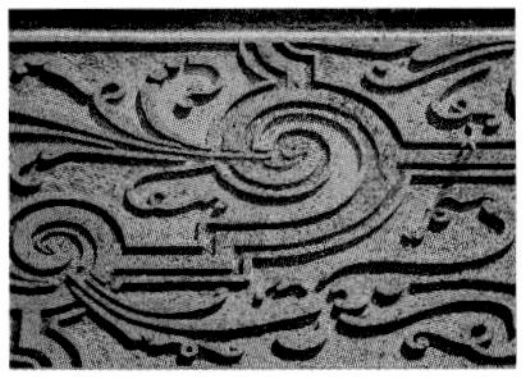

N 48°34' E 2°43'

JARDINES BORDADOS DEL CASTILLO DE VAUX-LE-VICOMTE, MAINCY, SEINE-ET-MARNE, FRANCIA.

Los "tapetes de influencia turca", o jardines bordados con arriates de boj del castillo de Vaux-le-Vicomte, son, como el conjunto del parque, la obra del arquitecto y jardinero André Le Nôtre (1613-1700). Realizado para Nicolas Fouquet, superintendente general de finanzas, el castillo fue construido en 5 años por alrededor de 18 000 obreros. El jardín, adornado con varios planos de agua y con fuentes, ofrece una perspectiva de 2 500 m, que requirieron la destrucción de dos aldeas. Invitado por Fouquet en 1661, el joven rey Luis XIV, ofuscado por la fastuosidad de la fiesta, ordenó investigar al superintendente y lo mandó encarcelar. En cuanto a Le Nôtre, lo nombraron inspector general de los edificios del rey. Elaboró otros jardines clásicos, llamados "a la francesa" para los castillos de Saint-Germain-en-Laye, Saint-Cloud y Fontainebleau, pero su obra maestra sigue siendo los jardines del castillo de Versalles, palacio del "rey sol" Luis XIV.

PARTERRES OF BRODERIES AT THE CHATEAU DE VAUX-LE-VICOMTE, MAINCY, SEINE-ET-MARNE, FRANCE.

The "Oriental carpets", or parterres of broderies done in box hedges at the château de Vaux-le-Vicomte, are the work of the architect-gardener André Le Nôtre (1613-1700), as is the rest of the park. The castle was built in 5 years by some 18,000 workers under the direction of Nicolas Fouquet, general secretary of finances. The garden is embellished with several pools and fountains, and two hamlets were destroyed in order to offer a view stretching as far as 2,500 m (8,200 ft.). After having been invited by Fouquet to visit in 1661, young King Louis XIV became offended by the sumptuousness of the feast, ordered an investigation and had the secretary thrown in jail. As for Le Nôtre, he was granted the title of general supervisor for the king's buildings. He designed other classical, "French-style" gardens for the châteaux de Saint-Germain-en-Laye, Saint-Cloud and Fontainebleau, but his masterpiece still remains the gardens of the château de Versailles, the "Roi Soleil" Louis XIV's palace.

PARTERRES DE BRODERIES DU CHÂTEAU DE VAUX-LE-VICOMTE, MAINCY, SEINE-ET-MARNE, FRANCE.

Les « tapis de turquerie », ou parterres de broderies en haies de buis du château de Vaux-le-Vicomte, sont, comme l'ensemble du parc, l'œuvre de l'architecte-jardinier André Le Nôtre (1613-1700). Réalisé pour Nicolas Fouquet, surintendant général des Finances, le château a été construit en 5 ans par quelque 18 000 ouvriers. Le jardin, agrémenté de plusieurs plans d'eau et fontaines, offre une perspective de 2 500 m qui a nécessité la destruction de deux hameaux. Invité par Fouquet en 1661, le jeune roi Louis XIV, offusqué par le faste de la fête, ordonna une enquête sur le surintendant et le fit emprisonner. Le Nôtre, quant à lui, se vit confier le titre de contrôleur général des Bâtiments du roi. Il élabora d'autres jardins classiques dits « à la française » pour les châteaux de Saint-Germain-en-Laye, Saint-Cloud et Fontainebleau, mais son chef-d'œuvre reste les jardins du château de Versailles, palais du « Roi-Soleil » Louis XIV.

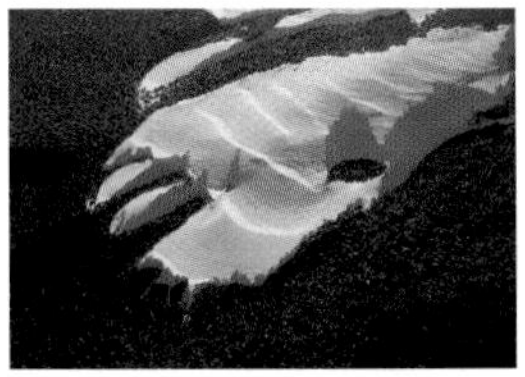

S 25°15' E 153°10'

DUNA DE ARENA EN EL CORAZÓN DE LA VEGETACIÓN EN LA ISLA FRASER, QUEENSLAND, AUSTRALIA.

Sobre las costas australianas de Queensland, la Isla Fraser lleva el nombre de una mujer, que se refugio ahí en 1836, después del naufragio de su barco. Con 120 km de ancho por 15 km de largo, es isla de arena más grande del mundo. Curiosamente, en este sustrato poco fértil se desarrolló una selva húmeda en medio de la cual se insinúan amplias dunas que se extienden al capricho del viento. La Isla Fraser dispone de importantes recursos hídricos, con cerca de 200 lagos de agua dulce, y alberga una fauna variada de marsupiales, de aves y de reptiles. Explotada desde 1860 por su madera, que se empleó sobre todo en la construcción del Canal de Suez, la isla fue posteriormente codiciada por compañías areneras en los años 1970 y hoy en día es una zona protegida, inscrita desde 1992 en la Lista del patrimonio mundial de la UNESCO.

SAND DUNE AT THE HEART OF THE VEGETATION ON FRASER ISLAND, QUEENSLAND, AUSTRALIA.

Off the Australian coasts of Queensland, Fraser Island bears the name of a woman who found shelter there in 1836 after the wreck of her ship. 120 km (75 mi.) long by 15 km (9 mi.) wide, it is the largest sand island in the world. Curiously enough, a tropical rainforest has grown up on this unfertile substratum, with large dunes creeping through the middle of it, progressing at the mercy of the wind. Fraser Island has important water resources, with close to 200 fresh-water lakes, and harbors a varied fauna of marsupials, birds and reptiles. Exploited since 1860 for its wood, which was used in particular for the construction of the Suez Canal, the island was then coveted by sand-producing companies in the 70's; today it is a protected zone, inscribed on the UNESCO World Heritage List since 1992.

DUNE DE SABLE AU CŒUR DE LA VÉGÉTATION SUR L'ÎLE FRASER, QUEENSLAND, AUSTRALIE.

Au large des côtes australiennes du Queensland, l'île Fraser porte le nom d'une femme qui y trouva refuge en 1836 après le naufrage de son navire. Avec 120 km de long sur 15 km de large, elle est la plus grande île de sable du monde. Curieusement, sur ce substrat peu fertile s'est développée une forêt tropicale humide au milieu de laquelle s'insinuent de larges dunes progressant au gré du vent. L'île Fraser dispose d'importantes ressources hydriques, avec près de 200 lacs d'eau douce, et abrite une faune variée de marsupiaux, d'oiseaux et de reptiles. Exploitée dès 1860 pour son bois, notamment utilisé pour la construction du canal de Suez, l'île fut ensuite convoitée par des compagnies sablières dans les années 1970 ; c'est aujourd'hui une zone protégée, inscrite depuis 1992 sur la Liste du patrimoine mondial de l'Unesco.

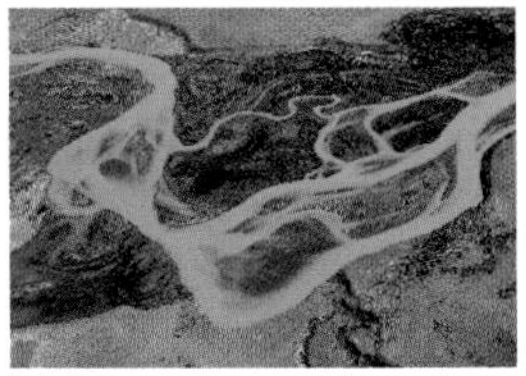

S 50°02' W 72°07'

RÍO LA LEONA, REGIÓN DE SANTA CRUZ, ARGENTINA.

En la Patagonia, al este del Parque Nacional de Los Glaciares, el Rio la Leona, que parte del sur del lago Viedma, serpentea a lo largo de unos cincuenta kilómetros entre los relieves de la cordillera de los Andes para desembocar en el lago argentino, el más importante del país (1 560 km²), del cual es la principal fuente de aprovisionamiento de agua. Río subglaciar, la Leona se alimenta con los bloques de un hielo ligeramente turquesa, en razón de antigüedad y de su gran densidad, que se desprendieron de los glaciares. Al derretirse, estos bloques le dan a la corriente de agua su coloración característica azul lechosa, que los argentinos llaman "dulce de glaciar". El contraste de los colores es tanto mas sobrecogedor cuanto que las riberas, sometidas a sucesivas crecidas, están prácticamente exentas de cualquier vegetación. El río fue bautizado la Leona en 1877 por el explorador argentino Francisco Pascasio Moreno, quien, durante una de sus expediciones en esta región, sobrevivió al ataque de un puma hembra, una "leona". Como la mayoría de los cursos de agua de la Patagonia, la Leona es rica en especies de peces, sobre todo salmones y truchas.

RIO LEONA, REGION OF SANTA CRUZ, ARGENTINA.

In Patagonia, east of Los Glaciares National Park, the Rio Leona, originating south of Lago Viedma, winds some fifty kilometers among the mountains of the Cordillera de los Andes to empty into Lago Argentino, the largest in the country (1,560 sq. km. (602 sq. mi.) and forming the main source of its water supply. A sub-glacial river, the Leona is fed by blocks of an ice that is slightly turquoise in color because it has detached from the glaciers and is old and very dense. As they melt, these blocks give the water of this river its characteristic milky-blue coloring, which Argentinians call dulce de glaciar, or "glacial milk". The contrast of colors is all the more striking in that the shores, which are subject to successive floodings, are nearly bare of all vegetation. The river was baptized the Leona in 1877 by the Argentinean explorer Francisco Pascasio Moreno who, during one of his expeditions to this region, survived the attack of a female puma, a "lioness". Like most rivers in Patagonia, the Leona is rich in various species of fish, especially salmon and trout.

RIVIÈRE LA LEONA, RÉGION DE SANTA CRUZ, ARGENTINE.

En Patagonie, à l'est du parc national de Los Glaciares, la rivière la Leona, partant du sud du lac Viedma, serpente sur une cinquantaine de kilomètres parmi les reliefs de la cordillère des Andes pour se jeter dans le lac Argentino, le plus important du pays (1 560 km²), dont elle est la principale source d'approvisionnement en eau. Rivière subglaciaire, la Leona est alimentée par des blocs d'une glace légèrement turquoise, parce qu'ancienne et très dense, détachés des glaciers. En fondant, ces blocs donnent au cours d'eau sa coloration caractéristique d'un bleu laiteux, que les Argentins appellent dulce de glaciar, « crème de glacier ». Le contraste des couleurs est d'autant plus saisissant que les berges, soumises à des crues sucessives, sont quasiment exemptes de toute végétation. La rivière fut baptisée la Leona en 1877 par l'explorateur argentin Francisco Pascasio Moreno qui, durant l'une de ses expéditions dans cette région, avait survécu à une attaque d'une femelle puma, une « lionne ». Comme la majorité des cours d'eau de Patagonie, la Leona est riche de diverses espèces de poissons, notamment de saumons et de truites.

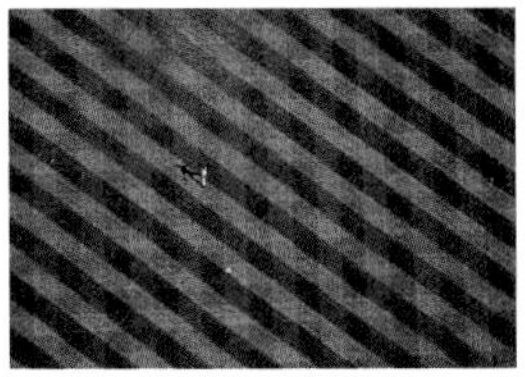

N 40°50' W 73°56'

EL YANKEE STADIUM DE NUEVA YORK, ESTADOS UNIDOS.

Ubicado en el corazón del Bronx, barrio pobre de Nueva York, el Yankee Stadium dispone de un pasto muy cuidado, mientras que cada vez más estadios norteamericanos adoptan revestimientos sintéticos; tiene una capacidad de 55 000 lugares. Este estadio de béisbol pertenece a los Yankees de Nueva York, el equipo con más títulos, cuenta con 23 victorias en finales desde que se creó esta competencia en 1903, de entre las 26 con que cuenta el campeonato norteamericano. Nacido en los Estados Unidos poco antes de 1850, el béisbol se profesionalizó rápidamente aunque siguió siendo el entretenimiento favorito de una mayoría de norteamericanos, que con gusto lo califican como el national passtime (pasatiempo nacional). Representado por 80 federaciones en el mundo y practicado por mas de 150 millones de profesionales, lo que lo convierte en el segundo deporte mas practicado después del volibol (210 federaciones y 180 millones de profesionales), el béisbol fue reconocido como disciplina olímpica en 1986.

YANKEE STADIUM IN NEW YORK, UNITED STATES.

Situated in the heart of the Bronx, one of New York's poor districts, Yankee Stadium has a carefully groomed natural turf, while more and more American stadiums are adopting synthetic surfaces. Home to the New York Yankees, this baseball stadium offers a 55,000 seating capacity. Since the creation of the World Series championship in 1903, this team has won the most titles, with 23 victories out of 26. Originating in the United States shortly before 1850, baseball quickly became a professional sport while still remaining the favorite leisure-time activity for a majority of Americans who happily describe it as their national passtime. Represented by 80 federations in the world, and practiced by more than 150 million members - making it the second most practiced sport after volleyball (210 federations and 180 million members) -, baseball was recognized as an Olympic discipline in 1986.

LE YANKEE STADIUM À NEW YORK, ÉTATS-UNIS.

Situé au cœur du Bronx, quartier pauvre de New York, le Yankee Stadium dispose d'un terrain en gazon soigneusement entretenu, alors que de plus en plus de stades américains adoptent des revêtements synthétiques ; il offre une capacité d'accueil de 55 000 places. Ce stade de base-ball est celui des New York Yankees, équipe la plus titrée - avec 23 victoires en finale depuis la création de cette compétition en 1905 - parmi les 26 que compte le championnat nord-américain. Né aux États-Unis peu avant 1850, le base-ball s'est très tôt professionnalisé tout en restant le loisir favori d'une majorité d'Américains qui le qualifient volontiers de national passtime (passe-temps national). Représenté par 80 fédérations dans le monde et pratiqué par plus de 150 millions de licenciés - ce qui en fait le deuxième sport le plus pratiqué après le volley-ball (210 fédérations et 180 millions de licenciés) -, le base-ball a été reconnu discipline olympique en 1986.

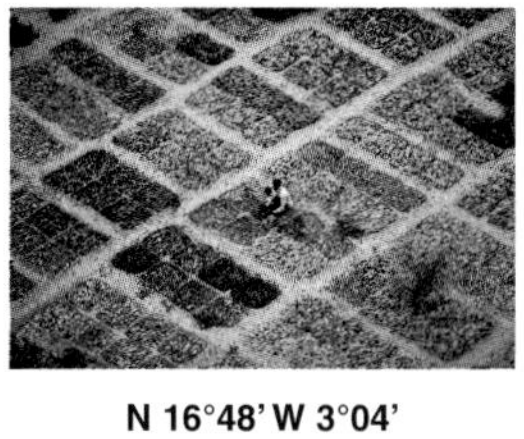

N 16°48' W 3°04'

CULTIVOS DE HORTALIZAS EN LOS ALREDEDORES DE TUMBUKTU, MALI.

En la región árida de Tumbuktu, en el corazón de Mali, el cultivo de hortalizas se vuelve difícil por el suelo arenoso poco fértil y por las condiciones climatológicas: las temperaturas diurnas pueden alcanzar los 50° C y las precipitaciones apenas superan los 150 mm por año. Constituidos de una yuxtaposición de parcelas de aproximadamente un metro de ancho, en las que el agua se utiliza con parsimonia, estos jardines de arena producen legumbres (chícharos, habas, lentejas, frijoles, coles, lechugas, cacahuates) que están principalmente destinadas al consumo local. El creciente desarrollo de las hortalizas en Mali es una consecuencia de las grandes sequías de los años 1973-1975 que, al diezmar el ganado de los criadores nómadas del norte del país, obligaron a una parte de ellos a volverse sedentarios y convertirse a la agricultura.

MARKET GARDENS IN THE VICINITY OF TIMBUKTU, MALI.

In the arid region of Timbuktu, in the heart of Mali, market gardening is made difficult by an unproductive, sandy soil and by climatic conditions : temperatures can reach 50°C (122 °F) during the day and precipitation rarely surpasses 150 mm annually. These sand gardens consist of many adjacent parcels each about one meter (3 feet) long, where water is used sparingly. They produce vegetables (peas, broad beans, lentils, green beans, cabbages, salads, peanuts...) mainly intended for local consumption. The increasing development of market gardening in Mali is a consequence of the great droughts of 1973-1975 and 1983-1985, which decimated the livestock of nomadic breeders in the northern part of the country and forced some of them to become sedentary in order to shift to agriculture.

CULTURES MARAÎCHÈRES AUX ENVIRONS DE TOMBOUCTOU, MALI.

Dans la région aride de Tombouctou, au cœur du Mali, la culture maraîchère est rendue difficile par un sol sableux peu fertile et par les conditions climatiques : les températures diurnes peuvent atteindre 50°C et les précipitations n'excèdent guère 150 mm par an. Constitués d'une juxtaposition de parcelles d'environ un mètre de côté dans lesquelles l'eau est utilisée avec parcimonie, ces jardins des sables produisent des légumes (pois, fèves, lentilles, haricots, choux, salades, arachides...) principalement destinés à la consommation locale. Le développement croissant du maraîchage au Mali est une conséquence des grandes sécheresses des années 1973-1975 et 1983-1985 qui, en décimant le cheptel des éleveurs nomades du nord du pays, ont contraint une partie d'entre eux à se sédentariser pour se reconvertir dans l'agriculture.

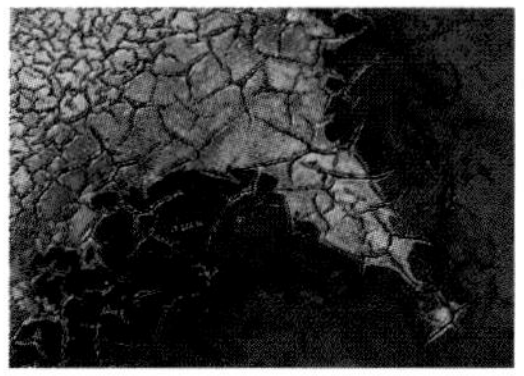

N 43°27'W 4°34'

FANGO AGRIETADO EN CAMARGA, BOUCHES-DU-RHÔNE, FRANCIA.

Antes de adentrarse en el Mar Mediterráneo, el Ródano (812 km) se separa en dos brazos que forman un delta de 750 km² formado esencialmente de depósitos aluviales: la Camarga. Esta amplia zona húmeda está cubierta en un 40% de terrenos pantanosos y de estanques de aguas más o menos salobres (de 0 a 12 gr de sal por litro), de los cuales algunos, llamados baisses, se secan durante el verano, dejando aparecer un suelo fangoso que se agrieta y se cubre de depósitos salinos bajo el efecto del sol. La Camarga alberga una fauna variada, principalmente numerosas aves: zancudas, anátidas, limícolas... y está clasificada en parte como reserva natural desde 1927. El hombre, que también aprovecha la riqueza de este medio natural, practica diversas actividades en el delta: cultivo de arroz, viticultura, pesca, ganadería (caballos y toros) y explotación de más de 100 km² de salinas, las más grandes de Europa, de las cuales se extraen cerca de un millón de toneladas de sal cada año.

CRACKED VASE IN CAMARGUE, BOUCHES-DU-RHÔNE, FRANCE.

Before emptying into the Mediterranean Sea, the Rhône (812 km (505 mi.) long) splits into two arms forming a delta with a surface of 750 sq. km. (290 sq. mi.), basically made of alluvial deposits, called the Camargue. 40% of this vast wetland is covered in marshes and ponds with more or less brackish waters (0 to 12 g of salt per liter), some of which, called "baisses" (or "falls"), are drained in the summer, revealing a muddy soil that is cracked and covered over in saline deposits by the effects of the sun. Partially classified as a natural reserve since 1927, the Camargue harbors varied fauna, in particular a great many birds, including waders, anatidae, benthos... Also taking advantage of the wealth of this natural habitat, man practises various activities in the delta: rice-growing, wine-growing, fishing, breeding (horses and bulls) and the exploitation of over 100 sq. km. of salt marsh - the most extensive in Europe - from which close to a million metric tons of salt are extracted per year.

VASE CRAQUELÉE EN CAMARGUE, BOUCHES-DU-RHÔNE, FRANCE.

Avant de se jeter dans la mer Méditerranée, le Rhône (812 km) se sépare en deux bras qui forment un delta de 750 km² essentiellement composé de dépôts alluvionnaires : la Camargue. Cette vaste zone humide est à 40 % couverte de marécages et d'étangs aux eaux plus au moins saumâtres (0 à 12 g de sel par litre), dont certains, appelés « baisses », s'assèchent en été, laissant apparaître un sol vaseux qui se craquelle et se couvre de dépôts salins sous l'effet du soleil. En partie classée réserve naturelle depuis 1927, la Camargue abrite une faune variée, notamment de nombreux oiseaux : échassiers, anatidés, limicoles... Profitant également de la richesse de ce milieu naturel, l'homme pratique diverses activités dans le delta : riziculture, viticulture, pêche, élevage (chevaux et taureaux) et exploitation de plus de 100 km² de marais salants – les plus vastes d'Europe – dont on extrait près d'un million de tonnes de sel par an.

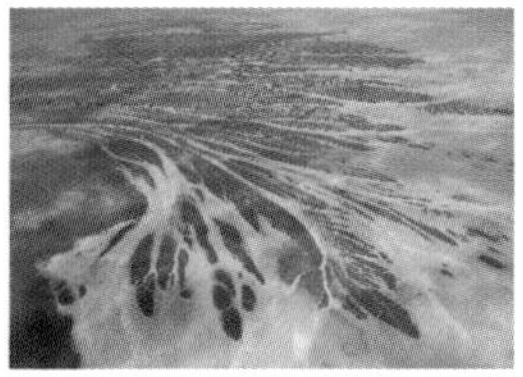

N 26°12' W 14°05'

SEBKHET ARIDAL, CERCA DEL CABO BOUJDOUR, SAHARA OCCIDENTAL, MARRUECOS.

Cuando se retiran las aguas del ued Lemnaider, que alimentan esta sebkha (lago salado temporal) en época de lluvias, cavan canales en donde afloran depósitos de sal. La sebkha, característica de zonas áridas de Magreb, se encuentra en el corazón de Marruecos, al sur del Sahara Occidental. Esta parte de desierto, antiguamente colonia española, que abarca 2 500 km a lo largo del Atlántico y que cubre 252 000 km², fue reivindicada por Marruecos durante la retirada de los españoles en 1975. Sin embargo, el Frente Polisario (Frente popular para la liberación de Saguia-el-Hamra y Río de Oro) proclamó la independencia del Sahara Occidental y tomó las armas. Incluso se creó y se admitió en el seno del la Organización de la Unidad Africana (OUA), una República Árabe Saharaui Democrática (RASD); reconocida por más de setenta Estados africanos y asiáticos, sin embargo, las instancias internacionales no la consideran como la administradora oficial de dicho territorio.

SEBKHET ARIDAL, NEAR CAPE BOUJDOUR, WESTERN SAHARA, MOROCCO.

The waters of the Lemnaider wadi feed this sebkha (temporary salt lake) in the rainy period and create sand gullies where salt deposits appear when the waters withdraw. Typical of the arid zones in the Maghreb, this sebkha is located in southern Morocco, at the heart of the Western Sahara. Once a Spanish colony, this section of desert, which stretches 2,500 km along the Atlantic coast and covers an area of 252,000 sq. km. (97,000 sq. mi.), was claimed by Morocco when the Spaniards left in 1975. However, with the support of Algeria, the Polisario Front (Popular Front for the Liberation of Saguia el Hamra and Rio de Oro) proclaimed the independence of Western Sahara and took up arms. A democratic Sahrawi Arab Democratic Republic (SADR) was even created and admitted to the Organization of African Unity (OAU); recognized by over seventy African and Asian States, it is not however considered the official administrator of this territory by international authorities.

SEBKHET ARIDAL, PRÈS DU CAP BOUJDOUR, SAHARA OCCIDENTAL, MAROC.

En se retirant, les eaux de l'oued Lemnaider, qui alimentent cette sebkha (lac salé temporaire) en période de pluie, ont creusé des rigoles dans le sable où affleurent des dépôts de sel. Caractéristique de zones arides du Maghreb, la sebkha se trouve dans le sud du Maroc, au cœur du Sahara occidental. Autrefois colonie espagnole, cette partie de désert, qui s'étire sur 2 500 km le long de l'Atlantique et couvre 252 000 km², a été revendiquée par le Maroc lors du départ des Espagnols, en 1975. Cependant, soutenu par l'Algérie, le Front Polisario (Front populaire pour la libération de la Saguia al-Hamra et du Rio de Oro) a proclamé l'indépendance du Sahara occidental et pris les armes. Une République arabe sahraouie démocratique (RASD) a même été créée et admise au sein de l'Organisation de l'unité africaine (OUA) ; reconnue par plus de soixante-dix États africains et asiatiques, elle n'est pourtant pas considérée comme administrateur officiel de ce territoire par les instances internationales.

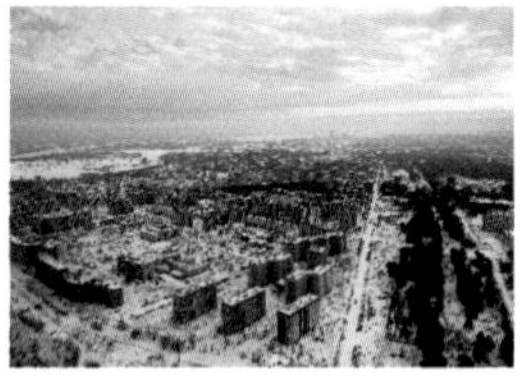

N 51°21' E 30°09'

PRIPRIAT, CIUDAD ABANDONADA CERCA DE LA CENTRAL NUCLEAR DE CHERNOBIL, UCRANIA.

La explosión, en abril de 1986, de uno de los reactores de la central de Chernobil, en Ucrania (que entonces formaba parte de la URSS), generó la mayor catástrofe nuclear civil de todos los tiempos. Una nube radiactiva se escapó del reactor destruido y contaminó extensas zonas como manchas de leopardo, no solamente en Ucrania, sino también en Bielorrusia y en la Rusia vecina. Aunque de manera tardía, las 120 localidades circunvecinas, como Pripriat (50 000 habitantes), a 3 km del epicentro, fueron evacuadas. La nube, empujada por el viento, se propagó después por toda Europa. Actualmente no se conoce el número exacto de víctimas pero se considera que varios millones de personas sufren enfermedades vinculadas a la irradiación (cánceres, deficiencias inmunitarias...). En diciembre de 2000 se detuvo definitivamente el último reactor de la central, que permanecía en actividad para producir el 9% de la electricidad del país, a cambio de una ayuda occidental de 2 300 millones de dólares que permitirá la construcción de otras dos centrales nucleares. La industria nuclear no ha resuelto todavía el problema del futuro de los desechos altamente radiactivos de larga vida, generados por 433 reactores en 32 países y que se acumulan en los centros de almacenamiento.

PRIPYAT, AN ABANDONED CITY CLOSE TO THE CHERNOBYL NUCLEAR POWER PLANT, UKRAINE.

The explosion in April 1986, of one of the reactors of the Chernobyl power plant in Ukraine (part of the USSR at the time) produced the greatest civilian nuclear disaster of all times. A radioactive cloud escaped from the destroyed reactor and contaminated large areas in the form of polka dots, not only in Ukraine, but also in Byelorussia and in neighboring Russia. The 120 surrounding localities, such as Pripyat (50,000 inhabitants), 3 km (2 mi.) from the epicenter, were evacuated, although very late. Driven by winds, the cloud then spread to the rest of Europe. Today, the exact number of victims is not known, but it is estimated that several million people are suffering from radiation-related illnesses (cancers, immune deficiencies...). In December of 2000, the power plant's last functioning reactor, which had remained active in order to produce 9% of the country's electricity, was stopped permanently, in exchange for Western aid amounting to $2.3 billion (US), which will permit the construction of two other nuclear power plants. The nuclear industry has still not solved the problem of what to do with the long-lived, highly radioactive waste, generated by 433 reactors in 32 countries, which is accumulating in storage centers.

PRIPRIAT, VILLE ABANDONNÉE PRÈS DE LA CENTRALE NUCLÉAIRE DE TCHERNOBYL, UKRAINE.

L'explosion en avril 1986 d'un des réacteurs de la centrale de Tchernobyl, en Ukraine (alors faisant partie de l'URSS), a engendré la plus grande catastrophe nucléaire civile de tous les temps. Un nuage radioactif s'est échappé du réacteur détruit et a contaminé de larges zones en taches de léopard, non seulement en Ukraine, mais aussi en Biélorussie et en Russie voisine. Les 120 localités environnantes, comme Pripiat (50 000 habitants), à 3 km de l'épicentre, ont été évacuées, bien que tardivement. Poussé par les vents, le nuage s'est ensuite propagé à toute l'Europe. Aujourd'hui, le nombre exact de victimes n'est pas connu mais on estime que plusieurs millions de personnes souffrent de maladies liées à l'irradiation (cancers, déficiences immunitaires...). En décembre 2000, le dernier réacteur de la centrale, demeuré en activité pour produire 9 % de l'électricité du pays, a définitivement été arrêté, en échange d'une aide occidentale de 2,3 milliards de dollars qui permettra la construction de deux autres centrales nucléaires. L'industrie nucléaire n'a toujours pas résolu le problème du devenir des déchets hautement radioactifs à vie longue, générés par 433 réacteurs dans 32 pays, qui s'accumulent dans les centres de stockage.

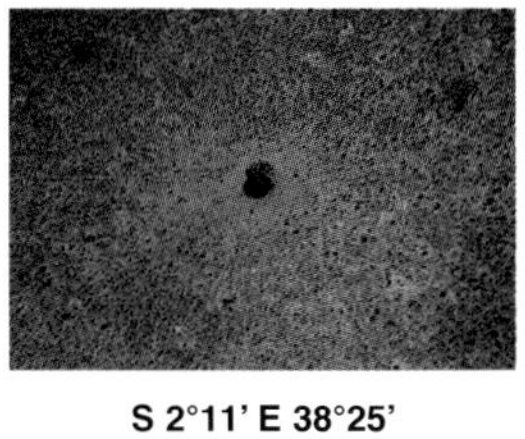

S 2°11' E 38°25'

"EL ÁRBOL DE LA VIDA", PARQUE NACIONAL DE TSAVO ESTE, KENIA.

El parque nacional de Tsavo Este al sureste de Kenia, clasificado en 1948, es el mayor conjunto protegido del país (21 000 km²). Atravesado por la vía carretera y ferroviaria Nairobi-Mombasa, el parque se encuentra abierto al público en su parte oeste, mientras que dos tercios de su parte este, formada de sabana espinosa, están reservados para los científicos. Esta acacia de Tsavo Este, símbolo de vida entre las grandes extensiones desoladas, es el punto de convergencia de caminos de animales salvajes que vienen a aprovechar sus hojas o su sombra. Siendo ya famoso por sus numerosos elefantes, Tsavo tuvo en los años 1970 una afluencia masiva de paquidermos que huían de la sequía. Estos paquidermos dañaron seriamente el medio natural, puesto que diariamente consumen más de 200 kg de vegetación, creando una controversia sobre la necesidad de una matanza selectiva. ¡Los cazadores furtivos terminaron con el asunto exterminando a cerca del 80% de los 36 000 elefantes del parque! Sus rinocerontes, codiciados por su cuerno, que en Asia es famoso como afrodisiaco, sufrieron la misma suerte. Si bien la prohibición del comercio internacional de marfil y de cuerno de rinoceronte ha permitido que algunas poblaciones de animales salvajes se reconstituyan, el tráfico, y sobretodo la desaparición del hábitat natural, siguen siendo amenazas preocupantes. El comercio mundial de la flora y de la fauna salvajes todavía representa cada año 100 000 millones de francos (14 000 millones de dólares) del volumen de negocios.

"TREE OF LIFE", TSAVO EAST NATIONAL PARK, KENYA.

The Tsavo National Park in southeastern Kenya, classified as such in 1948, is the largest protected area in the country (21,000 sq. km.). Divided by the Nairobi-Mombassa road and railway, the western section of the park is open to the public, while two-thirds of the eastern section, made up of thorn-bush savanna, is reserved for scientists. A symbol of life in these vast, desolate expanses, this acacia from Tsavo-East is a point of convergence for the tracks of wild animals that come to take advantage of its leaves or shade. Already well known for its many elephants, Tsavo experienced a massive influx in the 70's of pachyderms fleeing from drought. Consuming more than 200 kg (440 lb) of vegetation daily, they seriously damaged the natural habitat, creating controversy over the possible need for selective slaughtering. Poachers settled the problem by wiping out close to 80% of the park's 36,000 elephants! Its rhinoceroses, coveted for their horn, which is perceived as an aphrodisiac in Asia, met the same fate. Although the prohibition of international ivory and rhinoceros-horn trade has allowed certain wild animal populations to recover, this traffic, and especially the disappearance of their natural habitat, are still alarming threats. The world trade of exotic plants and wildlife still represents $14 billion dollars (US) in yearly sales' figures.

« L'ARBRE DE VIE », PARC NATIONAL DE TSAVO-EST, KENYA.

Le parc national de Tsavo au sud-est du Kenya, classé en 1948, est le plus vaste ensemble protégé du pays (21 000 km²). Traversé par l'axe routier et ferroviaire Nairobi-Mombasa, le parc est ouvert au public dans sa partie ouest, alors que les deux tiers de sa partie est, constituée de savane épineuse, sont réservés aux scientifiques. Symbole de vie parmi les vastes étendues désolées, cet acacia de Tsavo-Est est le point de convergence des pistes d'animaux sauvages venus profiter de ses feuilles ou de son ombre. Déjà réputé pour ses nombreux éléphants, Tsavo a connu dans les années 1970 un afflux massif de pachydermes fuyant la sécheresse. Consommant quotidiennement plus de 200 kg de végétation, ils ont sérieusement endommagé le milieu naturel, suscitant une controverse sur la nécessité d'un abattage sélectif. Les braconniers ont tranché en exterminant près de 80 % des 36 000 éléphants du parc ! Ses rhinocéros, convoités pour leur corne réputée aphrodisiaque en Asie, ont subi le même sort. Si l'interdiction du commerce international de l'ivoire et de la corne de rhinocéros a permis à certaines populations d'animaux sauvages de se reconstituer, le trafic, et surtout la disparition de l'habitat naturel, demeurent des menaces préoccupantes. Le commerce mondial de la flore et de la faune sauvages représente encore chaque année 100 milliards de francs (14 milliards de dollars) de chiffre d'affaires.

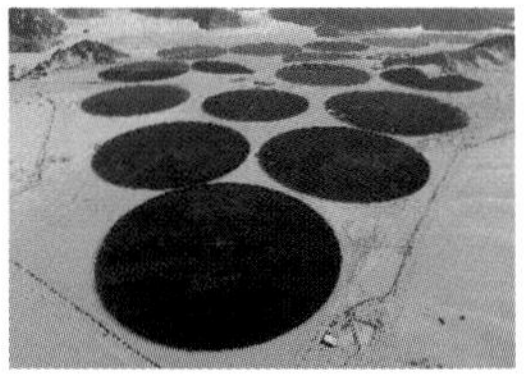

N 29°43' E 35°33'

IRRIGACIÓN EN CARRUSEL, MA'AN, WADI RUM, JORDANIA.

En el desierto, en donde los suelos aluviales ricos en elementos nutritivos permanecen estériles a falta de agua fertilizante, invertir en un sistema de irrigación permite crear una real prosperidad agrícola. En 1952, Franck Zybach, el inventor norteamericano de este carrusel de riego autopropulsado, no imaginaba que se convertiría en una instalación automática programada por computadora. La perforación busca agua en las capas profundas (de 30 a 400 m), y la distribuye en las diferentes áreas de riego. Ahí, la electricidad asegura el movimiento de un brazo giratorio, formado de varios segmentos puestos punta con punta, montados en ruedas de tractor y sosteniendo los tubos de riego. Esta rampa, de alrededor de 500 m de largo, suministra el agua a los cultivos sobre una superficie de riego discoidal de 78 hectáreas. La producción de una tonelada de cereales necesita cerca de 1 000 toneladas de agua. Los países de Africa del Norte y del Medio Oriente, confrontados simultáneamente con una escasez de agua y con necesidades alimentarias cada vez mayores, tienden a darle privilegio a la importación de cereales más que a la producción nacional, que es una gran consumidora de un agua escasa y preciosa. Así, estos países representan la región del mundo en donde las importaciones de cereales han aumentado más durante el pasado decenio.

CENTER-PIVOT IRRIGATION, MA'AN, WADI RUM, JORDAN.

In the desert, where alluvial soils rich in nutrients remain unproductive due to a lack of fertilizing water, investing in an irrigation system makes it possible to generate real agricultural prosperity. In 1952, Frank Zybach, the American inventor of this self-propelled, center-pivot sprinkler, could not imagine that it would become an automatic fixture, programmed by computer. The drill looks for water in the deep strata (from 30 to 400 m (115 to 1,300 ft)), and distributes it to the different sprinkling areas. There, electricity runs the movement of a rotating arm, made up of several segments placed end to end that are mounted on tractor wheels and carry spray-nozzles. This spray boom, about 500 m (1,600 ft.) long, distributes water to crops over a circular irrigated surface of 78 hectares (188 acres). The production of one metric ton of cereals requires approximately 1,000 metric tons (110 tons) of water. Countries in Northern Africa and in the Middle East, faced simultaneously with a shortage of water and increasing food demands, tend to favor the importing of cereals over national production, which consumes high quantities of rare, precious water. These countries thus represent the region of the world where cereal imports have most increased over the past decade.

IRRIGATION EN CARROUSEL, MA'AN, WADI RUM, JORDANIE.

Dans le désert où les sols alluviaux riches en éléments nutritifs demeurent stériles faute d'eau fertilisante, investir dans un système d'irrigation permet d'engendrer une réelle prospérité agricole. En 1952, Franck Zybach, l'inventeur américain de ce carrousel d'arrosage autopropulsé, n'imaginait pas qu'il deviendrait une installation automatique programmée par ordinateur. Le forage va chercher l'eau dans les couches profondes (de 30 à 400 m), et la distribue aux différentes aires d'arrosage. Là, l'électricité assure le mouvement d'un bras pivotant, constitué de plusieurs segments mis bout à bout montés sur des roues de tracteur et portant les buses d'arrosage. Cette rampe, longue d'environ 500 m, restitue l'eau aux cultures sur une surface irriguée discoïde de 78 hectares. La production d'une tonne de céréales nécessite environ 1000 tonnes d'eau. Les pays d'Afrique du Nord et du Moyen-Orient, confrontés simultanément à une pénurie d'eau et à des besoins alimentaires croissants, tendent à privilégier l'importation de céréales plutôt que la production nationale, forte consommatrice d'une eau rare et précieuse. Ces pays représentent ainsi la région du monde où les importations de céréales ont le plus augmenté durant la décennie écoulée.

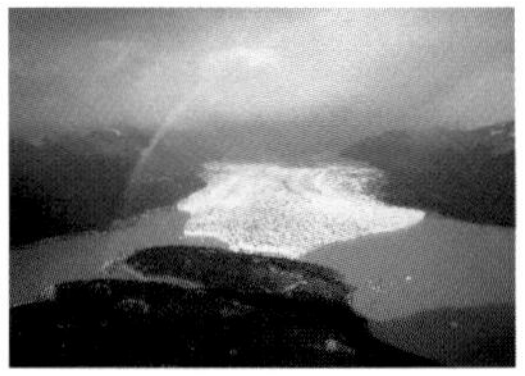

S 46°36' W 70°56'

GLACIAR PERITO MORENO, SANTA CRUZ, ARGENTINA.

En el sur de Argentina, cerca de la frontera chilena, se encuentra el parque nacional de Los Glaciares, creado en 1937, e inscrito en 1981 en la Lista del patrimonio mundial de la UNESCO. Con una superficie de 4 459 km², este espacio protegido alberga 47 glaciares que nacen del manto glaciar continental de Patagonia, el más grande del mundo después de la Antártida y Groenlandia. Con un largo frontal de 5 000 m y una altura de 60 m, el Perito Moreno gana terreno sobre uno de los brazos del lago argentino, que lleva en su cauce pedazos de rocas arrancadas de las orillas, que erosionan y modelan el paisaje. Cada tres o cuatro años, en la confluencia de los dos brazos del lago, el glaciar interrumpe el flujo de agua; la presión constante de ésta sobre la barrera de hielo termina por romperla, produciendo una detonación que puede escucharse a varios kilómetros a la redonda. Los glaciares y los cascos polares representan un 9% de las tierras sobre el nivel del mar del globo. El calentamiento global del planeta, vinculado en parte a las actividades humanas, puede elevar el nivel de los océanos y ahogar litorales fértiles por el derretimiento de los glaciares. También la ubicación de grandes ecosistemas podría verse modificada por la misma causa.

PERITO MORENO GLACIER, SANTA CRUZ, ARGENTINA.

Located in southern Argentina, close to the Chilean border, Los Glaciares National Park was created in 1937 and inscribed on the UNESCO World Heritage List in 1981. Covering a total of 4,459 sq. km. (1,721 sq. mi.), this protected area contains 47 glaciers from the continental glacier mantle of Patagonia, the largest in the world after the Antarctic and Greenland. 5,000 m (16,000 ft) wide at the front and 60 m (200 ft) high, the Perito Moreno is moving along one of the arms of Lago Argentino, dragging rock debris in its course, torn from the edges, eroding and sculpting the landscape. Every three or four years, at the confluence of the two arms of the lake, the glacier blocks the out-flow of water; this increasing pressure on the ice barrier eventually breaks it, producing an explosion that can be heard several kilometers away. Glaciers and polar icecaps represent 9% of the emerged land on the globe. The planet's global warming, partly due to human activities, could provoke the melting of the ice and thus a rise in the level of the oceans. Fertile coastal areas could be submerged and the position of large ecosystems modified.

GLACIER PERITO MORENO, SANTA CRUZ, ARGENTINE.

Dans le Sud de l'Argentine, près de la frontière chilienne, se trouve le parc national de Los Glaciares, créé en 1937, et inscrit en 1981 sur la Liste du patrimoine mondial de l'Unesco. D'une superficie de 4 459 km², cet espace protégé abrite 47 glaciers issus du manteau glaciaire continental de Patagonie, le plus grand au monde après l'Antarctique et le Grœnland. D'une largeur frontale de 5 000 m et d'une hauteur de 60 m, le Perito Moreno progresse sur l'un des bras du lac Argentino, entraînant dans sa course des débris de roches arrachés aux berges qui érodent et modèlent le paysage. Tous les trois ou quatre ans, à la confluence des deux bras du lac, le glacier interrompt l'écoulement de l'eau ; la pression croissante de celle-ci sur la barrière de glace finit par la rompre, en produisant une détonation qui peut être entendue à plusieurs kilomètres alentour. Les glaciers et les calottes polaires représentent 9 % des terres émergées du globe. Le réchauffement global de la planète, en partie lié aux activités humaines, est susceptible, par la fonte des glaces, d'élever le niveau des océans et de noyer des littoraux fertiles. L'emplacement des grands écosystèmes pourrait également s'en trouver modifié.

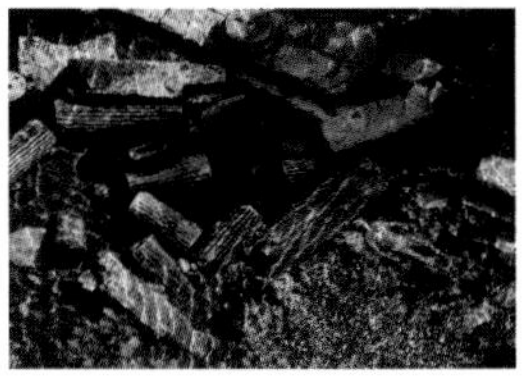

N 37°58' E 29°19'

TURISTA EN UNA ALBERCA EN PAMUKKALE (HIERÁPOLIS), ANATOLIA, TURQUÍA.

La ciudad de Pamukkale, al oeste de Anatolia, en Turquía, posee manantiales de agua rica en sales minerales cuyas propiedades curativas se conocen desde la antigüedad. En 129 a.c., los romanos establecieron ahí la ciudad termal de Hierápolis que, víctima de cuatro terremotos, fue reconstruida varias veces antes de conocer la decadencia frente al Imperio bizantino. Actualmente, el sitio arqueológico de Hierápolis recibe a numerosos visitantes. Incluso se construyó un hotel sobre los vestigios de una antigua fuente sagrada, su alberca, cuyo fondo está cubierto de fragmentos de columnas romanas, constituye una apreciada atracción para los turistas. Inscrito en la Lista del Patrimonio Mundial de la UNESCO en 1988, el sitio de Hierápolis-Pamukkale se ha desnaturalizado por la presencia de numerosas infraestructuras hoteleras, cuya demolición prevista desde 1992 todavía no se ha efectuado.

TOURIST IN A SWIMMING POOL IN PAMUKKALE (HIERAPOLIS), ANATOLIA, TURKEY.

The city of Pamukkale, in western Anatolia, Turkey, has hot water springs that are rich in mineral salts, whose curative properties have been known since Antiquity. In 129 B.C., the Romans established the spa of Hierapolis here, which was rebuilt several times following four earthquakes, before its decline under the Byzantine Empire. Today, the archaeological site of Hierapolis receives many visitors. A motel was even built on vestiges of an old sacred fountain; its swimming pool, whose bottom is strewn with fragments of Roman columns, constitutes an attraction that is much appreciated by tourists. Inscribed on the UNESCO World Heritage List in 1988, the site of Hierapolis-Pamukkale is spoiled by the presence of several hotel infrastructures, whose demolition, programmed since 1992, has still not been carried out.

TOURISTE DANS UNE PISCINE À PAMUKKALE (HIERAPOLIS), ANATOLIE, TURQUIE.

La ville de Pamukkale, dans l'Ouest de l'Anatolie, en Turquie, dispose de sources d'eau chaude riche en sels minéraux dont les propriétés curatives sont connues depuis l'Antiquité. En 129 av. J.-C., les Romains y établirent la cité thermale de Hierapolis qui, victime de quatre tremblements de terre, fut reconstruite plusieurs fois avant de connaître le déclin sous l'Empire byzantin. Aujourd'hui, le site archéologique de Hierapolis accueille de nombreux visiteurs. Un motel a même été bâti sur les vestiges d'une ancienne fontaine sacrée ; sa piscine, dont le fond est jonché de fragments de colonnes romaines, constitue une attraction appréciée des touristes. Inscrit sur la Liste du patrimoine mondial de l'Unesco en 1988, le site de Hierapolis-Pamukkale est dénaturé par la présence de nombreuses infrastructures hôtelières, dont la démolition prévue depuis 1992 n'a toujours pas été effectuée.

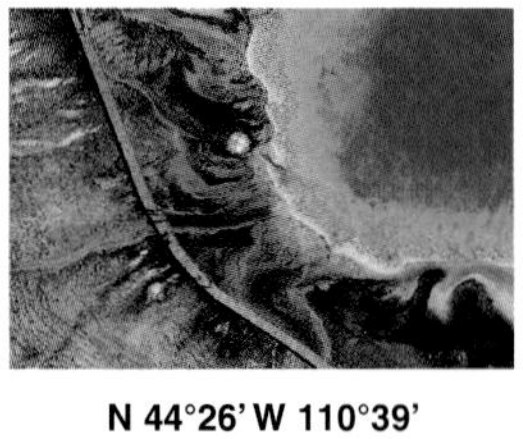

N 44°26' W 110°39'

GÉISER DEL GRAND PRISMATIC, PARQUE NACIONAL DE YELLOWSTONE, WYOMING, ESTADOS UNIDOS.

Situado en una planicie volcánica que cubre los estados de Montana, de Idaho y de Wyoming, Yellowstone es el parque nacional más antiguo. Creado en 1872, se extiende sobre 9 000 km² y presenta la mayor concentración de sitios geotérmicos del mundo, con más de 3 000 géisers, fumarolas y manantiales calientes. Con un diámetro de 112 m, el Grand Prismatic Spring es la fuente termal más grande del parque, y la tercera del mundo por su tamaño. El espectro de colores, que le ha valido su nombre, se debe a la presencia de algas microscópicas cuyo crecimiento en el agua caliente, en el corazón de la pila, difiere del de la periferia en donde la temperatura es menos elevada. Inscrito en la Lista del Patrimonio Mundial de la UNESCO desde 1978, el Parque Nacional de Yellowstone recibe a un promedio de 3 millones de visitantes cada año. Por otra parte, en los Estados Unidos y en Canadá se sitúan los cinco sitios naturales más frecuentados del mundo. Así, el continente norteamericano recibe anualmente a más de 60 millones de turistas (una décima parte del turismo mundial), que, sin embargo, le aportan anualmente la quinta parte de los ingresos mundiales de la actividad turística.

GRAND PRISMATIC GEYSER, YELLOWSTONE NATIONAL PARK, WYOMING, UNITED STATES.

Yellowstone, created in 1872, is the oldest of all national parks. It is situated on a volcanic plateau straddling the states of Montana, Idaho and Wyoming, spreads over 9,000 sq. km. (3,500 sq. mi.) and is home to the greatest concentration of geothermal sites in the world, with more than 3,000 geysers, fumaroles and hot springs. Grand Prismatic Spring, with a diameter of 112 m. (367 ft.), is the largest hot-spring basin in the park, and the third widest in the world. The spectrum of colors that earned it its name is due to the presence of microscopic algae whose growth in hot water, at the center of the bowl, differs from those at the periphery where the temperature is lower. Inscribed on the UNESCO World Heritage List since 1978, Yellowstone National Park receives an average of 3 million visitors per year. The five most-visited natural sites in the world are located in the United States and Canada. The North American continent thus receives over 60 million tourists annually (one-tenth of all world tourism) bringing in one-fifth of the worldwide income for tourist activity.

GEYSER DU GRAND PRISMATIC, PARC NATIONAL DE YELLOWSTONE, WYOMING, ÉTATS-UNIS.

Situé sur un plateau volcanique qui chevauche les Etats du Montana, de l'Idaho et du Wyoming, Yellowstone est le plus ancien des parcs nationaux. Créé en 1872, il s'étend sur 9 000 km² et présente la plus grande concentration de sites géothermiques du monde, avec plus de 3 000 geysers, fumerolles et sources chaudes. D'un diamètre de 112 m, le Grand Prismatic Spring est le bassin thermal le plus vaste du parc, et le troisième au monde par sa taille. Le spectre de couleurs qui lui a valu son nom est dû à la présence d'algues microscopiques dont la croissance dans l'eau chaude, au cœur de la vasque, diffère de celles de la périphérie où la température est moins élevée. Inscrit sur la Liste du patrimoine mondial de l'Unesco depuis 1978, le parc national de Yellow-stone accueille en moyenne 3 millions de visiteurs par an. C'est d'ailleurs aux États-Unis et au Canada que sont situés les cinq sites naturels les plus fréquentés du monde. Le continent nord-américain accueille ainsi annuellement plus de 60 millions de touristes (un dixième du tourisme mondial), qui lui apportent néanmoins le cinquième des recettes mondiales de l'activité touristique.

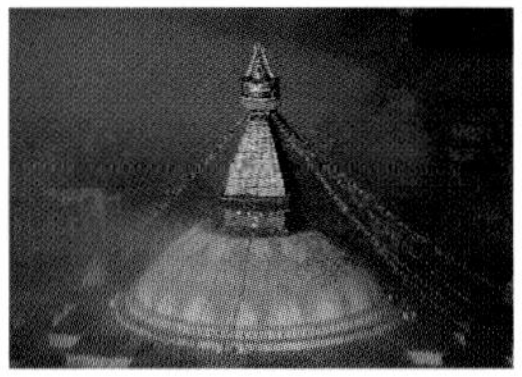

N 27°43' E 85°22'

EL STUPA DE BODNATH, SANTUARIO BUDISTA, KATMANDÚ, NEPAL.

La ciudad de Bodnath alberga uno de los santuarios budistas más venerados de Nepal, principalmente por los millones de tibetanos exiliados de ese país vecino. Dicho stupa, monumento relicario en forma de túmulos coronado con una torre, guarda un fragmento de hueso de Buda. Con 40 m de altura y de diámetro, es el más grande de Nepal. En la arquitectura de este santuario todo es alegoría: el cosmos y los elementos del universo (tierra, agua, aire, fuego, aire, éter) están simbolizados; los ojos de Buda fijan los cuatro puntos cardinales; los diversos estados de acceso al conocimiento supremo, el nirvana, están representados por los 13 escalones de la torre. Durante las fiestas religiosas, el monumento se decora con arcilla amarilla y se adorna con banderas de oración. El budismo es la cuarta religión en el mundo después del cristianismo, del islam y del hinduismo, agrupa a 350 millones de adeptos, de los cuales un 99% se encuentra en Asia. En Europa se cuentan actualmente 2.5 millones de practicantes, como consecuencia de un suceso repentino, particularmente marcado en Francia: los adeptos al budismo pasaron de 200 000 en 1976 a 700 000 veinte años más tarde.

THE BAUDHANATH STÛPA, BUDDHIST SANCTUARY, KATMANDU, NEPAL.

The city of Baudhanath shelters one of the most venerated Buddhist sanctuaries in Nepal, where thousands of Tibetans have found refuge. This stûpa, a monument-shrine in the shape of a tumulus topped with a tower, is said to conceal a fragment of bone of the Buddha. 40 m (130 ft) in height and diameter, it is the largest in Nepal. Everything is allegorical in the architecture of this sanctuary: the cosmos and the elements of the universe (earth, water, fire, air, and ether) are symbolized here; the Buddha's eyes are fixed on the four cardinal points; the tower's 13 steps represent the various stages leading to supreme knowledge, or nirvâna. During religious feasts, the monument is decorated in yellow clay and is adorned with prayer flags. Buddhism, the fourth largest religion in the world after Christianity, Islam and Hinduism, has 350 million adherents, 99% of which are in Asia. In Europe, there are 2.5 million believers today, after a brilliant success that was particularly noticeable in France: the number of followers of Buddhism rose from 200,000 in 1976 to 700,000 twenty years later.

LE STÛPA DE BODNATH, SANCTUAIRE BOUDDHISTE, KATMANDOU, NÉPAL.

La ville de Bodnath abrite l'un des sanctuaires bouddhistes les plus vénérés du Népal, notamment par les milliers de Tibétains exilés dans ce pays voisin. Ce stûpa, monument reliquaire en forme de tumulus surmonté d'une tour, recèlerait un fragment d'os du Bouddha. Avec 40 m de hauteur et de diamètre, il est le plus grand du Népal. Dans l'architecture de ce sanctuaire, tout est allégorie : le cosmos et les éléments de l'univers (terre, eau, feu, air, éther) y sont symbolisés ; les yeux du Bouddha fixent les quatre points cardinaux ; les divers stades d'accès à la connaissance suprême, le nirvâna, sont représentés par les 13 marches de la tour. Lors des fêtes religieuses, le monument est décoré d'argile jaune et orné de drapeaux de prière. Le bouddhisme, quatrième religion dans le monde après le christianisme, l'islam et l'hindouisme, rassemble 350 millions d'adeptes, dont 99 % en Asie. En Europe, on compte aujourd'hui 2,5 millions de pratiquants, suite à un succès fulgurant, particulièrement prononcé en France : de 200 000 en 1976, les adeptes du bouddhisme sont passés à 700 000 vingt ans plus tard.

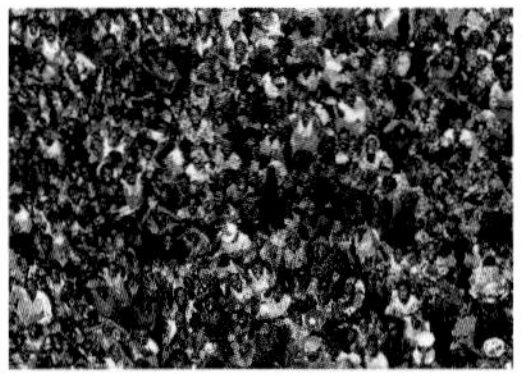

N 6°44' W 3°29'

MULTITUD EN ABENGOUROU, COSTA DE MARFIL.

Esta multitud heterogénea, que manifiesta su entusiasmo saludando al fotógrafo, fue inmortalizada en Abengourou, en el este de Costa de Marfil. Formada principalmente de niños y adolescentes, la multitud nos recuerda que este país es joven puesto que, al igual que en todo el continente africano, el 81% de la población tiene menos de 15 años de edad. Además, el país presenta una tasa total de fecundidad de 5.1 representativa de la media del continente, la cual es ampliamente superior a la media mundial (2.7). La modernización y la evolución de las preocupaciones culturales y socioeconómicas acarrean una baja progresiva de la fecundidad, pero aún serán necesarias varias décadas antes de que la población se estabilice en África, como lo demuestra la tasa media de crecimiento de la población, estimada en un 2.4% entre 1995 y 2000, y que sigue siendo la más elevada de todos los continentes. África cuenta en este inicio de milenio con cerca de 800 millones de habitantes, es decir el 13% de la humanidad; y en cuanto al continente asiático, éste alberga el 60%.

CROWD IN ABENGOUROU, CÔTE-D'IVOIRE.

This colourful crowd, showing its enthusiasm by waving at the photographer, has been immortalized in Abengourou, eastern Côte-d'Ivoire. Made up mainly of children and teenagers, they remind us that this country is young since, like the rest of the African continent, 81% of the population are under 15 years of age. Moreover, this country has a total fertility rate of 5.1, representative of the continent's average, which is much higher than the world average (2.7). Modernization and new cultural and socio-economic concern have brought about a progressive decrease in fertility, but several more decades will be needed before the population is stabilized in Africa, as witnessed by the average rate of population growth, estimated at 2.4% between 1995 and 2000, and still the highest of all continents. Africa at the beginning of this new millennium has close to 800 million inhabitants, or 13% of humankind; the Asian continent however has 60%.

FOULE À ABENGOUROU, CÔTE-D'IVOIRE.

Cette foule bigarrée, qui manifeste son enthousiasme en saluant le photographe, a été immortalisée à Abengourou, dans l'est de la Côte-d'Ivoire. Principalement constituée d'enfants et d'adolescents, elle nous rappelle que ce pays est jeune puisque, comme pour l'ensemble du continent africain, 81 % de la population est âgé de moins de 15 ans. Le pays présente en outre un taux total de fécondité de 5,1 représentatif de la moyenne du continent, laquelle est largement supérieure à la moyenne mondiale (2,7). La modernisation et l'évolution des préoccupations culturelles et socio-économiques entraînent une baisse progressive de la fécondité, mais il faudra encore plusieurs décennies avant que la population ne soit stabilisée en Afrique, comme en témoigne le taux moyen de croissance de la population, estimé à 2,4 % entre 1995 et 2000, et qui demeure le plus élevé de tous les continents. L'Afrique compte en ce début de millénaire près de 800 millions d'habitants, soit 13 % de l'humanité ; le continent asiatique en héberge, lui, 60 %.

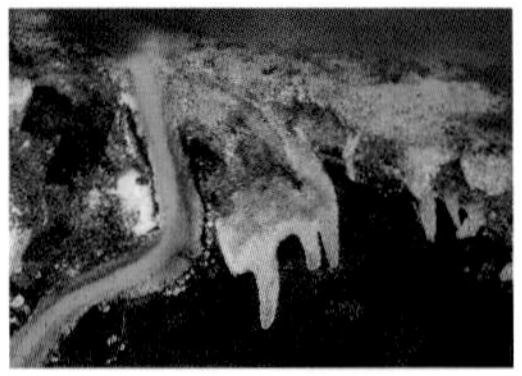

N 6°15' E 120°36'

CIUDAD CERCA DE LA ISLA DE PANDUCAN, FILIPINAS.

La región de Panducan, situada en el grupo de islas de Pangutaran, forma parte del archipiélago de Sulú anteriormente considerado como un hogar de piratería, de contrabando y de tráfico de todos tipo con los países vecinos. Alberga una población 95% musulmana, minoritaria en el país, que durante mucho tiempo ha estado en conflicto con el poder central. En estas islas viven, entre otros, los Tausug, el "pueblo de las corrientes marinas". Repartidos en pequeñas aldeas con casas de bambú sobre pilotes dispersadas en las costas, los Tausug, hasta hace poco contrabandistas o herreros, ahora se han convertido al cultivo seco del arroz, pero viven principalmente del negocio y de la pesca. La autosuficiencia alimentaria de muchas de estas comunidades costeras se reduce debido a los efectos devastadores sobre la fauna marina, particularmente sobre los arrecifes coralíferos, de la práctica común de la pesca con cianuro o con explosivo. Los depósitos de sedimentos y de aluviones, que resultan de la disminución de vegetación fijadora, son igualmente devastadores. Cerca del 70% de los arrecifes coralíferos de las Filipinas se encuentran dañados por esta causa.

VILLAGE CLOSE TO THE ISLAND OF PANDUCAN, PHILIPPINES.

The region of Panducan, situated in the group of islands of Pangutaran, forms part of the Sulu Archipelago formerly considered a haven for piracy, smuggling and trafficking of all kinds with neighboring countries. It accommodates a 95% Moslem population who has long been in conflict with the central power and is a minority in this country. The Tausug, amongst others, or "people of the ocean currents", live on these islands. Spread throughout small hamlets of bamboo houses on poles dispersed along the coasts, the Tausug, formerly smugglers or blacksmiths, have now changed over to dry rice-growing, but basically live on trade and fishing. The self-sufficiency in food production of a number of these coastal communities is reduced by the devastating effects on marine fauna, and especially on coral reefs, caused by the current practice of fishing with cyanide or explosives. The deposits of sediments and alluvium, left by the withdrawal of fixing vegetation, are also devastating. Close to 70% of all coral reefs in the Philippines have been damaged.

VILLAGE PRÈS DE L'ÎLE DE PANDUCAN, PHILIPPINES.

La région de Panducan, située dans le groupe d'îles de Pangutaran, fait partie de l'archipel de Sulu auparavant considéré comme un foyer de piraterie, de contrebande et de trafics en tous genres avec les pays voisins. Elle abrite une population à 95% musulmane, minoritaire dans le pays, qui a longtemps été en conflit avec le pouvoir central. Dans ces îles vivent entre autres les Tausug, le « peuple des courants marins ». Répartis dans des petits hameaux de maisons en bambou sur pilotis, dispersés sur les côtes, les Tausug, naguère contrebandiers ou forgerons, se sont aujourd'hui reconvertis dans la culture sèche du riz mais vivent essentiellement du négoce et de la pêche. L'autosuffisance alimentaire de nombre de ces communautés côtières se réduit, en raison des effets dévastateurs sur la faune marine, notamment sur les récifs coralliens, de la pratique courante de la pêche au cyanure ou à l'explosif. Les dépôts de sédiments et d'alluvions, résultant du retrait de la végétation fixatrice, sont également ravageurs. Près de 70 % des récifs coralliens des Philippines s'en trouvent endommagés.

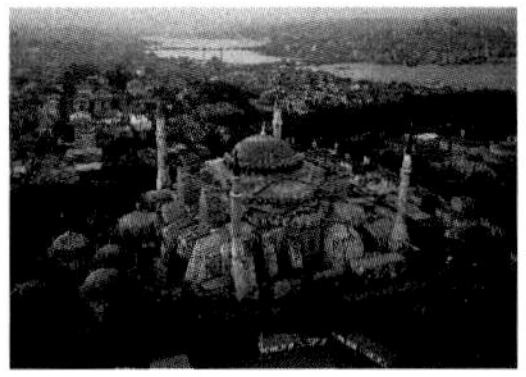

N 41°00' E 28°59'

BASÍLICA SANTA SOFÍA EN ESTAMBUL, TURQUÍA.

En Estambul, la antigua Constantinopla o Bizancio, sobre la ribera occidental del estrecho de Bósforo que separa Europa y Asia, se eleva la basílica Santa Sofía, construida de 532 a 537 en tiempos del reinado del emperador bizantino Justiniano. Considerada durante mucho tiempo como el monumento sagrado más importante de la cristiandad, esta construcción está coronada con una majestuosa cúpula de más de 30 m de diámetro que culmina a 56 m del suelo, cuya construcción representa una proeza técnica para la época. Después de que los turcos tomaran Constantinopla en 1453, Santa Sofía se transformó en mezquita; se añadieron cuatro alminares y varios contrafuertes a su estructura inicial. En 1934 ,el gobierno de la República turca laica decide convertirla en museo, permitiéndole así al público admirar, entre otras cosas, algunos extraordinarios mosaicos bizantinos.

SAINT SOPHIA BASILICA IN ISTANBUL, TURKEY.

Saint Sophia Basilica, built from 532 to 537 under the reign of the Byzantine emperor Justinian is located on the western bank of the Bosphorus Strait, which separates Europe and Asia, in Istanbul, formerly Constantinople or Byzantium. Long considered the most important sacred monument in Christendom, this building is crowned by a majestic dome of over 30 m in diameter that reaches a height of 56 m (184 ft.) above ground level, and whose erection constituted a technical feat for that time. After the capture of Constantinople by the Turks in 1453, Saint Sophia was transformed into a mosque; four minarets and several buttresses were added to its original structure. In 1934, the government of the secular republic of Turkey decided to turn it into a museum, thereby allowing the public to admire, among other things there, some remarkable Byzantine mosaics.

BASILIQUE SAINTE-SOPHIE À ISTANBUL, TURQUIE.

À Istanbul, l'ancienne Constantinople ou Byzance, sur la rive occidentale du détroit du Bosphore qui sépare l'Europe et l'Asie, s'élève la basilique Sainte-Sophie, construite de 532 à 537 sous le règne de l'empereur byzantin Justinien. Longtemps considéré comme le monument sacré le plus important de la Chrétienté, ce bâtiment est couronné d'une majestueuse coupole de plus de 30 m de diamètre culminant à 56 m au-dessus du sol, dont l'édification constitue une prouesse technique pour l'époque. Après la prise de Constantinople par les Turcs en 1453, Sainte-Sophie est transformée en mosquée ; quatre minarets et plusieurs contreforts sont ajoutés à sa structure initiale. En 1934, le gouvernement de la République turque laïque décide d'en faire un musée, permettant ainsi au public d'y admirer, entre autres, de remarquables mosaïques byzantines.

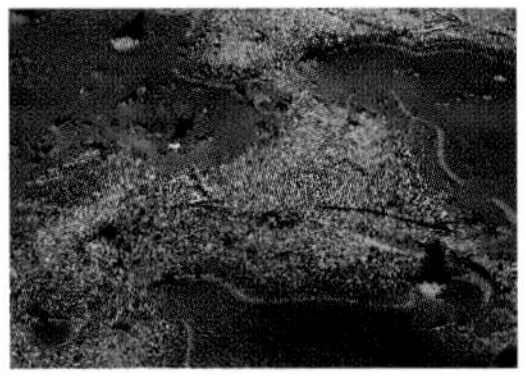

S 24°39' E 15°07'

ORIX EN EL DESIERTO DE NAMIB, REGIÓN DE SWAKOPMUND, NAMIBIA.

Sobre el lado atlántico de África austral, el desierto de Namib cubre la totalidad de los 1 300 km del litoral namibio y se extiende cerca de 100 km hacia el interior de las tierras, ocupando una quinta parte del país. A pesar de que en lengua nama su nombre significa, "lugar en donde no hay nada", la riqueza biológica hace de éste un lugar único en el mundo. Porque el Namib tiene un secreto: las masas de aire húmedo que provienen del Atlántico se condensan al contacto con la superficie del desierto que se refresca durante la noche, envolviéndolo con una densa niebla matinal cerca de 100 días por año. Esta bruma representa 30 mm de precipitaciones anuales y constituye la principal fuente de agua y por lo tanto de vida. La bruma humecta la arena roja-anaranjada, lo cual permite que numerosas especies vegetales y animales subsistan en el desierto de Namib, principalmente una fauna de insectos especializados en la captura de dicho vapor de agua providencial. Fruto de la evolución, sólo las especies que presentan las características mejores adaptadas a las condiciones extremas de los medios desérticos (aridez, temperatura, escasos recursos alimentarios) pueden sobrevivir ahí, como el gran antílope llamado orix o gemsbock.

ORYX IN THE NAMIB DESERT, SWAKOPMUND REGION, NAMIBIA.

Along the southern African coast facing the Atlantic, the Namib Desert covers the entire 1,300 km of the Namibian coastline and extends inland nearly 100 km (62 mi.), occupying one-fifth of the country. Although its name means "place where there is nothing" in the Nama language, its biological wealth makes this place unique in the world, for the Namib has a secret: masses of humid air from the Atlantic condense upon contact with the surface of the desert, which cools off at night, enveloping it in a thick morning fog, nearly 100 days a year. This mist represents 30 mm (over 1 in.) of annual precipitation and constitutes the main source of water, and thus of life. By moistening the red-orange sand, it allows many plant and animal species to subsist in the Namib Desert, in particular a fauna of insects specialized in capturing this providential water vapor. The fruits of evolution, only those species that exhibit features best adapted to the extreme conditions of desert environments (aridness, temperature, poor food resources) can survive here, such as this large antelope called oryx or gemsbock.

ORYX DANS LE DÉSERT DU NAMIB, RÉGION DE SWAKOPMUND, NAMIBIE.

Sur la façade atlantique de l'Afrique australe, le désert du Namib couvre la totalité des 1 300 km du littoral namibien et s'étire sur près de 100 km de largeur à l'intérieur des terres, occupant un cinquième du pays. Bien que son nom signifie, en langue Nama, « endroit où il n'y a rien », sa richesse biologique en fait un lieu unique au monde. Car le Namib a un secret : les masses d'air humide provenant de l'Atlantique se condensent au contact de la surface du désert qui se rafraîchit durant la nuit, l'enveloppant d'un épais brouillard matinal près de 100 jours par an. Cette brume représente 30 mm de précipitations annuelles et constitue la principale source d'eau, donc de vie. En humectant le sable rouge orangé, elle permet à de nombreuses espèces végétales et animales de subsister dans le désert du Namib, notamment une faune d'insectes spécialisés dans la capture de cette vapeur d'eau providentielle. Fruit de l'évolution, seules les espèces présentant les caractéristiques les mieux adaptées aux conditions extrêmes des milieux désertiques (aridité, température, faibles ressources alimentaires) peuvent y survivre, comme cette grande antilope appelée oryx ou gemsbock.

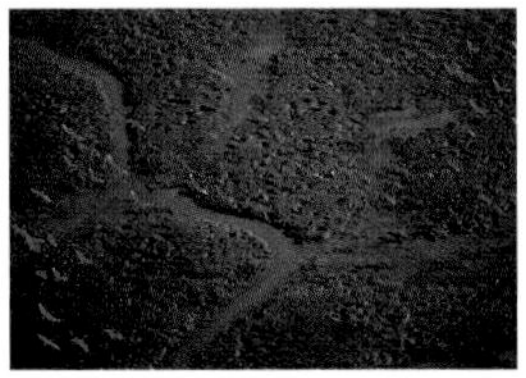

N 9°57' W 62°21'

VUELO DE IBIS ROJOS CERCA DE PEDERNALES, DELTA AMACURO, VENEZUELA.

Desde la región de los Llanos hasta el delta Amacuro que constituye la desembocadura del Río Orinoco, más de una tercera parte de la superficie de Venezuela está formada de zonas húmedas, hábitat favorito de los ibis rojos (Eudocimus ruber). Estas zancudas anidan en grandes colonias en los manglares y no se desplazan más de unos cuantos kilómetros para alimentarse. El caroteno proveniente de los camarones, cangrejos y otros crustáceos que consumen contribuye a darle a la especie su pigmentación característica. Las plumas de ibis rojos, hasta hace poco utilizadas por las poblaciones autóctonas para confeccionar abrigos y adornos, toman parte desde ahora en la elaboración artesanal de flores artificiales. Codiciada tanto por sus plumas como por su carne, esta ave se encuentra hoy en día amenazada; actualmente podrían quedar menos de 200 000 representantes de la especie en toda su área de repartición, en América Central y en América del Sur.

FLIGHT OF SCARLET IBIS CLOSE TO PEDERNALES, DELTA AMACURO, VENEZUELA.

From the region of the Llanos to the Delta Amacuro, mouth of the Rio Orinoco, more than one-third of Venezuela's surface consists of wetlands, the scarlet ibis' (Eudocimus ruber) favorite habitat. Large colonies of these wading birds nest in the trees of the mangrove swamps and only move less than a few kilometers away for feeding. The carotene from shrimp, crabs and other crustaceans consumed contribute in giving the species its characteristic pigmentation. The scarlet ibis feathers, formerly used by indigenous populations to make coats and adornments, are now used in the handcrafting of artificial flowers. Coveted for both its feathers and its flesh, this bird is endangered today. There are thought to be fewer than 200,000 specimens of this species within its area of distribution, in Central and South America.

VOL D'IBIS ROUGES PRÈS DE PEDERNALES, DELTA AMACURO, VENEZUELA.

Depuis la région des Llanos jusqu'au delta Amacuro qui constitue l'embouchure du fleuve Orénoque, plus d'un tiers de la superficie du Venezuela est formé de zones humides, habitat favori des ibis rouges (Eudocimus ruber). Ces échassiers nichent en colonies importantes dans les palétuviers des mangroves et ne se déplacent que de quelques kilomètres pour se nourrir. Le carotène issu des crevettes, crabes et autres crustacés qu'ils consomment contribue à donner à l'espèce sa pigmentation caractéristique. Les plumes d'ibis rouges, naguère utilisées par les populations autochtones pour confectionner des manteaux et des parures, entrent désormais dans la fabrication artisanale de fleurs artificielles. Convoité tant pour ses plumes que pour sa chair, cet oiseau est aujourd'hui menacé ; il resterait actuellement moins de 200 000 représentants de l'espèce dans l'ensemble de son aire de répartition, en Amérique Centrale et en Amérique du Sud.

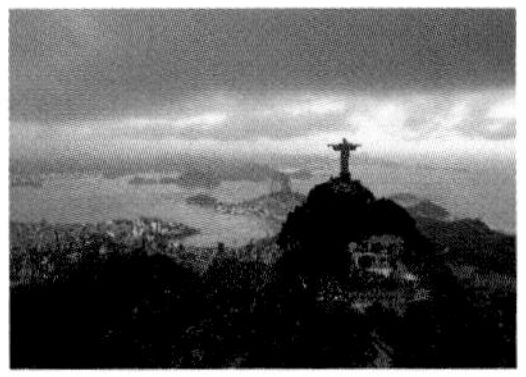

S 22°54' W 43°14'

EL CORCOVADO DOMINANDO DESDE LO ALTO LA CIUDAD DE RÍO DE JANEIRO, BRASIL.

Colocada sobre un pico rocoso de 704 m llamado Corcovado ("jorobado"), la estatua del Cristo redentor domina la bahía de Guanabara y su célebre "Pan de azúcar", así como a toda la ciudad de Río de Janeiro. La ciudad debe su nombre de "río de enero" a una equivocación de los primeros navegantes portugueses que anclaron en la bahía, en enero de 1502, puesto que creyeron penetrar en la desembocadura de una corriente de agua. Capital de Brasil de 1763 a 1960, Río de Janeiro se ha convertido actualmente en una megalópolis que abarca 50 km y alberga a más de 10 millones de habitantes. El Cristo redentor del Corcovado recuerda que Brasil es el primer país católico del planeta, con alrededor de 121 millones de personas bautizadas (75% de la población). El catolicismo (cerca de mil millones de fieles) es en sí mismo mayoritario en el seno de la religión cristiana la cual, con casi 2 mil millones de adeptos, es la más practicada en el mundo.

CORCOVADO MOUNTAIN OVERLOOKING THE CITY OF RIO DE JANEIRO, BRAZIL.

Perched on a rocky summit 704 m high called the Corcovado ("hunchback"), the statue of Christ overlooks Guanabara Bay with its famous Sugar Loaf Mountain, as well as the entire metropolitan area of Rio de Janeiro. The city owes its name of "January river" to a mistake made by the first Portuguese navigators who dropped anchor in the bay in January 1502. They believed they were entering the mouth of a river. Capital of Brazil from 1763 to 1960, Rio de Janeiro has become today a megalopolis that spreads over 50 km and accommodates over 10 million inhabitants. The Christ on the Corcovado reminds us that Brazil was the first Catholic country on the planet, with about 121 million baptized (75% of the population). Catholicism (with close to a billion followers) is itself a majority within the Christian religion, which is the most widely practised religion in the world, with nearly 2 billion adherents.

LE CORCOVADO SURPLOMBANT LA VILLE DE RIO DE JANEIRO, BRÉSIL.

Perchée sur un piton rocheux de 704 m appelé Corcovado (« bossu »), la statue du Christ rédempteur domine la baie de Guanabara et son célèbre « Pain de sucre », ainsi que l'ensemble de l'agglomération de Rio de Janeiro. C'est à une méprise des premiers navigateurs portugais qui jetèrent l'ancre dans la baie, en janvier 1502, que la ville doit son nom de « fleuve de janvier », ces derniers croyant pénétrer dans l'embouchure d'un cours d'eau. Capitale du Brésil de 1763 à 1960, Rio de Janeiro est aujourd'hui devenue une mégalopole qui s'étend sur 50 km et abrite plus de 10 millions d'habitants. Le Christ rédempteur du Corcovado rappelle que le Brésil est le premier pays catholique de la planète, avec environ 121 millions de baptisés (75 % de la population). Le catholicisme (près d'un milliard de fidèles) est lui-même majoritaire au sein de la religion chrétienne laquelle, avec presque 2 milliards d'adeptes, est la plus pratiquée dans le monde.

BULTOS DE ALGODÓN, THONAKAHA, KORHOGO, COSTA DE MARFIL.

En el siglo XIX se introdujeron en África del Oeste las primeras semillas de la variedad de algodoneros *Gossypium hirsutum*, originaria de las Antillas británicas, que es todavía la más cultivada en el mundo. La producción de algodón, originalmente destinada solamente a las necesidades locales, fue fomentada por las potencias coloniales europeas a principios del siglo XX para oponerse al monopolio de exportación de los Estados Unidos y de Egipto, en una época en la cual dicha materia prima representaba un 80% del mercado mundial de textiles. Recolectado manualmente a razón de 15 a 40 kg por día y por obrero en el África tropical, el grano de algodón pasa después por desgranadoras para separar las fibras, los granos y los desechos. Una tonelada de grano de algodón produce 400 kg de fibras y 560 kg de granos, que son transformados para el consumo humano (aceite) o animal (orujo). La ciudad de Korhogo, situada al norte de Costa de Marfil, en el corazón de la zona algodonera, cuenta con una de las nueve fábricas de desgrane del país; además es conocida por su artesanado senoufo de pinturas tradicionales en telas de algodón. Actualmente, a pesar del desarrollo de materiales sintéticos, el algodón aún representa el 47% del mercado mundial de textiles. Costa de Marfil se sitúa en la decimoctava posición mundial de los productores de fibra.

BALES OF COTTON, THONAKAHA, KORHOGO, CÔTE-D'IVOIRE.

The first seeds of the variety of cotton known as *Gossypium hirsutum*, originally from the British Antilles and still the most generally cultivated in the world, were introduced into West Africa in the 19th century. The production of cotton, originally intended for local needs only, was encouraged by the European colonial powers at the beginning of the 20th century in order to put an end to the export monopoly of the United States and Egypt at a time when this raw material represented 80% of the world textile market. Harvested manually at the rate of 15 to 40 kg (33 to 88 lb) per day per worker in tropical Africa, the cotton is then passed through cotton gins in order to separate fibers, seeds and waste. A ton of cotton produces 400 kg (880 lb) of fiber and 560 kg (1,230 lb) of seeds, which are processed for human consumption (oil) or animal feed (cattle cakes). The city of Korhogo, situated in northern Côte-d'Ivoire, in the heart of the cotton-producing area, has one of the country's nine cotton mills, and is known for its Senoufo handicraft, traditional paintings on cotton fabrics. Today, in spite of the development of synthetic materials, cotton still represents 47% of the world textile market. Côte-d'Ivoire ranks in eighteenth place worldwide among fiber producers.

BALLOTS DE COTON, THONAKAHA, KORHOGO, CÔTE-D'IVOIRE.

Au XIXe siècle furent introduites en Afrique de l'Ouest les premières semences de la variété de cotonniers *Gossypium hirsutum*, originaire des Antilles britanniques, qui est encore la plus cultivée dans le monde. La production de coton, originellement destinée aux seuls besoins locaux, fut encouragée par les puissances coloniales européennes au début du XXe siècle afin de contrer le monopole d'exportation des États-Unis et de l'Égypte, à une époque où cette matière première représentait 80 % du marché mondial du textile. Récolté manuellement à raison de 15 à 40 kg par jour et par ouvrier en Afrique tropicale, le coton-graine est ensuite passé dans des égreneuses afin de séparer fibres, graines et déchets. Une tonne de coton-graine produit 400 kg de fibres et 560 kg de graines, qui sont transformées pour la consommation humaine (huile) ou animale (tourteaux). La ville de Korhogo, située au nord de la Côte-d'Ivoire, au cœur de la zone de production cotonnière, compte l'une des neuf usines d'égrenage du pays ; elle est par ailleurs connue pour son artisanat sénoufo de peintures traditionnelles sur toiles de coton. Aujourd'hui, en dépit du développement des matières synthétiques, le coton représente encore 47 % du marché mondial du textile. La Côte-d'Ivoire se place au dix-huitième rang mondial des producteurs de fibre.

N 8°53' W 5°49'

INVASIÓN DE LANGOSTAS CERCA DE RANOHIRA, REGIÓN DE FIANARANTOSA, MAGADASCAR.

Desde hace siglos, miríadas de langostas devastan de manera crónica los cultivos de cereales y los pastizales de Magadascar. A partir de 1992, las invasiones de langostas migratorias africanas (*Locusta migratoria*) y de langostas rojas de África (*Nomadacris septemfasciata*), hasta entonces localizadas en el suroeste, se extendieron progresivamente a cuatro quintas partes de la isla. Alcanzando densidades de 5 millones de insectos por hectárea, los enjambres de varios kilómetros de largo avanzan a un ritmo de 40 km por día, devastando toda la vegetación que encuentran a su paso. A pesar del esparcimiento masivo de insecticidas, que por otra parte son nocivos para el medio ambiente, esta plaga no ha podido ser detenida y provoca que se cierna sobre la isla el espectro de la escasez alimentaria. La mayoría de los países del globo, sobre todo los del hemisferio sur, son víctimas de tales invasiones; en el mundo existen diez especies de langostas que devastan cultivos.

LOCUST INVASION CLOSE TO RANOHIRA, IN THE REGION OF FIANARANTSOA, MADAGASCAR.

For centuries, cereal crops and pasture lands in Madagascar have been chronically devastated by myriads of locusts. Since 1992, invasions of migratory locusts (*Locusta migratoria*) and of nomadic locusts (*Nomadacris septemfasciata*), until then located in the southwest, have spread progressively over 4/5 of the island. Reaching densities of 5 million insects per hectare, clouds of locusts several kilometers long advance at a rate of 40 km (24 mi.) per day, devastating all vegetation in their path. In spite of the massive spreading of insecticides - which is harmful to the environment -, it has been impossible to stop this plague, and the threat of food shortage looms over the island. Most countries around the globe, especially those in the southern hemisphere, are victims of these invasions. Ten species of crop-devastating locusts exist in the world.

INVASION DE CRIQUETS PRÈS DE RANOHIRA, RÉGION DE FIANARANTSOA, MADAGASCAR.

Depuis des siècles, les cultures céréalières et les pâturages de Madagascar sont dévastés de manière chronique par des myriades de criquets. À partir de 1992, les invasions de criquets migrateurs (*Locusta migratoria*) et de criquets nomades (*Nomadacris septemfasciata*), jusqu'alors localisées au sud-ouest, se sont progressivement étendues aux 4/5 de l'île. Atteignant des densités de 5 millions d'insectes à l'hectare, les essaims de plusieurs kilomètres de long progressent au rythme de 40 km par jour, dévastant toute végétation sur leur passage. Malgré l'épandage massif d'insecticides - par ailleurs nocifs pour l'environnement -, ce fléau n'a pu être enrayé et fait planer sur l'île le spectre de pénuries alimentaires. La plupart des pays du globe, surtout ceux de l'hémisphère Sud, sont victimes de telles invasions ; il existe dans le monde dix espèces de criquets ravageurs de cultures.

S 22°27' E 45°21'

BASURERO DE LA CIUDAD DE MÉXICO, MÉXICO

Los desechos domésticos se van amontonando en todos los continentes y constituyen desde ahora un problema mayor para todos los grandes centros urbanos, al igual que la contaminación del aire que resulta de la circulación de los vehículos y de las emanaciones industriales. La Ciudad de México, que cuenta con cerca de 20 millones de habitantes, produce diariamente cerca de 20 000 toneladas de basura doméstica. Al igual que en muchos países, la mitad de estos desperdicios se lleva a basureros a cielo abierto. El volumen de desechos aumenta en el planeta con el crecimiento de la población mundial, y con el ingreso. Así pues, un norteamericano produce anualmente más de 700 kg de desechos domésticos, o sea cuatro veces más que un habitante de un país en vías de desarrollo, y dos veces más que un mexicano. Frente a los problemas de contaminación ocasionados por tirar basura e incinerarla (que aún ahora absorben el 50% y el 35% respectivamente del volumen anual de la basura doméstica en Francia), se recurre cada vez más al reciclaje y a la disminución del volumen de empaques.

GARBAGE DUMP IN THE CITY OF MEXICO, MEXICO.

Domestic garbage is piling up on all continents and now constitutes a major problem for all large urban centers, as does air pollution produced by traffic and industrial emissions. Mexico City, with approximately 20 million inhabitants, produces nearly 20,000 metric tons (22,000 tons) of domestic garbage per day. As in many countries, half of this waste is taken to open-air garbage dumps. The volume of garbage on the planet is increasing with the rise in world population and income. Therefore, an American produces more than 700 kg (1540 lb) of domestic garbage annually, or about four times as much as an inhabitant of a developing country, and two times as much as a Mexican. In the face of pollution problems caused by dumping and incineration (which still absorb 50% and 35% respectively of the yearly volume of domestic garbage in France), recycling and package compacting are more frequently used.

DÉCHARGE DE LA VILLE DE MEXICO, MEXIQUE.

Les déchets ménagers s'amoncellent sur l'ensemble des continents et constituent désormais un problème majeur pour tous les grands centres urbains, tout comme la pollution de l'air résultant de la circulation des véhicules et des émanations industrielles. Mexico, qui compte environ 20 millions d'habitants, produit ainsi près de 20 000 tonnes d'ordures ménagères par jour. Comme dans de nombreux pays, la moitié de ces détritus est dirigée vers des décharges à ciel ouvert. Le volume des déchets augmente sur la planète avec la croissance de la population mondiale, et avec le revenu. Ainsi, un Américain produit annuellement plus de 700 kg de déchets domestiques, soit environ quatre fois plus qu'un habitant dans un pays en développement, et deux fois plus qu'un Mexicain. Face aux problèmes de pollution occasionnés par la mise en décharge et l'incinération (qui absorbent encore respectivement 50 % et 35 % du volume annuel d'ordures ménagères en France), le recyclage et la réduction du volume des emballages sont de plus en plus utilisés.

N 19°24' W 99°01'

IGLESIA A LAS FALDAS DEL VOLCÁN PARICUTÍN, SAN JUAN PARANGARICUTIRO, MICHOACÁN, MÉXICO.

El eje volcánico transmexicano que corre a lo largo de la costa suroeste del país cuenta con más de 300 volcanes, de los cuales el más reciente, el Paricutín, culmina a 2 800 m. En febrero de 1943, un campesino de Michoacán vio salir volutas de humo de un campo de maíz, signo precursor de la aparición del volcán. Efectivamente, unos meses más tarde, se erigía en ese lugar un cono de cenizas de 450 m, y corrientes de lavas se habían tragado las casas de los alrededores. El joven volcán permaneció activo durante 9 años, y respetó toda vida humana. Sin embargo, del pueblo de Paricutín, solo queda el nombre, con que se bautizó al volcán, y del pueblo de San Juan Parangaricutiro solo quedan el campanario y la nave de la iglesia, que emergen de un lecho solidificado de lava negra. Visitantes, turistas u ocasionalmente peregrinos religiosos, como en este caso, un día antes de Pascua, vienen a alegrar con su presencia este paisaje lunar. En México, en donde el 90% de la población es católica, las fiestas religiosas tienen un lugar importante. Así pues, la Virgen de Guadalupe, santa patrona de México, que se festeja el 12 de diciembre, provoca cerca de 1 500 procesiones por todo el país, y las más grandes llegan a reunir hasta 100 000 peregrinos.

CHURCH AT THE FOOT OF PARICUTÍN VOLCANO, SAN JUAN PARANGARICUTIRO, MICHOACÁN, MEXICO.

The trans-Mexican volcanic belt that runs along the southwestern coast of the country harbors more than 300 volcanoes, the most recent being the Paricutín, which reaches a height of 2,800 m. (10,700 ft.). In February of 1943, a peasant in Michoacán saw smoke spirals rising from a cornfield, a forewarning of the formation of a volcano. A few months later, a cone of ashes 450 m (1480 ft.) high stood in this same place, and lava flows had swallowed up the surrounding dwellings. The young volcano remained active for 9 years, but spared all human life. However, what remains of the village of Paricutín is only its name, which was given to the volcano; what remains of the village of San Juan Parangaricutiro is the bell-tower and the nave of the church, which emerge from a bed of black, solidified lava. Visitors, tourists or occasionally religious pilgrims, come to cheer this moonscape with their presence, as seen here on the eve of Easter Sunday. In Mexico, where 90% of the population is Catholic, religious feasts and rituals are a predominant part of the culture. The Virgin of Guadalupe, the holy patroness of Mexico celebrated on December 12th, is thus honored by about 1500 processions throughout the country, the largest ones of which attract as many as 100,000 pilgrims.

EGLISE AU PIED DU VOLCAN PARICUTÍN, SAN JUAN PARANGARICUTIRO, MICHOACÁN, MEXIQUE.

L'axe volcanique transmexicain qui longe la côte sud-ouest du pays compte plus de 300 volcans, dont le dernier-né, le Paricutín, culmine à 2 800 m. En février 1943, un paysan du Michoacán aperçut des volutes de fumée s'élever d'un champ de maïs, signe précurseur de l'apparition du volcan. Quelques mois plus tard en ce lieu se dressait en effet un cône de cendres de 450 m, et des coulées de lave avaient englouti les habitations alentour. Le jeune volcan demeura en activité durant 9 années, et épargna toute vie humaine. Cependant, du hameau de Paricutín, il ne subsiste aujourd'hui que le nom, donné au volcan, et du village de San Juan Parangaricutiro, le clocher et la nef de l'église, émergeant d'un lit de lave noire solidifiée. Des visiteurs, touristes ou occasionnellement pèlerins religieux, comme ici, à la veille de Pâques, viennent égayer de leur présence ce paysage lunaire. Au Mexique, où 90 % de la population est catholique, les fêtes et rites religieux tiennent une place prépondérante dans la culture. La Vierge de Guadalupe, sainte patronne du Mexique, célébrée le 12 décembre, suscite ainsi environ 1500 processions à travers le pays, dont les plus grandes rassemblent jusqu'à 100 000 pèlerins.

N 19°27' W 102°14'

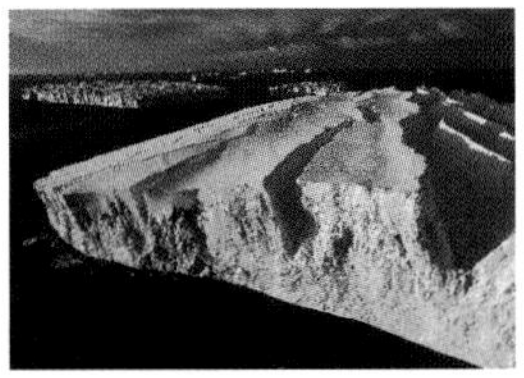

S 67°00' E 139°00'

ICEBERGS A LO LARGO DE TIERRA ADELIA, ANTÁRTIDA (POLO SUR).

Estos icebergs que van a la deriva al capricho de las corrientes marinas se separaron recientemente de las plataformas glaciares de la Antártida, como lo comprueban su forma tabular y los estratos de hielo aún visibles en sus flancos angulosos. Sólo emerge una pequeña parte del volumen de cada uno, ya que más del 80% queda bajo el nivel del agua. De la misma forma que los 2 000 km³ de hielo separados cada año de la Antártida, dichos icebergs sufrirán lentamente la erosión de los vientos y de las olas antes de desquebrajarse y después derretirse por completo. La Antártida, continente de extremos con una superficie de 14 millones de km², temperaturas que descienden hasta los -70°C y vientos que alcanzan los 300 km/hr, tiene el 90% de los icebergs y de las reservas de agua dulce del planeta. Objeto de reivindicaciones territoriales desde el siglo xx, la Antártida está regida desde 1959 por el tratado de Washington que le confiere un estatuto internacional y limita su utilización sólo a las actividades pacíficas y científicas. Así, la estación rusa Vostok ha obtenido, hasta a 3 623 m de profundidad, muestras de hielo que han permitido reconstituir más de 420 000 años de historia del clima y de la composición de la atmósfera. Actualmente, la concentración atmosférica de CO_2, gas principal del efecto de invernadero, responsable del calentamiento climático, está en su nivel más elevado desde hace 160 000 años.

ICEBERGS OFF THE ADÉLIE COAST, ANTARCTIC (SOUTH POLE).

These icebergs that are drifting at the mercy of the ocean currents recently detached themselves from glacier shelves in the Antarctic, as witnessed by their slab-shaped form, and by the ice strata still visible on their angular sides. Only a small part of the volume of each one emerges, with more than 80% remaining below water level. Like the 2,000 cu. km. of ice detached every year in the Antarctic, these icebergs will gradually undergo erosion from the winds and waves before foundering and melting completely. A continent of extremes with a surface of 14 million sq. km., temperatures that fall to -70°C (-94°F), and winds that reach 300 km/hr (190 mph), Antarctica hoards 90% of the planet's ice and fresh water reserves. Target of territorial claims since the 19th century, it has been governed since 1959 by the Antarctic Treaty, which grants it an international status and limits its use to peaceful and scientific activities only. The Russian station Vostok has thus taken ice core samples up to 3623 m (11,890 ft) in depth that have made it possible to reconstruct more than 420,000 years of history of the climate and composition of the atmosphere. Today, the atmospheric content of CO_2, the main greenhouse gas responsible for global warming, is at its highest level in 160,000 years.

ICEBERGS AU LARGE DE LA TERRE ADÉLIE, ANTARCTIQUE (PÔLE SUD).

Ces icebergs qui dérivent au gré des courants marins se sont récemment détachés des plates-formes glaciaires de l'Antarctique, comme en témoignent leur forme tabulaire et les strates de glace encore visibles sur leurs flancs anguleux. Seule émerge une faible partie du volume de chacun, plus de 80 % restant sous le niveau de l'eau. Comme les 2 000 km³ de glace détachés chaque année de l'Antarctique, ces icebergs subiront lentement l'érosion des vents et des vagues avant de basculer puis de fondre complètement. Continent des extrêmes avec une superficie de 14 millions de km², des températures descendant jusqu'à -70°C et des vents atteignant 300 km/h, l'Antarctique recèle 90 % des glaces et des réserves d'eau douce de la planète. Enjeu de revendications territoriales dès le xxe siècle, il est régi depuis 1959 par le traité de Washington qui lui confère un statut international et limite son utilisation aux seules activités pacifiques et scientifiques. La station russe Vostok a ainsi prélevé, jusqu'à 3623 m de profondeur, des carottes de glace qui ont permis de reconstituer plus de 420 000 ans d'histoire du climat et de la composition de l'atmosphère. Aujourd'hui, la teneur atmosphérique en CO_2, principal gaz à effet de serre responsable du réchauffement climatique, est à son niveau le plus élevé depuis 160 000 ans.

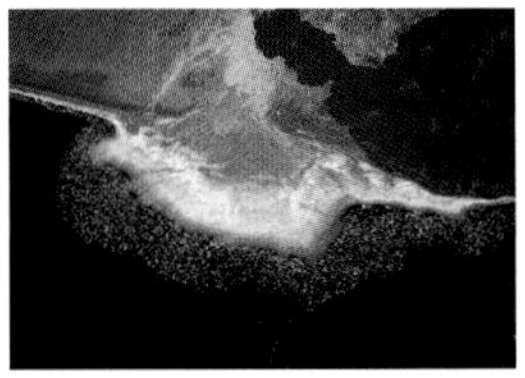

N 2°15' E 36°35'

FLAMENCOS EN LA ORILLA DEL LAGO LOGIPI, VALLE DE SUGUTA, KENIA.

La blancura del natrón (carbonato de sodio) cristalizado sobre la ribera negra volcánica del lago Logipi contrasta con el azul vedoso de las algas que proliferan en el agua alcalina y salobre. Vista desde el cielo, esta parte de la orilla dibuja curiosamente la forma de una ostra gigante, bordeada con algunas perlas nacaradas que corresponden probablemente a brotes de agua dulce sobre las que los flamencos se aglutinan. Estas zancudas vienen a alimentarse en las aguas poco profundas del lago en donde abundan algas y pequeños crustáceos, que les dan su característico color rosa. Así, inmensas colonias de flamencos rosas siguen su curso de un lago al otro del Rift-Valley a merced de la pluviometría anual que modifica la concentración de sodio y por lo tanto la disponibilidad de alimento. Los flamencos abandonaron la región después de la cruel sequía que, durante cerca de 5 años, castigó a África Oriental hasta 1998. A principios de ese mismo año, las grandes lluvias debidas al fenómeno meteorológico El Niño incitaron a pequeños flamencos y flamencos rosas a volver a poblar el Rift-Valley, que hoy podría albergar cerca de 3 millones de ellos, es decir más de la mitad del efectivo mundial.

GREATER (OR ROSE-COLORED) FLAMINGOS ON THE SHORE OF LOGIPI LAKE, SUGUTA VALLEY, KENYA.

The whiteness of the natron (sodium carbonate) crystallized on the black volcanic bank of the Logipi Lake contrasts with the blue-green of the algae that proliferate in the brackish, alkaline water. Seen from the sky, this part of the beach, curiously enough, forms the shape of a giant oyster bordered with some iridescent pearls probably due to some resurgences of fresh water, above which the flamingos gather. These wading birds come to feed in the shallow waters of the lake, abounding in algae and small crustaceans that give flamingos their characteristic color. Huge colonies of greater flamingos thus move around from one lake to the other in the Rift Valley at the mercy of the yearly precipitation, which modifies the concentration of soda and thus the availability of food. They deserted the region at the time of the merciless drought that persisted for nearly 5 years in East Africa until 1998. At the beginning of that same year, heavy rains caused by the climatic phenomenon El Niño, encouraged the lesser and greater flamingos to return to populate the Rift Valley, which today is thought to harbor close to 3 million, or more than half the world's population.

FLAMANTS ROSES AU BORD DU LAC LOGIPI, VALLÉE DE SUGUTA, KENYA.

La blancheur du natron (carbonate de sodium) cristallisé sur la berge noire volcanique du lac Logipi contraste avec le bleu-vert des algues qui prolifèrent dans l'eau alcaline et saumâtre. Vue du ciel, cette partie du rivage dessine curieusement une forme d'huître géante, bordée de quelques perles nacrées correspondant probablement à des résurgences d'eau douce au-dessus desquelles les flamants s'agglutinent. Ces échassiers viennent se nourrir dans les eaux peu profondes du lac où foisonnent des algues et de petits crustacés, qui donnent aux flamants leur couleur caractéristique. D'immenses colonies de flamants roses évoluent ainsi d'un lac à l'autre de la vallée du Rift, au gré de la pluviométrie annuelle qui modifie la concentration en soude donc la disponibilité alimentaire. Ils ont déserté la région lors de la cruelle sécheresse qui, pendant près de 5 ans, a sévi en Afrique orientale jusqu'en 1998. Au début de cette même année, les pluies importantes dues au phénomène climatique El Niño ont incité petits flamants et flamants roses à revenir peupler la vallée du Rift, qui en abriterait aujourd'hui près de 3 millions, soit plus de la moitié de l'effectif mondial.

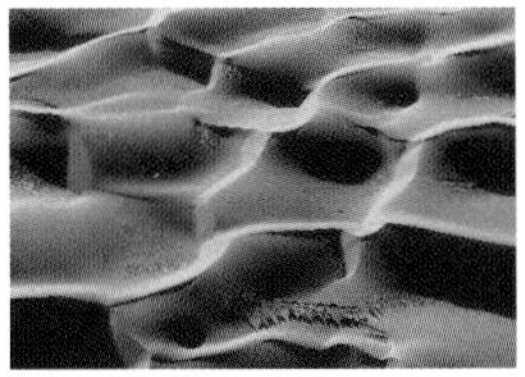

N 18°09' W 15°29'

CARAVANA DE DROMEDARIOS EN LAS DUNAS DE NUAKCHOTT, MURITANIA

El Sahara, el desierto de arena más grande del mundo, cubre 9 000 000 km² (el equivalente de los Estados Unidos) repartidos en 11 países. En su borde oeste se encuentra Mauritania, desértica en dos terceras partes, país particularmente afectado por el fenómeno de desertización provocado por el hombre. El sobrepastoreo, la extracción de leña y la expansión agrícola suprimen poco a poco la vegetación fijadora situada en el contorno de los grandes macizos dunares, facilitando así la propagación de arena, que hoy amenaza ciudades como Nuakchott, la capital. En las zonas áridas y semiáridas (las dos terceras partes del continente africano), las frágiles tierras cultivables se deterioran rápidamente si las prácticas de cultivo y la explotación de la cubierta vegetal no son lo suficientemente intensas. Así, en el curso del último medio siglo, el 65% de las tierras arables africanas se han degradado. Esta deterioración acarrea una baja de rendimientos agrícolas que repercute en la seguridad alimentaria. En este círculo vicioso difícil de romper, la pobreza es a la vez causa y consecuencia de la degradación de las tierras cultivables y de la baja de su productividad agrícola.

CARAVAN OF DROMEDARIES IN DUNES CLOSE TO NOUAKCHOTT, MAURITANIA.

The Sahara, largest sand desert in the world, covers 9,000,000 sq. km. (3,500,000 sq. mi.) - the size of the United States-, distributed over 11 countries. On its western border, Mauritania, which is three-quarters desert, is especially affected by the phenomenon of desertification of anthropic origin. Over-grazing, collecting of fire-wood, and agricultural expansion have gradually reduced the fixing vegetation situated around the large expanses of dunes, thus facilitating the progression of the sand that today threatens cities such as Nouakchott, the capital. In the arid and semi-arid zones (2/3 of the African continent), fragile arable lands deteriorate quickly if farming practices and the exploitation of the natural vegetation are too intensive. Over the past half-century, 65% of African arable lands have degraded in this way. This deterioration brings about a drop in agricultural yield that affects food security. In this vicious circle, which is so difficult to break, poverty is both the cause and the consequence of the degradation of arable lands and their decrease in agricultural productivity.

CARAVANE DE DROMADAIRES DANS LES DUNES PRÈS DE NOUAKCHOTT, MAURITANIE.

Le Sahara, plus grand désert de sable du monde, couvre 9 000 000 km² (l'équivalent des États-Unis) répartis sur 11 pays. Sur sa bordure ouest, la Mauritanie, aux trois-quarts désertiques, est particulièrement touchée par le phénomène de désertification d'origine anthropique. Le surpâturage, la récolte de bois de feu et l'expansion agricole suppriment peu à peu la végétation fixatrice située sur le pourtour des grands massifs dunaires, facilitant ainsi la progression du sable, qui menace aujourd'hui des villes comme Nouakchott, la capitale. Dans les zones arides et semi-arides (les 2/3 du continent africain), les terres cultivables, fragiles, se détériorent rapidement si les pratiques culturales et l'exploitation du couvert végétal sont trop intensives. Au cours du dernier demi-siècle, 65 % des terres arables africaines ont ainsi été dégradées. Cette détérioration entraîne une baisse des rendements agricoles, qui se répercute sur la sécurité alimentaire. Dans ce cercle vicieux difficile à rompre, la pauvreté est à la fois cause et conséquence de la dégradation des terres cultivables et de la baisse de leur productivité agricole.

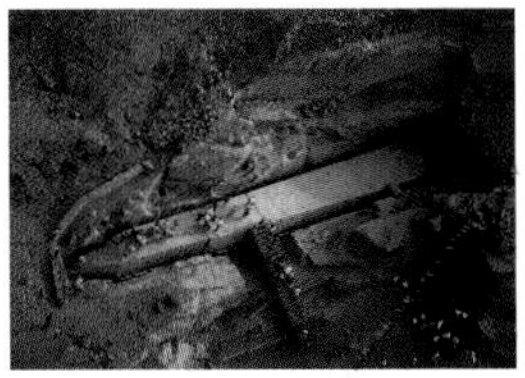

N 24°01' E 32°58'

EL OBELISCO INCONCLUSO, ASUÁN, EGIPTO.

La potencia inmóvil que manifiesta el obelisco extendido sobre su enorme cama y cuya base parece salir de la sombra de las profundidades terrestres es la de un símbolo en construcción que todavía forma parte de la naturaleza. No se le escapará sino hasta que le retiren su ganga y lo transporten a fuerza de hombre hasta su lugar de ejercicio. Sólo entonces el obelisco alcanzará su pleno significado y, gracias a su levantamiento, tomará lugar en el cortejo se los símbolos grandiosos de las sociedades humanas. Alzado majestuosamente, sin importar cual sea el texto eventualmente escrito en su pedestal, se convertirá en testigo eficaz de la ingeniosidad y del orgullo de un grupo de humanos. Este obelisco fue abandonado después de un accidente durante la extracción. Para Egipto, el turismo es una fuente tradicional de divisas. Un atentado perpetuado en noviembre de 1997 en Luxor (62 muertos de los cuales 58 eran turistas) hizo que a este país se le frecuentara menos (2 mil millones de dólares en pérdidas en 1998).

UNFINISHED OBELISK, ASWAN, EGYPT.

The immobile power expressed by the obelisk, stretched lengthwise on its cutting bed and whose base seems to rise out of the shadowy bowels of the earth, is that of a symbol undergoing construction, yet still forming part of nature. It will not completely escape until it is extracted from its source and transported forcibly by man to its proper place. Only then will the obelisk reach its full significance and, once erect, will take its place in the cortege of awe-inspiring symbols of human societies. Towering majestically, with whatever text is eventually inscribed on its pedestal, it will become a testimony to the ingenuity and pride of a group of human beings. This obelisk was abandoned after an accident during its extraction. For Egypt, tourism is a traditional source of currency. An attack perpetrated in November of 1997 at Luxor (with 62 deaths, including 58 tourists) caused a decline in visits and a resulting loss of 2 billion dollars in 1998.

L'OBÉLISQUE INACHEVÉ, ASSOUAN, ÉGYPTE.

La puissance immobile qu'exprime l'obélisque allongé sur son lit de taille et dont la base semble sortir de l'ombre des profondeurs terrestres est celle d'un symbole en construction faisant toujours partie de la nature. Il ne lui échappera que lorsqu'il sera extrait de sa gangue, transporté à force d'homme jusqu'à son lieu d'exercice. Alors seulement l'obélisque atteindra sa pleine signification et, par son érection, prendra place dans le cortège des symboles grandioses des sociétés humaines. Dressé en majesté, quel que soit le texte éventuellement écrit sur son socle, il deviendra le témoin efficace de l'ingéniosité et de l'orgueil d'un groupe d'humains. Cet obélisque a été abandonné à la suite d'un accident en cours d'extraction. Pour l'Egypte, le tourisme est une source traditionnelle de devises. Un attentat perpétré en novembre 1997 à Louxor (62 morts dont 58 touristes) a fait chuter la fréquentation (2 milliards de dollars de pertes en 1998).

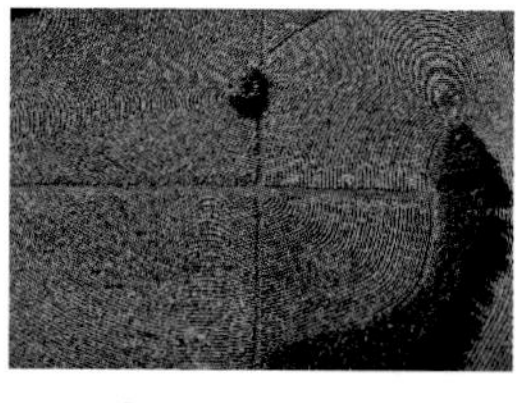

S 27°50' W 56°01'

CULTIVO DEL TÉ EN LA PROVINCIA DE CORRIENTES, ARGENTINA.

La fertilidad de la tierra roja y las lluvias regulares de la región de Corrientes proporcionan las condiciones óptimas para el cultivo del té. Teniendo cuidado de proteger de los suelos contra la erosión, los arbustos de té son plantados siguiendo las curvas del nivel y resguardados del viento por setos. Contrariamente a los países de Asia y de África, en donde los pequeños retoños se recolectan manualmente, en Argentina se lleva a cabo una recolección mecánica, principalmente con tractores de chasis elevado que surcan las plantaciones regulares de arbustos. El té híbrido de la variedad india Assam, que se cultiva en este país y se recolecta en verano, tiene una débil producción (50 000 toneladas por año) que completa la importante producción invernal de mate tradicional, especie de acebo que se consume como infusión y que es llamado "té de los jesuitas". Actualmente, el té se cultiva en 40 países, India, China, Sri Lanka y Kenia abastecen entre ellos solos el 60% de la producción mundial.

TEA-GROWING IN THE PROVINCE OF CORRIENTES, ARGENTINA.

The fertility of the red earth and regular rains in the Corrientes region provide optimal conditions for tea-growing. Out of a concern to protect soils against erosion, tea-plants are planted along contour levels and protected from the wind by hedges. Unlike countries in Asia and Africa where young shoots are harvested manually, picking in Argentina is done mechanically, using high-clearance tractors, which cross the regular plantations of bushes. Hybrid tea of the Indian variety Assam, cultivated in this country, has a low level of production (50,000 metric tons (55,000 tons) per year); harvested in the summer, it complements the substantial winter production of traditional maté, a type of holly drunk as herbal tea and known as the "tea of the Jesuits". Today, tea is cultivated in 40 countries, with India, China, Sri Lanka and Kenya providing 60% of world production alone.

CULTURE DE THÉ DANS LA PROVINCE DE CORRIENTES, ARGENTINE.

La fertilité de la terre rouge et les pluies régulières de la région de Corrientes fournissent les conditions optimales pour la culture du thé. Dans un souci de protection des sols contre l'érosion, les théiers sont plantés suivant les courbes de niveau et protégés du vent par des haies. Contrairement aux pays d'Asie et d'Afrique, où les jeunes pousses sont récoltées manuellement, on procède, en Argentine, à une cueillette mécanique, notamment au moyen de tracteurs enjambeurs qui sillonnent les plantations régulières d'arbustes. Le thé hybride de la variété indienne Assam, cultivé dans ce pays, fait l'objet d'une faible production (50 000 tonnes par an) ; récolté en été, il complète l'importante production hivernale de maté traditionnel, sorte de houx consommé en infusion et dit « thé des jésuites ». Aujourd'hui, le thé est cultivé dans 40 pays, l'Inde, la Chine, Sri Lanka et le Kenya fournissant à eux seuls 60 % de la production mondiale.

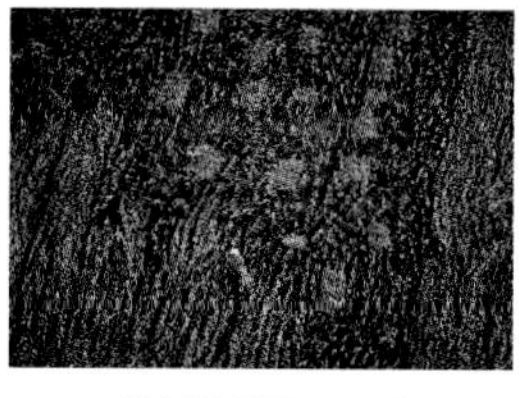

N 19°32' E 99°43'

TRABAJO DE LOS CAMPOS EN LA REGIÓN DE PHITSANULOK, TAILANDIA.

Fértil y favorecida por un clima tropical húmedo, la planicie central de Tailandia, en donde se encuentra Phitsanulok, es el granero de arroz del país. Como en cualquier otra parte del territorio, este cereal se cosecha y recolecta sobre todo a mano. Desde hace cincuenta años, con el deseo de incrementar sus exportaciones, Tailandia triplicó la superficie de sus tierras arables, ganando espacios cultivables en las zonas arboladas. Mientras que los bosques representaban la mitad del territorio en los años 1960, ahora sólo cubren el 28% del país. Sin embargo, si bien el fenómeno de la deforestación vinculado a la agricultura afecta a todo los países de Asia, Tailandia es el país en donde más se manifiesta. La tala acelerada conduce a una degradación preocupante de los suelos puestos al desnudo, rápidamente limpiados por la erosión. Asia del Sur que tiene el 30% de las tierras sobre el nivel del mar del globo y que alberga a cerca del 60% de la población mundial, ve cómo se ejercen grandes presiones sobre los recursos de sus tierras.

WORK IN THE FIELDS OF THE PHITSANULOK REGION, THAILAND.

Fertile and enjoying a moist, tropical climate, the central plain of Thailand, where Phitsanulok is located, is the rice granary of the country. As in the rest of the territory, this cereal is especially reaped and harvested by hand. In the last fifty years, concerned with its export growth, Thailand has tripled the area of its arable lands, taking over arable space from wooded areas. While forests represented half of the territory in the 60's, they cover today only 28% of the country. Although the phenomenon of deforestation related to farming affects all countries in Asia, this is most apparent in Thailand. Accelerated deforestation leads to an alarming degradation of the exposed soils, which are quickly washed away by erosion. Southern Asia, which accommodates 30% of the emerged land on the globe and about 60% of the world's population, thus has considerable pressures exerted on its lands' resources.

TRAVAUX DES CHAMPS DANS LA RÉGION DE PHITSANULOK, THAÏLANDE.

Fertile et bénéficiant d'un climat tropical humide, la plaine centrale de Thaïlande, où se trouve Phitsanulok, est le grenier à riz du pays. Comme partout ailleurs sur le territoire, cette céréale est surtout moissonnée et récoltée à la main. Depuis cinquante ans, dans un souci d'accroissement de ses exportations, la Thaïlande a triplé la superficie de ses terres arables, gagnant des espaces cultivables sur les zones boisées. Alors qu'elles représentaient la moitié du territoire dans les années 1960, les forêts ne couvrent plus aujourd'hui que 28 % du pays. Si le phénomène de déforestation lié à l'agriculture touche l'ensemble des pays d'Asie, c'est cependant en Thaïlande qu'il est le plus manifeste. Le déboisement accéléré conduit à une dégradation inquiétante des sols mis à nu, vite lessivés par l'érosion. L'Asie du Sud, qui héberge sur 30 % des terres émergées du globe environ 60 % de la population mondiale, voit ainsi des pressions considérables s'exercer sur les ressources de ses terres.

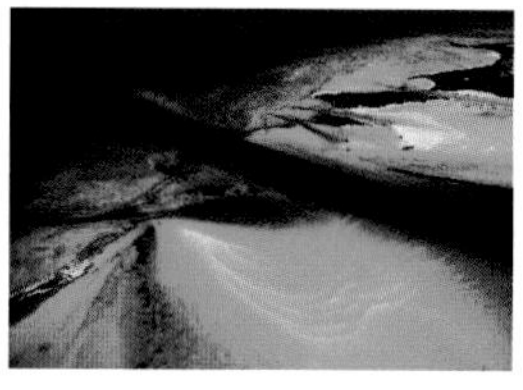

N 24°26' W 76°44'

ISLOTES Y FONDOS MARINOS, EXUMA CAYS, BAHAMAS.

El archipiélago de las Bahamas que obtiene su nombre de las palabras baja mar, se extiende en forma de arco sobre cerca de 14 000 km² de tierras sobre el nivel del mar en el océano Atlántico, desde Florida hasta Santo Domingo. Está formado por más de 700 islas, de las cuales menos de cincuenta están habitadas, y por algunos miles de arrecifes coralíferos, llamados cayes. Fue en estas islas, más precisamente en Samana Cay, en donde Cristóbal Colón atracó el 12 de octubre de 1492 durante el primer viaje hacia el Nuevo Mundo. Importante centro de piratería del siglo XVI al XVII, las Bahamas se volvieron posesión inglesa en 1718 hasta su independencia, en 1973. El país es hoy un "paraíso fiscal" en el cual no existe ningún impuesto sobre los ingresos. Obtiene lo necesario de sus recursos en las actividades bancarias (20% del PNB), pero sobre todo en el turismo (60% del PNB), que emplea a dos de cada tres isleños. Además, más de un millar de navíos, es decir cerca del 3% de la flota de comercio internacional, están registrados con el pabellón de conveniencia de Bahamas. De la misma forma, las Bahamas se han convertido en uno de los centros para el tránsito de la droga (cannabis, cocaína) que tiene como destino los Estados Unidos.

ISLETS AND SEAFLOORS, EXUMA AND CAYS ISLANDS, BAHAMAS.

The archipelago of the Bahamas, which takes its name from the Spanish baja mar (shallow sea), extends from Florida to Santo Domingo. In the shape of a crescent, it represents nearly 14,000 sq. km. (5,400 sq. mi.) of emerged land in the Atlantic Ocean, and is made of several thousands of coral reefs called cays, as well as more than 700 islands, fewer than fifty of which are inhabited. On his first journey to the New World, Christopher Columbus landed on one of these islands, Samana Cay, on October 12th 1492. A major center for piracy from the 16th to the 17th centuries, the Bahamas became an English possession in 1718 until their independence in 1973. The country is today a "fiscal paradise" in which there is no income tax. It draws the main part of its resources from banking activities (20% of the GNP) and, to an even greater extent, from tourism (60% of the GNP), which employs two of the islands' inhabitants out of three. In addition, more than a thousand ships, or nearly 3% of the international trade fleet, are registered under the Bahamian flag of convenience. The Bahamas have also become a hub for drug transit (cannabis, cocaine) to the United States.

ILOTS ET FONDS MARINS, EXUMA CAYS, BAHAMAS.

L'archipel des Bahamas, qui tire son nom de l'espagnol baja mar (hauts-fonds), s'étend en arc de cercle sur près de 14 000 km² de terres émergées dans l'océan Atlantique, de la Floride à Saint-Domingue. Il est constitué de plus de 700 îles, dont moins d'une cinquantaine habitées, et de quelques milliers de récifs coralliens, appelés cayes. C'est dans ces îles, plus précisément à Samana Cay, que Christophe Colomb accosta le 12 octobre 1492 lors de son premier voyage vers le Nouveau Monde. Centre de piraterie important du XVIe au XVIIe siècle, les Bahamas devinrent possession anglaise en 1718 jusqu'à leur indépendance, en 1973. Le pays est aujourd'hui un « paradis fiscal » dans lequel n'existe aucun impôt sur le revenu. Il tire l'essentiel de ses ressources des activités bancaires (20 % du PNB), mais surtout du tourisme (60 % du PNB), qui emploie deux insulaires sur trois. En outre, plus d'un millier de navires, soit près de 3 % de la flotte de commerce internationale, sont enregistrés sous pavillon de complaisance bahaméen. Les Bahamas sont également devenues l'une des plaques tournantes pour le transit de la drogue (cannabis, cocaïne) à destination des États-Unis.

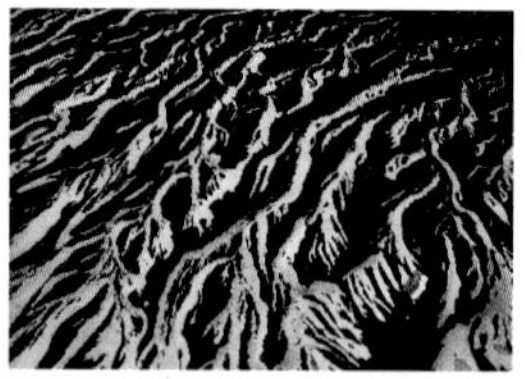

N 56°00' E 160°00'

FLANCOS NEVADOS DEL VOLCÁN KRONOTKSAYA, KAMCHATKA, RUSIA.

En el extremo oriental de Siberia, la casi isla de Kamchatka se extiende sobre cerca de 370 000 km². En esta región de la Federación de Rusia, la naturaleza reina y el hombre está poco presente (la densidad es inferior a un habitante por km²). La península de Kamchatka es muy joven geológicamente, cuenta con menos de un millón de años de existencia y alberga 160 volcanes, de los cuales 30 están todavía activos, inscritos en la Lista del Patrimonio Mundial de la UNESCO desde 1996. En esta porción del "cinturón de fuego" del Pacífico, el cono perfecto del volcán Kronotskaya, uno de los más elevados, culmina a 3 528 m. La región comprende también numerosos manantiales termales, caídas de agua y géisers, ríos violentos y torrentes. En un área de 9 000 km² alberga la reserva natural de Kronotsky en donde viven, protegidos, los osos pardos de Kamchatka, linces, martas cibelinas y zorros. Al frente, Alaska, que se encuentra separada por el Mar de Bering, presenta el mismo aspecto. Hace 26 000 años, pequeños grupos de hombres franquearon el estrecho entonces seco y progresivamente poblaron toda América. Los Sioux, los Incas y los Guaraní son sus descendientes: venían de Kamchatka.

SNOW-COVERED SIDE OF THE KRONOTSKAYA VOLCANO, KAMCHATKA, RUSSIA.

At the easternmost end of Siberia, the Kamchatka Peninsula spreads over close to 370,000 sq. km. In this part of the Russian Federation, nature reigns supreme and man is nearly absent (the population density is less than one inhabitant per sq. km.). Existing for less than a million years, and therefore geologically very young, the Kamchatka Peninsula contains 160 volcanoes - 30 of which are still active - which have been inscribed on the UNESCO World Heritage List since 1996. In this portion of the "Ring of Fire" in the Pacific, the Kronotskaya Volcano's perfect cone, which is one of the highest, reaches a peak height of 3528 m (11,580 ft). The region also includes numerous hot springs, waterfalls and geysers, fast-flowing rivers and streams. Over an area of 9,000 sq. km. (3,500 sq. mi.), it harbors the Kronotski National Park, a protected area for the Kamchatka brown bear, lynx, sable and fox. Opposite to it, and separated by Behring Strait, American Alaska exhibits the same appearance. 26,000 years ago, small groups of men crossed the strait, which was then dry, and progressively populated all of America. The Sioux, Inca, and Guarani are their descendants: they came from Kamchatka.

FLANCS ENNEIGÉS DU VOLCAN KRONOTSKAYA, KAMTCHATKA, RUSSIE.

À l'extrémité orientale de la Sibérie, la presqu'île du Kamtchatka s'étend sur près de 370 000 km². Dans cette région de la Fédération de Russie, la nature est reine et l'homme peu présent (la densité est inférieure à un habitant par km²). Géologiquement très jeune, avec moins d'un million d'années d'existence, la péninsule du Kamtchatka abrite 160 volcans, dont 30 encore actifs, inscrits sur la Liste du patrimoine mondial de l'Unesco depuis 1996. Dans cette portion de la « ceinture de feu » du Pacifique, le cône parfait du volcan Kronotskaya, l'un des plus élevés, culmine à 3528 m. La région comprend aussi de nombreuses sources thermales chaudes, des chutes d'eau et des geysers, des fleuves violents et des torrents. Elle abrite sur 9000 km² la réserve naturelle de Kronotski où vivent, protégés, les ours bruns du Kamtchatka, des lynx, des zibelines et des renards. En face, séparé par le détroit de Behring, l'Alaska américain présente le même aspect. Il y a 26 000 ans, de petits groupes d'hommes franchirent le détroit alors à sec et progressivement peuplèrent toute l'Amérique. Les Sioux, les Incas, les Guarani sont leurs descendants : ils venaient du Kamtchatka.

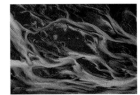

N 63°56' W 20°57'

DETALLE DEL RÍO PJORSA, ISLANDIA.

El Río Pjorsa (o Thjorsa), que fluye con un caudal de 385 m³/seg a lo largo de 230 km, es el más largo de Islandia. Cava su lecho en terrenos recubiertos de lava y acarrea hasta el océano múltiples desechos orgánicos y minerales, de donde proviene su color característico. Todo el país está cubierto de una gran red de ríos no navegables, la mayoría nacidos de torrentes subglaciares, cuyos trayectos variables y tortuosos vuelven delicada cualquier construcción de obras permanentes tales como puentes o presas. Sin embargo, la energía hidráulica permite satisfacer el 20% de las necesidades en electricidad, y las posibilidades siguen siendo considerables, ya que sólo se ha explotado una sexta parte del potencial hidráulico.

DETAIL OF THE PJORSA RIVER, ICELAND.

The Pjorsa (or Thjorsa) river, which flows at a rate of 385 cu. m. (13,600 cu ft.)/sec. over a distance of 230 km (143 mi.), is the longest in Iceland. It hollows out its bed in lava-covered land and carries great quantities of organic and mineral waste to the ocean, hence its characteristic color. The entire country is covered by a vast network of non-navigable rivers, for the most part originating from sub-glacial streams, whose changing and tormented courses make all permanent construction work, such as bridges or dams, very problematic. Hydraulic energy however meets 20% of the electricity needs, and has considerable promise, since only one-sixth of the water potential has so far been exploited.

DÉTAIL DE LA RIVIÈRE PJORSA, ISLANDE.

La rivière Pjorsa (ou Thjorsa), qui coule avec un débit de 385 m³/s sur une distance de 230 km, est la plus longue d'Islande. Elle creuse son lit dans des terrains recouverts de lave et charrie jusqu'à l'océan de multiples déchets organiques et minéraux, d'où sa couleur caractéristique. L'ensemble du pays est couvert d'un vaste réseau de rivières non navigables, pour la plupart issues de torrents subglaciaires, dont les parcours variables et torturés rendent délicate toute construction d'ouvrages permanents tels que ponts ou barrages. L'énergie hydraulique permet néanmoins de satisfaire 20 % des besoins en électricité, et les possibilités demeurent considérables, puisque seul un sixième du potentiel hydraulique a été exploité.

N 16°12' W 0°01'

PIRAGUA SOBRE EL RÍO NÍGER EN LA REGIÓN DE GAO, MALI.

El Río Níger que nace en el macizo de Futa Djalon, en Guinea, es el tercer corriente de agua más larga del continente africano, con 4 184 km. Atravesando Mali a lo largo de 1 700 km, forma una amplia curva que alcanza el límite sur del Sahara, abasteciendo de agua a poblaciones importantes como Tumbuktu y Gao. La corta estación de lluvias estimula la regeneración de vegetación acuática entre la cual circulan piraguas, medios comunes de desplazamiento, de transporte y de intercambio entre poblaciones ribereñas. Debido a que se encuentran sometidos a un movimiento de crecidas de temporada, el Niger permite también irrigar cerca de 5 000 km² de tierras, sobre las cuales se practican el cultivo de arroz y de hortalizas. Se trata de la principal fuente hídrica para cerca del 80% de la población de Mali, que vive de la agricultura y de la ganadería.

PIROGUE ON THE NIGER RIVER NEAR GAO, MALI.

The Niger River, whose source is in the Fouta Djallon massif, Guinea, is the third longest river on the African continent, with a length of 4,184 km. (2,600 mi.). Crossing Mali over a distance of 1,700 km (1,060 mi.), it forms a large loop that reaches the southern limit of the Sahara, providing water for large urban areas such as Tombouctou and Gao. The short rainy season stimulates the regeneration of aquatic plants among which navigate the pirogues, a usual means of travel, transport and exchange between populations bordering the river. Subject to a movement of seasonal floods, the Niger enables irrigation of close to 5,000 sq. km. (1,900 sq. mi.) of land, used for rice-growing and market-gardening. It constitutes the main water resource for close to 80% of Mali's population, who live on agriculture and raising livestock.

PIROGUE SUR LE FLEUVE NIGER DANS LA RÉGION DE GAO, MALI.

Le fleuve Niger, qui prend sa source dans le massif du Fouta Djalon, en Guinée, est, avec 4 184 km, le 3e plus long cours d'eau du continent africain. Traversant le Mali sur une distance de 1 700 km, il forme une large boucle qui atteint la limite sud du Sahara, alimentant en eau des agglomérations importantes comme Tombouctou et Gao. La courte saison des pluies stimule la régénération des végétaux aquatiques parmi lesquels circulent des pirogues, moyens usuels de déplacement, de transport et d'échange entre les populations riveraines du fleuve. Soumis à un mouvement de crues saisonnières, le Niger permet par ailleurs d'irriguer près de 5 000 km² de terres, sur lesquelles sont pratiquées la riziculture et le maraîchage. Il constitue la principale ressource hydrique pour près de 80 % de la population malienne, qui vit d'agriculture et d'élevage.

S 3°03' W 60°06'

ARMADÍAS SOBRE EL AMAZONAS, REGIÓN DE MANAOS, AMAZONAS, BRASIL.

En esta región en donde la densidad de la vegetación no permite otro acceso a las zonas de explotación, las armadías son el medio más rentable para transportar la madera. Los troncos amarrados unos con otros se almacenan en el Río Amazonas antes de ser remolcados hacia los aserraderos. Brasil es el quinto productor mundial de madera industrial y el primer productor de maderas tropicales, pero este gran aporte económico se hace a costa de una deforestación preocupante de cerca de 22 000 km² cada año. Así, la selva amazónica ha perdido el 15% de su superficie original, debido, principalmente, a la roturación de tierras cultivables, a la explotación minera, y a la explotación de la madera de construcción, del combustible y de los productos forestales. Desde 1961, la utilización por persona de papel y de cartón, productos de origen forestal, casise ha triplicado, principalmente en los países ricos. Así, Europa, Japón y América del Norte, que no representan sino un 19% de la población mundial, consumen el 63% de la madera y del cartón que se producen, y casi la mitad de la madera industrial.

LOG RUNNING ON THE AMAZON, NEAR MANAUS, AMAZONAS, BRAZIL.

In this region, where the density of the vegetation does not permit any access to the areas of exploitation, log running is the most cost-effective means of transporting wood. Logs tied together are stockpiled on the Amazon River before being towed to sawmills. Brazil is the fifth largest producer of industrial wood in the world, and the greatest producer of tropical wood, but the price paid for this major economic contribution is an alarming deforestation rate of 22,000 sq. km. (8,500 sq. mi.) per year. The Amazon Rain Forest has thus already lost 15% of its original surface area, mainly due to the clearing of arable land, mining exploitation, as well as exploitation for lumber, fuel and forest products. The use of paper and cardboard from forest products per person has nearly tripled since 1961, especially in the richer countries. Thus Europe, Japan and North America, which represent only 19% of the world population, consume 63% of all wood and cardboard products, and nearly half the industrial wood.

FLOTTAGE DU BOIS SUR L'AMAZONE, RÉGION DE MANAUS, AMAZONAS, BRÉSIL.

Dans cette région où la densité du couvert végétal ne permet pas d'autre accès aux zones d'exploitation, le flottage est le moyen de transport de bois le plus rentable. Les grumes liées entre elles sont stockées sur le fleuve Amazone avant d'être remorquées vers les scieries. Le Brésil est le cinquième producteur mondial de bois industriel et le premier producteur de bois tropicaux, mais cet apport économique majeur se fait au prix d'une déforestation inquiétante de près de 22 000 km² chaque année. La forêt amazonienne a ainsi déjà perdu 15 % de sa superficie originelle, en raison, principalement, du défrichement des terres cultivables, de l'exploitation minière, et de l'exploitation pour le bois d'œuvre, le combustible et les produits forestiers. L'utilisation par personne de papier et de carton, issus de produits forestiers, a presque triplé depuis 1961, essentiellement dans les pays riches. Ainsi l'Europe, le Japon et l'Amérique du Nord, qui ne représentent que 19 % de la population mondiale, consomment 63 % du bois et du carton produits, et presque la moitié du bois d'industrie.

N 30°49' E 30°28'

UN FELLAH DEL VALLE DEL NILO HACIENDO HACES DE TRIGO, EGIPTO.

Desde hace siglos, los campesinos egipcios del valle del Nilo, los fellah, utilizan las mismas técnicas agrícolas ancestrales, aran los campos con azada, siegan el trigo con una hoz y transportan los haces a lomo de burro o de camello. El valle del Nilo dibuja una franja muy fértil que atraviesa el país de sur a norte. Ahí se concentra la población agrícola más densa del mundo: en efecto, las tierras cultivables no representan sino el 3% del territorio, y la totalidad, es decir 33 000 km², recibe agua, lo que hace de Egipto el país más irrigado de África. La producción de trigo, aunque en progreso (+ 50% entre 1990 y 2000) gracias principalmente al empleo de abono, cubre menos de la mitad de las necesidades de una población en rápido crecimiento. Egipto se sitúa entre los mayores importadores de cereales en el mundo (9.6 millones de toneladas en 1999).

FELLAH SHEAVING WHEAT IN THE NILE VALLEY, EGYPT.

The fellahin, Egyptian peasants in the Nile Valley, have been using the same ancestral farming techniques for centuries. They plough fields with a hoe, reap wheat with a sickle, and transport sheaves on donkey or camel-back. The Nile Valley forms a very fertile strip that crosses the country from south to north. The densest farming population in the world is concentrated here: arable lands represent in fact only 3% of the territory, and the entire area, 33,000 sq. km. (12,700 sq. mi.), is irrigated, making Egypt the most irrigated country in Africa. Wheat production, though increasing (up 50% from 1990 to 2000), especially thanks to the use of manure, meets less than half the needs of a fast-growing population. Egypt is among the major importers of cereals in the world (9.6 million metric tons (10.6 tons) in 1999).

MISE EN GERBES DU BLÉ PAR UN FELLAH DE LA VALLÉE DU NIL, ÉGYPTE.

Depuis des siècles, les paysans égyptiens de la vallée du Nil, les fellahs, utilisent les mêmes techniques agricoles ancestrales, labourant les champs à la houe, moissonnant le blé à la faucille et transportant les gerbes à dos d'âne ou de chameau. La vallée du Nil dessine un ruban très fertile qui traverse le pays du sud au nord. Là, se concentre la population agricole qui est la plus dense du monde : les terres cultivables ne représentent en effet que 3 % du territoire, et la totalité, soit 33 000 km², est irriguée, faisant de l'Égypte le pays le plus irrigué d'Afrique. La production de blé, bien qu'en progression (+ 50 % entre 1990 et 2000) grâce notamment à l'emploi d'engrais, couvre moins de la moitié des besoins d'une population en rapide augmentation. L'Égypte se situe parmi les plus importants importateurs de céréales au monde (9,6 millions de tonnes en 1999).

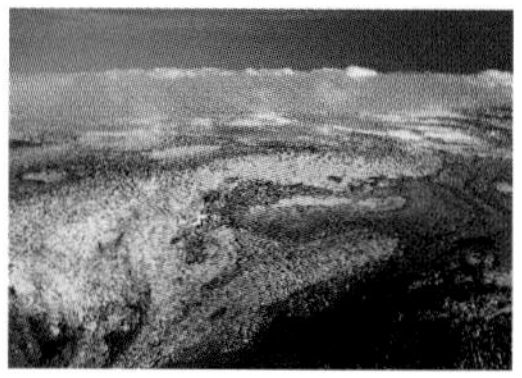

N 60°14' E 6°44'

GLACIAR DE FOLGEFONN EN LOS ALTIPLANOS DE SORFJORDEN, NORUEGA.

Enclavado entre los fiordos Hardangerfjord y Sorfjord, al sur de Noruega, el Folgefonn es por su superficie (212 km²), el tercero de los 1 500 glaciares del país. Glaciar de planicie característica de las regiones con influencia climática templada, esta cúpula nevada aplanada se desliza sobre una capa de agua formada entre la roca y el hielo. En verano, el derretimiento parcial del hielo abastece de limo y arcilla el agua de los fiordos, dándole un color verde completamente particular. Independientemente de los cambios de las estaciones, la superficie y el espesor de los glaciares podría adelgazarse constantemente a causa del calentamiento del planeta, esto debido principalmente al aumento del efecto invernadero provocado por las actividades humanas. Esta hipótesis del calentamiento del clima ha suscitado desde 1992, durante la "Cumbre de la Tierra" en Río de Janeiro, una toma de conciencia internacional. El Protocolo de Kyoto, cuyo objetivo es obligar a los países industrializados a reducir sus emisiones de gas de efecto invernadero a partir de 2002, estaba en el centro de las conferencias de Kyoto (1997) y de La Haya (2000). Pero en 2001, los Estados Unidos se rehusan a comprometerse con esta medida, a pesar de emitir más gases de efecto invernadero que ningún otro país del mundo.

FOLGEFONN GLACIER ON THE HIGH PLATEAUS OF SØRFJORDEN, NORWAY.

Enclosed between the Hardangerfjorden and Sørfjorden fjords, in southern Norway, the Folgefonn is the third largest of the 1,500 glaciers in the country, with a surface of 212 sq. km. (82. sq. mi.). A plateau glacier characteristic of regions subject to the influence of moderate climate, this flattened, snowy dome slips over a film of water formed between rock and ice. In the summer, the partial melting of the ice feeds the water in fjords with silt and clay, giving them quite a particular green color. It is believed that global warming, which is particularly due to the increase in the greenhouse effect caused by human activities, is constantly reducing the surface and thickness of the glaciers, independently of seasonal variations. This global warming hypothesis has been producing more international awareness since 1992, beginning with the "Earth Summit" in Rio de Janeiro. The Kyoto Protocol, whose objective is to force industrialized countries to reduce their greenhouse gas emissions starting in 2002, was at the heart of the Kyoto (1997) and The Hague Conferences (2000). But in 2001, the United States - who emits more greenhouse gases than any other country in the world - refused to make this commitment.

GLACIER FOLGEFONN SUR LES HAUTS PLATEAUX DE SORFJORDEN, NORVÈGE.

Enclavé entre les fjords Hardangerfjord et Sorfjord, au sud de la Norvège, le Folgefonn, est, par sa superficie (212 km²), le troisième des 1 500 glaciers du pays. Glacier de plateau caractéristique des régions à influence climatique tempérée, cette coupole neigeuse aplatie glisse sur un film d'eau formé entre la roche et la glace. En été, la fonte partielle des glaces alimente l'eau des fjords en limon et argile, leur donnant une couleur verte tout à fait particulière. Indépendamment des variations saisonnières, la surface et l'épaisseur des glaciers s'amenuiseraient constamment en raison du réchauffement de la planète, notamment dû à l'accroissement de l'effet de serre provoqué par les activités humaines. Cette hypothèse de réchauffement du climat a suscité dès 1992, lors du « Sommet de la Terre » à Rio de Janeiro, une prise de conscience internationale. Le Protocole de Kyoto, dont l'objectif est d'obliger les pays industrialisés à réduire leurs émissions de gaz à effet de serre à partir de 2002, était au cœur des conférences de Kyoto (1997) et de La Haye (2000). Mais en 2001, les Etats-Unis, qui émettent pourtant plus de gaz à effet de serre qu'aucun autre pays au monde, refusent de s'engager dans cette voie.

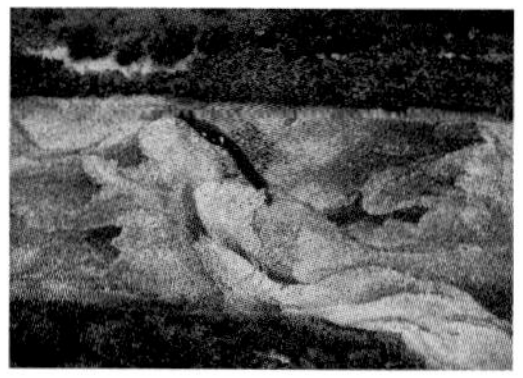

S 2°59' E 38°31'

RÍO ATHI DESECADO EN EL OESTE DEL PARQUE NACIONAL DE TSAVO, KENIA.

Como la mayoría de las corrientes de agua kenianas, el Río Athi, que atraviesa el parque nacional de Tsavo, no es perenne. Sin embargo, en temporada de sequía los pastores masai llevan sus rebaños de bovinos y de cabras al lecho desecado de este río, para que el ganado pueda beber en los charcos de aguas providenciales que se conservan en las depresiones rocosas. Cuando las aguas del río se retiran revelan su obra, un sorprendente fresco que es el resultado del depósito de los diferentes tipos de arenas graníticas según su densidad y su forma. Los Masai, que suman todavía 15 000 personas, son pastores seminómadas cuya subsistencia depende sólo del producto de la ganadería y recorren largas distancias entre Kenia y Tanzania en busca de puntos de agua y de pastizales para sus rebaños. De acuerdo con las creencias de este pueblo, En-kai, creador del mundo, les habría ofrecido el ganado. Actualmente existen programas de "desarrollo" que incitan a los Masai a convertirse a la agricultura y, por lo tanto, a volverse sedentarios.

THE DRIED UP ATHI RIVER, TSAVO WEST NATIONAL PARK, KENYA.

Like most Kenyan rivers, the Athi, which crosses Tsavo National Park, is not perennial. In the dry season, Masai shepherds still lead their herd of cattle and goats to this dry riverbed, so that their livestock can drink from the providential puddles collected in rocky depressions. In withdrawing, the river waters reveal their artwork, a surprising fresco resulting from the deposit of different types of granitic sands according to their density and shape. Semi-nomadic shepherds whose subsistence depends entirely on the product of their livestock-raising, 15,000 Masai continue to travel long distances between Kenya and Tanzania in search of water-holes and pasture for their herds. According to their beliefs, their livestock was given to them by En-kai, the creator of the world. Today, "development" programs are encouraging the Masai to change over to farming and thus become sedentary.

RIVIÈRE ATHI ASSÉCHÉE DANS L'OUEST DU PARC NATIONAL DE TSAVO, KENYA.

Comme la plupart des cours d'eau kenyans, la rivière Athi, qui traverse le parc national de Tsavo, n'est pas pérenne. En période de sécheresse, les bergers Masaï mènent néanmoins leur troupeau de bovins et de chèvres dans le lit asséché de cette rivière, afin que le bétail puisse s'abreuver dans les flaques d'eau providentielles maintenues dans des cuvettes rocheuses. En se retirant, les eaux de la rivière ont révélé leur œuvre, surprenante fresque résultant du dépôt des différents types de sables granitiques selon leur densité et leur forme. Pasteurs semi-nomades dont la subsistance dépend du seul produit de l'élevage, les Masaï sont encore 15 000 à parcourir de longues distances entre le Kenya et la Tanzanie à la recherche de points d'eau et de pâturages pour leurs troupeaux. Selon les croyances de ce peuple, le bétail lui aurait été offert par En-kai, créateur du monde. Aujourd'hui, des programmes de « développement » incitent les Masaï à se reconvertir dans l'agriculture et donc à se sédentariser.

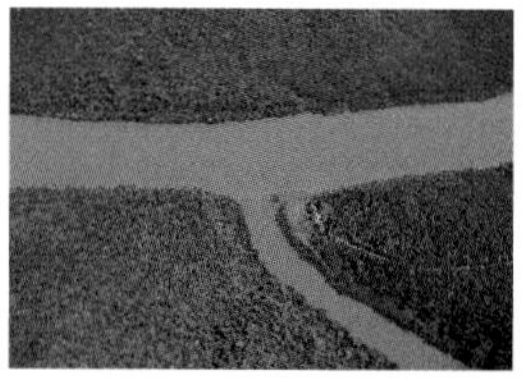

S 27°15' W 54°03'

ENCUENTRO DEL RÍO URUGUAY CON UNO DE SUS AFLUENTES, MISIONES, ARGENTINA.

El bosque tropical argentino, considerablemente talada en beneficio de la agricultura, ya no constituye en algunos sitios una barrera antierosión tan eficaz como hasta hace poco. Las fuertes lluvias que se abaten sobre la provincia de Misiones (2 000 mm por año) limpian el suelo y arrastran de aquí en adelante cantidades importantes de tierras ferruginosas al Río Uruguay, que se tiñe de color ocre rojizo. Crecido por afluentes cargados de restos vegetales, el Río Uruguay (1 612 km) se lanza al océano Atlántico a la altura de Río de la Plata, el mayor estero del planeta (200 km de largo) en donde se depositan los sedimentos que el río acarrea. Estos llenan los canales de acceso al puerto de Buenos Aires que se dragan regularmente para que sigan siendo navegables. Los aluviones que se acumulan en las desembocaduras de los ríos pueden modificar los paisajes al formar deltas o al ganarle terreno al mar.

MEETING OF THE URUGUAY RIVER AND ONE OF ITS TRIBUTARIES, MISIONES, ARGENTINA.

The Argentinian tropical forest, considerably cleared for farming, no longer constitutes as efficient an anti-erosion barrier as it once did in many places. The heavy rains that beat down on the province of Misiones (2,000 mm (80 in.) per year) wash the soil away and now drag large quantities of ferruginous earth into the Rio Uruguay, which is taking on an ocher-red tinge. Swollen by its tributaries carrying plant debris, the Rio Uruguay (1,612 km (1,006 mi.)) empties into the Atlantic Ocean at the level of the Rio de la Plata - the most extensive estuary on the planet (200 km (124 mi.) wide) - where sediments carried by the river are deposited. These fill access channels to the harbor of Buenos Aires, which are dragged regularly in order to remain navigable. Alluvium accumulated in the mouths of the rivers can modify landscapes by forming deltas or by reclaiming land from the sea.

RENCONTRE DU RIO URUGUAY ET D'UN DE SES AFFLUENTS, MISIONES, ARGENTINE.

La forêt tropicale argentine, considérablement déboisée au profit de l'agriculture, ne constitue plus par endroit une barrière anti-érosion aussi efficace que naguère. Les fortes pluies qui s'abattent sur la province de Misiones (2 000 mm par an) lessivent le sol et entraînent désormais des quantités importantes de terre ferrugineuse dans le rio Uruguay, qui se teinte en ocre-rouge. Gonflé par des affluents chargés de débris végétaux, le rio Uruguay (1 612 km) se jette dans l'océan Atlantique au niveau du rio de la Plata – le plus vaste estuaire de la planète (200 km de large) – où se déposent les sédiments charriés par le fleuve. Ceux-ci comblent les chenaux d'accès au port de Buenos Aires qui sont dragués régulièrement afin de rester navigables. Les alluvions accumulées aux embouchures des fleuves peuvent modifier les paysages en formant des deltas ou en gagnant du terrain sur la mer.

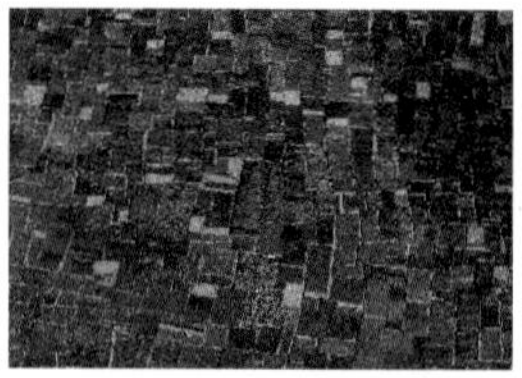

S 8°43' E 115°26'

CULTIVO DE ALGAS EN BALI, INDONESIA.

En la antigüedad las algas se utilizaban exclusivamente como abono, después, en el siglo XVI, se incorporaron en forma de cenizas a la fabricación del vidrio y actualmente se producen con fines alimentarios en un 97%. De las cerca de 30 000 especies de algas conocidas en el mundo solamente se explotan algunas decenas. Entre ellas, las algas carragenositas (Florideas ricas en mucílagos), igualmente llamadas chondrus o líquen de Irlanda, se utilizan para gelificar, espesar o como estabilizadores en las industrias agroalimentaria, farmacéutica y cosmética. En el Lejano Oriente, el cultivo de este tipo de algas verdes se practica sobre cuerdas o redes sumergidas. Los principales productores de dicha alga son Indonesia y las Filipinas, con el 23 y el 65% de la producción mundial respectivamente. En cambio, con todas las especies de algas incluidas (verdes, rojas y pardas), China va a la cabeza de los países productores y Japón es el principal consumidor.

ALGAE GROWING IN BALI, INDONESIA.

Used exclusively as a fertilizer in Antiquity, then incorporated in the form of ashes into the glass-making process of the 16th century, 97% of all algae produced today are intended for food purposes. Of the approximately 30,000 known species of algae in the world, only a few dozen are exploited. These include the rhodophyte algae (red algae, rich in gums), also called carrageen or Irish moss, which are used as gelling agents, thickeners or stabilizers by the food, pharmaceutical and cosmetic industries. In the Far East, this type of green alga is grown using immersed strings or nets. The main producers are Indonesia and Philippines, with 23% and 65% of the world production, respectively. On the other hand, if all species of algae are taken together (green, red, and brown), China then takes the lead among the producing countries, with Japan being foremost among consuming countries.

CULTURE D'ALGUES À BALI, INDONÉSIE.

Exclusivement utilisées comme engrais dans l'Antiquité, puis incorporées sous forme de cendres dans la fabrication du verre au XVIe siècle, les algues sont aujourd'hui produites à 97 % à des fins alimentaires. Des quelque 30 000 espèces d'algues connues dans le monde seulement quelques dizaines sont exploitées. Parmi elles, les algues carraghénophytes (Floridées riches en mucilages), également appelées chondrus ou lichens d'Irlande, sont utilisées comme gélifiants, épaississants ou stabilisants par les industries agro-alimentaire, pharmaceutique et cosmétique. En Extrême-Orient, la culture de ce type d'algues vertes se pratique sur des cordages ou des filets immergés. Les principaux producteurs en sont l'Indonésie et les Philippines, avec respectivement 23 % et 65 % de la production mondiale. En revanche, toutes espèces d'algues confondues (vertes, rouges, et brunes), c'est la Chine qui arrive en tête des pays producteurs, le Japon étant le premier pays consommateur.

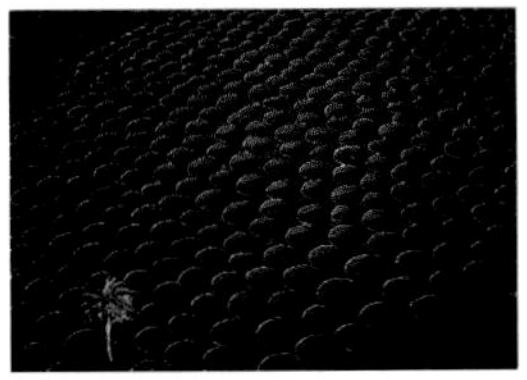

N 28°48' W 13°41'

VIDES, REGIÓN DE LA GERIA, LANZAROTE, ISLAS CANARIAS, ESPAÑA.

De las siete islas del archipiélago español de la Canarias, Lanzarote es la más cercana al continente africano. Su clima desértico y la ausencia total de manantiales y de ríos sobre este territorio de 813 km^2 vuelven difícil cualquier práctica agrícola. Sin embargo, debido a su origen volcánico, la isla se beneficia de un suelo negro fértil formado de cenizas y lapilli (grava volcánica), sobre un suelo arcilloso poco permeable. Aquí se empleó una singular técnica vitícola, perfectamente adaptada a las condiciones naturales originales: las cepas de vides se plantan individualmente en medio de hoyos cavados en los lapilli, con el fin de sacar la humedad recogida, y se protegen de los vientos secos del noroeste y del Sahara con pequeñas bardas de piedra que se edifican en semicírculo. El viñedo de La Geria produce un vino rojo dulce de Malvasía. El total de la producción vinícola española representa alrededor del 13% de los cerca de 275 millones de hectolitros de vino producidos anualmente en el mundo, y se sitúa así en la tercera posición de los países productores, pero igualmente de los países exportadores detrás de Francia y de Italia.

VINEYARDS, NEAR GERIA, LANZAROTE, CANARY ISLANDS, SPAIN.

Among the seven islands in the Spanish archipelago of the Canary Islands, Lanzarote is the one closest to the African continent. The desert climate and total absence of springs and rivers on this 813 sq. km. (314 sq. mi.) territory make any farming activity difficult. However, the volcanic origin of the island provides it with a fertile black soil, consisting of ash and lapilli (volcanic gravel), covering a clay subsoil of little permeability. An unusual wine-growing technique has been developed to suit to these unusual natural conditions : vine-stocks are planted individually at the center of funnels dug in the lapilli, and draw the moisture collected there, while stone walls built in a semi-circle protect them from the dry northeast and Saharan winds. The Geria vineyard produces a sweet red Malvoisie wine. The total Spanish wine production represents approximately 13% of the annual world production - about 275 million hectoliters (7.23 billion gallons) of wine worldwide - and thus ranks third, after France and Italy, among wine-producing and wine-exporting countries.

VIGNES, RÉGION DE GERIA, LANZAROTE, ÎLES CANARIES, ESPAGNE.

Des sept îles de l'archipel espagnol des Canaries, Lanzarote est la plus proche du continent africain. Son climat désertique et l'absence totale de source et de rivière sur ce territoire de 813 km^2 rendent difficile toute pratique agricole. Cependant, en raison de son origine volcanique, l'île bénéficie d'un sol noir fertile constitué de cendres et de lapilli (graviers volcaniques), sur un sous-sol argileux peu perméable. S'adaptant parfaitement à ces conditions naturelles originales, une technique viticole singulière a été adoptée : les ceps de vigne sont plantés individuellement au milieu d'entonnoirs creusés dans les lapilli, afin d'y puiser l'humidité recueillie, et sont protégés des vents secs du nord-est et du Sahara par des murets de pierre édifiés en demi-cercle. Le vignoble de Geria produit un vin rouge doux de Malvoisie. L'ensemble de la production vinicole espagnole représente environ 13 % des quelque 275 millions d'hectolitres de vin produits annuellement dans le monde, et se situe ainsi au troisième rang des pays producteurs – mais également des pays exportateurs –, derrière la France et l'Italie.

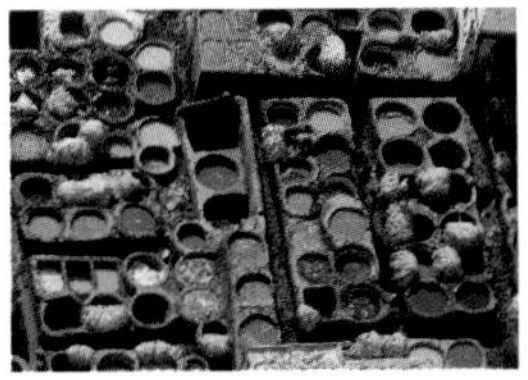

N 34°05' W 4°57'

TALLERES Y TINAS DE TINTOREROS EN FEZ, MARRUECOS.

El barrio de los tintoreros en Marruecos ha conservado su autenticidad: desde hace siglos se emplean las mismas técnicas ancestrales de coloración que se transmiten de manera hereditaria. Las fibras textiles de lana o de algodón y las pieles curtidas de borrego, de cabra, de vaca o de dromedario, se sumergen en tinas de tinturas con paredes de cerámica, los batanes, en donde los artesanos pisotean las pieles. Los colorantes se elaboran en los molinos del ued Fez a partir de pigmentos naturales: amapola, índigo, azafrán, hueso de dátil y antimonio se usan para obtener los colores rojo, azul, amarillo, café claro y negro respectivamente. Los materiales teñidos servirán para confeccionar los célebres tapetes y objetos de cuero de fama internacional, que constituyen los dos principales productos artesanales de exportación de Marruecos.

DYE SHOPS AND VATS IN FÈS, MOROCCO.

The district of dye-shops in Fès, Morocco, has maintained its authenticity: for centuries the same ancestral coloring techniques have been used, passed down from generation to generation. The textile wool or cotton fibers and tanned sheep, goat, cow or dromedary hides are immersed in dye-vats with ceramic partitions, or fullers, where they are stomped on by craftsmen. Colorings are prepared from natural pigments in mills at the Fès wadi. Poppy, indigo, saffron, date pit and antimony are used to obtain the colors red, blue, yellow, beige and black respectively. The dyed fabrics will be used to make the famous tapestries and leather objects of international renown that constitute Morocco's two main export handicrafts.

ATELIERS ET CUVES DES TEINTURIERS À FÈS, MAROC.

Le quartier des teinturiers de Fès, au Maroc, a gardé son authenticité : depuis des siècles sont employées les mêmes techniques ancestrales de coloration, transmises de manière héréditaire. Les fibres textiles de laine ou de coton et les peaux tannées de mouton, de chèvre, de vache ou de dromadaire, sont immergées dans des cuves de teintures aux parois de céramique, les foulons, où elles sont piétinées par les artisans. Les colorants sont élaborés dans les moulins de l'oued Fès à partir de pigments naturels : coquelicot, indigo, safran, noyau de datte et antimoine sont respectivement utilisés pour obtenir les couleurs rouge, bleu, jaune, beige et noir. Les matières teintées serviront à confectionner les fameux tapis et objets de cuir, de renommée internationale, qui constituent les deux principaux produits artisanaux d'exportation du Maroc.

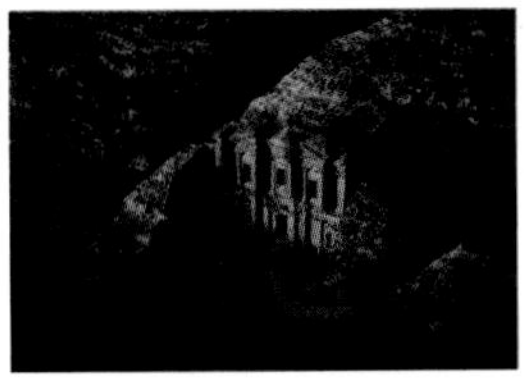

N 30°20' E 35°26'

TEMPLO DE ED-DEIR, PETRA, REGIÓN DE MA'AN, JORDANIA.

País casi completamente encerrado, Jordania, ocupa no obstante una posición estratégica entre el Mediterráneo y el Mar Rojo. En el siglo VII antes de nuestra era, los nabateos, pueblo de mercaderes nómadas, emprendieron la talla en la arenisca de los acantilados del sur del país una ciudad troglodítica que se convertiría en su capital: Petra, "la piedra" en griego. Al mantenerse del comercio de productos raros (incienso, especias, piedras y metales preciosos, marfiles) y del peaje de las rutas de las caravanas, la civilización nabatea extendió su influencia mucho más allá de la región transjordana, antes de caer bajo el yugo de Roma en 106 d. c. Situado en las alturas de la ciudad, el templo de Ed-Deir, construido entre los siglos I y III a. c., domina con su imponente estatura (47 m de alto y 40 m de ancho) los cerca de 800 monumentos de Petra. Lugar de culto desde su origen, fue ocupado, después de la decadencia de la civilización nabatea, por religiosos cristianos bizantinos, de donde su nombre de Ed-Deir: "el monasterio". Petra, ciudad inscrita en la lista del patrimonio mundial de la UNESCO en 1985, se enfrenta desde hace algunos años a una amenaza inquietante: las sales minerales disueltas en el manto freático alcanzan la base de los monumentos por capilaridad, se incrustan en la piedra y la debilitan. El viento completa la degradación progresiva de los monumentos.

ED-DEIR TEMPLE, PETRA, NEAR MA'AN, JORDAN.

Although this country is nearly completely land-locked, Jordan occupies a strategic position between the Mediterranean and the Red Sea. In the 7th century before our era, the Nabateans, a nomadic trading people, undertook to dig, in the sandstone of cliffs located in the southern part of their country, a city carved in rock that was to become their capital: Petra, or "rock", in Greek. Living on the trade of rare products (incense, spices, precious stones and metals, ivory...) and on taxation of the caravan routes, Nabatean civilization extended its influence far beyond the trans-Jordanian region, before coming under the yoke of Rome in 106 A. D.. Situated on the heights of the city, the Ed-Deir temple, built between the 1st and 3rd century B. C., dominates the approximately 800 monuments of Petra with its imposing height (47 m (154 ft.) high by 40 m (131 ft.) wide). A place of worship since its origin, it was occupied by Byzantine Christian monks after the decline of Nabatean civilization, hence its name of Ed-Deir: "the monastery". Petra, a city inscribed on the UNESCO World Heritage List in 1985, has been subject, for several years, to an alarming threat: the mineral salts dissolved in the water table are reaching the base of monuments by capillarity, are becoming encrusted in the rock and are weakening it. The winds also play a part in the progressive deterioration of the monuments.

TEMPLE DE ED-DEIR, PETRA, RÉGION DE MA'AN, JORDANIE.

Pays presque totalement enclavé, la Jordanie occupe cependant une position stratégique entre Méditerranée et mer Rouge. Au VIIe siècle avant notre ère, les Nabatéens, peuple de marchands nomades, entreprirent de tailler dans le grès des falaises du sud du pays une ville troglodytique qui allait devenir leur capitale : Petra, « la pierre », en grec. Vivant du commerce de produits rares (encens, épices, pierres et métaux précieux, ivoire...) et de la taxation des routes caravanières, la civilisation nabatéenne étendit son influence bien au-delà de la région transjordanienne, avant de tomber sous le joug de Rome en 106 après J.-C. Situé sur les hauteurs de la ville, le temple de Ed-Deir, construit entre le Ier et le IIIe siècle avant J.-C., domine de sa stature imposante (47 m de haut et 40 m de large) les quelque 800 monuments de Petra. Lieu de culte dès son origine, il fut, après le déclin de la civilisation nabatéenne, occupé par des religieux chrétiens byzantins, d'où son nom de Ed-Deir : « le monastère ». Petra, ville inscrite sur la Liste du patrimoine mondial de l'Unesco en 1985, est confrontée depuis quelques années à une menace inquiétante : les sels minéraux dissous dans la nappe phréatique atteignent la base des monuments par capillarité, s'incrustent dans la pierre et la fragilisent. Le vent complète la dégradation progressive des monuments.

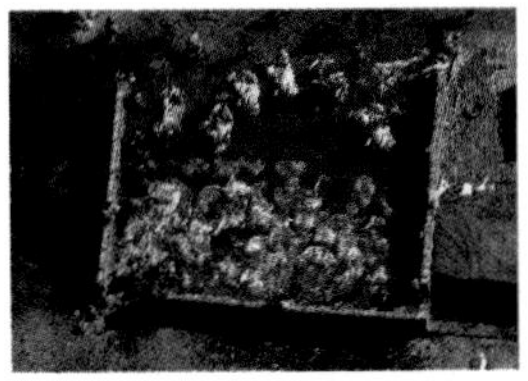

Localización no especificada.
Exact localisation not specified.
Localisation non précisée.

RASTRO EN UN PAÍS EN DESARROLLO.

Los últimos cincuenta años han visto pasar la producción mundial de carne de 44 a 216 millones de toneladas, lo que representa un crecimiento dos veces más rápido que la población. Constituida esencialmente de porcinos (40%), aves (28%) y bovinos (26%), esta producción consume más de un tercio de la cosecha mundial de cereales. En efecto, en la cría industrial sin pasturas y en fase de engorda, la producción de 1 kg de carne necesita consumir el equivalente de 7 kg de cereales (2 kg de cereales para 1 kg de ave). En un mundo en el que la desnutrición todavía afecta a una de cada cinco personas, y en el que el aumento de la producción mundial de cereales se desacelera, el consumo animal de cereales forrajeros es criticable para algunos. El escándalo de las "vacas locas" (encefalitis espongiforme bovina – EEB, que dio pie para que se hiciera el proceso de las "harinas animales", nutrimentos que utilizan desechos de animales muertos) y los litigios relativos al uso de hormonas para acelerar el crecimiento de los animales han suscitado además en los últimos años inquietudes crecientes en cuanto a las desviaciones y los límites de ciertos modelos de producción.

SLAUGHTERHOUSE IN A DEVELOPING COUNTRY.

The past fifty years have seen an increase in world production of meat from 44 to 216 million metric tons (48 to 238 million tons), which represents a growth two times faster than that of the population. Made up essentially of pork (40%), poultry (28%) and beef (26%), this production uses over a third of the world's cereals crops. In actual fact, in industrial "off-land" raising (without grazing) and during the fattening phase, the production of 1 kg (2 lb) of beef requires the consumption of the equivalent of 7 kg (over 15 lb) of cereals (2 kg (over 4 lb) of cereals for 1 kg (2 lb) of poultry). In a world where malnutrition affects 1 person out of 5, and where the increase in world cereal production is slowing down, this animal consumption of fodder cereals is, to some people, reprehensible. The "mad cow" disease scandal (Bovine Spongiform Encephalopathy - BSE, which provided the opportunity to make a case against "animal flours", nutrients using waste from dead animals) and the disputes about the use of hormones to accelerate animal growth have raised concern these past few years regarding leeway and limits for certain production models.

ABATTOIR DANS UN PAYS EN DÉVELOPPEMENT.

Les cinquante dernières années ont vu la production mondiale de viande passer de 44 à 216 millions de tonnes, ce qui représente une croissance deux fois plus rapide que la population. Constituée pour l'essentiel de porcins (40 %), de volailles (28 %) et de bovins (26 %), cette production consomme plus d'un tiers de la récolte mondiale de céréales. En effet, en élevage industriel « hors sol » (sans pâturage) et en phase d'engraissement, la production de 1 kg de bœuf nécessite la consommation de l'équivalent de 7 kg de céréales (2 kg de céréales pour 1 kg de volaille). Dans un monde où la malnutrition affecte encore 1 personne sur 5, et où l'augmentation de la production mondiale de céréales ralentit, cette consommation animale de céréales fourragères est pour certains critiquable. Le scandale de la « vache folle » (encéphalite spongiforme bovine - ESB, qui a été l'occasion de faire le procès des « farines animales », nutriments utilisant des déchets d'animaux morts) et les litiges relatifs au recours aux hormones pour accélérer la croissance des animaux ont par ailleurs suscité ces dernières années des inquiétudes croissantes quant aux dérives et limites de certains modèles de production.

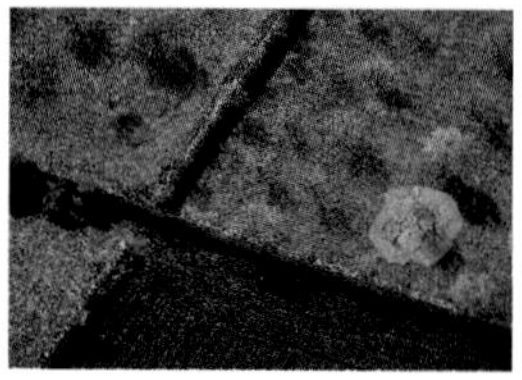

N 39°36' E 3°02'

COSECHA DE ALMENDRAS EN LA ISLA DE MALLORCA, ISLAS BALEARES, ESPAÑA.

Muy antigua, como en todos los países mediterráneos, el cultivo de la almendra en el archipiélago español de las Baleares sigue siendo tradicional. Las almendras se cosechan después del vareo manual en lonas extendidas bajo los árboles. La escasa productividad de los almendros (2 a 5 kg de frutos por árbol) se compensa generalmente con la importancia de las superficies sembradas; no obstante, ésta ha disminuido considerablemente, pues los árboles viejos rara vez se reemplazaron. La producción de almendras de estas islas, que antes constituía lo esencial de la producción española, apenas representa hoy en día el 3%, con una cosecha de 7 000 toneladas al año. España es sin embargo el segundo productor de almendra del mundo, con una producción anual de cerca de 227 000 toneladas consumidas en casi el 80% por el conjunto de los países europeos en diversas formas: en confitería y pastelería en cuanto a almendras dulces secas, como agente aromatizante (esencia de almendras amargas), o en cosmetología (aceite de almendras dulces).

ALMOND HARVEST ON THE ISLAND OF MALLORCA, BALEARIC ISLANDS, SPAIN.

Almond growing is a very ancient practice and still carried out in a traditional manner in the Spanish archipelago of the Balearics, as in all Mediterranean countries. Almonds are generally harvested by being hand-shaked out of trees into tarpaulins spread underneath. The low productivity of almond trees (2 to 5 kg (4 to 11 lb) of fruits per tree) is generally compensated by the large areas planted; however this has decreased considerably since the old trees have rarely been replaced. The almond production on these islands, which formerly constituted the main element in Spanish production, today barely represents 3%, with a harvest of 7,000 metric tons (7,700 tons) per year. Nevertheless, Spain is the second largest producer of almonds in the world, with a yearly production of nearly 227,000 metric tons (250,000 tons), almost 80% of which is consumed in various forms throughout European countries: candy and desserts for dried, sweet almonds, flavoring (essence of bitter almond) or cosmetology (sweet almond oil).

RÉCOLTES DES AMANDES SUR L'ÎLE DE MAJORQUE, ÎLES BALÉARES, ESPAGNE.

Très ancienne, comme dans tous les pays méditerranéens, la culture des amandes dans l'archipel espagnol des Baléares est restée traditionnelle. Les amandes sont généralement récoltées après gaulage manuel dans des bâches étendues sous les arbres. La faible productivité des amandiers (2 à 5 kg de fruits par arbre) est généralement compensée par l'importance des surfaces plantées ; cependant celle-ci a considérablement diminué, les vieux arbres ayant rarement été remplacés. La production d'amandes de ces îles, qui jadis constituait l'essentiel de la production espagnole, n'en représente plus guère que 3 % aujourd'hui, avec une récolte de 7 000 tonnes par an. L'Espagne est néanmoins le deuxième producteur d'amandes au monde, avec une production annuelle d'environ 227 000 tonnes consommées à près de 80 % par l'ensemble des pays européens sous diverses formes : en confiserie et pâtisserie pour les amandes douces séchées, comme agent aromatisant (essence d'amande amère), ou en cosmétologie (huile d'amande douce).

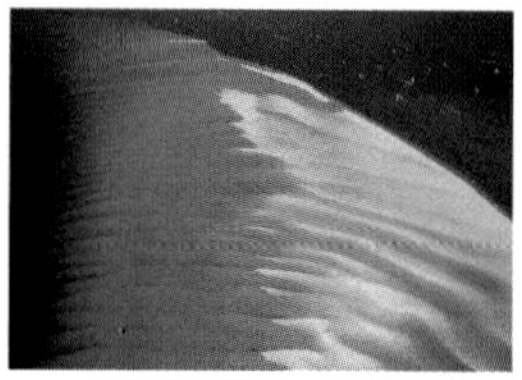

N 44°39' W 1°15'

RESERVA NATURAL DEL BANCO DE ARGUIN, GIRONDA, FRANCIA.

En la desembocadura de la cuenca de Arcachon, entre el cabo Ferret y la duna del Pilato (la más alta de Francia, 106 m) el banco de Arguin aflora bajo las aguas del Océano Atlántico. Constituido por un conjunto de islotes arenosos que cambian de forma y de lugar a merced de los vientos y las corrientes marinas, siguiendo un ciclo relativamente regular de alrededor de 80 años, este sitio, de una superficie variable de 150 a 500 ha, fue clasificado como reserva natural en 1972. El banco de Arguin es en efecto una escala, un lugar de hibernación o de anidamiento para numerosas especies de aves migratorias; ahí se encuentra especialmente una colonia de 4 000 a 5 000 parejas de charranes patinegros (*Sterna sandvicensis*) entre los tres más importantes de Europa. A pesar de su estatuto de protección, la reserva natural está amenazada por la importancia de la afluencia turística y el desarrollo creciente de actividades ostreícolas en su periferia. En Mauritania existe un área protegida homónima: el parque nacional del Banco de Arguin, que acoge igualmente numerosas colonias de aves migratorias.

BANC D'ARGUIN NATURAL RESERVE, GIRONDE, FRANCE.

At the mouth of the Arcachon Basin, between Cap-Ferret and the Pilat sand dune (highest in France, 106 m), the Banc d'Arguin sandbank appears just above the Atlantic Ocean's surface. This site was classified as a natural reserve in 1972 and has a variable surface area of 150 to 500 hectares (405 to 1235 acres) : its sandy islets regularly change shape and place with the whims of winds and ocean currents. The Banc d'Arguin happens to be a stopover, a place where many species of migratory birds spend the winter or nest : a colony of 4,000 to 5,000 pairs of sterns (*Sterna sandvicensis*), among the three most important in Europe, can be seen here in particular. In spite of its protective status, the Natural Reserve is threatened by a large number of tourists and by an increasing development of oyster-farming activities on its outer fringes. In Mauritania there is a protected area by the same name : the Banc d'Arguin National Park, which is also home to numerous colonies of migratory birds.

RÉSERVE NATURELLE DU BANC D'ARGUIN, GIRONDE, FRANCE.

À l'embouchure du bassin d'Arcachon, entre le Cap-Ferret et la dune du Pilat (la plus haute de France, 106 m), le banc d'Arguin affleure sous les eaux de l'océan Atlantique. Constitué d'un ensemble d'îlots sableux qui changent de forme et de place au gré des vents et courants marins, suivant un cycle relativement régulier d'environ 80 ans, ce site, d'une superficie variable de 150 à 500 ha, a été classé en réserve naturelle en 1972. Le banc d'Arguin est en effet une escale, un lieu d'hivernage ou de nidification pour de nombreuses espèces d'oiseaux migrateurs ; on y rencontre notamment une colonie de 4 000 à 5 000 couples de sternes (*Sterna sandvicensis*) parmi les trois plus importantes d'Europe. Malgré son statut de protection, la réserve naturelle est menacée par l'importance de l'affluence touristique et le développement croissant d'activités ostréicoles à sa périphérie. En Mauritanie existe une aire protégée homonyme : le parc national du Banc d'Arguin, qui accueille également de nombreuses colonies d'oiseaux migrateurs.

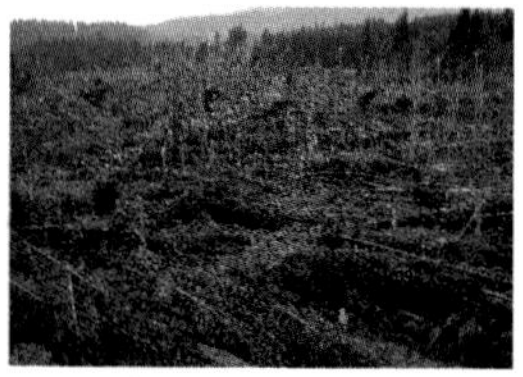

N 48°39' E 7°14'

ÁRBOLES DERRIBADOS POR LA TEMPESTAD EN EL BOSQUE DE LOS VOSGOS, FRANCIA.

El 26 de diciembre de 1999, el departamento de los Vosgos se despertó con 348 de sus 515 comunas privadas de electricidad, el 10% de sus bosques por tierra, el tráfico ferroviario totalmente interrumpido y 60 000 líneas telefónicas cortadas. La región de Lorena fue en efecto la más gravemente afectada por las tormentas que atravesaron a Francia el 26 y el 27 de diciembre y provocaron 79 muertos. En la escala nacional, más de 300 millones de árboles fueron derribados, lo que representó, para los bosques públicos, el equivalente a tres años de cosechas (de los cuales el 70% se venderían de todos modos). La Oficina Nacional de Bosques, que debe hacer frente a la reconstitución del dominio forestal público en los años venideros, tiene la intención a partir de ahora de favorecer la diversidad biológica sin comprometer la economía de mercado, privilegiando las especies mejor adaptadas y mezcladas, y evitando el alineamiento sistemático. En este sentido, las consecuencias de la catástrofe no habrían sido todas negativas. La violencia de los vientos (169 km/h en París-Montsouris) y la amplitud de los estragos y del territorio devastado constituyen no obstante un acontecimiento sin precedente en Francia en el curso de los últimos siglos, que revive las interrogaciones sobre el papel que desempeña el calentamiento climático.

TREES FELLED BY A STORM IN THE VOSGES FOREST, FRANCE.

On December 26th, 1999, the department of Vosges woke up to find 348 of its 515 municipalities without electricity, 10% of its forests on the ground, railway traffic completely interrupted and 60,000 telephone lines down. The Lorraine region was in fact the most seriously affected by the storms that blew across France on December 26th and 27th, provoking 79 deaths. On a national scale, more than 300 million trees fell, representing, for public forests, the equivalent of three years' production (70% of which will be sold, however). The National Forest Department, which must deal with the reconstruction of national public forests in the years to come, intends to encourage biodiversity from now on, without compromising the market economy, while privileging the better adapted, mixed species, and avoiding systematic alignment. As such, the consequences of this disaster will not have been all negative. The high wind velocity (169 km/hr (102 mph) at Paris-Montsouris) and the extent of the damages and of the territory devastated, however, constitutes an event without precedent in the last few centuries in France, all of which rekindles questions as to the role played by global warming.

ARBRES ABATTUS PAR LA TEMPÊTE DANS LA FORÊT DES VOSGES, FRANCE.

Le 26 Décembre 1999, le département des Vosges s'est réveillé avec 348 de ses 515 communes privées d'électricité, 10 % de ses forêts à terre, le trafic ferroviaire totalement interrompu et 60 000 lignes téléphoniques coupées. La région Lorraine fut en effet la plus gravement touchée par les tempêtes qui ont traversé la France les 26 et 27 décembre et provoqué 79 morts. À l'échelle nationale, plus de 300 millions d'arbres ont été couchés, représentant, pour les forêts publiques, l'équivalent de trois années de récolte (dont 70 % seront toutefois vendus). L'Office National des Forêts, qui doit faire face à la reconstitution du domaine forestier publique dans les années à venir, entend désormais favoriser la diversité biologique sans compromettre l'économie marchande, en privilégiant des essences mieux adaptées et mélangées, et en évitant l'alignement systématique. En ce sens, les conséquences de la catastrophe n'auront pas été toutes négatives. La violence des vents (169 km/h à Paris-Montsouris) et l'ampleur des dégâts et du territoire dévasté constituent cependant un événement sans précédent en France au cours des derniers siècles, qui ravive les interrogations sur le rôle joué par le réchauffement climatique.

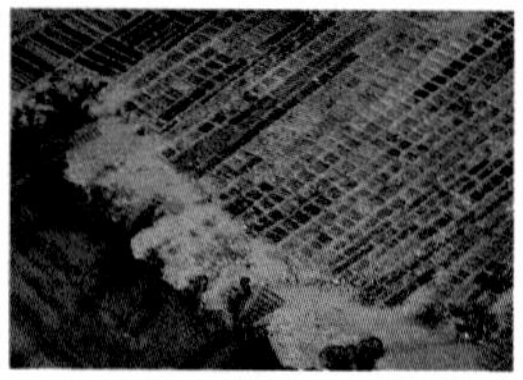

N 14°34' W 11°46'

CULTIVOS DE HORTALIZAS EN EL RÍO SENEGAL EN LOS ALREDEDORES DE KAYES, MALI.

Al oeste de Mali, cerca de las fronteras senegalesa y mauritana, la ciudad de Kayes es un importante cruce étnico y comercial; toda la región está atravesada por el Río Senegal, en cuyas riberas los cultivos de hortalizas son numerosos. Recurso providencial en esta zona saheliana, el agua del río, que las mujeres recolectan y transportan en diversos recipientes, permite el riego manual de las pequeñas parcelas (o casilleros) donde se plantan las frutas y legumbres destinadas al mercado local. El río Senegal, que lleva ese nombre a partir de la confluencia del Bafing ("río negro") y del Bakoy ("río blanco"), un poco hacia arriba de Kayes, recorre 1 600 km a través de cuatro países. Los acondicionamientos hidráulicos instalados en su curso sólo permiten irrigar 600 km^2 de cultivos, pero su cuenca de 350 000 km^2 alimenta de agua a cerca de 10 millones de personas.

MARKET GARDENING ON THE SENEGAL RIVER IN THE VICINITY OF KAYES, MALI.

In western Mali, near the borders of Senegal and Mauritania, the city of Kayes is an important ethnic and commercial crossroads; the Senegal River, with large numbers of market gardens on its banks, flows through the entire region. The river water is a providential resource in this Sahelian zone. It is collected and transported in various containers by women, making the manual irrigation of small parcels (or border strips) where fruits and vegetables for the local market are planted possible. The Senegal River, which only bears this name after the confluence of the Bafing ("black river") and the Bakoy ("white river"), slightly upstream from Kayes, covers a distance of 1,600 km (1,000 mi.) through four countries. The water resource developments along its course permit the irrigation of 600 sq. km. (230 sq. mi.) of crops, but its basin, with an area of 350,000 sq. km. (135,000 sq. mi.), supplies water to nearly 10 million people.

CULTURES MARAÎCHÈRES SUR LE FLEUVE SÉNÉGAL AUX ENVIRONS DE KAYES, MALI.

A l'ouest du Mali, près des frontières sénégalaise et mauritanienne, la ville de Kayes est un important carrefour ethnique et commercial ; toute la région est traversée par le fleuve Sénégal sur les berges duquel les cultures maraîchères sont nombreuses. Ressource providentielle dans cette zone sahélienne, l'eau du fleuve, collectée et transportée dans divers récipients par les femmes, permet l'arrosage manuel des petites parcelles (ou casiers) où sont plantés les fruits et légumes destinés au marché local. Le fleuve Sénégal, qui ne porte ce nom qu'à partir du confluent du Bafing (« rivière noire ») et du Bakoy (« rivière blanche »), un peu en amont de Kayes, parcourt 1 600 km à travers quatre pays. Les aménagements hydrauliques installés sur son cours ne permettent d'irriguer que 600 km^2 de cultures, mais son bassin de 350 000 km^2 alimente en eau près de 10 millions de personnes.

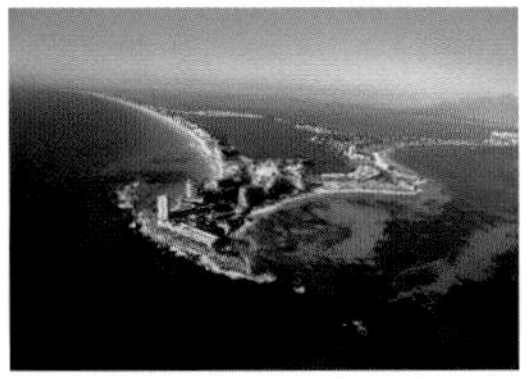

N 21°05' W 86°46'

PUNTA CANCÚN, CANCÚN, QUINTANA ROO, MÉXICO.

En la punta noreste de la Península de Yucatán, una estrecha franja de tierra se intercala entre una amplia laguna costera y el Mar Caribe. No fue sino hasta 1972 cuando aparecieron las primeras construcciones en este lugar excepcional, hoy convertido en el primer destino turístico de México, y en uno de los mayores balnearios del mundo, enlazado con los Estados Unidos y Europa por vuelos directos. Lujosos complejos hoteleros se encadenan a lo largo de 15 km a la orilla del mar, y el desarrollo turístico se prolonga a lo largo de 70 km al sur de Cancún, llamados Riviera Maya. El sector turístico, que ha generado 8 300 millones de dólares de ingresos en 2000, representa un importante recurso económico para el país. Sitio privilegiado del turismo en masa (3 millones de visitantes al año, de los cuales 74% son origen extranjero), Cancún fue también la sede, en 1999, de un taller norteamericano sobre el "turismo sustentable". Este lugar con gran futuro tiene como objetivo preservar los recursos naturales y los atractivos locales, a menudo alterados por el impacto ecológico de la expansión turística, y garantizar un reparto equitativo de la derrama económica.

PUNTA CANCÚN, CANCÚN, QUINTANA ROO, MEXICO.

At the northeastern tip of the peninsula of Yucatán, a narrow strip of earth separates a huge inland lagoon from the Caribbean Sea. It was not until 1972 that the first buildings appeared on this remarkable site, which has today become the leading tourist destination in Mexico, and one of the largest sea resorts in the world, linked to the United States and Europe by direct flights. Luxurious hotel complexes form a chain along 15 km (9 mi.) of seafront, and this rapid tourist expansion continues over 70 km (43 mi.) to the south of Cancún, nicknamed the Maya Riviera. The tourist sector, which generated $8.3 billion of income in the year 2000, represents an important economic resource for the country. A Mecca for mass tourism (3 million visitors per year, of which 74% are foreigners), Cancún also welcomed a North American workshop on "sustainable" tourism in 1999. This future course attempts to preserve the natural resources and local attractions, often altered by the ecological impact of tourist expansion, and to ensure an equitable distribution of economic benefits.

PUNTA CANCÚN, CANCÚN, QUINTANA ROO, MEXIQUE.

A la pointe nord-est de la péninsule du Yucatán, une étroite bande de terre s'intercale entre une vaste lagune côtière et la mer des Caraïbes. Ce n'est qu'en 1972 que les premiers bâtiments sont apparus sur ce site exceptionnel, aujourd'hui devenu la première destination touristique du Mexique, et l'une des plus vastes stations balnéaires du monde, reliée aux États-Unis et à l'Europe par des vols directs. De luxueux complexes hôteliers s'enchaînent sur 15 km de front de mer, et cet essor touristique se poursuit sur 70 km au sud de Cancún, baptisés Riviera Maya. Le secteur touristique, qui a généré 8,3 milliards de dollars de recettes en 2000, représente une importante ressource économique pour le pays. Haut-lieu du tourisme de masse (3 millions de visiteurs par an, dont 74 % d'étrangers), Cancún a également accueilli, en 1999, un atelier nord-américain sur le « tourisme durable ». Cette voie d'avenir s'attache à préserver les ressources naturelles et les attraits locaux, souvent altérés par l'impact écologique de l'expansion touristique, et à assurer une répartition équitable des retombées économiques.

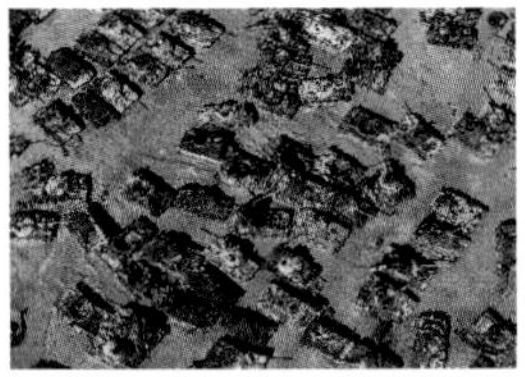

N 29°26' E 45°24'

CEMENTERIO DE CARROS IRAQUÍES EN EL DESIERTO CERCA DE JAHRA, KUWAIT.

Después de la invasión de Kuwait por Iraq el 2 de agosto de 1990, una coalición de 28 países dirigida por Estados Unidos, compuesta por cerca de 760 000 hombres, desencadena el 17 de enero de 1991 la operación bautizada "Tormenta del Desierto" con el fin de forzar a las fuerzas de ocupación a abandonar el emirato. Intensos bombardeos aéreos preceden a la ofensiva terrestre del 24 de febrero, que sólo durará 100 horas. Iraq se retira de Kuwait. La Guerra del Golfo, cubierta por todas las televisiones, aunque sin imágenes reales, impactó las mentes. Este conflicto habría producido miles de muertos y costado mil millones de dólares. Estados Unidos, Europa occidental, Japón y Australia totalizan cerca del 65% de esta suma, es decir, 517 mil millones de dólares. Este mismo grupo de países, que constituye el Comité de Ayuda al Desarrollo, aportó en 2000, a título de ayuda pública destinada al desarrollo de los países más pobres, 53 mil millones de dólares, es decir, alrededor de la décima parte del monto global de sus gastos militares.

IRAQI TANK CEMETERY IN THE DESERT, CLOSE TO AL JAHRA, KUWAIT.

After the invasion of Kuwait by Iraq on August 2, 1990, a coalition of 28 countries directed by the United States, nearly 760,000 strong, launched the operation baptized "Desert Storm" on January 17, 1991, in order to oblige the forces of occupation to withdraw from the emirate. Intense aerial bombing preceded the terrestrial offensive of February 24th, which only lasted 100 hours. Iraq withdrew from Kuwait. The Gulf War, followed by all television networks but without real images, made an impact on people's minds. This conflict is said to have caused thousand of deaths and cost a billion dollars per day while the war lasted. By the year 2000, the world budget for military expenses reached $798 billion. The United States, Western Europe, Japan and Australia make up close to 65% of this sum, or $517 billion. This same group of countries, which makes up the Development Aid Committee, spent a total of $53 billion (about one-tenth of the overall amount of its military expenses) in the year 2000 on public aid intended for the development of the poorest countries.

CIMETIÈRE DE CHARS IRAKIENS DANS LE DÉSERT PRÈS DE JAHRA, KOWEÏT.

Après l'invasion du Koweït par l'Irak le 2 août 1990, une coalition de 28 pays dirigée par les Etats-Unis, forte de près de 760 000 hommes, déclenche le 17 janvier 1991 l'opération baptisée « Tempête du désert » afin de contraindre les forces d'occupation à quitter l'émirat. D'intenses bombardements aériens précèdent l'offensive terrestre du 24 février, qui ne durera que 100 heures. L'Irak se retire du Koweït. La guerre du Golfe, suivie par toutes les télévisions bien que sans images réelles, a frappé les esprits. Ce conflit aurait fait des milliers de morts et coûté un milliard de dollars par jour de guerre. Pour l'année 2000, le budget mondial des dépenses militaires atteint 798 milliards de dollars. Les Etats-Unis, l'Europe occidentale, le Japon et l'Australie totalisent près de 65 % de cette somme, soit 517 milliards de dollars. Ce même groupe de pays, qui constitue le Comité d'Aide au Développement, a versé en 2000, au titre de l'aide publique destinée au développement des pays les plus pauvres, 53 milliards de dollars, soit environ le dixième du montant global de ses dépenses militaires.

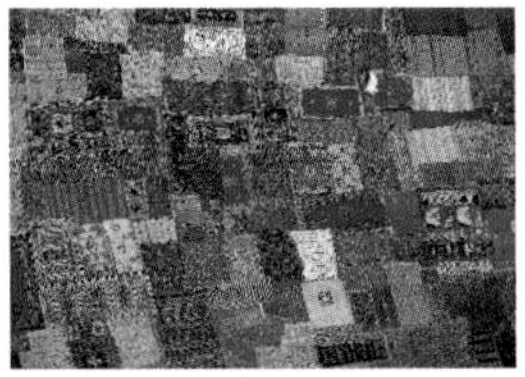

N 31°32' W 8°03'

TAPETES DE MARRAKECH, MARRUECOS.

Además de los países de Asia Central y ciertos países de América del Sur, en el norte de África (Egipto, Túnez, Marruecos, Argelia) se encuentran importantes centros de producción de tapetes. Si Marruecos ha logrado mantener una tradición de fabricación en el seno de células familiares y cooperativas artesanales, debe en lo sucesivo lo esencial de su producción a las manufacturas mecanizadas. Los tapetes se tejen tradicionalmente de lana, símbolo de protección y de felicidad, eventualmente combinada con seda, algodón y a veces pelo de camello o de cabra. Los colores y motivos son característicos de las regiones de fabricación, y es en el Gran Atlas, al pie del cual se encuentra Marrakech, donde los tonos son más cálidos: rojo, naranja, amarillo. El 90% de los tapetes del Gran Atlas se confeccionan en las ciudades de Tazenakht y Amerzgane por una mano de obra casi exclusivamente femenina. Reservado hasta hace poco sólo para el uso doméstico local, el tapete marroquí ha adquirido un renombre internacional que le permite ser en la actualidad el objeto de un comercio de exportación floreciente.

CARPETS FROM MARRAKECH, MOROCCO.

Aside from the countries in central Asia and a few countries in South America, important centers for carpet production exist in North Africa (Egypt, Tunisia, Morocco, Algeria). Although Morocco has succeeded in maintaining a tradition of carpet-making within family groups and cooperatives formed by craftsmen, it now owes the greater part of its production to mechanized manufacture. Carpets are traditionally woven in wool, a symbol of protection and good fortune, possibly combined with silk, cotton and sometimes camel or goat hair. Their colors and patterns are characteristic of the regions of manufacture, and the tones are warmest - red, orange, and yellow - in the High Atlas Mountains, overlooking Marrakech. 90% of the carpets from the High Atlas Mountains are made in the cities of Tazenakht and Amerzgane by almost exclusively female labour. Formerly reserved for local, domestic use only, the Moroccan carpet has acquired an international recognition that permits it today to be the object of a flourishing export trade.

TAPIS DE MARRAKECH, MAROC.

Outre les pays d'Asie centrale et certains pays d'Amérique du Sud, d'importants centres de production de tapis se trouvent au nord de l'Afrique (Égypte, Tunisie, Maroc, Algérie). Si le Maroc a réussi à maintenir une tradition de fabrication au sein de cellules familiales et de coopératives artisanales, il doit désormais l'essentiel de sa production à des manufactures mécanisées. Les tapis sont traditionnellement tissés en laine, symbole de protection et de bonheur, éventuellement associée à de la soie, du coton et parfois du poil de chameau ou de chèvre. Les couleurs et motifs sont caractéristiques des régions de fabrication, et c'est dans le Haut Atlas, au pied duquel se trouve Marrakech, que les tons sont les plus chauds : rouge, orange, jaune. 90 % des tapis du Haut Atlas sont confectionnés dans les villes de Tazenakht et Amerzgane par une main-d'œuvre presque exclusivement féminine. Naguère réservé au seul usage domestique local, le tapis marocain a acquis une renommée internationale qui lui permet de faire aujourd'hui l'objet d'un commerce d'exportation florissant.

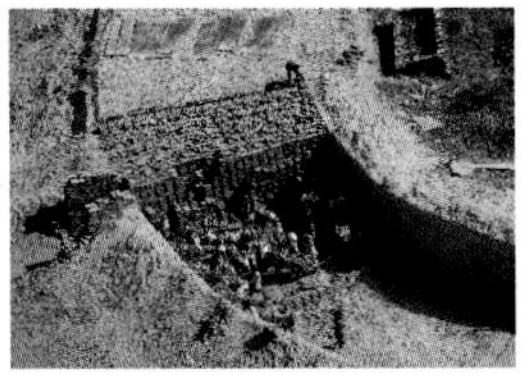

N 27°04' E 78°53'

LADRILLERA AL ESTE DE AGRA, UTTAR PRADESH, INDIA.

Numerosas ladrilleras se han desarrollado en la periferia de Agra, aglomeración de 1.2 millones de habitantes de Uttar Pradesh, estado que alberga un sexto de la población india. Estas pequeñas empresas son proveedoras de trabajo en una región fuertemente afectada por el desempleo y el subempleo, a imagen del conjunto del país. India se clasificaba en efecto en 1998 en el 141° lugar mundial por su PIB por habitante corregido por los diferenciales del poder adquisitivo de su moneda. La producción de estos ladrillos de tierra cocida está más particularmente destinada a los centro urbanos, los rurales se contentan generalmente con habitaciones de adobe (tierra arcillosa cruda), de menor costo, pero más sensibles a la intemperie. El importante crecimiento urbano de la aglomeración de Agra, que en veinte años ha visto aumentar su población en 50%, deja entrever un futuro próspero para las empresas de materiales de construcción de la región.

BRICKYARD IN EAST AGRA, UTTAR PRADESH, INDIA.

Many brickyards have sprung up on the outskirts of Agra, an urban area with 1.2 million inhabitants in Uttar Pradesh, which harbors one-sixth of the Indian population. These small businesses provide work in a region greatly affected by unemployment and underemployment, as in the rest of the country. In fact, India held in 1998 the 141st place worldwide for per capita GDP, corrected for differences in the buying power of its currency. The production of these terra-cotta bricks is intended especially for urban centers, as farmers are generally content with dwellings in pisé or rammed earth (raw, clayey earth), less expensive but more vulnerable to inclement climate. The high rate of urban growth in greater Agra, which in twenty years witnessed an increase by half in its population, would seem to indicate an auspicious future for regional businesses dealing in construction materials.

BRIQUETERIE À L'EST D'AGRA, UTTAR PRADESH, INDE.

De nombreuses briqueteries se sont développées dans la périphérie d'Agra, agglomération de 1,2 million d'habitants de l'Uttar Pradesh, État qui abrite un sixième de la population indienne. Ces petites entreprises sont pourvoyeuses de travail dans une région fortement touchée par le chômage et le sous-emploi, à l'image de l'ensemble du pays. L'Inde se classait en effet en 1998 au 14 1e rang mondial pour son PIB par habitant corrigé des différences de pouvoir d'achat de sa monnaie. La production de ces briques en terre cuite est plus particulièrement destinée aux centres urbains, les ruraux se contentant généralement d'habitations en pisé (terre argileuse crue), d'un moindre coût mais plus sensibles aux intempéries. L'importante croissance urbaine de l'agglomération d'Agra, qui en vingt ans a vu sa population augmenter de moitié, laisse entrevoir un avenir prospère pour les entreprises de matériaux de construction de la région.

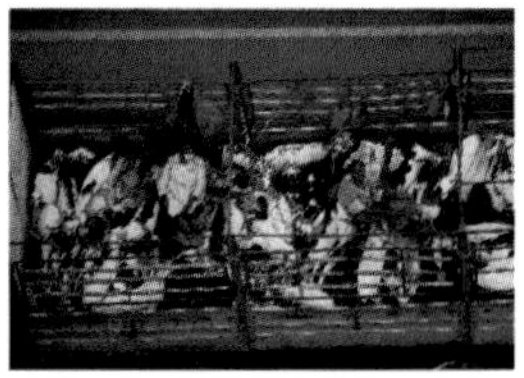

N 6°35' W 5°01'

TRANSPORTE DE CABRAS CERCA DE TOUMODI, REGIÓN DE YAMOUSSOUKRO, COSTA DE MARFIL.

En la región de Yamoussoukro, capital política de Costa de Marfil desde 1983, estos criadores viajan en el remolque de un camión en compañía de su rebaño de cabras, probablemente para venderlas en uno de los numerosos mercados del país. En toda África Occidental, son tradicionalmente los pueblos nómadas de los países sahelianos, más particularmente los peuls, quienes se dedican a la cría extensiva de ganado, y exportan una parte importante de éste hacia los países costeros. Desde hace una treintena de años, el mejoramiento de las infraestructuras carreteras en esta región ha contribuido ampliamente al desarrollo de los intercambios comerciales. Es en particular el caso en Costa de Marfil que, desde los años 1970, ha más que triplicado la superficie de sus carreteras asfaltadas. Pero actualmente, el desarrollo de las comunicaciones pasa también por la telefonía móvil y por Internet, en plena expansión en las principales ciudades de África Occidental.

TRANSPORTING GOATS CLOSE TO TOUMODI, NEAR YAMOUSSOUKRO, CÔTE-D'IVOIRE.

Near Yamoussoukro, the political capital of Côte-d'Ivoire since 1983, these livestock breeders are traveling by tow truck, accompanying their goatherd, certainly to sell them at one of the many markets in the country. Traditionally, in all of West Africa, the nomadic peoples from the Sahalian countries, more particularly the Peul, are devoted to the extensive raising of livestock, exporting a large part of it to coastal countries. For about thirty years, the improvement of road infrastructures in this region has contributed considerably to the development of trade. This is particularly the case of Côte-d'Ivoire, which, since the 1970's, has more that tripled the total length of its paved roads. But today, the development of communications also includes mobile telephones and Internet, which are enjoying a boom in the main cities of West Africa.

TRANSPORT DE CHÈVRES PRÈS DE TOUMODI, RÉGION DE YAMOUSSOUKRO, CÔTE-D'IVOIRE.

Dans la région de Yamoussoukro, capitale politique de la Côte-d'Ivoire depuis 1983, ces éleveurs voyagent dans la remorque d'un camion en compagnie de leur troupeau de chèvres, sans doute pour les vendre sur l'un des nombreux marchés du pays. Dans toute l'Afrique de l'Ouest, ce sont traditionnellement les peuples nomades des pays sahéliens, plus particulièrement les Peuls, qui se consacrent à l'élevage extensif du bétail, exportant une partie importante de celui-ci vers les pays côtiers. Depuis une trentaine d'années, l'amélioration des infrastructures routières dans cette région a largement contribué au développement des échanges commerciaux. C'est en particulier le cas en Côte-d'Ivoire qui, depuis les années 1970, a plus que triplé la superficie de ses routes bitumées. Mais aujourd'hui, le développement des communications passe aussi par la téléphonie mobile et par Internet, en plein essor dans les principales villes d'Afrique de l'Ouest.

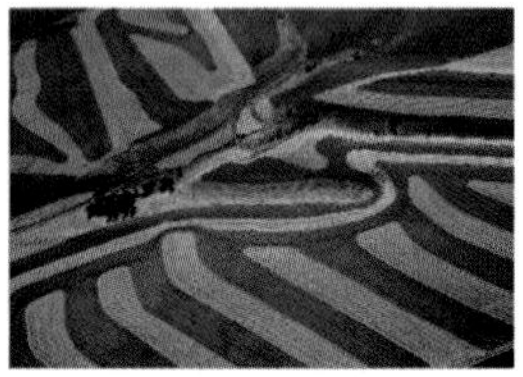

N 46°42' W 117°12'

AGRICULTURA CERCA DE PULLMAN, ESTADO DE WASHINGTON, ESTADOS UNIDOS.

Llamado el Evergreen State, "estado siempre verde", el Estado de Washington desarrolla desde hace decenios el cultivo del trigo, esforzándose hoy en adaptarlo a la topografía del terreno con el fin de componer un suelo debilitado por viejas prácticas agrícolas erosivas. El "agrobusiness", que conjunta agricultura, industria, investigación e inversiones financieras, mantiene a Estados Unidos en el primer lugar mundial en cuanto a las exportaciones de cereales (alrededor del 35% del total mundial), la producción de maíz (40% del total) y de soya (cerca de la mitad de la cosecha del planeta). Modificaciones genéticas efectuadas especialmente en semillas de maíz y de soya han permitido crear variedades resistentes a los parásitos o tolerantes a los herbicidas, que supuestamente aumentan los rendimientos. Mientras que estos organismos genéticamente modificados (OGM) son todavía objeto de prohibiciones y de vivas controversias a través del mundo, especialmente en razón de los pocos conocimientos relativos a sus efectos en el medio ambiente y la salud, su cultivo ya está ampliamente extendido en Argentina, Canadá y sobre todo en Estados Unidos, donde la mitad de la soya está genéticamente modificada.

AGRICULTURE CLOSE TO PULLMAN, WASHINGTON STATE, UNITED STATES.

Nicknamed the "Evergreen State", the state of Washington has been cultivating wheat for decades, striving to adapt it today to the topography of the land in order to manage a soil that is debilitated by old, erosive farming practices. "Agro business", which combines farming, industry, research and financial investments, maintains the United States in first place worldwide in cereal exports (about 35% of total world production), corn production (40% of the total) and soy production (almost half of the planet's crops). Genetic modifications carried out on corn and soy seeds in particular have made it possible to create varieties that are resistant to parasites or tolerant of herbicides and that are expected to increase output. In spite of the fact that these genetically modified organisms (GMO's) are still the target of prohibitions and bitter controversies around the world, especially because of the little knowledge available as to their effects on the environment and health, these crops are already being introduced extensively throughout Argentina, Canada and especially the United States, where half of the soya grown is genetically modified.

AGRICULTURE PRÈS DE PULLMAN, ÉTAT DE WASHINGTON, ÉTATS-UNIS.

Surnommé Evergreen state, « État toujours vert », l'État de Washington développe depuis des décennies la culture du blé, s'efforçant aujourd'hui de l'adapter à la topographie du terrain afin de ménager un sol fragilisé par d'anciennes pratiques agricoles érosives. « L' agro-business », qui allie agriculture, industrie, recherche et investissements financiers, maintient les États-Unis au premier rang mondial pour les exportations de céréales (environ 35 % du total mondial), la production de maïs (40 % du total) et de soja (près de la moitié de la récolte planétaire). Des modifications génétiques effectuées notamment sur des semences de maïs et de soja ont permis de créer des variétés résistantes aux parasites ou tolérantes aux herbicides, censées augmenter les rendements. Alors que ces organismes génétiquement modifiés (OGM) sont encore l'objet d'interdictions et de vives controverses à travers le monde, notamment en raison du peu de connaissances relatives à leurs effets sur l'environnement et la santé, leur mise en culture est déjà largement répandue en Argentine, au Canada et surtout aux Etats-Unis, où la moitié du soja est génétiquement modifiée.

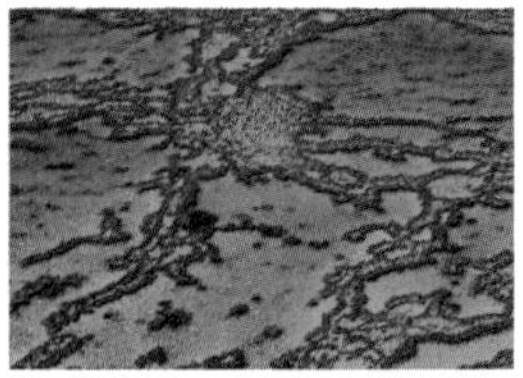

S 16°55' E 146°03'

GRAN BARRERA DE CORAL, QUEENSLAND, AUSTRALIA.

Al noreste de las costas australianas, los 2 500 km de la Gran Barrera constituyen la mayor formación coralina del mundo, incluyendo más de 400 especies de corales. Parque marino desde 1979, (que representa el 15% de la superficie marina protegida mundial), inscrito en 1981 en la Lista del Patrimonio Mundial de la UNESCO, este rico santuario silencioso de vida submarina es el refugio de más de 1500 especies de peces y de 4000 especies de moluscos, del dugón, en peligro de extinción, y de seis especies de tortugas marinas, de las 7 con las que cuenta el planeta. Los ingresos anuales de la pesca y del turismo (2 millones de visitantes al año) se evalúan en mil millones de dólares. Único relieve de origen biológico en el mundo, los corales son pólipos vivientes en simbiosis con algas fotosensibles, las rodofitas, que participan en la elaboración del esqueleto calcáreo de sus anfitriones. A pesar de su papel primordial de protección de las costas y de mantenimiento de la riqueza de la fauna oceánica, las formaciones coralinas del mundo padecen diversas amenazas. Una de ellas, contemporánea, es un ínfimo aumento de temperatura del agua: éste provoca la extinción del alga simbiótica y trae consigo el blanqueo y la muerte de los corales. El calentamiento del planeta podría ser responsable de este fenómeno, particularmente pronunciado en 1998, que causó la perdida de corales milenarios.

GREAT BARRIER REEF, QUEENSLAND, AUSTRALIA.

On the northeastern coast of Australia, the Great Barrier Reef (2,500 km (1,500 mi.) long) is the largest coral reef in the world, and includes more than 400 species of corals. Classified as a marine park since 1979 – it represents 15% of the protected marine surface in the world – and inscribed in 1981 on the UNESCO World Heritage List, this underwater sanctuary, silent though teeming with life, shelters 1,500 species of fish and 4,000 species of mollusks, as well as the dugong – an endangered species -, and six of the seven existing species of marine turtles. The annual income for fishing and tourism (with 2 million visitors per year) is equivalent to $1 billion. Corals are the only rocky formation of biological origin in the world. They consist of polyps living in symbiosis with photosensitive algae, zooxanthellae, which participate in the development of the calcareous skeleton of their hosts. Although they play an essential role in the protection of coasts and in preserving the ocean fauna wealth, coral formations are faced with various threats throughout the world. One of them, a contemporary one, is a minute increase in water temperature, causing the loss of symbiotic algae, leading to bleaching and death of the coral. Global warming could be responsible for this phenomenon, which was particularly pronounced in 1998, and caused the loss of thousand-year-old corals.

GRANDE BARRIÈRE DE CORAIL, QUEENSLAND, AUSTRALIE.

Au nord-est des côtes australiennes, les 2 500 km de la Grande Barrière constituent la plus grande formation corallienne du monde, comportant plus de 400 espèces de coraux. Parc marin depuis 1979 (représentant 15 % de la surface marine protégée mondiale), inscrit en 1981 sur la Liste du patrimoine mondial de l'Unesco, ce riche sanctuaire silencieux de vie sous-marine est le refuge de plus de 1 500 espèces de poissons et 4 000 espèces de mollusques, du dugong, menacé d'extinction, et de six espèces de tortues marines, sur les 7 que compte la planète. Les recettes annuelles de la pêche et du tourisme (2 millions de visiteurs par an) s'évaluent à 1 milliard de dollars. Seul relief d'origine biologique au monde, les coraux sont des polypes vivant en symbiose avec des algues photosensibles, les zooxhantelles, qui participent à l'élaboration du squelette calcaire de leurs hôtes. Malgré leur rôle primordial de protection des côtes et de maintien de la richesse de la faune océanique, les formations coralliennes du monde souffrent de diverses menaces. L'une d'elles, contemporaine, est une infime augmentation de température de l'eau : elle provoque l'expulsion de l'algue symbiotique, entraînant le blanchiment et la mort des coraux. Le réchauffement de la planète pourrait être responsable de ce phénomène, particulièrement prononcé en 1998, et qui a causé la perte de coraux millénaires.

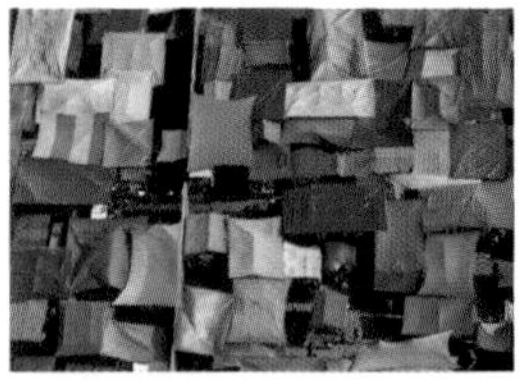

N 19°20' W 99°05'

MERCADO CERCA DEL BARRIO DE XOCHIMILCO, CIUDAD DE MÉXICO, MÉXICO.

Bajo este mosaico de sombrillas multicolores se oculta un mercado popular animado y ruidoso, que se establece por un día en una calle de la capital. Así protegidos del sol, los puestos de frutas y legumbres, de plantas medicinales o especias, colindan con los de telas y productos artesanales. Verdadera institución en México, los mercados florecen diariamente en todo el país. Así como la artesanía, las tradiciones del vestido o las fachadas de las casas, traducen el apego de los mexicanos por los colores brillantes y alegres, como ese rosa fuerte llamado "rosa mexicano". En el escenario internacional, México es el campeón mundial del desarrollo comercial, con exportaciones que crecen un 18% cada año, de las que más del 85% van hacia los Estados Unidos. Pero, si bien la liberalización económica generó que el PIB por habitante se duplicara entre 1985 y 1999, agravó en cambio las desigualdades en la distribución del ingreso. En el campo, donde la agricultura no puede enfrentar la competencia de los productos importados, el ingreso promedio puede ser hasta cuatro veces menor al ingreso nacional. Los problemas sociales que desde 1994 agitan al Estado de Chiapas están en parte relacionados con ello.

MARKET CLOSE TO XOCHIMILCO, MEXICO CITY, MEXICO.

Under this colorful mosaic of parasols is hidden a loud, animated, working-class market, set up for the day in one of the capital's city streets. Thus protected from the sun, fruit and vegetable stalls, medicinal plants or spices, adjoin those of fabrics and handicrafts. A real institution in Mexico, these markets blossom every day throughout the country. Like handicrafts, dress traditions or house facades, they portray the strong attachment Mexicans have for vivid, cheerful colors, such as this bright pink named "rosa mexicano". On an international scale, Mexico is world champion in commercial expansion, with exports growing 18% per year, 85% of which is directed to the United States. Although this economic liberalization has doubled the per capita GDP from 1985 to 1999, it has on the other hand accentuated existing inequalities in the distribution of income. In rural areas, where agriculture cannot face the competition of imported production, the average income is as much as four times less than the national income. The social unrest that has been troubling the state of Chiapas since 1994 is partly due to this.

MARCHÉ PRÈS DU QUARTIER DE XOCHIMILCO, MEXICO, MEXIQUE.

Sous cette mosaïque de parasols colorés se dissimule un marché populaire animé et bruyant, établi pour la journée dans une rue de la capitale. Ainsi protégés du soleil, les étals de fruits et légumes, plantes médicinales ou épices, jouxtent ceux des tissus et produits artisanaux. Véritable institution au Mexique, les marchés fleurissent quotidiennement dans tout le pays. Comme l'artisanat, les traditions vestimentaires ou les façades des habitations, ils traduisent l'attachement des Mexicains aux couleurs éclatantes et gaies, telles que ce rose vif dénommé « rosa mexican ». Sur la scène internationale, le Mexique est champion mondial de l'essor commercial, avec des exportations en croissance de 18 % par an, en direction des États-Unis pour plus de 85 %. Mais cette libéralisation économique, si elle a entraîné le doublement du PIB par habitant entre 1985 et 1999, a par contre aggravé les inégalités dans la distribution du revenu. Dans les campagnes, où l'agriculture ne peut faire face à la concurrence des productions importées, le revenu moyen est jusqu'à quatre fois inférieur au revenu national. Les troubles sociaux qui agitent l'Etat du Chiapas depuis 1994 y sont en partie liés.

CASAS INUNDADAS AL SUR DE DACCA, BANGLADESH.

N 23°21' E 90°31'

Recorrido por una vasta red de 300 corrientes de agua, entre ellas los ríos Ganges, Brahmaputra y Meghna, que descienden las pendientes del Himalaya para precipitarse en el Golfo de Bengala, Bangladesh es una planicie deltaica sujeta a los monzones estacionales. De junio a septiembre, las lluvias diluvianas aumentan a veces hasta 50 000 m³/s el caudal de los ríos, que salen de su lecho e inundan cerca de la mitad del territorio devastando todo a su paso. Para tratar de escapar de la violencia de las crecidas, una parte de la población del país vive permanentemente en *chars*, islotes fluviales efímeros formados por arena y limo acumulados por las corrientes; no obstante, estos últimos son regularmente arrasados y llevados por las olas. Cada año, de 1000 a 2000 personas perecen en estas inundaciones y cerca del 25% de los 123 millones de bengalíes se encuentran sin hogar. Los estragos ocasionados a la agricultura son igualmente considerables en este país 80% rural. Territorio entre los más densamente poblados del mundo, con 922 habitantes por km², Bangladesh es igualmente uno de los países más pobres: el 32% de la población vive con menos de un dólar al día. Hoy, casi la mitad de la humanidad vive con menos de dos dólares diarios.

HOUSES FLOODED IN THE SOUTHERN PART OF DACCA, BANGLADESH.

With a vast network of 300 rivers, including the Ganges, Brahmaputra and Meghna Rivers, which descend the slopes of the Himalayas to empty into the gulf of Bengal, Bangladesh is a delta plain that is subject to seasonal monsoons. From June to September, torrential rains sometimes increase the rivers' flow to as much as 50 000 cu. m./sec, whose beds overflow flooding close to half of the territory, devastating everything that lies in their path. In its attempt to escape from these violent floods, part of the country's population permanently lives on *chars*, temporary fluvial islets made of sand and silt accumulated by currents; however, they are regularly leveled and washed away by the tides. Every year, 1,000 to 2,000 people perish in these floods and close to 25% of the 123 million Bangladeshis find themselves again without shelter. Damages caused to farming are also considerable in this 80% rural country. Among the most densely populated territory in the world, with 922 inhabitants per sq. km., Bangladesh is also one of the poorest countries: 32% of the population live on less than one dollar per day. Today, nearly half of humankind lives on less than two dollars a day.

MAISONS INONDÉES AU SUD DE DACCA, BANGLADESH.

Parcouru par un vaste réseau de 300 cours d'eau, dont les fleuves Gange, Brahmapoutre et Meghna, qui dévalent les pentes de l'Himalaya pour se jeter dans le golfe du Bengale, le Bangladesh est une plaine deltaïque soumise à des moussons saisonnières. De juin à septembre, des pluies diluviennes augmentent parfois jusqu'à 50 000 m³/s le débit des fleuves, qui sortent de leur lit et inondent près de la moitié du territoire en dévastant tout sur leur passage. Pour tenter d'échapper à la violence des crues, une partie de la population du pays vit en permanence sur des *chars*, îlots fluviaux éphémères formés de sable et de limon accumulés par les courants ; cependant, ces derniers sont régulièrement arasés et emportés par les flots. Chaque année, de 1 000 à 2 000 personnes périssent dans ces inondations et près de 25 % des 123 millions de Bangladais se retrouvent sans abri. Les dégâts occasionnés à l'agriculture sont également considérables dans ce pays à 80 % rural. Territoire parmi les plus densément peuplés du monde, avec 922 habitants par km², le Bangladesh est également l'un des pays les plus pauvres : 32 % de la population vit avec moins d'un dollar par jour. Aujourd'hui, presque la moitié de l'humanité vit avec moins de deux dollars par jour (environ 15FF).

PAISAJE AGRÍCOLA CERCA DE COÑAC, CHARENTE, FRANCIA.

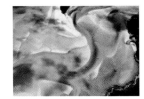

N 48°34' W 2°43'

En el siglo XIX, los viñedos de Charente, gran región vinícola, fueron devastados, como cerca de la mitad del viñedo francés, por el filoxera, enfermedad causada por un pulgón parásito. Una parte importante de las cepas de esta región se reemplazó con cultivos de cereales que dominan todavía el paisaje actual. El viñedo, sin embargo, se fue reconstituyendo alrededor de la ciudad de Coñac, donde la producción de alcohol del mismo nombre no ha dejado de aumentar. Nacida en un suelo gredoso, la cepa Ugni blanca produce un vino que, después de la destilación y el envejecimiento en barricas de roble, da vida al coñac. El inventario actualmente en proceso de envejecimiento rebasa el equivalente de mil millones de botellas. La apelación Coñac está reservada solamente para esta región, delimitada por decreto desde 1909, y dividida en seis caldos. Con más de 15 000 explotaciones en 900 m², la región de Coñac produce más de 190 millones de botellas al año de este prestigioso alcohol; nueve décimos se exportan, principalmente a Estados Unidos y Japón, pero también a los otros países de Europa.

AGRICULTURAL LANDSCAPE CLOSE TO COGNAC, CHARENTE, FRANCE.

In the 19th century, the grapevines of Charente, a large wine-growing region, were ravaged, as was nearly half of the French wine-growing region, by phylloxera, an illness caused by a parasitic aphid. A large number of the vines in this region were replaced by cereal crops, which are still predominant in the present landscape. Nevertheless, the wine-growing areas are gradually being restored around the city of Cognac, where production of the alcoholic drink bearing the same name (or Brandy) has continued to increase. Growing in chalky soil, the vine variety, Ugni blanc, produces a wine that, after distillation and ageing in oak casks, gives origin to cognac. The stock currently being aged is in excess of the equivalent of a billion bottles. The appellation Cognac is reserved for this soil alone, delimited by decree since 1909, and divided into six vineyards. With more than 15,000 vineyards covering an area of 900 sq. km. (350 sq. mi.), the region of Cognac produces over 190 million bottles of this prestigious alcohol per year; nine-tenths of it is exported, mainly to the United States and Japan, but also to the other countries in Europe.

PAYSAGE AGRICOLE PRÈS DE COGNAC, CHARENTE, FRANCE.

Au XIXe siècle, les vignes de Charente, grande région viticole, furent ravagées, comme près de la moitié du vignoble français, par le phylloxera, maladie causée par un puceron parasite. Une partie importante des cépages de cette région fut remplacée par des cultures céréalières qui dominent encore dans le paysage actuel. Le vignoble s'est néanmoins peu à peu reconstitué autour de la ville de Cognac, où la production d'alcool du même nom n'a cessé d'augmenter. Poussant sur un sol crayeux, le cépage Ugni blanc fournit un vin qui, après distillation et vieillissement en fûts de chêne, donne naissance au cognac. Le stock actuellement en cours de vieillissement dépasse l'équivalent d'un milliard de bouteilles. L'appellation Cognac est réservée à ce seul terroir, délimité par décret depuis 1909, et divisé en six crus. Avec plus de 15 000 exploitations sur 900 km², la région de Cognac produit plus de 190 millions de bouteilles par an de ce prestigieux alcool ; les neuf-dixièmes sont exportés, principalement vers les États-Unis et le Japon, mais aussi vers les autres pays d'Europe.

CAMPESINO TRABAJANDO SU CAMPO, REGIÓN DE LASSITHI, CRETA, GRECIA.

N 35°09' E 25°35'

Granero de trigo de Creta en la Antigüedad, la planicie fértil de la meseta de Lassithi es todavía hoy un lugar de cultivo intensivo de cereales, pero también de papas. En Creta, la práctica de la agricultura y el acceso a los campos se dificultan por el relieve escarpado; el burro, medio tradicional de locomoción, de transporte y de tracción, es ciertamente el animal mejor adaptado a la topografía de la isla, y su utilización todavía está generalizada ahí. El clima local, considerado como uno de los más saludables y templados de Europa, favorecería la longevidad excepcional de los habitantes de Creta. Pero las virtudes del régimen alimenticio cretense, en el que las aceitunas y el aceite de olivo tienen un sitio de honor, contribuyen igualmente. Los cretenses no son sin embargo los únicos en atravesar comúnmente un siglo entero: el valle de Vilcabamba, en Ecuador, cuenta igualmente numerosos centenarios. Los progresos de la medicina y el mejoramiento de la situación sanitaria mundial alargan progresivamente la esperanza de vida media de la humanidad, que en la actualidad es de 66 años. Pero la duración de la existencia en la tierra sigue siendo muy desigual: en Japón o en Canadá, se vive en promedio 80 años, mientras que 3 personas de cada 4 mueren a la edad de 50 años en los países menos adelantados.

PEASANT PLOUGHING HIS FIELD, NEAR LASSITHI, CRETE, GREECE.

The fertile plain of the Lassithi plateau, known as the wheat granary for Crete in Antiquity, remains an area where cereals and potatoes are intensively grown. In Crete, where sheer slopes render cultivation and access to fields difficult, the donkey, a traditional means of transportation also used for carrying and hauling loads, remains the best adapted animal to put up with the topography of the island. The local climate, considered to be one of healthiest and mildest of Europe, is said to encourage the exceptional longevity of Crete's inhabitants. The virtues of the Cretan diet, consisting of large quantities of olives and olive oil, also supposedly contribute. The Cretans are not however the only ones to live commonly past a whole century: the valley of Vilcabamba, in Ecuador, also has a number of centenarians. Progress in medicine and improvement of sanitary conditions throughout the world progressively lengthen the average life expectancy of mankind, which is now 66 years of age. But the length of people's existence on earth is still very variable: in Japan or Canada, people live until 80 years of age on the average, whereas 3 people out of 4 die before the age of 50 in less advanced countries.

PAYSAN LABOURANT SON CHAMP, RÉGION DE LASSITHI, CRÈTE, GRÈCE.

Grenier à blé de la Crète dans l'Antiquité, la plaine fertile du plateau de Lassithi est aujourd'hui encore un lieu de culture intensive de céréales mais aussi de pommes de terre. En Crète, la pratique de l'agriculture et l'accès aux champs sont rendus difficiles par le relief escarpé ; l'âne, moyen traditionnel de locomotion, de transport et de traction, est certainement l'animal le mieux adapté à la topographie de l'île, et son utilisation y est encore généralisée. Le climat local, considéré comme l'un des plus salubres et des plus doux d'Europe, favoriserait la longévité exceptionnelle des habitants de la Crète. Mais les vertus du régime alimentaire Crétois, où les olives et l'huile d'olive sont à l'honneur, y contribueraient également. Les Crétois ne sont cependant pas les seuls à traverser communément un siècle entier : la vallée de Vilcabamba, en Equateur, compte également nombre de centenaires. Les progrès de la médecine et l'amélioration de la situation sanitaire mondiale allongent progressivement l'espérance de vie moyenne de l'humanité, actuellement de 66 ans. Mais la durée d'existence sur terre demeure très inégale : au Japon ou au Canada, on vit en moyenne jusqu'à 80 ans, alors que 3 personnes sur 4 meurent avant l'âge de 50 ans dans les pays les moins avancés.

BANCO DE ARENA EN EL LITORAL DE LA ISLA DE WHITSUNDAY, QUEENSLAND, AUSTRALIA.

S 20°17' E 148°59'

A lo largo de la costa oeste de Australia, Whitsunday es, con 109 km², la mayor de las 74 islas que constituyen el archipiélago del mismo nombre. Como en esta playa de White Haven, el litoral de las islas se caracteriza por la excepcional blancura de la arena, esencialmente compuesta de sedimentos coralinos que provienen especialmente de la Gran Barrera, unos kilómetros al este. En los meandros de la costa, la arena se amontonó para formar dunas que se desplazan a merced de las corrientes, y entre las cuales el agua del Pacífico se insinúa con la marea creciente. Descubiertas en 1770 por el navegante británico James Cook, las islas del archipiélago permanecen en su mayoría deshabitadas y sin explotar. No obstante, a partir de 1930, algunas se han acondicionado como estaciones balnearias.

SANDBANK ON THE COAST OF WHITSUNDAY ISLAND, QUEENSLAND, AUSTRALIA.

Off the west coast of Australia, Whitsunday is, with a surface of 109 sq. km. (42 sq. mi.), the largest of the 74 islands forming the archipelago bearing the same name. As can be seen on this White Haven's beach, the islands' coastline is characterized by the outstanding whiteness of the sand, essentially composed of coral sediments originating mainly from the Great Barrier Reef, a few kilometers to the East. In the meanders of the coastline, the sand has accumulated into dunes, moving according to the currents, and among which the waters of the Pacific wind their way at flood tide. Discovered in 1770 by the British navigator James Cook, the archipelago's islands have mostly remained uninhabited and unexploited. However, since 1930, some have been increasingly converted to sea resorts.

BANC DE SABLE SUR LE LITTORAL DE L'ÎLE DE WHITSUNDAY, QUEENSLAND, AUSTRALIE.

Au large de la côte ouest de l'Australie, Whitsunday est, avec 109 km², la plus grande des 74 îles qui constituent l'archipel du même nom. Comme sur cette plage de White Haven, le littoral des îles se caractérise par l'exceptionnelle blancheur du sable, essentiellement composé de sédiments coralliens provenant notamment de la Grande Barrière, à quelques kilomètres à l'est. Dans les méandres de la côte, le sable s'est amoncelé pour former des dunes qui se déplacent au gré des courants et entre lesquelles l'eau du Pacifique s'insinue à marée montante. Découvertes en 1770 par le navigateur britannique James Cook, les îles de l'archipel sont en majorité restées inhabitées et inexploitées. Cependant, à partir de 1930, quelques unes ont progressivement été aménagées en stations balnéaires.

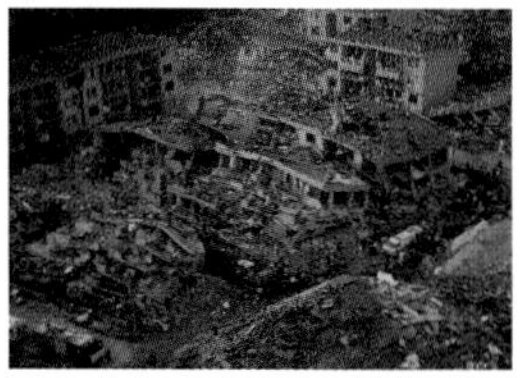

N 40°43' E 29°48'

TEMBLOR DE TIERRA EN GOLÇÜK, RIBERA DEL MAR DE MÁRMARA, TURQUÍA.

El sismo que asoló la región de Izmit el 17 de agosto de 1999 a las 3:02 horas, tenía una magnitud de 7.4 grados en la escala de Richter, que llega hasta el 9. El epicentro se localizó en Golçük, ciudad industrial de 65 000 habitantes (4 600 muertos). Este temblor de tierra provocó oficialmente la muerte de al menos 15 500 personas, sepultadas mientras dormían. El derrumbamiento parcial o total de 50 000 inmuebles suscitó una polémica que puso en tela de juicio a los empresarios acusados de no haber respetado las normas de construcción antisísmica. El sur y el norte de Turquía corren a lo largo de la falla del norte de Anatolia a una velocidad relativa media de 2.5 cm al año, pero las avanzadas se producen en realidad de manera brutal, bajo la forma de sismos: 3 m en menos de 1 minuto por lo que respecta al de Izmit. La actividad sísmica afecta regularmente a Turquía (1992: 500 muertos; 1995: 100 muertos, 50 000 sin hogar), pero otras zonas en los bordes de placas teutónicas están particularmente expuestas a los riesgos, como la zona transasiática que corre de las Azores a Indonesia pasando por Turquía, Armenia (25 000 muertos en 1988) o Irán (45 000 en 1990).

EARTHQUAKE IN GOLÇÜK, COAST OF THE MARMARA SEA, TURKEY.

The earthquake that hit the region of Izmit on August 17th, 1999 at 3:02 a.m., measured 7.4 degrees on the Richter scale, out of a maximum of 9. The epicenter was located in Golçük, an industrial city of 65,000 inhabitants, where 4,600 people died. This earthquake officially caused the death of at least 15,500 people, who were buried while they slept. The partial or total collapse of 50,000 buildings caused a controversy: building contractors were accused of not having respected anti-seismic construction standards. Northern and southern Turkey are sliding along the north Anatolian fault at a relative average speed of 2.5 cm per year, but this movement actually occurs violently, in the form of earthquakes: 3 m in less than one minute for the Izmit quake. Seismic activity hits Turkey regularly (1992 toll: 500 dead; 1995 toll: 100 dead, 50,000 homeless), but other zones on the edges of tectonic plates are especially exposed to risks, such as the trans-Asiatic zone, which runs from the Azores to Indonesia by way of Turkey, Armenia (25,000 deaths in 1988) or Iran (45,000 in 1990).

TREMBLEMENT DE TERRE À GOLÇÜK, RIVAGE DE LA MER DE MARMARA, TURQUIE.

Le séisme qui a frappé la région d'Izmit, le 17 août 1999 à 3 h 02, avait une magnitude de 7,4 degrés sur l'échelle de Richter, qui en compte 9. L'épicentre était situé à Golçük, ville industrielle de 65 000 habitants (4 600 morts). Ce tremblement de terre a officiellement provoqué la mort d'au moins 15 500 personnes, ensevelies pendant leur sommeil. L'effondrement partiel ou total de 50 000 immeubles a suscité une polémique mettant en cause les entrepreneurs accusés de ne pas avoir respecté les normes de construction antisismique. Le sud et le nord de la Turquie coulissent le long de la faille nord-anatolienne à une vitesse relative moyenne de 2,5 cm par an, mais les avancées se produisent en réalité de façon brutale, sous la forme de séismes : 3 m en moins d'une minute pour celui d'Izmit. L'activité sismique frappe régulièrement la Turquie (1992 : 500 morts ; 1995 : 100 morts, 50 000 sans-abri), mais d'autres zones en bordure de plaques tectoniques sont particulièrement exposées aux risques, comme la zone transasiatique qui court des Açores à l'Indonésie en passant par la Turquie, l'Arménie (25 000 morts en 1988) ou l'Iran (45 000 en 1990).

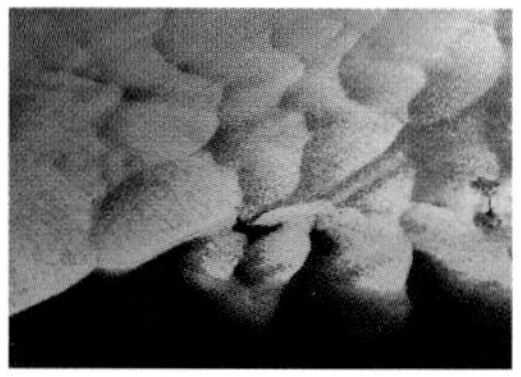

N 6°00' W 62°52'

BANCO DE ARENA DEL RÍO CARONI, ESTADO DE BOLÍVAR, VENEZUELA.

Con 690 km de largo, el río Caroni atraviesa de sur a norte el Estado de Bolívar (a la región se la llama más comúnmente Guayana, en Venezuela, desciende a través de una sucesión de cascadas y encuentra en su recorrido anchos bancos de arena. El Caroni, y todas las otras corrientes de agua que atraviesan la Guayana, son ricos en alcaloides y taninos provenientes de la degradación de los vegetales de la selva espesa. Por tal razón, se agrupan bajo la apelación de "ríos negros" en contraste con los "ríos blancos" que descienden de los macizos andinos acarreando numerosos sedimentos. Antes de terminar su recorrido en el Río Orinoco, el Caroni va a alimentar la presa hidroeléctrica de Guri (puesta en servicio en 1986), segunda en el mundo en cuanto a la potencia hidroeléctrica (10 300 megawatts, siendo la potencia de una central nuclear del parque francés del orden de 1 000 megawatts), que provee el 60% de la electricidad de Venezuela. La energía hidráulica se desarrolla en el continente sudamericano, y suministra ya el 50% de su electricidad a una decena de países.

SANDBANK ON THE RÍO CARONÍ, BOLÍVAR STATE, VENEZUELA.

690 km long, the Río Caroní crosses Bolívar state (the region is more commonly called Guayana) from south to north, to Venezuela, then descends through a succession of waterfalls, meeting wide sandbars on its course. The Caroní, and all other rivers that cross Guayana, are rich in alkaloids and in tannins produced by the degradation of the plants in the dense forest. They are thus grouped under the name "black rivers" as opposed to "white rivers", which come down from the Andean massifs carrying many types of sediment. Before reaching the end of its course in the Río Orinoco, the Caroní feeds the hydroelectric dam of Guri (which started operating in 1986), with the second highest hydroelectric strength in the world (10,300 megawatts - the strength of France's nuclear power stations being in the order of 1,000 megawatts), which provides 60% of Venezuela's electricity. Hydraulic energy is developing on the South American continent, and already provides about ten countries with 50% of their electricity.

BANC DE SABLE DU RIO CARONI, ÉTAT DE BOLIVAR, VENEZUELA.

Long de 690 km, le rio Caroni traverse du sud au nord l'État de Bolivar (la région est plus communément appelée Guayana) au Venezuela, dévale à travers une succession de cascades, rencontrant sur son parcours de larges bancs de sable. Le Caroni, et tous les autres cours d'eau qui traversent le Guayana, sont riches en alcaloïdes et en tanins issus de la dégradation des végétaux de la forêt dense. Aussi sont-ils regroupés sous l'appellation de « rivières noires », en contraste avec les « rivières blanches » qui descendent des massifs andins en charriant de nombreux sédiments. Avant de finir sa course dans le fleuve Orénoque, le Caroni vient alimenter le barrage hydroélectrique de Guri (mis en service en 1986), 2e au monde pour la puissance hydroélectrique (10 300 mégawatts – la puissance d'une centrale nucléaire du parc français étant de l'ordre de 1 000 mégawatts), qui fournit 60 % de l'électricité du Venezuela. L'énergie hydraulique se développe sur le continent sud-américain, et fournit déjà 50 % de leur électricité à une dizaine de pays.

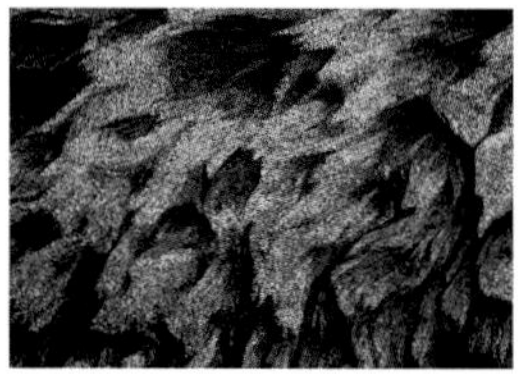

N 46°27' E 3°59'

VEGETACIÓN SUBACUÁTICA EN EL LOIRA CERCA DE DIGOIN, SAÔNE-ET-LOIRE, FRANCIA.

Con un largo de 1 012 km, el Loira tiene su origen en Ardèche, al sureste de la región, y atraviesa una gran parte del territorio antes de lanzarse al Atlántico, al oeste. Esta corriente de agua, considerada como el último río salvaje de Francia, está sujeto a un régimen muy irregular de crecidas y estiajes de gran amplitud. En verano, se reduce a veces a estrechos riachuelos poco profundos que serpentean entre los bancos de arena, y donde proliferan salteadas plantas subacuáticas, como aquí, cerca de Digoin. En invierno, sus crecidas pueden provocar importantes inundaciones que afectan las ciudades ribereñas. Con el fin de domar este río imprevisible preservando al mismo tiempo su equilibrio ecológico, un plan de acondicionamiento empezó en 1994. Se han desmantelado así dos presas en 1998, con la restauración de los ríos de salmón del Haut-Allier y Vienne, afluentes del Loira. El Estado y las 10 regiones francesas comprendidas en la cuenca del Loira se lanzaron, para el periodo 2000-2006, en una nueva etapa del plan: más de 715 millones de francos (109 millones de euros) van a servir para mejorar la prevención de las crecidas y el manejo del agua, y a valorizar el patrimonio natural y cultural.

UNDERWATER VEGETATION IN THE LOIRE, CLOSE TO DIGOIN, SAÔNE-ET-LOIRE, FRANCE.

1,012 km long, the source of the Loire is in Ardèche, in the southeastern part of the country, and crosses a large part of the territory before emptying into the Atlantic, to the west. This river, considered the last unspoiled one in France, is subject to a very irregular schedule of extreme high and low levels. In the summer, it is sometimes reduced to fine, shallow trickles of water that flow in and out among the sandbanks, and where underwater plants proliferate in places, as seen here, close to Digoin. In winter, its flooding can provoke large inundations affecting cities and villages along the shores. In order to tame this unpredictable river, while preserving its ecological balance, a development plan was implemented in 1994. Two dams were thus dismantled in 1998, restoring the salmon rivers of the Haut-Allier and Vienne, tributaries of the Loire. The state and its 10 French regions, alarmed over the Loire basin, rushed into a new stage of the plan for the period 2000-2006: more than $100 million are to be used to improve flood prevention and water management, and to develop the value of this natural and cultural heritage.

VÉGÉTATION SUBAQUATIQUE DANS LA LOIRE PRÈS DE DIGOIN, SAÔNE-ET-LOIRE, FRANCE.

Longue de 1 012 km, la Loire prend sa source en Ardèche, au sud-est du pays, et traverse une grande partie du territoire avant de se jeter dans l'Atlantique, à l'ouest. Ce cours d'eau, considéré comme le dernier fleuve sauvage de France, est soumis à un régime très irrégulier de crues et d'étiages de grande ampleur. En été, il est parfois réduit à d'étroits filets d'eau peu profonds qui ruissellent parmi les bancs de sable, et où prolifèrent par endroits des plantes subaquatiques, comme ici près de Digoin. En hiver, ses crues peuvent provoquer d'importantes inondations touchant les villes et villages riverains. Afin de dompter ce fleuve imprévisible tout en préservant son équilibre écologique, un plan d'aménagement a débuté en 1994. Deux barrages ont ainsi été démantelés en 1998, restaurant les rivières à saumons du Haut-Allier et de la Vienne, affluents de la Loire. L'Etat et les 10 régions françaises concernées par le bassin ligérien se sont lancés, pour la période 2000-2006, dans une nouvelle étape du plan : plus de 715 millions de francs (109 millions d'Euros) vont servir à améliorer la prévention des crues et la gestion de l'eau, et à valoriser le patrimoine naturel et culturel.

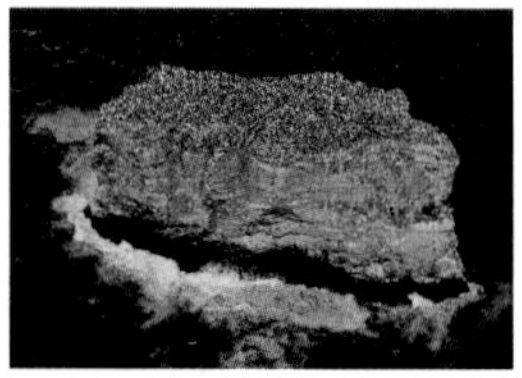

N 63°43' W 22°58'

COLONIA DE FOUS DE BASSAN ISLA DE ELDEY, ISLANDIA.

Situada en el cruce de las áreas geográficas ártica, americana y europea, Islandia alberga una población de aves variada; 70 especies vienen a anidar aquí con regularidad, y 300 otras pasan una temporada puntualmente. A 14 km al sur de las costas islandesas, la isla de Eldey, pico rocoso de 70 m de altura clasificada como reserva natural, acoge cada año una de las colonias más importantes de alcatraces (*Morus bassanus*) del mundo, compuesta por cerca de 40 000 individuos. Llegados a la isla entre enero y febrero para la anidación, las aves la abandonan en septiembre para ir a hibernar a lo largo de las costas africanas, después de haber dado vida a un solo pichón por pareja. Como cerca de un cuarto de las especies de aves de la región paleártica, los alcatraces efectúan su migración con destino a África, recorriendo más de 300 km diarios y arrostrando los riesgos naturales (vientos contrarios, predadores), así como los peligros resultantes de las actividades humanas (desecación de los medios, pesticidas). Es en la Isla de Eldey donde se exterminaron en 1844 los dos últimos especímenes del gran pingüino (Alca impennis), especie hasta hace poco extendida y desde entonces desaparecida.

COLONY OF GANNETS, ELDEY ISLAND, ICELAND.

Located at the crossroads of Arctic, American and European geographical areas, Iceland harbors various bird populations. 70 species regularly come here to nest, and another 300 sojourn here at irregular intervals. 14 km (9 mi.) off the southern coast of Iceland, Eldey Island, a 70 m (230 mi.) high rocky peak classified as a natural reserve, is home to one of the largest colonies of northern gannets (*Morus bassanus*) in the world - nearly 40,000 every year -. After arriving on the island in January-February to nest, the birds leave in September to spend the winter off the African coasts, after giving birth to one chick per pair. As with nearly a quarter of the species of birds in the palearctic region, gannets migrate towards Africa, traveling over 300 km (about 200 mi.) per day and braving natural risks (head winds, predators…) as well as threats resulting from human activities (drainage of environments, pesticides…). The last two specimens of the great auk or garefowl (Pinguinus impennis) were exterminated in 1844 on Eldey Island, leaving this once plentiful species now extinct.

COLONIE DE FOUS DE BASSAN, ÎLE D'ELDEY, ISLANDE.

Située au carrefour des aires géographiques arctique, américaine et européenne, l'Islande abrite une population d'oiseaux variée ; 70 espèces viennent y nicher régulièrement, et 300 autres y séjournent ponctuellement. À 14 km au sud des côtes islandaises, l'île d'Eldey, piton rocheux de 70 m de hauteur classé réserve naturelle, accueille chaque année l'une des plus importantes colonies de fous de Bassan (*Morus bassanus*) du monde, forte de près de 40 000 individus. Arrivés sur l'île en janvier-février pour la nidification, les oiseaux la quittent en septembre pour partir hiverner au large des côtes africaines, après avoir donné naissance à un seul petit par couple. Comme près d'un quart des espèces d'oiseaux de la région paléarctique, les fous de Bassan effectuent leur migration à destination de l'Afrique, parcourant plus de 300 km par jour et bravant les risques naturels (vents contraires, prédateurs…) ainsi que les périls résultant des activités humaines (assèchement des milieux, pesticides…). C'est sur l'île d'Eldey que furent exterminés en 1844 les deux derniers spécimens de grand pingouin (Alca impennis), espèce naguère répandue et désormais disparue.

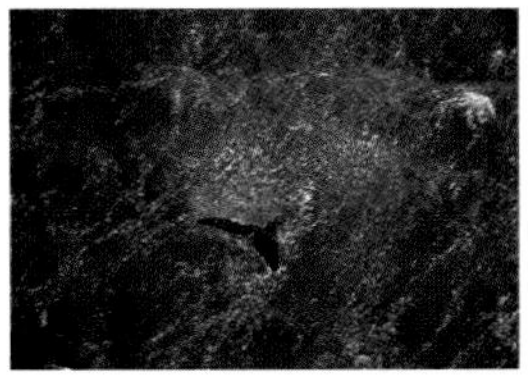

S 42°23' W 64°29'

BALLENA A LO LARGO DE LA PENÍNSULA DE VALDÉS, ARGENTINA.

Tras veranear en el Ártico, las ballenas vuelven a los mares del sur en invierno para reproducirse en ellos. De julio a noviembre, las costas de la península de Valdés, en Argentina, se convierten en el lugar de acoplamiento y de parto de las ballenas francas. Mamífero marino migratorio, la ballena fue víctima hasta los años cincuenta de una explotación intensiva por su carne y el aceite extraído de su grasa, que la ha llevado al borde de la extinción. Medidas de protección acompañan a la toma de conciencia internacional desde 1937. En 1982, se declaró una moratoria prohibiendo la caza con fines comerciales, y en 1994, el santuario ballenero de los mares australes viene a sumarse al del Océano Índico, establecido quince años antes. A pesar de esta movilización, se estima que en 2001 se dio muerte a más de 21 000 ballenas, principalmente por parte de Japón y Noruega, desde la puesta en práctica de la moratoria en 1986. Después de decenios de protección, 7 de las 13 especies de ballenas, que todavía no cuentan más que unos cuantos miles de individuos (10 a 60 veces menos que a principios del siglo xx), siguen estando amenazadas.

WHALE OFF THE VALDÉS PENINSULA, ARGENTINA.

After spending the summer in the Arctic, whales return to the South Seas in winter to reproduce. From July to November, the coasts of the Valdés Peninsula, Argentina, become mating and calving grounds for right whales. The whale, a migratory marine mammal, was a victim of intensive exploitation for its meat and for the oil extracted from its blubber until the fifties, thus bringing it on the brink of extinction. Since 1937, conservation initiatives have accompanied the increasing international awareness. In 1982, a moratorium forbidding hunting for commercial purposes was declared, and in 1994, the South Sea Whale Sanctuary was added to the Indian Ocean Sanctuary, established fifteen years earlier. In spite of this mobilization, it was estimated in 2001 that over 21,000 whales were killed mainly by Japan and Norway, since the moratorium came into effect in 1986. After decades of protection, 7 of the 13 species of whales, comprising only a few thousand individuals (10 to 60 times fewer than at the beginning of the 20th century), are still endangered.

BALEINE AU LARGE DE LA PÉNINSULE DE VALDÉS, ARGENTINE.

Estivant dans l'Arctique, les baleines rejoignent les mers du Sud en hiver pour s'y reproduire. De juillet à novembre, les côtes de la presqu'île de Valdés, en Argentine, deviennent le lieu d'accouplement et de mise bas des baleines franches. Mammifère marin migrateur, la baleine a été victime jusqu'aux années cinquante d'une exploitation intensive pour sa viande et l'huile extraite de sa graisse, qui l'a menée au bord de l'extinction. Des mesures de protection accompagnent la prise de conscience internationale dès 1937. En 1982, un moratoire interdisant la chasse à des fins commerciales est déclaré, et en 1994, le sanctuaire baleinier des mers australes vient s'ajouter à celui de l'Océan indien établi quinze ans plus tôt. En dépit de cette mobilisation, on estime en 2001 que plus de 21 000 baleines ont été tuées, principalement par le Japon et la Norvège, depuis la mise en oeuvre du moratoire en 1986. Après des décennies de protection, 7 des 13 espèces de baleines, qui ne comptent encore que quelques milliers d'individus (10 à 60 fois moins qu'au début du xxe siècle), sont toujours menacées.

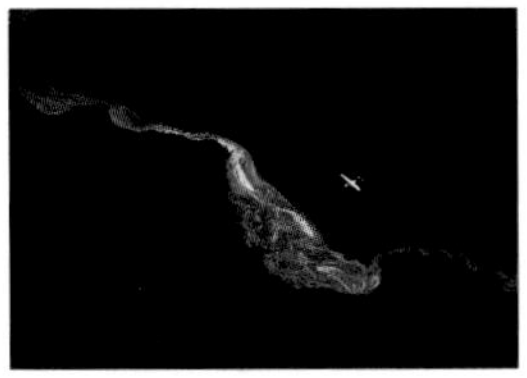

S 1°52' E 36°17'

FORMACIÓN CRISTALINA EN EL LAGO MAGADI, KENYA.

Nacida de un desgarramiento de la corteza terrestre que sobrevino alrededor de 40 millones de años antes de nuestra era, la gran fractura del rift se extiende sobre cerca de 7 000 km al este de África. Bordeada de altas mesetas volcánicas, su vasta fosa de hundimiento, sucesión de depresiones (valles rift) que van del Mar Rojo hasta Mozambique, abriga un rosario de grandes lagos (Turkana, Victoria, Tanganyika, ...) y planos de agua, como el Lago Magadi, el más meridional de Kenya. Alimentado por las aguas de las lluvias que lavan las pendientes volcánicas vecinas arrastrando sales minerales, éste contiene un agua con alto contenido de sal. En diferentes partes, su superficie está marmoleada de licks, depósitos salinos cristalizados mezclados al agua salobre. Aunque inhospitalario, este medio no siempre está exento de vida: millones de flamencos enanos vienen a alimentarse con microalgas, camarones y otros crustáceos que proliferan en las aguas del lago.

CRYSTALLINE FORMATION ON LAKE MAGADI, KENYA.

Produced by a split in the earth's crust that took place 40 million years before our era, the large fracture in the Rift Valley extends over close to 7,000 km (4,350 mi.) in East Africa. Bordered by high volcanic plateaus, its immense fault trough, a succession of depressions (rift valleys or grabens) extending from the Red Sea to Mozambique, harbors a string of large lakes (Lakes Turkana, Victoria, Tanganyika,...) and ponds, such as Lake Magadi, the southernmost lake in Kenya. Fed by rainwater that falls on the neighboring volcanic slopes, washing away the mineral salts, this lake contains water with a high salt content. In places, its surface is veined with licks, crystallized saline deposits mixed with brackish water. Though inhospitable, this environment is not however without life : millions of lesser flamingos come to feed on microalgae, shrimp and other crustaceans proliferating in the waters of the lake.

FORMATION CRISTALLINE SUR LE LAC MAGADI, KENYA.

Née d'une déchirure de la croûte terrestre survenue 40 millions d'années environ avant notre ère, la grande fracture du Rift s'étend sur près de 7 000 km à l'est de l'Afrique. Bordée de hauts plateaux volcaniques, son vaste fossé d'effondrement, succession de dépressions (Rift valleys) allant de la mer Rouge jusqu'au Mozambique, abrite un chapelet de grands lacs (Turkana, Victoria, Tanganyika,...) et de plans d'eau, comme le lac Magadi, le plus méridional du Kenya. Alimenté par les eaux des pluies qui lessivent les pentes volcaniques avoisinantes en emportant des sels minéraux, celui-ci contient une eau à haute teneur en sel. Par endroits, sa surface est marbrée de licks, dépôts salins cristallisés mêlés à l'eau saumâtre. Bien qu'inhospitalier, ce milieu n'est toutefois pas exempt de vie : des millions de petits flamants viennent se nourrir des microalgues, crevettes et autres crustacés qui prolifèrent dans les eaux du lac.

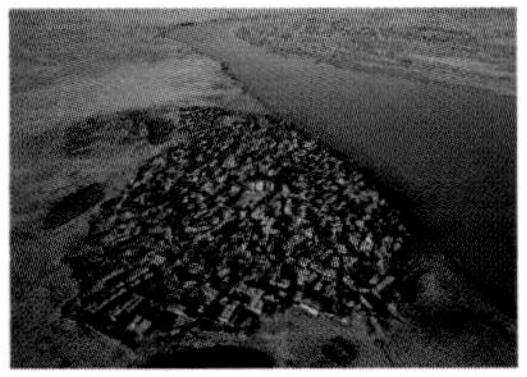

N 14°28' W 4°12'

PUEBLO EN LAS RIBERAS DE UN BRAZO DEL NÍGER, REGIÓN DE MOPTI, MALI.

Al atravesar Mali, el Río Níger se ramifica y forma un vasto delta interior en la planicie de Massina. Con un caudal de 7 000 m^3/s, constituye un maná para los habitantes de esta región árida que, en la mayor parte, se han instalado en las riberas de sus numerosos brazos. Viviendo al ritmo de las crecidas estacionales que sobrevienen entre agosto y enero, los habitantes practican el comercio fluvial, la pesca, la cría de animales y la agricultura. La región de Mopti se ha convertido no sólo en un centro comercial importante, sino igualmente un cruce donde se codean las diversas poblaciones de la región; ahí se encuentran pescadores bozo, pastores nómadas peuls, campesinos bambara, pero también songhais, tuaregs, dogons, tukulores. En este país con un 90% de población musulmana, la mezquita constituye generalmente el edificio central de cada ciudad o pueblo, que domina con su imponente estatura.

VILLAGE ON THE BANKS OF AN ARM OF THE NIGER, NEAR MOPTI, MALI.

As it crosses Mali, the Niger River branches, forming an enormous inland delta in the Massina plain. With a flow of 7,000 cu. m. (1,840 gal.)/sec., it represents a providential resource for the inhabitants of this arid region, who, for the most part, have settled on the banks of its numerous arms. Living at the pace of the seasonal flooding that occurs between August and January, inhabitants practice river trading, fishing, raising livestock and growing crops. The region of Mopti has not only become an important business center but also a crossroads where various populations of the region intermingle; one finds Bozo fishermen, nomadic Peul shepherds, Bambara farmers, but also Songhai, Tuareg, Dogon, and Toucouleur. In this 90% Moslem country, the mosque generally represents the central building. Its imposing stature towers every city or village.

VILLAGE SUR LES RIVES D'UN BRAS DU NIGER, RÉGION DE MOPTI, MALI.

En traversant le Mali, le fleuve Niger se ramifie, formant un vaste delta intérieur dans la plaine de Massina. D'un débit de 7 000 m^3/s, il constitue une manne pour les habitants de cette région aride qui, pour la plupart, se sont installés sur les rives de ses nombreux bras. Vivant au rythme des crues saisonnières qui surviennent entre août et janvier, les habitants pratiquent le commerce fluvial, la pêche, l'élevage et l'agriculture. La région de Mopti est devenue non seulement un centre commercial important mais également un carrefour où se côtoient les diverses populations de la région ; on y rencontre des pêcheurs bozo, des pasteurs nomades peuls, des cultivateurs bambara, mais aussi des Songhaï, des Touareg, des Dogons, des Toucouleurs. Dans ce pays à 90 % musulman, la mosquée constitue généralement le bâtiment central de chaque ville ou village qu'elle domine de sa stature imposante.

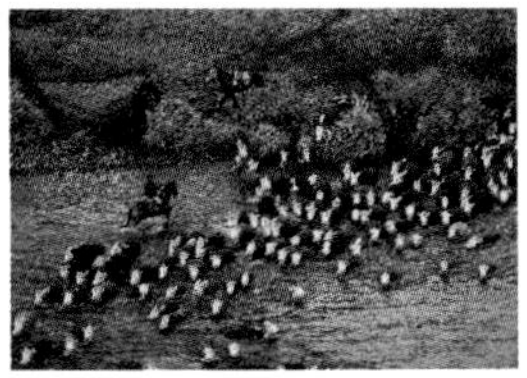

S 40°03' W 71°04'

VADEO DEL RÍO CHIMEHUIN, PROVINCIA DE NEUQUÉN, ARGENTINA.

Atravesando el Río Chimehuin, este rebaño de vacas de raza Hereford, rodeado de gauchos, regresa a su tierra (campo) de origen después de una trashumancia estacional hacia los pastizales de altitud de la cordillera de los Andes. Cubierto en parte de estepa espinosa, el Neuquén ha privilegiado, como el conjunto de la Patagonia la cría de ovinos con respecto a la de los bovinos, que siguen siendo minoritarios en esta región. Más al norte, en las vastas planicies herbosas de la Pampa, es donde vive lo esencial de la cabaña bovina del país, constituido por razas originarias especialmente de Gran Bretaña y que cuenta con cerca de 55 millones de cabezas. Cuarto productor mundial, Argentina exporta al mundo entero su carne de res, afamada por su sabor. Los argentinos, los mayores consumidores del mundo, la degustan en las parrillas, restaurantes especializados, a razón de cerca de 70 kg por habitante al año. Característica en Occidente de un régimen alimenticio "rico", el consumo anual de carne bovina representa 43 kg para un norteamericano, 41 kg para un australiano, contra 4.4 kg para un chino (consumo más que duplicado en cuatro años), 3.4 kg para un filipino, 1.5 kg para un indonesio...

FORDING THE CHIMEHUIN RIVER, NEUQUÉN PROVINCE, ARGENTINA.

Crossing the Chimehuin River, this herd of Hereford cows, flanked by gauchos, is returning to its field (campo) of origin after a seasonal transhumance to the high-altitude pastures of the Cordillera de los Andes. Partly covered by prickly steppe, Neuquén, like the rest of Patagonia, has encouraged sheep rather than cattle raising, which is barely developed in this region. The greater part of the country's cattle population, made up especially of breeds from Great Britain and numbering close to 55 million heads, live farther north in the immense grassy plains of the Pampa. Argentina exports its flavored beef all over the world, making it the fourth largest producer worldwide. Argentineans, among the foremost consumers of beef in the world, enjoy steak dinners at parrillas, or specialized restaurants, at a rate of close to 70 kg per inhabitant per year. Characteristic of a "nutritious" diet in the West, the yearly consumption of beef represents 43 kg (95 lb.) for an American, 41 kg (90 lb.) for an Australian, as opposed to 4.4 kg (9.7 lb.) for a Chinese person (consumption that has more than doubled in four years), 3.4 kg (7.5 lb.) for a Filipino, 1.5 kg (3.3 lb.) for an Indonesian...

PASSAGE À GUÉ DE LA RIVIÈRE CHIMEHUIN, PROVINCE DU NEUQUÉN, ARGENTINE.

Traversant la rivière Chimehuin, ce troupeau de vaches de race Hereford, encadré par des gauchos, rejoint son domaine (campo) d'origine après une transhumance saisonnière vers les pâturages d'altitude de la cordillère des Andes. En partie couvert de steppe épineuse, le Neuquén a privilégié, comme l'ensemble de la Patagonie, l'élevage des ovins par rapport à celui des bovins qui demeurent minoritaires dans cette région. C'est plus au nord, dans les vastes plaines herbeuses de la Pampa, que vit l'essentiel du cheptel bovin du pays, constitué de races originaires notamment de Grande-Bretagne et riche de près de 55 millions de têtes. Quatrième producteur mondial, l'Argentine exporte dans le monde entier sa viande de bœuf réputée savoureuse. Les Argentins, parmi les plus gros consommateurs du monde, la dégustent dans les parillas, restaurants spécialisés, à raison de près de 70 kg par habitant et par an. Caractéristique en Occident d'un régime alimentaire « riche », la consommation annuelle de viande bovine représente 43 kg pour un Américain, 41 kg pour un Australien, contre 4,4 kg pour un Chinois (consommation plus que doublée en quatre ans), 3,4 kg pour un Philippin, 1,5 kg pour un Indonésien...

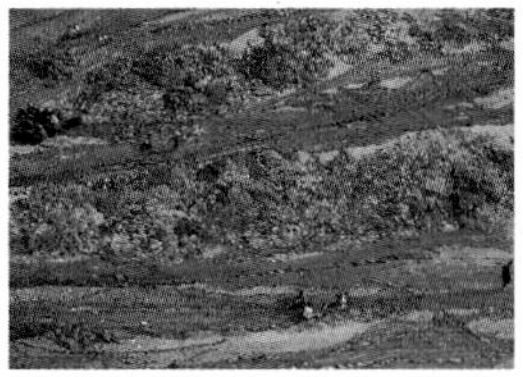

S 40°03' W 71°04'

REDES DE PESCA EN EL PUERTO DE AGADIR, MARRUECOS.

En Agadir, primer puerto pesquero de Marruecos, redes de varios centenares de metros se tienden en el suelo para repararlas antes de las próximas salidas al mar. Con 3 500 km de litoral, el país dispones de importantes recursos halièuticos; sus aguas albergan cerca de 250 especies de peces, especialmente sardinas que migran a lo largo de las costas, aprovechando los upwellings, subidas de aguas ricas en nutrimentos. La pesca marroquí, con sus bous y sus barquitos de motor, se conserva 75% artesanal. Las sardinas constituyen más del 80% de la captura, y Agadir se ha convertido en el primer puerto sardinero del mundo. Desde 1970, la flota mundial de pesca se ha sextuplicado, y la producción se ha duplicado, alcanzando 97 millones de toneladas. Frente a este volumen anual de capturas, los recursos halièuticos disminuyen, y 11 de las 15 grandes zonas de pesca en el mundo están hoy en decadencia. Paralelamente, la producción de la acuicultura ha aumentado de manera espectacular: multiplicada por cuatro en 12 años, asegura el 20% de la producción mundial.

FISHING NETS IN THE PORT OF AGADIR, MOROCCO.

In Agadir, Morocco's most important fishing port, nets several hundred meters long are spread out on the ground in order to be repaired before going out to sea again. With 3,500 km of coastline, the country has important fishing resources; its waters harbor close to 250 species of fish, especially sardines that migrate along the coasts, taking advantage of the upwellings - rising waters rich in nutrients. Moroccan fishing, with its trawlers and small motorboats, remains 75% traditional. Sardines make up over 80% of catches, and Agadir has become the most important port for sardine-fishing in the world. Since 1970, the world fishing fleet has sextupled and production has doubled, reaching 97 million metric tons (107 metric tons). Due to this yearly volume, fishing resources are decreasing, and 11 of the 15 major fishing grounds in the world are declining today. At the same time, the aquaculture production has increased spectacularly. It now represents 20% of world production, providing four times more than 12 years ago.

FILETS DE PÊCHE DANS LE PORT D'AGADIR, MAROC.

À Agadir, premier port de pêche du Maroc, des filets de plusieurs centaines de mètres sont tendus sur le sol pour y être réparés avant les prochaines sorties en mer. Avec 3 500 km de littoral, le pays dispose d'importantes ressources halieutiques ; ses eaux abritent près de 250 espèces de poissons, notamment des sardines qui migrent le long des côtes, profitant des upwellings, remontées d'eaux riches en nutriments. La pêche marocaine, avec ses chalutiers et ses petites barques à moteur, reste à 75 % artisanale. Les sardines constituent plus de 80 % des prises, et Agadir est devenu le premier port sardinier du monde. Depuis 1970, la flotte mondiale de pêche a sextuplé et la production a doublé, atteignant 97 millions de tonnes. Face à ce volume annuel de prises, les ressources halieutiques diminuent, et 11 des 15 grandes zones de pêche dans le monde sont aujourd'hui en déclin. Parallèlement, la production de l'aquaculture a spectaculairement augmenté : multipliée par quatre en 12 ans, elle assure 20 % de la production mondiale.

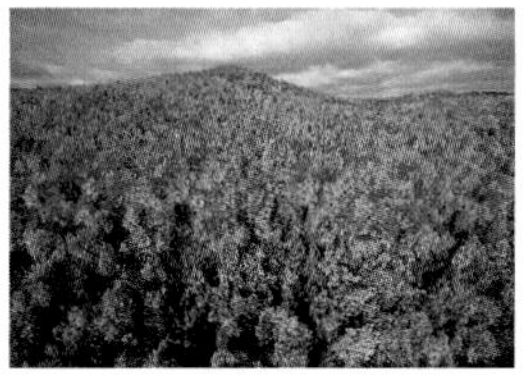

N 47°40' W 71°02'

BOSQUE DE OTOÑO EN LA REGIÓN DE CHARLEVOIX, QUÉBEC, CANADÁ.

Las colinas de la región de Charlevoix, en los bordes del Río San Lorenzo, en Québec, las domina un bosque mixto de frondosos y coníferas, de los cuales 4 600 km^2 fueron clasificados como Reserva de la Biósfera por la UNESCO en 1998. Cubriendo cerca de dos tercios de la provincia, el bosque quebequense, boreal al norte y templado al sur, se explota desde finales del siglo XVII. Actualmente, contribuye a la prosperidad económica de Canadá, que ocupa los lugares primero, segundo y tercero en la producción de papel de periódico, de pulpa de madera y de madera de Suvre. Sobreexplotado por largo tiempo, pero igualmente carcomido por insectos parásitos y lluvias ácidas, el bosque canadiense ha visto disminuir su superficie de manera considerable. No obstante, cubre todavía 2.4 millones de km^2, de los cuales 12% son protegidos. Comprometido desde 1992 en la vía del desarrollo durable de los bosques, Canadá se esfuerza en hacer evolucionar las prácticas forestales hacia una mejor armonización de las expectativas medioambientales, económicas, sociales y culturales expresadas en relación con los bosques.

FALL FOREST IN THE REGION OF CHARLEVOIX, QUEBEC, CANADA.

The hills in the region of Charlevoix, on the shore of the Saint Lawrence River, Quebec, are predominantly covered in a mixed forest of broad-leaved trees and conifers, 4,600 sq. km. (1775 sq. mi.) of which were classified as a Biosphere Reserve by UNESCO in 1988. Covering close to two-thirds of the province, the Quebec forest, boreal in the north and temperate in the south, has been exploited since the end of the 17th century. Today, it contributes to the econmic prosperity of Canada, which ranks first, second and third worldwide for newsprint, pulp and lumber production respectively. Long overexploited but also eaten away by parasitic bugs and by acid rain, the Canadian forest has undergone a considerable decrease in its surface area. However, it still covers 2.4 million sq. km. (0.93 million sq. mi.) today, 12% of which are protected. Having undertaken a commitment to the sustainable development of its forests since 1992, Canada is striving to help forestry practices evolve towards a better harmonization of the environmental, economic, social and cultural expectations concerning forests.

FORÊT D'AUTOMNE DANS LA RÉGION DE CHARLEVOIX, QUÉBEC, CANADA.

Les collines de la région de Charlevoix, en bordure du fleuve Saint-Laurent, au Québec, sont dominées par une forêt mixte de feuillus et de conifères, dont 4 600 km^2 ont été classés comme Réserve de la Biosphère par l'Unesco en 1988. Couvrant près des deux tiers de la province, la forêt québécoise, boréale au nord et tempérée au sud, est exploitée depuis la fin du XVIIe siècle. Aujourd'hui, elle contribue à la prospérité économique du Canada qui occupe les premier, deuxième et troisième rangs mondiaux pour les productions de papier journal, de pâte à papier et de bois d'œuvre. Longtemps surexploitée mais également rongée par des insectes parasites et par les pluies acides, la forêt canadienne a vu sa superficie diminuer de manière considérable. Cependant, elle couvre encore aujourd'hui 2,4 millions de km^2, dont 12 % sont protégés. Engagé depuis 1992 dans la voie du développement durable des forêts, le Canada s'efforce de faire évoluer les pratiques forestières vers une meilleure harmonisation des attentes environnementales, économiques, sociales et culturelles exprimées à l'égard des forêts.

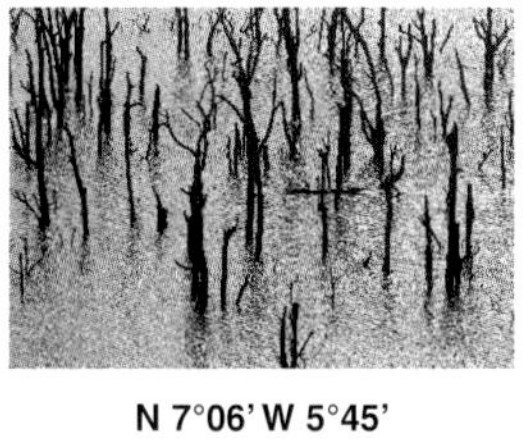

N 7°06' W 5°45'

PESCADOR EN EL LAGO DE KOSSOU CERCA DE BOUAFLÉ, COSTA DE MARFIL.

El Lago de Kossou, que cubre 1 500 km^2 en el centro de Costa de Marfil, es una contención de agua artificial concebida para regular el caudal del Río Bandam y permitir la construcción, hacia abajo, de una presa hidroeléctrica. La inundación de esta zona, realizada entre 1969 y 1971, se hizo al precio de 200 pueblos devorados y de 75 000 personas desplazadas. Paralelamente, un vasto programa de reinstalación de las poblaciones evacuadas y de desarrollo se puso en práctica en la periferia de este lago: construcción de 63 poblados, electrificación, acondicionamiento de centros piscícolas y formación de alrededor 3 000 campesinos de la región en las técnicas de pesca. En 2000, el mundo cuenta con más de 45 000 presas, de las cuales la mitad están en China. Si las presas pueden desempeñar un papel importante en el control de las crecidas y la satisfacción de las necesidades de energía y agua, especialmente en los países en desarrollo donde se encuentran 2/3 de las contenciones, sus impactos ecológicos y sociales (de 40 a 80 millones de personas en el mundo han sido desplazadas para la creación de reservorios) siguen siendo considerables. Una mejor integración de las dimensiones social, ecológica y económica podría no obstante hacer de ellas un verdadero elemento de desarrollo humano y de manejo sustentable de los preciosos recursos de agua.

FISHERMAN ON KOSSOU LAKE CLOSE TO BOUAFLÉ, CÔTE-D'IVOIRE.

Kossou Lake, which covers 1,500 sq. km. in central Côte-d'Ivoire, is an artificial water reservoir conceived to regulate the flow of the Bandama River and to enable the downstream construction of a hydroelectric dam. This zone was flooded between 1969 and 1971, wiping 200 villages out and displacing 75,000 people. Simultaneously, the evacuated populations were relocated, and an extensive development program was implemented : 63 villages were constructed, electricity was provided, fishing centers were installed and approximately 3,000 farmers were trained in fishing techniques. As of 2000, there are over 45,000 dams throughout the world, half of them in China. Although dams can play an important role in flood control and in meeting energy and water needs, especially in the developing countries, where 2/3 of the reservoirs are located, their ecological and social impacts (40 to 80 million people in the world have been displaced in order to create reservoirs) are still substantial. A better integration of the social, ecological and economic dimensions could however make dams a real element of human development and sustainable management of our precious water resources.

PÊCHEUR SUR LE LAC DE KOSSOU PRÈS DE BOUAFLÉ, CÔTE-D'IVOIRE.

Le lac de Kossou, qui couvre 1 500 km^2 au centre de la Côte-d'Ivoire, est une retenue d'eau artificielle conçue pour réguler le débit du fleuve Bandama et permettre la construction, en aval, d'un barrage hydroélectrique. La mise en eau de cette zone, réalisée entre 1969 et 1971, s'est faite au prix de 200 villages engloutis et de 75 000 personnes déplacées. Parallèlement, un vaste programme de réinstallation des populations évacuées et de développement a été mis en place en périphérie de ce lac : construction de 63 villages, électrification, aménagement de centres piscicoles et formation d'environ 3 000 paysans de la région aux techniques de pêche. En 2000, le monde compte plus de 45 000 barrages, dont la moitié en Chine. Si les barrages peuvent jouer un rôle important dans la maîtrise des crues et la satisfaction des besoins en énergie et en eau, notamment dans les pays en développement où se trouvent les 2/3 des retenues, leurs impacts écologiques et sociaux (40 à 80 millions de personnes dans le monde ont été déplacées pour la création de réservoirs) demeurent considérables. Une meilleure intégration des dimensions sociale, écologique et économique pourrait cependant en faire un véritable élément de développement humain et de gestion durable des précieuses ressources en eau.

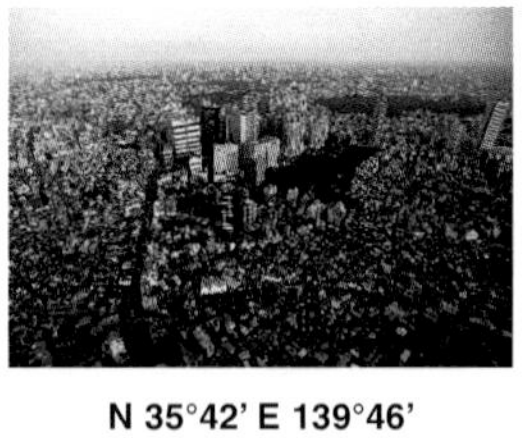

N 35°42' E 139°46'

BARRIO DE SHINJUKU, TOKIO, JAPÓN.

Pueblo de pescadores construido en medio de los pantanos en su origen, Edo se convierte en Tokio, "Capital del Este" en 1868. Sin dejar de agrandarse bajo el impulso de sus comerciantes, la ciudad, devastada por un temblor de tierra en 1923 y por los bombardeos en 1945, renace dos veces de sus cenizas. Hoy, la megalópolis de Tokio (incluyendo Yokohama, Kawasaki, Chiba...) que se extiende de sobre 70 km y cuenta con 28 millones de habitantes (6.4 millones en 1950), se ha convertido en la zona urbana más vasta del mundo. Construida sin esquema global de urbanización, dispone de varios centros que satelizan los diferentes barrios. Shinjuku, barrio de los negocios, está dominado por una serie impresionante de edificios administrativos, entre los cuales está el ayuntamiento, estructura de 243 m de alto inspirada en la Catedral de Nuestra Señora de París. En 1800, sólo Londres superaba el millón de habitantes. Hoy, 326 aglomeraciones del planeta se han unido a ella, de las cuales 180 están en países en desarrollo y 16 megalópolis, como Tokio, cuentan más de 10 millones de residentes. La urbanización, convertida en la tendencia demográfica mayor, ha engendrado la triplicación de la población que vive en la ciudad desde 1950.

DISTRICT OF SHINJUKU, TOKYO, JAPAN.

Originally a fishing village built among marshes, Edo became Tokyo, the "Capital of the East", in 1868. Continuing to expand under impetus from its businessmen, the city, devastated by an earthquake in 1923 and by bombardments in 1945, has twice been reborn from its ashes. Today, the megalopolis of Tokyo (including Yokohama, Kawasaki, Chiba...), which spreads over 70 km and includes 28 million inhabitants (6.4 million in 1950), has become the most extensive urban zone in the world. Constructed without any overall urbanization plan, it has several centers with different district satellites. Shinjuku, the business district, is dominated by an impressive cluster of administrative buildings, one of which is City Hall, a structure 243 m (798 ft) high inspired by Notre-Dame Cathedral in Paris. In 1800, only London had a population in excess of one million inhabitants. Today, 326 urban areas on the planet have caught up, including 180 in developing countries. 16 megalopolises, like Tokyo, have over 10 million residents. Urbanization, which has become the major demographic tendency, has tripled the amount of people living in cities since 1950.

QUARTIER DE SHINJUKU, TOKYO, JAPON.

À l'origine village de pêcheurs bâti au milieu des marécages, Edo devient Tokyo, « Capitale de l'Est », en 1868. Ne cessant de s'agrandir sous l'impulsion de ses commerçants, la ville, dévastée par un tremblement de terre en 1923 et par les bombardements en 1945, renaît par deux fois de ses cendres. Aujourd'hui, la mégalopole de Tokyo (incluant Yokohama, Kawasaki, Chiba...) qui s'étend sur 70 km et compte 28 millions d'habitants (6,4 millions en 1950), est devenue la plus vaste zone urbaine du monde. Construite sans schéma global d'urbanisation, elle dispose de plusieurs centres qui satellisent les différents quartiers. Shinjuku, quartier des affaires, est dominé par un ensemble impressionnant de bâtiments administratifs, parmi lesquels l'hôtel de ville, structure de 243 m de haut inspirée de la cathédrale Notre-Dame de Paris. En 1800, seule Londres dépassait le million d'habitants. Aujourd'hui, 326 agglomérations de la planète l'ont rejointe, dont 180 dans les pays en développement, et 16 mégalopoles, comme Tokyo, comptent plus de 10 millions de résidents. L'urbanisation, devenue la tendance démographique majeure, a engendré le triplement de la population vivant en ville depuis 1950.

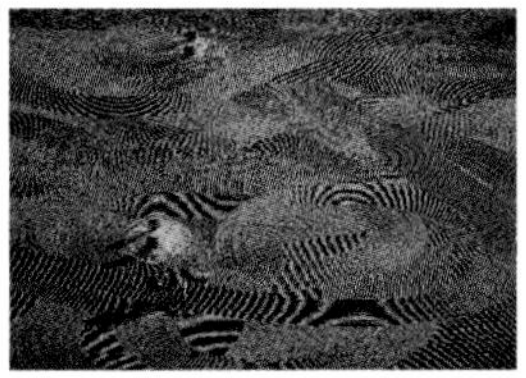

N 36°24' E 10°23'

RONDA DE ENTRENAMIENTO DEL HIPÓDROMO DE MAISONS-LAFFITTE, YVELINES, FRANCIA.

El Hipódromo de Maisons-Laffitte, cerca de París, posee uno de los más importantes centros de entrenamiento hípico de Francia, las pistas y las caballerizas acogen cerca de 800 caballos. En las rondas de entrenamiento - aquí apreciamos la ronda Adam - cotidianamente niveladas por rastrilllaje, los lads calientan a los potros y los preparan para el salto de obstáculos antes de permitirles correr en las pistas de entrenamiento y luego en los campos de carreras. El Hipódromo de Maisons-Laffitte es anualmente el marco de más de 250 carreras, con un total cercano a los 3 000 competidores. Las carreras hípicas constituyen una parte no desdeñable de la industria del juego; más de 100 mil millones de dólares se apuestan a los caballos de carreras cada año en el mundo, cerca de la mitad de esta suma (44 mil millones de dólares) la comprometen los japoneses, primeros apostadores del mundo.

TRAINING RINGS AT THE MAISONS-LAFFITTE RACETRACK, YVELINES, FRANCE.

The Maisons-Laffitte racetrack, close to Paris, houses one of the most important centers for equestrian training in France, with tracks and stables accommodating close to 800 horses. Stable boys warm up the young horses in these training rings - the Adam ring in this case - which are leveled daily by harrows. They train them to obstacle jump and run, before competing on the race course. The Maisons-Laffitte racetrack hosts 250 races annually, amounting to 3,000 starters altogether. Horse races represent a significant part of the gambling industry: more than $100 billion are bet on racehorses every year throughout the world. Nearly half of this sum ($44 billion) is wagered by the Japanese, the world's leading betters.

ROND D'ENTRAÎNEMENT DE L'HIPPODROME DE MAISONS-LAFFITTE, YVELINES, FRANCE.

L'hippodrome de Maisons-Laffitte, près de Paris, possède l'un des plus importants centres d'entraînement hippique de France, les pistes et les écuries accueillant près de 800 chevaux. Dans les ronds d'entraînement - ici le rond Adam - quotidiennement nivelés par hersage, les lads échauffent les jeunes chevaux et les préparent au saut d'obstacles avant de leur permettre de courir sur les pistes d'entraînement, puis sur les champs de courses. L'hippodrome de Maisons-Laffitte est annuellement le cadre de plus de 250 courses, avec au total près de 3 000 partants. Les courses hippiques constituent une part non négligeable de l'industrie du jeu ; plus de 100 milliards de dollars sont misés sur les chevaux de course chaque année dans le monde, près de la moitié de cette somme (44 milliards de dollars) étant engagée par les Japonais, premiers parieurs au monde.

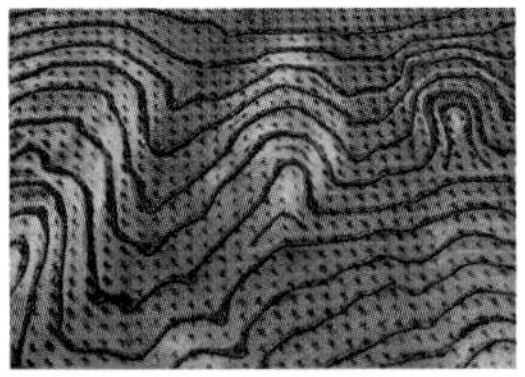

N 8°43' W 2°39'

NUEVAS PLANTACIONES DE OLIVOS, GUBERNORATO DE ZAGHOUAN, TÚNEZ.

Los taludes edificados para retener el agua de chorreo y limitar la erosión subrayan el relieve, a la manera de las curvas de nivel de un mapa. Las plantaciones de olivos se realizan en tierras laborables, frecuentemente en franjas de relieve como ésta en los suelos superficiales llamados "bayoth" al pie de Yebel (1 295 m), situado al noreste de Túnez. Originario del contorno mediterráneo, donde quedan hoy el 90% de los olivos del planeta, este árbol, símbolo de paz, puede vivir hasta 1000 años, y da anualmente de 5 a 30 kg de aceitunas. Su aceite servía antes para alumbrar en lamparitas de arcilla, antes de ser reemplazado por el petróleo. En la actualidad se consumen las aceitunas de mesa y el aceite de olivo, afamado por sus virtudes dietéticas y medicinales, igualmente explotado en cosmetología. La producción de 1 litro de aceite de olivo necesita de 5 a 6 kg de aceitunas. Con un millón de toneladas de aceitunas producidas en 2000, Túnez duplicó su producción de 1997, y se posiciona en el cuarto lugar mundial después de España (4 182 000 toneladas), Italia (2 775 000 toneladas) y Grecia (dos millones de toneladas). Estos países son también los principales consumidores de aceite de olivo: 20 litros por habitante al año en Grecia, 15 litros en España e Italia, y solamente 0.5 litros en Francia.

NEW OLIVE TREE PLANTATIONS, ZAGHWAN GOVERNORATE, TUNISIA.

Embankments built to prevent erosion caused by runoff enhance the landscape, similar to contour lines on a map. Olive tree plantations are established on plowable land, often at the edges of mountains, as seen here on surface soils called "bayoths" at the foot of the Djebel Zaghwan (1,295 m (4,250 ft.) high), situated in northeast Tunisia. Originating from lands surrounding the Mediterranean, where 90% of the planet's olive trees are found today, this tree is a symbol of peace and can live up to 1,000 years, yielding 5 to 30 kg (11 to 66 lb.) of olives annually. Its oil was formerly used in small clay lamps for lighting, before being replaced by kerosene. Today olive oil is well known for its dietary and medicinal virtues and is also exploited in cosmetology. The production of 1 liter (1 quart) of olive oil requires 5 to 6 kg (11 to 13 lb.) of olives. With 1 million metric tons (1.1 million tons) of olives produced in the year 2000, Tunisia doubled its 1997 production, and is now in fourth place worldwide after Spain (4,182,000 metric tons (4,600,000 tons)), Italy (2,775,000 metric tons (3,052,500 tons)) and Greece (2 million metric tons (2.2 million tons)). These countries are also the main consumers of olive oil: 20 liters (1.3 gal.) per inhabitant per year for Greece, 15 liters (4 gal.) in Spain and Italy, and only 0.5 liter (1 pint) in France.

NOUVELLES PLANTATIONS D'OLIVIERS, GOUVERNORAT DE ZAGHOUAN, TUNISIE.

Les talus édifiés pour retenir l'eau de ruissellement et limiter l'érosion soulignent le relief, à la manière des courbes de niveau d'une carte. Les plantations d'oliviers sont effectuées sur des terres labourables, souvent sur des franges de relief comme ici sur des sols superficiels dits « bayoth » au pied du Djebel Zaghouan (1 295m), situé au nord-est de la Tunisie. Originaire du pourtour méditerranéen, où demeurent aujourd'hui 90 % des oliviers de la planète, cet arbre, symbole de paix, peut vivre jusqu'à 1000 ans, et donne annuellement 5 à 30 kg d'olives. Son huile servait jadis dans de petites lampes d'argile pour l'éclairage, avant d'être remplacée par le pétrole. On consomme aujourd'hui les olives de table et l'huile d'olive, réputée pour ses vertus diététiques et médicinales, également exploitée en cosmétologie. La production d'1 litre d'huile d'olive nécessite 5 à 6 kg d'olives. Avec un million de tonnes d'olives produites en 2000, la Tunisie a doublé sa production de 1997, et se positionne au quatrième rang mondial derrière l'Espagne (4 182 000 tonnes), l'Italie (2 775 000 tonnes) et la Grèce (deux millions de tonnes). Ces pays sont aussi les principaux consommateurs d'huile d'olive : 20 litres par habitant et par an pour la Grèce, 15 litres en Espagne et en Italie, et seulement 0,5 litre en France.

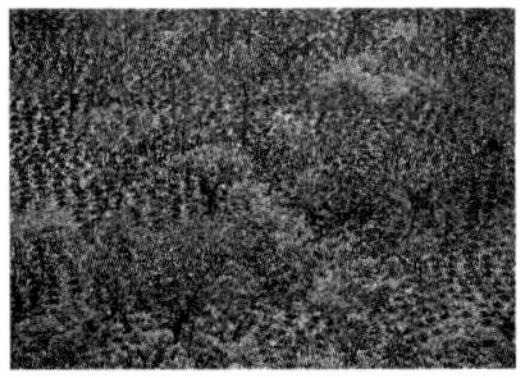

N 8°43' W 2°39'

CULLTIVO DE ÑAMES AL NORTE DE TAGADI, REGIÓN DE BONDOUKOU, COSTA DE MARFIL.

Enterrado según técnicas agrícolas tradicionales bajo montículos de tierra, como en este campo cerca de Bondoukou, al este de Costa de Marfil, el ñame se cultiva para el consumo local en la mayoría de los países tropicales del mundo. En África, este tubérculo rico en almidón y en proteínas, está particularmente extendido en las zonas situadas en el límite septentrional de las regiones boscosas, de Costa de Marfil hasta Camerún. Ingrediente básico de uno de los principales platos de la gastronomía marfileña, el foutou (especie de puré compacto), este feculento está muy presente en la alimentación rural, así como en la citadina, que representa desde ahora cerca de la mitad de la población del país. Costa de Marfil sigue siendo el tercer productor africano de ñames (después de Nigeria, que sola asegura el 70% de la producción africana, y Ghana). En toda África, la agricultura ocupa más del 60% de la población activa, y representa el 40% de los ingresos del continente.

YAM CROP, NORTH OF TAGADI, IN THE REGION OF BONDOUKOU, CÔTE-D'IVOIRE.

Yams are grown for local consumption in most tropical countries of the world. According to traditional farming techniques, they are buried under mounds of earth, as in this field close to Bondoukou, in eastern Côte-d'Ivoire. In Africa, this tuber, which is rich in starch and proteins, is especially common in zones situated at the northern edges of the forest regions, from Côte-d'Ivoire to Cameroon. It is a basic ingredient in foutou (a type of compact purée), one of the main dishes of Ivoirian gastronomy. This starchy food is very common in both the countryside and the city, where now close to half the population of the country lives. Côte-d'Ivoire is still the third greatest yam producer in Africa (after Nigeria - which provides 70% of all African production alone, and Ghana). Throughout Africa, farming is the occupation of over 60% of the labor force, and represents 40% of the incomes on the continent.

CULTURE D'IGNAMES AU NORD DE TAGADI, RÉGION DE BONDOUKOU, CÔTE-D'IVOIRE.

Enfouie selon des techniques agricoles traditionnelles sous des monticules de terre, comme dans ce champ près de Bondoukou, à l'est de la Côte-d'Ivoire, l'igname est cultivée pour la consommation locale dans la plupart des pays tropicaux du monde. En Afrique, ce tubercule, riche en amidon et en protéines, est particulièrement répandu dans les zones situées à la limite septentrionale des régions forestières, de la Côte-d'Ivoire jusqu'au Cameroun. Ingrédient de base d'un des principaux plats de la gastronomie ivoirienne, le foutou (sorte de purée compacte), ce féculent est très présent dans l'alimentation des ruraux comme des citadins, qui représentent désormais près de la moitié de la population du pays. La Côte-d'Ivoire demeure le troisième producteur africain d'ignames (après le Nigeria, qui assure à lui seul 70 % de la production africaine, et le Ghana). Dans toute l'Afrique, l'agriculture occupe plus de 60 % de la population active, et représente 40 % des revenus du continent.

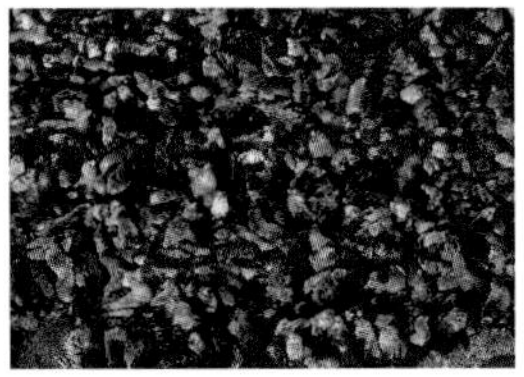

S 34°05' E 18°19'

OTARIAS EN UNA ROCA CERCA DE DUIKER ISLAND, PROVINCIA DEL CABO, REPÚBLICA DE SUDÁFRICA.

Muy gregarias, las otarias - con las que se fabrican abrigos de pieles - de Sudáfrica (Arctocephalus pucillus pucillus) se agrupan en las costas, en colonias de varios centenares de individuos, principalmente para acoplarse y parir. Más cómodas en el medio marino que en tierra firme, estos mamíferos semiacuáticos pasan la mayor parte de su tiempo recorriendo las aguas litorales en busca de alimento: peces, calamares y crustáceos. La especie presente en el Cabo de Buena Esperanza no se encuentra sino en las costas de África austral, del Cabo Cross (Namibia) a la Bahía de Algoa (Sudáfrica), y cuenta 850 000 representantes. Las otarias, 14 especies en total, pertenecen a la familia de los pinnípedos que engloba también 19 especies de focas y una de morsas; presente en la mayoría de los mares, los pinnípedos representan un efectivo total de 50 millones de individuos, de los cuales 45 millones son focas.

SEALS ON A ROCK CLOSE TO DUIKER ISLAND, WESTERN CAPE PROVINCE, REPUBLIC OF SOUTH AFRICA.

South African fur seals (Arctocephalus pucillus pucillus) are very gregarious. They herd together on coasts, mostly to mate and calve, in colonies of several hundred individuals. Preferring a sea environment over dry land, these semi-aquatic mammals spend the greater part of their time traveling through coastal waters in search of food: fish, squid and crustaceans. The species found on the Cape of Good-Hope is only seen on the coasts of South Africa, from Cape Cross (Namibia) to Algoa Bay (South Africa), and includes 850,000 specimens. Eared seals (including fur seals and sea lions), with 14 species in all, belong to the family of pinnipeds, which also include 19 species of true seals and one of walruses; found in most seas, pinnipeds represent a total of 50 million individuals, 45 million of which are true seals.

OTARIES SUR UN ROCHER PRÈS DE DUIKER ISLAND, PROVINCE DU CAP, RÉPUBLIQUE D'AFRIQUE DU SUD.

Très grégaires, les otaries à fourrure d'Afrique du Sud (Arctocephalus pucillus pucillus) se regroupent sur les côtes, en colonies de plusieurs centaines d'individus, principalement pour s'accoupler et mettre bas. Plus à l'aise en milieu marin que sur la terre ferme, ces mammifères semi-aquatiques passent la majeure partie de leur temps à parcourir les eaux littorales en quête de nourriture : poissons, calmars et crustacés. L'espèce présente au cap de Bonne-Espérance ne se rencontre que sur les côtes d'Afrique australe, du cap Cross (Namibie) à la baie d'Algoa (Afrique du Sud), et compte 850 000 représentants. Les otaries, 14 espèces au total, appartiennent à la famille des pinnipèdes qui englobe aussi 19 espèces de phoques et une de morses ; présents dans la plupart des mers, les pinnipèdes représentent un effectif total de 50 millions d'individus, dont 45 millions de phoques.

POBLADO SOBRE PILOTES EN TONGCQUIL, GRUPO DE ISLAS DE SAMALES, FILIPINAS.

N 6° 07' E 121°81'

Al sur de Filipinas, especialmente en el archipiélago de Sulu, en cuyo seno se sitúan las Islas de Samales, viven los badjaos, llamados "gitanos del mar". Si algunos de ellos viven permanentemente en sus barcos, verdaderas casas flotantes, otros ocupan pueblos aislados sobre pilotes, como aquí, donde tallaron un canal en el arrecife coralino con el fin de salir a alta mar a bordo de sus embarcaciones. Viviendo de la cosecha de mariscos y de madreperlas recogidas al zambullirse conteniendo la respiración a profundidades que rebasan los 80 m, este pueblo practica también la pesca y el comercio marítimo. En un número de alrededor de 30 000, los badjaos pertenecen a una minoría musulmana de las Filipinas, los moros, que no representan sino el 4% de la población y se concentran principalmente en la parte sur del país.

TONGCQUIL, VILLAGE ON POLES IN THE SAMALES ISLANDS, PHILIPPINES.

The Samales Islands located in the Sulu archipelago, southern Philippines, are home to the Badjaos, nicknamed "Gypsies of the sea". Although some of them live permanently on their boats, which are floating houses, others live in isolated villages on poles, as seen here, where they have carved a channel in the coral reef in order to reach high sea with their boats. They live off the harvest of shellfish and oyster pearls, by diving to depths of over 80 m (260 ft.) without breathing apparatus, and also traditionally fish and trade. Numbering approximately 30,000, the Badjaos belong to a Muslim minority in the Philippines - the Moro - who represent only 4% of the population and are concentrated mainly in the southern part of the country.

VILLAGE SUR PILOTIS DE TONGCQUIL, GROUPE D'ÎLES DE SAMALES, PHILIPPINES.

Au sud des Philippines, notamment dans l'archipel de Sulu au sein duquel sont situées les îles de Samales, vivent les Badjaos, surnommés « Gitans de la mer ». Si certains d'entre eux habitent en permanence sur leurs bateaux, véritables maisons flottantes, d'autres occupent des villages isolés sur pilotis, comme ici où ils ont taillé un chenal dans le récif corallien afin de rejoindre la haute mer à bord de leurs embarcations. Vivant de la récolte de coquillages et d'huîtres perlières prélevées en plongeant en apnée jusqu'à des profondeurs dépassant 80 m, ce peuple pratique aussi la pêche et le commerce maritime. Au nombre d'environ 30 000, les Badjaos appartiennent à une minorité musulmane des Philippines, les Moros, qui ne représentent que 4 % de la population et sont principalement concentrés dans la partie sud du pays.

ACANTILADOS DE INISHMORE, ISLAS DE ARAN, CONDADO DE CLARE, IRLANDA.

N 53°7' W 9°45'

A lo largo de las costas irlandesas, las Islas de Aran, Inishmore, Inishman e Inisheer, cuyos acantilados alcanzan 90 m de altura, protegen la bahía de Galway de los vientos y las corrientes violentas del Atlántico. Inishmore, la mayor (14.5 km por 4 km). Es también la más poblada, con cerca de un millar de habitantes. Desde hace siglos, las poblaciones mismas han contribuido a fertilizar el suelo de estas islas al esparcir regularmente en la roca una mezcla de arena y algas destinada a constituir la delgada capa de humus necesaria para la agricultura. Con el fin de proteger sus parcelas de la erosión eólica, los isleños han construido una vasta red de muros rompevientos, que representan en total cerca de 12 000 km, que da a estas tierras la apariencia de un gigantesco mosaico. Obteniendo lo esencial de sus recursos de la pesca, de la agricultura y de la ganadería, las Islas de Aran acogen un número creciente de turistas, atraídos especialmente por los numerosos vestigios arqueológicos.

INISHMORE CLIFFS, ARAN ISLANDS, COUNTY CLARE, IRELAND.

Off the Irish coasts, the Aran Islands - Inishmore, Inishmaan and Inisheer, whose cliffs reach a height of 90 m (300 ft.), protect Galway Bay from the winds and the strong currents of the Atlantic. Inishmore, the largest in area (14.5 km by 4 km (10 x 2,5 mi.), is also the most populated, with close to a thousand inhabitants. For centuries, the populations have helped fertilize these islands' soil by regularly spreading a mixture of sand and algae intended to form the thin humus layer necessary for farming, over the rock. In order to protect their parcels from wind erosion, the islanders have constructed a vast network of low stone walls as a windbreak, representing altogether close to 12,000 km (7,500 mi.), which gives these lands the appearance of a giant mosaic. Drawing the greater part of their resources from fishing, farming and raising livestock, the Aran Islands are welcoming an increasing number of tourists, attracted particularly by the many archaeological remains.

FALAISES D'INISHMORE, ÎLES D'ARAN, COMTÉ DE CLARE, IRLANDE.

Au large des côtes irlandaises, les îles d'Aran - Inishmore, Inishmaan et Inisheer, dont les falaises atteignent 90 m de hauteur, protègent la baie de Galway des vents et des courants violents de l'Atlantique. Inishmore, la plus grande (14,5 km sur 4 km), est aussi la plus peuplée, avec près d'un millier d'habitants. Depuis des siècles, les populations ont elles-mêmes contribué à fertiliser le sol de ces îles en épandant régulièrement sur la roche un mélange de sable et d'algues destiné à constituer la mince couche d'humus nécessaire à l'agriculture. Afin de protéger leurs parcelles de l'érosion éolienne, les îliens ont construit un vaste réseau de murets brise-vent, représentant au total près de 12 000 km, qui donne à ces terres l'apparence d'une gigantesque mosaïque. Tirant l'essentiel de leurs ressources de la pêche, de l'agriculture et de l'élevage, les îles d'Aran accueillent un nombre croissant de touristes, attirés notamment par de nombreux vestiges archéologiques.

TRABAJOS DE LOS CAMPOS AL NORTE DE JODHPUR, RAJASTHAN, INDIA.

N 26°22' E 73°02'

Segundo estado indio por su superficie (342 240 km²), Rajasthan, al noroeste del país, está cubierto en un 65% de formaciones desérticas arenosas. La rareza de las aguas de superficie es grandemente responsable de la baja productividad de las tierras. No obstante, la irrigación, que beneficia al 27% de las tierras cultivables en India, ha permitido desarrollar la agricultura del mijo, el sorgo, el trigo y la cebada. La cosecha de estos cereales, al final de la estación de la seca, es una tarea que incumbe generalmente a las mujeres, quienes, incluso cuando trabajan en los campos, se tocan con el tradicional orhni, largo chal de color vivo específico de la región. La agricultura india suministra 1/4 del PIB y ocupa más de la mitad del territorio. El país cosecha cada año alrededor de 220 millones de toneladas de cereales, es decir, más de un décimo de la producción mundial, y se coloca en el 2º lugar mundial en cuanto al trigo y al arroz. Pero la batalla, añeja ya, entre el aumento de la producción y el crecimiento demográfico va a tener que integrar ahora el manejo de las reservas de agua subterráneas, que están mermando y sufren los azares climáticos como la severa sequía de abril de 2000 que afectó a 20 millones de personas en Rajasthan.

WORKING IN THE FIELDS, NORTH OF JODHPUR, RAJASTHAN, INDIA.

Second largest Indian state in area (342,240 sq. km.), 65% of Rajasthan, located in the northwestern part of the country, is covered by sandy, desert formations. The scarcity of surface waters is largely responsible for the low productivity of these lands. However, irrigation, which benefits 27% of the arable lands in India, makes it possible to cultivate millet, sorghum, wheat and barley. Harvesting these cereals at the end of the dry season, is generally a task for women, who, even when working in the fields, wear the traditional orhni, a long, bright-colored shawl typical of the region. Indian agriculture provides 1/4th of the GDP and takes up more the half the territory. The country harvests about 220 million metric tons (242 million tons) of cereals annually, or more than a tenth of the world production, and is the second producer worldwide for wheat and rice. Nevertheless, the age-old battle between increasing agricultural production and using land for population growth will now have to take into account the management of underground water reserves, which are diminishing and subject to climatic hazards such as the severe drought of April 2000, which affected 20 million people in Rajasthan.

TRAVAUX DES CHAMPS AU NORD DE JODHPUR, RAJASTHAN, INDE.

Deuxième État indien par sa superficie (342 240 km²), le Rajasthan, au nord-ouest du pays, est à 65 % couvert de formations désertiques sableuses. La rareté des eaux de surface est grandement responsable de la faible productivité des terres. Cependant l'irrigation, qui profite à 27 % des terres cultivables en Inde, a permis de développer l'agriculture du millet, du sorgho, du blé et de l'orge. La récolte de ces céréales, à la fin de la saison sèche, est une tâche incombant généralement aux femmes qui, même lors des travaux des champs, sont coiffées du traditionnel orhni, long châle de couleur vive spécifique à la région. L'agriculture indienne fournit 1/4 du PIB et occupe plus de la moitié du territoire. Le pays récolte chaque année environ 220 millions de tonnes de céréales, soit plus d'un dixième de la production mondiale, et se place au 2e rang mondial pour le blé et le riz. Mais la bataille déjà ancienne entre l'augmentation de la production et l'accroissement démographique va maintenant devoir intégrer la gestion des réserves d'eau souterraines, qui s'amenuisent et subissent les aléas climatiques comme la sévère sécheresse d'avril 2000 qui a affecté 20 millions de personnes dans le Rajasthan.

CRÁTER METEÓRICO GOSSES BLUFF, TERRITORIO DEL NORTE, AUSTRALIA.

S 23°49' E 132°19'

Hace alrededor de 135 millones de años, la caída de un meteorito en el suelo australiano devastó más de 20 km² en el actual Territorio del Norte. Actualmente queda de ello un cráter de 5 km de diámetro y 150 m de alto, el Gosses Bluff, también llamado Tnorala por los aborígenes. Las caídas de meteoritos de poco tamaño en la tierra son fenómenos frecuentes, que se producen miles de veces cada año. Generalmente, de un diámetro inferior a un metro, no causan estragos, puesto que se fragmentan y arden en el momento de su entrada en la atmósfera y alcanzan el suelo en forma de polvo. En cambio, aunque rara y aleatoria, la llegada de meteoritos de un diámetro superior a 10 m puede causar estragos importantes. Los más grandes de entre unos 150 cráteres de impacto conocidos alcanzan 200 km de diámetro. Si la extinción masiva de especies que sobrevino hace alrededor de 65 millones de años y que eliminó los dinosaurios del planeta se atribuye, según una hipótesis recientemente propuesta, al impacto devastador de un asteroide, ésta que se desarrolla en la actualidad, la más importante desde entonces, es imputable a la acción del hombre.

GOSSES BLUFF METEORIC CRATER, NORTHERN TERRITORY, AUSTRALIA.

Close to 135 million years ago, a meteorite hit Australian soil devastating more than 20 sq. km. of what is now the Northern Territory. Today, Gosses Bluff, also called Tnorala by the Aborigines, bares testimony to this event, with a crater 5 km (3 mi.) in diameter and 150 m (570 ft) high. Small-size meteorites that hit the earth are a frequent phenomenon that occurs thousands of times a year. Generally less than one meter in diameter, they do not provoke any damage since they fragment and burn up as they enter the atmosphere, and fall to the ground in the form of dust. On the other hand, meteorites over 10 m (33 ft) in diameter, though rare and random, can provoke considerable damage. Of about 150 known craters resulting from these impacts, the largest ones can reach up to 200 km (124 mi.) in diameter. While the massive extinction of species that occurred nearly 65 million years ago and eliminated dinosaurs from the planet is attributed to the devastating impact of an asteroid (according to a recently proposed hypothesis), the current one, the greatest since that time, is due to human activity.

CRATÈRE MÉTÉORIQUE GOSSES BLUFF, TERRITOIRE DU NORD, AUSTRALIE.

Il y a environ 135 millions d'années, la chute d'une météorite sur le sol australien a dévasté plus de 20 km² dans l'actuel territoire du Nord. Il en reste aujourd'hui un cratère de 5 km de diamètre et 150 m de haut, le Gosses Bluff, aussi appelé Tnorala par les Aborigènes. Les chutes de météorites de petite taille sur terre sont des phénomènes fréquents, se produisent des milliers de fois chaque année. Généralement d'un diamètre inférieur à un mètre, elles ne provoquent pas de dégâts puisqu'elles se fragmentent et brûlent lors de leur entrée dans l'atmosphère et atteignent le sol sous forme de poussière. En revanche, bien que rare et aléatoire, l'arrivée de météorites d'un diamètre supérieur à 10 m peut provoquer des dégâts importants. Les plus grands des quelque 150 cratères d'impact connus atteignent 200 km de diamètre. Si l'extinction massive d'espèces survenue il y a environ 65 millions d'années et qui élimina les dinosaures de la planète est attribuée, selon une hypothèse récemment avancée, à l'impact dévastateur d'un astéroïde, celle qui se déroule aujourd'hui, la plus importante depuis, est imputable à l'action de l'homme.

ISLOTE EN LOS ARROZALES EN TERRAZAS DE BALI, INDONESIA.

S 8°34' E 115°13'

Organizados en subaks (cooperativas agrícolas), los balineses ha explotado el relieve volcánico y las cerca de 150 corrientes de agua de su isla acondicionando un vasto sistema de irrigación que permite practicar el cultivo del arroz. El agua retenida en las colinas es conducida a los campos en terrazas por un red de canales surcados según las curvas de nivel. Considerado como un don de los dioses por los agricultores indonesios, el arroz da lugar a un verdadero ritual religioso: en cada etapa de la cosecha, se depositan ofrendas en los templos edificados en medio de los arrozales en honor de Dewi Sri, diosa de este cereal. La introducción, en 1976, de una nueva variedad de crecimiento rápido permitió pasar de dos a tres cosechas anuales, y el país se coloca actualmente en el tercer lugar mundial de los productores (51 millones de toneladas en 2000, es decir, 8% de la producción total del planeta), después de China e India.

ISLET IN TERRACED RICE FIELDS IN BALI, INDONESIA.

Organized in subaks (farming cooperatives), the Balinese have exploited the volcanic mountainsides and the 150 or so rivers on their island by installing a vast irrigation system that makes rice-growing possible. The water collected in the hills is conveyed to terraced fields through a network of canals dug along contour levels. Considered a gift from the gods by Indonesian farmers, rice is the motive for an authentic religious ritual: at each stage of the harvest, offerings are placed in temples built in the middle of the rice-fields to honor Dewi Sri, the goddess of this cereal. The introduction in 1976 of a new, fast-growing variety made it possible to increase the harvests from two to three per year, and the country is today the third producer worldwide after China and India (51 million metric tons (56 million tons) in 2000, or 8% of the total production on the planet).

ILOT DANS LES RIZIÈRES EN TERRASSE DE BALI, INDONÉSIE.

Organisés en subaks (coopératives agricoles), les Balinais ont exploité le relief volcanique et les quelque 150 cours d'eau de leur île en aménageant un vaste système d'irrigation qui permet de pratiquer la riziculture. L'eau retenue dans les collines est conduite dans les champs en terrasse par un réseau de canaux creusés selon les courbes de niveau. Considéré comme un don des dieux par les agriculteurs indonésiens, le riz donne lieu à un véritable rituel religieux: à chaque étape de la récolte, des offrandes sont déposées dans les temples édifiés au milieu des rizières en l'honneur de Dewi Sri, déesse de cette céréale. L'introduction, en 1976, d'une nouvelle variété à croissance rapide a permis de passer de deux à trois récoltes annuelles, et le pays se place aujourd'hui au troisième rang mondial des producteurs (51 millions de tonnes en 2000, soit 8 % de la production totale de la planète), après la Chine et l'Inde.

PLANTACIÓN DE PALMERAS DE ACEITE, REGIÓN DE KUALA, MALASIA.

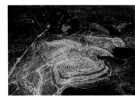

N 3°14' E 101°58'

Originarias de África occidental, las palmeras de aceite se introdujeron en Malasia en los años 1970 con el fin de diversificar una actividad agrícola que descansa casi exclusivamente en el cultivo de las heveas. Al sustituir a la selva ecuatorial en más de 27 000 km2 en 30 años, es decir, el 8% del país, estas palmeras se cultivan en las pendientes de las colinas, acondicionadas en terrazas que siguen las curvas de nivel con el fin de evitar la erosión provocada por el chorreo del agua. Clasificada en primer lugar de los países productores y exportadores, Malasia suministra la mitad del aceite de palma que se consume en el mundo. En 1999 el aceite de palma produjo más de 3.5 mil millones de dólares a Malasia, es decir, un aumento del 100% en 10 años. Los intereses económicos a corto plazo son tales, que rebasan por mucho las preocupaciones ecológicas vinculadas a la desaparición de la cubierta forestal. Este aceite, cuya producción mundial se ha cuadruplicado en 20 años, se ha convertido en el segundo cuerpo graso vegetal más utilizado después del aceite de soya. Destinado principalmente a la alimentación, entra igualmente en la fabricación de jabones, cosméticos y productos farmacéuticos.

OIL PALM PLANTATION, NEAR KUALA, MALAYSIA.

Originating from West Africa, oil palms were introduced to Malaysia in the 1970's in order to diversify a farming activity that depended nearly exclusively on rubber tree growing. Replacing the equatorial forest over more than 27,000 sq. km. (about 17,000 sq. mi.) in 30 years, or 8% of the country, these palm trees are cultivated on hillsides arranged in terraces according to contour lines, in order to prevent erosion caused by run-off. Ranking in first place among producing and exporting countries, Malaysia provides half the palm oil consumed around the world. In 1999, palm oil brought over $3.5 billion to Malaysia, or an increase of 100% in 10 years. The short-term economic interests outweigh any ecological concern about the disappearance of the forest. This oil, whose world production has quadrupled in 20 years, has become the second most used vegetable fat after soy oil. Mainly intended for food, it is also used in the manufacture of soaps, cosmetics and pharmaceutical products.

PLANTATION DE PALMIERS À HUILE, RÉGION DE KUALA, MALAISIE.

Originaires d'Afrique occidentale, les palmiers à huile ont été introduits en Malaisie dans les années 1970 afin de diversifier une activité agricole reposant presque exclusivement sur la culture d'hévéas. Se substituant à la forêt équatoriale sur plus de 27 000 km2 en 30 ans, soit 8 % du pays, ces palmiers sont cultivés sur les pentes des collines, aménagées en terrasses suivant les courbes de niveau afin d'éviter l'érosion provoquée par le ruissellement de l'eau. Classée au premier rang des pays producteurs et exportateurs, la Malaisie fournit la moitié de l'huile de palme consommée dans le monde. En 1999, l'huile de palme a rapporté plus de 3,5 milliards de dollars à la Malaisie, soit une augmentation de 100 % en 10 ans. Les intérêts économiques à court terme sont tels qu'ils dépassent de loin les préoccupations écologiques liées à la disparition du couvert forestier. Cette huile, dont la production mondiale a quadruplé en 20 ans, est devenue la deuxième corps gras végétal le plus utilisé après l'huile de soja. Principalement destinée à l'alimentation, elle entre également dans la fabrication de savons, cosmétiques et produits pharmaceutiques.

BARCO ENCALLADO AL NORTE DE LA ISLA DE ZAKINTOS (ZANTE), ISLAS JÓNICAS, GRECIA.

N 37°54' E 20°39'

A 16 km a lo largo de las costas del Peloponeso, Zante, la más meridional de las Islas Jónicas y la segunda por su superficie, debe su nombre a la abundancia de jacintos salvajes que se desarrollan ahí. Una parte de la isla presenta imponentes acantilados calizos veteados de yeso blanco que bajo el efecto de la erosión y de numerosos temblores de tierra, de los cuales el más importante tuvo lugar en 1953, se desmoronaron para dar nacimiento a playas de arena fina. La densidad de las posturas de las tortugas marinas careyes (*Caretta caretta*) en esta playas es una de las más elevadas del mundo. No obstante, las hélices de los barcos, la contaminación, la urbanización de las costas y los trastornos causados por los turistas, han hecho que cayeran los efectivos de tortugas marinas que vienen a reproducirse en la Isla de Zakinthos, de cerca de 2 000 individuos a finales de los años 1980 a menos de un millar a finales de los años 1990. Las medidas de conservación y la sensibilización del público, emprendidas desde 1981, apenas comienzan a dar frutos. Algunas especies emblemáticas amenazadas, como las tortugas marinas, se benefician de vastos programas de protección, pero no representan sino la punta del iceberg: un cuarto de las especies de mamíferos y 12% de las especies de aves del planeta están actualmente bajo amenaza de extinción.

BOAT ABANDONED IN THE NORTHERN PART OF THE ISLAND OF ZÁKINTHOS (ZANTE), IONIAN ISLANDS, GREECE.

Zante, 16 km (10 mi.) off the coasts of Peloponnisos, the southernmost of the Ionian Islands and second largest, owes its name to the abundance of wild hyacinth that grow there. Part of the island exhibits imposing calcareous cliffs, with veins of white gypsum. They have been crumbling under the effect of erosion and several earthquakes - the most important occurred in 1953 - creating beaches of fine sand, where egg-laying by loggerhead sea turtles (*Caretta caretta*) is one of the most dense in the world. However boat propellers, pollution, urbanization of the coasts and inconveniences caused by tourists have caused the decline of the population of marine turtles who come to reproduce on the island of Zákinthos. Their number fell from almost 2,000 specimens at the end of the 1980's, to less than a thousand at the end of the 1990's. Conservation measures and campaigns to increase public awareness, undertaken since 1981, are just beginning to bear fruit. Some token endangered species, such as sea turtles, benefit from vast protective programs, but they only represent the tip of the iceberg: one-quarter of all mammals and 12% of all bird species on the planet are in danger of extinction today.

BATEAU ÉCHOUÉ AU NORD DE L'ÎLE DE ZAKINTHOS (ZANTE), ÎLES IONIENNES, GRÈCE.

À 16 km au large des côtes du Péloponnèse, Zante, la plus méridionale des îles Ioniennes et la deuxième par sa superficie, doit son nom à l'abondance des jacinthes sauvages qui s'y développent. Une partie de l'île présente d'imposantes falaises calcaires veinées de gypse blanc qui, sous l'effet de l'érosion et de plusieurs tremblements de terre, dont le plus important eut lieu en 1953, se sont effritées pour donner naissance à des plages de sable fin. La densité de ponte des tortues marines caouannes (*Caretta caretta*) sur ces plages est l'une des plus élevées du monde. Cependant les hélices des bateaux, la pollution, l'urbanisation des côtes et les dérangements occasionnés par les touristes, ont fait chuter les effectifs de tortues marines venant se reproduire sur l'île de Zakinthos, de près de 2 000 individus à la fin des années 1980, à moins d'un millier à la fin des années 1990. Les mesures de conservation et la sensibilisation du public, entreprises dès 1981, commencent seulement à porter leurs fruits. Quelques espèces emblématiques menacées, comme les tortues marines, bénéficient de vastes programmes de protection, mais elles ne représentent que la partie émergée de l'iceberg: un quart des espèces de mammifères et 12 % des espèces d'oiseaux de la planète sont aujourd'hui menacées d'extinction.

COSECHA DE TRIGO EN LA REGIÓN DE MATHURA, UTTAR PRADESH, INDIA.

N 27°21' E 77°51'

Beneficiándose de terrenos aluviales irrigados permanentemente por las aguas del Ganges y de sus numerosos afluentes perennes que alimentan las nieves del Himalaya, la planicie del norte de India, en la cual se encuentra el estado de Uttar Pradesh, es la región más fértil del país. Su clima, marcado por inviernos templados y veranos calurosos y húmedos, contribuye igualmente a hacer de ella una de las regiones agrícolas más importantes del territorio. Muy cultivado en la región para el mercado interior, el trigo, como aquí, cerca de Mathura, lo cosechan manualmente las mujeres al final de la estación de la seca. Con una producción de 74 millones de toneladas en 2000 (12% de la cosecha mundial), India se coloca en el 2° lugar mundial, justo entre China y Estados Unidos. Desde 1960, el consumo global de cereales, destinado a la alimentación humana y a la cría de animales, se ha más que duplicado. No obstante, representa menos de 200 kg al año por persona en India (principalmente bajo la forma de arroz), mientras que un norteamericano consume, indirectamente, el equivalente de 900 kg de cereales cada año, bajo la forma de productos animales (carne o lácteos).

HARVESTING WHEAT NEAR MATHURA, UTTAR PRADESH, INDIA.

Uttar Pradesh is located in the northern Indian plain. Benefiting from alluvial lands permanently irrigated by the waters of the Ganges and its numerous perennial tributaries that are fed by the snows of the Himalayas, it is the most fertile region in the country. Its climate, characterized by mild winters and hot, humid summers, also contributes towards making it one of the most important agricultural regions in this territory. Extensively grown in the region for domestic markets, wheat is harvested manually by women at the end of the dry season, as seen here, close to Mathura. With a production of 74 million metric tons (81 million tons) in 2000 (12% of the world harvest), India ranks 2nd worldwide, just between China and the United States. Since 1960, the global consumption of cereals, intended for human food and for livestock, has more than doubled. However, this represents less than 200 kg (440 lb) per year per person in India (mainly in the form of rice), whereas an American consumes, indirectly, the equivalent of 900 kg (1,980 lb) of cereals every year, in the form of animal products (meat or milk).

RÉCOLTE DE BLÉ DANS LA RÉGION DE MATHURA, UTTAR PRADESH, INDE.

Bénéficiant de terrains alluviaux irrigués en permanence par les eaux du Gange et de ses nombreux affluents pérennes qu'alimentent les neiges de l'Himalaya, la plaine du nord de l'Inde, dans laquelle se trouve l'État de l'Uttar Pradesh, est la région la plus fertile du pays. Son climat, marqué par des hivers doux et des étés chauds et humides, contribue également à en faire l'une des plus importantes régions agricoles du territoire. Très cultivé dans la région pour le marché intérieur, le blé est, comme ici près de Mathura, récolté manuellement par les femmes à la fin de la saison sèche. Avec une production de 74 millions de tonnes en 2000 (12 % de la récolte mondiale), l'Inde se place au 2° rang mondial, juste entre la Chine et les Etats-Unis. Depuis 1960, la consommation globale de céréales, destinée à l'alimentation humaine et aux élevages, a plus que doublé. Cependant, elle représente moins de 200 kg par an et par personne en Inde (principalement sous forme de riz), alors qu'un Américain consomme, indirectement, l'équivalent de 900 kg de céréales chaque année, sous forme de produits animaux (viande ou laitages).

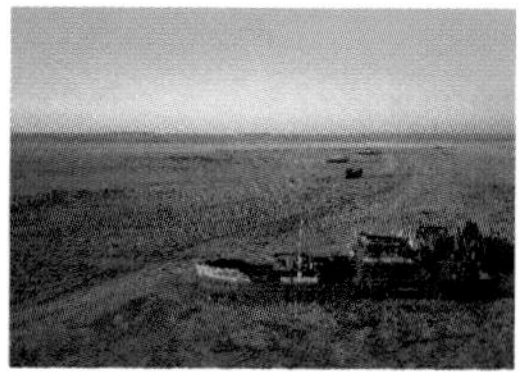

N 46°39' E 61°11'

BARCO ENCALLADO, MAR DE ARAL, REGIÓN DE ARAL'SK, KAZAJSTÁN.

En la primera parte de este siglo, el Mar de Aral, en Kazajstán, alcanzó una superficie de 66 500 km^2 que lo situaba por su importancia en el cuarto lugar mundial de los lagos endorreicos (o mares interiores); por otra parte, la pesca de arrastre se practicaba corrientemente en él. Después de la construcción, en los años 60, de una vasta red de irrigación destinada al monocultivo del algodón de la región, el caudal de las corrientes de agua Amú Daryá y Syr Daryá, que alimentaban el Mar de Aral, disminuyó de manera inquietante; el mar perdió el 50% de su superficie, el 75% de su volumen de agua, y sus bordes se retiraron de 60 a 80 km. Consecuencia directa de la disminución hídrica, su salinidad no ha dejado de aumentar en el curso de los últimos treinta años, para alcanzar en la actualidad 30 g/l, es decir, tres veces su concentración original de sal, trayendo consigo especialmente la desaparición de más de una veintena de variedades de peces. Adicionalmente, los polvos salados, llevados por el viento, queman toda vegetación en varios centenares de kilómetros a la redonda, y contribuyen así a la desertización de los medios. Si es uno de los más conocidos, el ejemplo del Mar de Aral no es único: 600 000 km^2 de tierras irrigadas en el mundo, de las cuales 75% están en Asia, estarían afectadas por un exceso de sal que reduce su productividad agrícola.

SHIPWRECK, ARAL SEA, NEAR ARAL'SK, KAZAKSTAN.

In the first part of this century, the Aral Sea in Kazakstan reached a surface area of 66,500 sq. km. (25,700 sq. mi.), making it the fourth widest endorheic lake (or inland sea) in the world, where dragnet fishing was commonly practiced. After the construction in the 60's of a huge irrigation network intended for the cotton monoculture in the region, the flow of the Amu Darya and Syr Darya rivers, which used to feed the Aral Sea, decreased to an alarming degree. The sea lost 50% of its surface area, 75% of its volume of water, and its shores receded by 60 to 80 km. (35 to 50 mi.). As a direct consequence of this water reduction, its saltiness has continued to increase over the last thirty years, reaching a level of 30 g/l today, three times its original salt concentration, which caused the disappearance of more than twenty species of fish. Moreover, the salty dusts carried by the winds, burnt all surrounding vegetation for several hundreds of kilometers, thus contributing to the desertification of the surrounding areas. Though one of the best known examples, the Aral Sea is not unique: 600,000 sq. km. (231,600 sq. mi.) of lands irrigated around the world, including 75% in Asia, are said to be affected by an excess of salt, thus reducing their agricultural productivity.

BATEAU ÉCHOUÉ, MER D'ARAL, RÉGION D'ARALSK, KAZAKHSTAN.

Dans la première partie de ce siècle, la mer d'Aral, au Kazakhstan, atteignait une superficie de 66 500 km^2 qui la situait par son importance au quatrième rang mondial des lacs endoréiques (ou mers intérieures) ; la pêche au chalut y était d'ailleurs couramment pratiquée. Après la construction, dans les années 60, d'un vaste réseau d'irrigation destiné à la monoculture du coton de la région, le débit des cours d'eau Amou Daria et Syr Daria, qui alimentaient la mer d'Aral, a diminué de manière inquiétante ; la mer a perdu 50 % de sa superficie, 75 % de son volume en eau, et ses bords se sont retirés de 60 à 80 km. Conséquence directe de la diminution hydrique, sa salinité n'a cessé d'augmenter au cours des trente dernières années, pour atteindre aujourd'hui 30 g/l, soit trois fois sa concentration originelle en sel, entraînant notamment la disparition de plus d'une vingtaine d'espèces de poissons. De plus, les poussières salées, portées par les vents, brûlent toute végétation sur plusieurs centaines de kilomètres alentour, contribuant ainsi à la désertification des milieux. S'il est l'un des plus connus, l'exemple de la mer d'Aral n'est pas unique : 600 000 km^2 de terres irriguées dans le monde, dont 75 % en Asie, seraient touchés par un excès de sel réduisant leur productivité agricole.

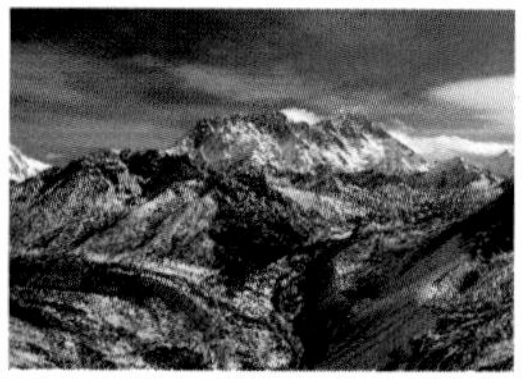

N 27°59' E 86°56'

MONTE EVEREST, HIMALAYA, NEPAL.

En el macizo del Himalaya, que forma la frontera entre Nepal y China, el Monte Everest es la cumbre más elevada del planeta, con una altitud de 8 848 m. Si los occidentales le dieron el nombre del coronel británico George Everest, encargado de establecer el trazo cartográfico de India, los nepaleses, en cambio, lo llaman Sagarmatha, "aquel cuya cabeza toca el cielo", y los chinos Jomolungma, nombre derivado del tibetano. Conquistado por primera vez el 29 de mayo de 1953 por el alpinista neozelandés Edmund Hillary y el sherpa nepalés Norkay Tensing, el Everest ha conocido desde entonces más de 300 ascensiones victoriosas; no obstante, un centenar de alpinistas, de los cuales la mitad eran cargadores sherpas, han perdido la vida en él. Cada año, son de 600 a 900 los que vienen a Nepal a escalar una de las 15 cumbres himalayas de más de 8 000 m; esta afluencia plantea problemas de contaminación, más de 30 toneladas de desechos han sido dejados en las laderas del Everest por las diversas expediciones en el curso de los últimos cincuenta años.

MOUNT EVEREST, HIMALAYAS, NEPAL.

In the massif of the Himalayas, which forms the border between Nepal and China, the highest peak on the planet, Mount Everest, rises at an altitude of 8,848 m (29,000 ft). Although Westerners named it after the British colonel, George Everest, who was assigned to establish a map of India in 1852, the Nepalese, on the other hand, call it Sagarmatha, "the one whose head touches the sky" and the Chinese, Chomolongma, a name derived from Tibetan. Conquered for the first time by the New Zealand mountaineer, Edmund Hillary, and the Nepalese Sherpa, Tenzing Norgay, on May 29th, 1953, the Everest has since been successfully climbed over 300 times; however, about one hundred mountaineers, nearly half of whom were Sherpa porters, have lost their lives there. Every year, between 600 and 900 climbers come to Nepal to conquer one of the 15 Himalayan peaks surpassing 8,000 m (26,000 ft); this amount of visits creates pollution problems : more than 30 metric tons (33 tons) of garbage have been abandoned on the Everest slopes by various expeditions over the past fifty years.

MONT EVEREST, HIMALAYA, NÉPAL.

Dans le massif de l'Himalaya, qui forme la frontière entre le Népal et la Chine, le mont Everest est le plus haut sommet de la planète, avec une altitude de 8 848 m. Si les Occidentaux lui ont donné le nom du colonel britannique Georges Everest, chargé en 1852 d'établir le relevé cartographique de l'Inde, les Népalais, en revanche, l'appellent Sagarmatha, « celui dont la tête touche le ciel » et les Chinois Chomolongma, nom dérivé du tibétain. Conquis pour la première fois le 29 mai 1953 par l'alpiniste néo-zélandais Edmund Hillary et le sherpa népalais Norkay Tensing, l'Everest a, depuis, connu plus de 300 ascensions victorieuses ; cependant une centaine d'alpinistes, dont près de la moitié étaient des porteurs sherpas, y ont perdu la vie. Chaque année, ils sont entre 600 et 900 à venir au Népal gravir l'un des 15 sommets himalayens de plus de 8 000 m ; cette affluence pose des problèmes de pollution, plus de 30 tonnes de déchets ayant été abandonnées sur les flancs de l'Everest par les diverses expéditions au cours des cinquante dernières années.

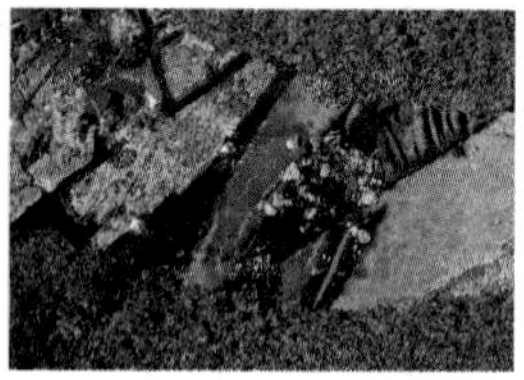

N 5°55' W 62°32'

RIBERA EN AUYÁN TEPUI, REGIÓN DE LA GRAN SABANA, VENEZUELA.

La región de la Gran Sabana, al sureste de Venezuela, es una vasta planicie cubierta de sabana y selva tupida de donde emergen imponentes relieves tabulares constituidos por rocas areniscas llamadas tepuyes. En uno de ellos, el Auyán Tepui o "montaña del diablo", que cubre 700 km^2 y culmina a 2 950 m, serpentea el Río Carrao. Al llegar al borde del tepui, este río se precipita en una cascada vertiginosa de 978 m, el Salto Ángel, caída de agua libre más alta del mundo. Rica en yacimientos de oro y diamantes, la región de la Gran Sabana y sus numerosas corrientes de agua suscitan desde 1930 la codicia de muchos exploradores, atraídos especialmente por ciudades como Icabarú, que se hizo célebre por el descubrimiento en 1942 de un diamante de 154 quilates, o como El Dorado, cuyo nombre evoca por sí solo la época de los conquistadores.

RIVER ON AUYÁN TEPUY, LA GRAN SABANA REGION, VENEZUELA.

The region of La Gran Sabana in southeastern Venezuela is a vast plain covered by savanna and dense forest, where imposing altiplanos made up of sandy rocks, called tepuyes, emerge. Río Carrao winds along one of them, the Auyán Tepuy or "Devil's Mountain", which covers 700 sq. km. (270 sq. mi.) and reaches a peak height of 2,950 m (9,735 ft.). Arriving at the edge of the tepuy, this river tumbles headlong in a dizzy cascade 978 m (3200 ft.) high, Angel Falls (Salto del Angel), the world's highest freefalling waterfall. Rich in gold and diamond deposits, the region of La Gran Sabana and its numerous rivers have attracted many prospectors since 1930. Indeed, cities became famous such as Icabaru where a 154-karat diamond was discovered in 1942, or El Dorado, whose name alone evokes the time of the conquistadors.

RIVIÈRE SUR L'AUYÁN TEPUY, RÉGION DE LA GRAN SABANA, VENEZUELA.

La région de la Gran Sabana, au sud-est du Venezuela, est une vaste plaine couverte de savane et de forêt dense d'où émergent d'imposants reliefs tabulaires constitués de roches gréseuses, appelés tepuyes. Sur l'un d'entre eux, l'Auyán Tepuy ou « montagne du diable », qui couvre 700 km^2 et culmine à 2 950 m, serpente le rio Carrao. Arrivée en bordure du tepui, cette rivière se précipite en une cascade vertigineuse de 978 m, le Salto Angel, chute d'eau libre la plus haute du monde. Riche en gisements d'or et de diamants, la région de la Gran Sabana et ses nombreux cours d'eau suscitent depuis 1930 la convoitise de maints prospecteurs, attirés notamment par des villes comme Icabaru, rendue célèbre par la découverte en 1942 d'un diamant de 154 carats, ou comme El Dorado, dont le nom évoque à lui seul l'époque des conquistadores.

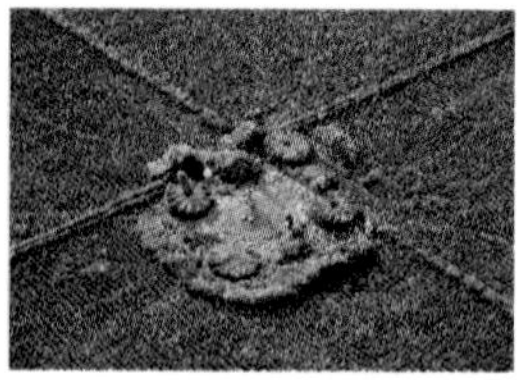

N 16°41' E 100°11'

TRABAJOS DE LOS CAMPOS ENTRE CHIANG MAI Y CHIANG RAI, TAILANDIA.

Ocupando cerca del 15% del territorio tailandés, las plantaciones de arroz dominan los paisajes del país hasta los valles del norte, alrededor de las ciudades de Chiang Mai y Chang Rai. Cosechado con mayor frecuencia de manera tradicional en pequeñas explotaciones familiares, el arroz se trilla a mano en medio de los campos antes de almacenarlo en los pueblos, y venderlo después. Tailandia, primer exportador de arroz del mundo, vende en la actualidad cada año al extranjero 6 millones de toneladas de arroz, es decir, un cuarto de su producción anual.. Este cereal constituye la base alimenticia de más de la mitad de la producción del globo, y Asia asegura el 92% de la cosecha anual mundial. Existen todavía cerca de 120 000 variedades de arroz, pero la expansión de la agricultura comercial moderna, que favorece la ocupación de vastas extensiones por las mismas variedades de alto rendimiento, que sustituyen a las múltiples variedades locales tradicionales, baja progresivamente la diversidad agrícola. Así, en China, cerca de 2000 variedades de arroz se han perdido desde hace 30 años. La seguridad alimenticia podría verse amenazada: con estas variedades salvajes desaparece un potencial genético vital para el mejoramiento de las plantas cultivadas, y el riesgo de malas cosechas que resulta de una vulnerabilidad uniforme de los monocultivos a nuevas enfermedades o desastres se precisan.

WORKING IN THE FIELDS BETWEEN CHIANG MAI AND CHIANG RAI, THAILAND.

Occupying close to 15% of Thai territory, rice plantations are predominant throughout the country up to valleys in the north, near the cities of Chiang Mai and Chiang Rai. Mostly harvested in the traditional way in small domestic farms, the rice is beaten by hand in the middle of the fields, stored in the villages, then sold. Thailand, the foremost exporter of rice in the world, today exports 6 million metric tons (6.6 million tons) of rice each year, representing one-quarter of its annual production. This cereal represents the basis of over half the world population's diet, with Asia providing 92% of the world's annual crops. There still exist close to 120,000 varieties of rice, but the expansion of modern commercial farming encourages the cultivation of high-yielding varieties in huge areas. They replace the many traditional local varieties, and progressively lower this agricultural diversity. Close to 2,000 varieties of rice in China have therefore been lost in the last 30 years. The loss of these wild varieties leads to the disappearance of a genetic potential vital for the improvement of cultivated plants, and increases the risk of bad harvests resulting from a uniform vulnerability of monocultures to new illnesses or ravagers. Food security could therefore seriously be threatened.

TRAVAUX DES CHAMPS ENTRE CHIANG MAÏ ET CHIANG RAÏ, THAÏLANDE.

Occupant près de 15 % du territoire thaïlandais, les plantations de riz dominent les paysages du pays jusque dans les vallées du Nord, autour des villes de Chiang Maï et Chiang Raï. Le plus souvent récolté de façon traditionnelle dans de petites exploitations familiales, le riz est battu manuellement au milieu des champs avant d'être stocké dans les villages, puis vendu. La Thaïlande, premier exportateur de riz au monde, vend aujourd'hui chaque année à l'étranger 6 millions de tonnes de riz, soit le quart de sa production annuelle. Cette céréale constitue la base alimentaire de plus de la moitié de la population du globe, et l'Asie assure 92 % de la récolte annuelle mondiale. Il existe encore près de 120 000 variétés de riz mais l'expansion de l'agriculture commerciale moderne, qui favorise l'occupation de vaste étendues par les mêmes variétés à haut rendement, se substituant aux multiples variétés locales traditionnelles, abaisse progressivement cette diversité agricole. Ainsi en Chine, près de 2000 variétés de riz ont été perdues depuis 30 ans. La sécurité alimentaire pourrait s'en trouver menacée : avec ces variétés sauvages disparaît un potentiel génétique vital pour l'amélioration des plantes cultivées, et le risque de mauvaises récoltes résultant d'une vulnérabilité uniforme des monocultures à de nouvelles maladies ou ravageurs se précise.

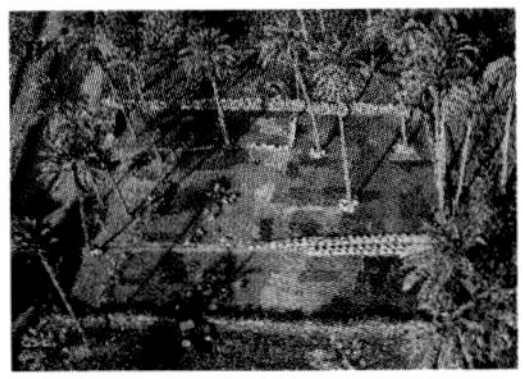

N 29°43' E 31°17'

SECADO DE DÁTILES, PALMAR AL SUR DE EL CAIRO, VALLE DEL NILO, EGIPTO.

Las palmeras datileras no se desarrollan sino en los medios áridos y calientes que disponen de algunos recursos hídricos, como los oasis. La producción mundial de dátiles alcanza 5 millones de toneladas al año. Lo esencial de la cosecha del Medio Oriente y el Magreb se destina al mercado interior de cada país, la exportación representa sólo una proporción del 5%. Egipto, segundo productor mundial después de Irán, cosecha cada año más de 800 000 toneladas de dátiles, que se consumen localmente a razón de 10 kg por persona anualmente. Estos dátiles se conservan habitualmente de manera artesanal: seleccionados por variedades, adquieren su color café progresivamente, secándose al sol, protegidos del viento y del agua por un murito de tierra y ramas, después se guardan en canastas trenzadas de palma. Aunque el consumo directo sea mayoritario, cierto número de productos derivados (jarabe, harina pasta, vinagre, azúcar, alcohol, repostería) se fabrican de manera artesanal o industrial a partir de esta fruta.

DATE DRYING, PALM GROVE SOUTH OF CAIRO, NILE VALLEY, EGYPT.

The date palms develop only in arid, hot surroundings with some water resources, such as oases. The world production of dates reaches 5 million metric tons per year. The greater part of the Middle East and Maghreb harvest is intended for the domestic market of each country, with exports representing only a proportion of 5%. Egypt, the second greatest world producer after Iran, harvests more than 800,000 metric tons (880,000 tons) of dates every year, consumed locally at the rate of 10 kg (22 lb) per person per year. These dates are usually preserved in the traditional way: sorted by varieties, they brown progressively as they dry in the sun, protected from wind and water by a low wall of earth and branches, and are then kept in baskets woven from palm leaves. Although most are used for direct consumption, a number of derivative products (syrup, flour, paste, vinegar, sugar, alcohol, desserts...) are manufactured in the traditional or industrial way, using this fruit.

SÉCHAGE DE DATTES, PALMERAIE AU SUD DU CAIRE, VALLÉE DU NIL, ÉGYPTE.

Les palmiers-dattiers ne se développent que dans les milieux arides et chauds disposant de quelques ressources hydriques, comme les oasis. La production mondiale de dattes atteint 5 millions de tonnes par an. L'essentiel de la récolte du Moyen-Orient et du Maghreb est destinée au marché intérieur de chaque pays, l'exportation ne représentant qu'une proportion de 5 %. L'Égypte, deuxième producteur mondial derrière l'Iran, récolte chaque année plus de 800 000 tonnes de dattes, consommées localement à raison de 10 kg par personne et par an. Ces dattes sont habituellement conservées de façon artisanale : triées par variétés, elles brunissent progressivement en séchant au soleil, protégées du vent et de l'eau par un muret de terre et de branches, puis sont confinées dans des paniers tressés de palmes. Bien que la consommation directe soit majoritaire, un certain nombre de produits dérivés (sirop, farine, pâte, vinaigre, sucre, alcool, pâtisseries...) sont fabriqués de façon artisanale ou industrielle à partir de ce fruit.

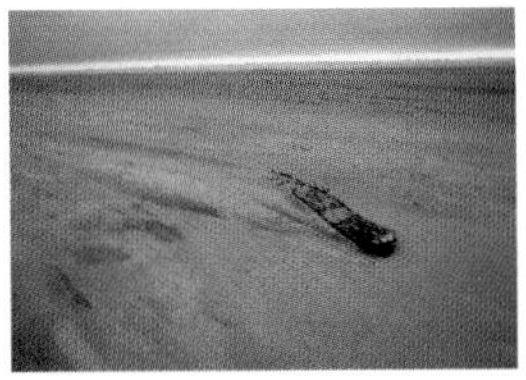

S 26°42' E 15°14'

BARCO ENCALLADO EN UNA PLAYA DE LA REGIÓN DE LÜDERITZ, NAMIBIA.

La corriente de Benguela, originada en la Antártica, corre a lo largo de la costa Namibia, donde se alternan playas, arrecifes y bajos fondos. Provoca una fuerte marejada, de corrientes violentas, y una espesa niebla que disimula los contornos de la costa. Por ello, esta última constituye un paso temido por los navegantes que cruzan de largo para llegar al Cabo de Buena Esperanza, en la punta sur del continente africano. Desde 1846, los marinos portugueses la califican como "arenas del infierno" y, en su parte norte, lleva desde 1933 el nombre evocador de "Costa de los Esqueletos". Innumerables restos oxidados de barcos, pero también de aviones y de vehículos todo-terreno, así como vestigios óseas de cetáceos encallados e incluso de hombres salpican este melancólico litoral. A veces algunos restos quedan enterrados en la arena a varios centenares de metros de la orilla, como aquí, cerca de la ciudad de Lüderitz, lo que atestigua la violencia de los naufragios. Si el mejoramiento de las técnicas de salvamento permite salvar más vidas que hace 50 años, el tributo que se paga a los mares del globo sigue siendo importante: al menos 65 marinos-pescadores desaparecen cotidianamente en el mundo, y cada semana 2 navíos grandes naufragan.

SHIPWRECK NEAR LÜDERITZ, NAMIBIA.

The Benguela current, coming from the Antarctic, follows the coastline of Namibia, where beaches, reefs and shoals alternate. It provokes strong waves, violent currents, and a thick fog that conceals coastal contours. Navigators crossing the open sea to return to Cape of Good Hope, the southern tip of the African continent, therefore dread this part of their journey. Since 1846, Portuguese sailors have described it as "sands of hell" and its northern part bears the evocative name of Skeleton Coast since 1933. Countless rusty shipwrecks, airplanes and cross-country vehicles carcasses, as well as the remaining bones of beached cetaceans, and even of men, are strewn along this melancholic coastline. At times, they can be found several hundred meters from the shore, proving how violent the shipwrecks can be, as seen here, close to the city of Lüderitz. Although improvements in lifesaving techniques enable more lives to be saved now than 50 years ago, a heavy toll is still paid to seas around the globe: at least 65 deep-sea fishermen lose their lives every day worldwide, and every week two large vessels are shipwrecked.

BATEAU ÉCHOUÉ SUR UNE PLAGE DANS LA RÉGION DE LÜDERITZ, NAMIBIE.

Le courant de Benguela, issu de l'Antarctique, longe la côte de Namibie, où alternent plages, récifs et hauts-fonds. Il provoque une forte houle, de violents courants, et un épais brouillard qui dissimule les contours de la côte. Aussi cette dernière constitue-t-elle un passage redouté par les navigateurs qui croisent au large pour rejoindre le cap de Bonne-Espérance, à la pointe sud du continent africain. Dès 1846, les marins portugais la qualifient de « sables de l'enfer » et, dans sa partie nord, elle porte depuis 1933 le nom évocateur de Côte des Squelettes. D'innombrables épaves rouillées de bateaux, mais aussi d'avions et de véhicules tout-terrain, ainsi que des vestiges osseux de cétacés échoués et même d'hommes parsèment ce mélancolique littoral. Certaines épaves sont parfois ensablées à plusieurs centaines de mètres du rivage, comme ici près de la ville de Lüderitz, témoignant de la violence des naufrages. Si l'amélioration des techniques de sauvetage permet d'épargner davantage de vies qu'il y a 50 ans, le tribut payé aux mers du globe demeure lourd : au moins 65 marins-pêcheurs disparaissent quotidiennement dans le monde, et chaque semaine 2 gros navires font naufrage.

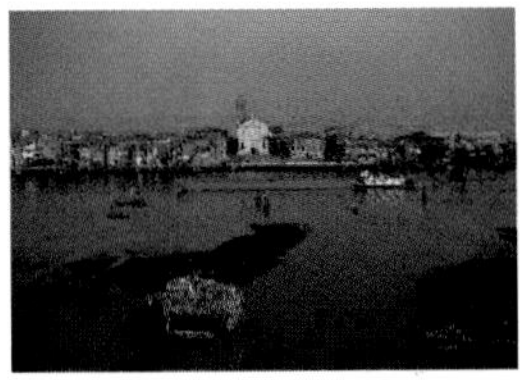

N 45°22' E 12°20'

PUEBLO DE PESCADORES DE MALAMOCCO, LAGUNA DE VENECIA, ITALIA.

La Laguna de Venecia, en Italia, está separada del Mar Adriático por un rosario de islas alargadas entre las cuales está la de Lido, donde se encuentra el pueblo de pescadores de Malamocco. Formada por 118 islotes, la ciudad histórica de Venecia, construida hace quince siglos, se ve sometida cada vez más frecuentemente al acqua alta, una subida de las aguas que la sumerge regularmente. Este fenómeno se ha agravado en el curso de los treinta últimos años, periodo durante el cual la ciudad se inunda a menudo, de las cuales un centenar de veces por más de un metro de agua. Con el fin de preservar este sitio altamente turístico, clasificado en la Lista del Patrimonio Mundial de la UNESCO en 1987, un proyecto ambicioso y costoso (el proyecto Moisés) se emprendió en 1988 teniendo como objetivo obturar periódicamente los tres pasos que unen al mar con la laguna por medio de unos cincuenta diques móviles.

FISHING VILLAGE IN MALAMOCCO, VENICE LAGOON, VENETO, ITALY.

Venice Lagoon, Italy, is separated from the Adriatic Sea by a string of long, narrow islands including the Lido, where the fishing village of Malamocco is located. Consisting of 118 islets, the historical city of Venice, built fifteen centuries ago, is becoming increasingly subject to acqua alta, a rise in the waters producing regular floods. This phenomenon has worsened over the last thirty years, a period in which the city has often been flooded, a hundred times or so by more than one meter of water. In order to preserve this important tourist site, inscribed on the UNESCO World Heritage List in 1987, an ambitious and expensive project (the Moses Project) was undertaken in 1988 in hopes of periodically closing the three passages that join the sea to the lagoon with fifty-some mobile floodgates.

VILLAGE DE PÊCHEURS DE MALAMOCCO, LAGUNE DE VENISE, VÉNÉTIE, ITALIE.

La lagune de Venise, en Italie, est séparée de la mer Adriatique par un chapelet d'îles longilignes parmi lesquelles celle du Lido, où se trouve le village de pêcheurs de Malamocco. Constituée de 118 îlots, la ville historique de Venise, construite il y a quinze siècles, est de plus en plus fréquemment soumise à l'acqua alta, une montée des eaux qui la submerge régulièrement. Ce phénomène s'est aggravé au cours des trente dernières années, période durant laquelle la ville a été inondée très souvent dont une centaine de fois par plus d'un mètre d'eau. Afin de préserver ce site hautement touristique, classé sur la Liste du patrimoine mondial de l'Unesco en 1987, un projet ambitieux et coûteux (le projet Moïse) a été engagé en 1988 avec pour objectif d'obturer périodiquement les trois passes qui relient la mer à la lagune au moyen d'une cinquantaine de digues mobiles.

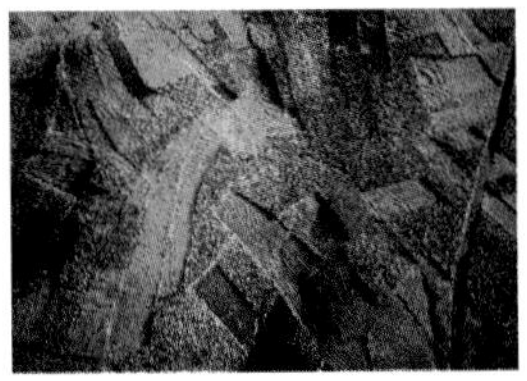

N 15°04' W 91°12'

PAISAJE AGRÍCOLA AL NOROESTE DE CIUDAD DE GUATEMALA, GUATEMALA.

La capital guatemalteca, Ciudad de Guatemala, está situada a 1 500 m de altitud en una zona montañosa que alberga 33 volcanes, algunos de los cuales todavía están activos. Cubiertos de lava fértil, los valles de esta región son regados por lluvias abundantes y regulares (de mayo a octubre) que hacen reverdecer las plantaciones. La agricultura, que constituye el recurso económico principal del país y ocupa al 55% de la población activa, se practica en pequeñas superficies, la mayoría de los agricultores (90%) disponen de menos de 7 hectáreas cada uno. El maíz, base de la alimentación, y el café, que representa el 50% de las exportaciones y con respecto al cual el país se sitúa en el noveno lugar mundial, son los principales cultivos productores de ingresos. Guatemala es igualmente productora de cannabis, de amapola y de coca, que alimentan de manera sustancial el tráfico internacional de la droga.

FARMING LANDSCAPE NORTHWEST OF GUATEMALA CITY, GUATEMALA.

The Guatemalan capital, Guatemala City, is situated at an altitude of 1,500 m (5,000 ft) in a mountainous zone that encompasses 33 volcanoes, some of which are still active. Covered by fertile lava, the valleys in this region are watered by regular, abundant rains (from May to October) that restore the greenness of the plantations. Farming constitutes the country's major economic resource and occupies 55% of the labor force. It is practiced over small areas, with most farmers (90%) having less than 7 hectares (17 acres) each. Corn - the basis of the country's diet, and coffee - which represents 50% of all exports and places the country as the ninth producer worldwide, are the main cash crops. Guatemala also produces cannabis, poppy and coca, which substantially contribute to the international drug traffic.

PAYSAGE AGRICOLE AU NORD-OUEST DE CIUDAD GUATEMALA, GUATEMALA.

La capitale guatémaltèque, Ciudad Guatemala, est située à 1 500 m d'altitude dans une zone montagneuse qui abrite 33 volcans, dont certains encore actifs. Couvertes de lave fertile, les vallées de cette région sont arrosées par des pluies abondantes et régulières (de mai à octobre) qui font reverdir les plantations. L'agriculture, qui constitue la ressource économique majeure du pays et occupe 55 % de la population active, est pratiquée sur de petites surfaces, la majorité des exploitants (90 %) disposant de moins de 7 hectares chacun. Le maïs, base de l'alimentation, et le café, qui représente 50 % des exportations et pour lequel le pays se situe au neuvième rang mondial, sont les principales cultures de rapport. Le Guatemala est également producteur de cannabis, de pavot et de coca, qui alimentent de manière substantielle le trafic international de la drogue.

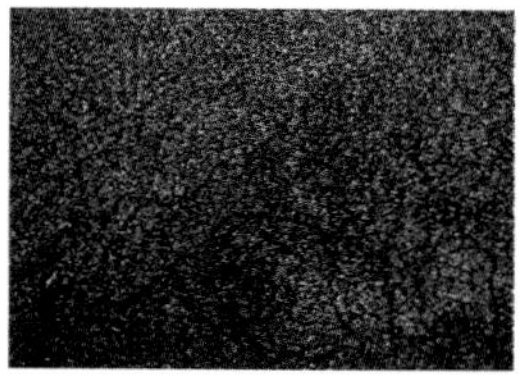

N 33°57' W 6°48'

VACAS EN UN RÍO PANTANOSO, REGIÓN DE RABAT, MARRUECOS.

La región de Rabat, como todo el norte de la costa atlántica marroquí, se beneficia con las precipitaciones relativamente abundantes (hasta 800 mm por año). En esta parte del país, considerada como una de las mejor drenadas de Marruecos, las lluvias de noviembre y de marzo alimentan las corrientes de agua y son el origen de las crecidas importantes. No obstante, a partir del mes de mayo, un viento del sureste, caliente y seco, el chergui, seca poco a poco su lecho. Éste, convertido temporalmente en pantanoso, se cubre de una alfombra efímera de hierbas y flores que recorren algunas vacas en busca de alimento que se escapan de los rebaños de los alrededores. La cabaña bovina de Marruecos, dominada por razas locales criadas a la vez por su leche y su carne, cuenta con un poco más de 2.6 millones de cabezas. La cría caprina (5.1 millones de cabezas) y, sobre todo, ovina (17.3 millones de cabezas) tienen efectivos mucho más importantes.

COWS IN A MARSHY RIVER, NEAR RABAT, MOROCCO.

The region of Rabat, like the rest of the Northern part along the Moroccan Atlantic coast, enjoys relatively abundant precipitation (up to 800 mm (32 in.) per year). In this area of the country, considered one of the best drained in Morocco, November and March rains feed the rivers and cause major flooding. However, from the month of May on, a warm, dry wind out of the southeast, the chergui, gradually dries up the river beds. They become temporarily marshy, covered by a temporary carpet of grass and flowers where cows wander in search of food, breaking away from the herds around them. Moroccan cattle, predominantly local breeds raised for milk and meat, numbers a little over 2.6 million. Goat, and especially sheep-raising, represent much larger numbers with 5.1 million and 17.3 million respectively.

VACHES DANS UNE RIVIÈRE MARÉCAGEUSE, RÉGION DE RABAT, MAROC.

La région de Rabat, comme tout le Nord de la côte atlantique marocaine, bénéficie de précipitations relativement abondantes (jusqu'à 800 mm par an). Dans cette partie du pays, considérée comme l'une des mieux drainées du Maroc, les pluies de novembre et de mars alimentent les cours d'eau et sont à l'origine de crues importantes. Cependant, à partir du mois de mai, un vent du sud-est chaud et sec, le chergui, assèche peu à peu leur lit. Celui-ci, devenu temporairement marécageux, se recouvre d'un tapis éphémère d'herbes et de fleurs que parcourent quelques vaches en quête de nourriture et échappées des troupeaux alentour. Le cheptel bovin du Maroc, dominé par des races locales élevées à la fois pour leur lait et leur viande, compte un peu plus de 2,6 millions de têtes. Les élevages caprin (5,1 millions de têtes) et, surtout, ovin (17,3 millions de têtes) ont des effectifs beaucoup plus importants.

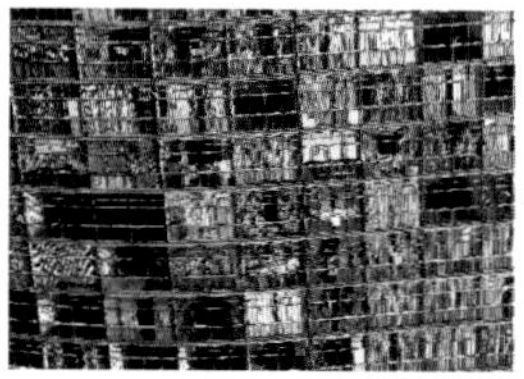

S 23°32' W 46°37'

DETALLE DE UN INMUEBLE DE SAO PAULO, BRASIL.

Más de 5 millones de paulistanos - habitantes de Sao Paulo - en Brasil viven en el seno de colonias obreras periféricas subequipadas, en inmuebles de confort precario llamados cortiços. Megalópolis de 18 millones de habitantes que crece cada año con 600 000 recién llegados, Sao Paulo es la mayor aglomeración de Brasil y de toda Sudamérica. Ciudad industrial y verdadero motor de la economía nacional, cuenta con más de 36 000 empresas, suministra la mitad de los productos manufacturados del país y alberga cerca del 45% de la fuerza de trabajo obrera brasileña. En esta ciudad, sin embargo la más próspera del país, cerca de un millón de niños viven en la calle (es decir, 1 de cada 5), entregados a la mendicidad, la delincuencia juvenil y la prostitución. En todo Brasil, se estima que de 7 a 9 millones de menores son abandonados a su suerte en las calles de los grandes centros urbanos.

DETAIL OF A BUILDING IN SÃO PAULO, BRAZIL.

More than 5 million Paulistanos – inhabitants of São Paulo, Brazil – live in underserviced, working-class suburbs, in buildings of precarious comfort called cortiços. A megalopolis with 18 million inhabitants that welcomes 600,000 newcomers every year, São Paulo is the largest urban area in Brazil and in all of South America. An industrial city and the true driving-force behind the national economy, it has over 36,000 businesses, provides half the manufactured products of the country and harbors close to 45% of the Brazilian working-class labor. In this city, which is the most prosperous one in the country, close to a million children are believed to live in the street (1 out of 5), leading a life of begging, petty crime and prostitution. It is estimated that 7 to 9 million minors are abandoned in the streets of large urban centers throughout Brazil.

DÉTAIL D'UN IMMEUBLE DE SÃO PAULO, BRÉSIL.

Plus de 5 millions de Paulistanos — habitants de São Paulo, au Brésil — vivent au sein de banlieues ouvrières sous-équipées, dans des immeubles au confort précaire appelés cortiços. Mégalopole de 18 millions d'habitants qui s'accroît chaque année de 600 000 nouveaux venus, São Paulo est la plus grande agglomération du Brésil et de toute l'Amérique du Sud. Ville industrielle et véritable moteur de l'économie nationale, elle compte plus de 36 000 entreprises, fournit la moitié des produits manufacturés du pays et abrite près de 45 % de la main-d'œuvre ouvrière brésilienne. Dans cette ville, pourtant la plus prospère du pays, près d'un million d'enfants vivraient dans la rue (soit 1 sur 5), livrés à la mendicité, la petite délinquance et la prostitution. Dans tout le Brésil, on estime que 7 à 9 millions de mineurs sont abandonnés à eux-mêmes dans les rues des grands centres urbains.

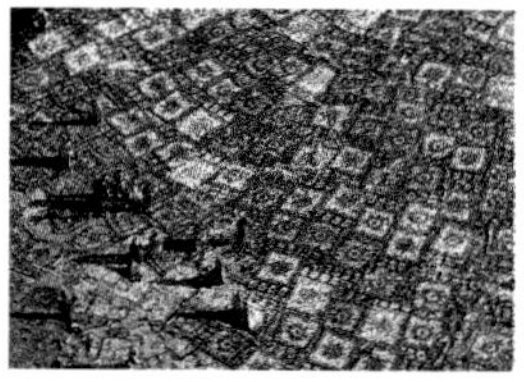

N 26°55' E 75°49'

ALGODONES SECÁNDOSE AL SOL EN JAIPUR, RAJASTHAN, INDIA.

Importante centro de producción textil, el Estado de Rajasthan, al noroeste de India, es afamado desde hace siglos por su artesanía de teñido y estampado en algodón y seda, practicado por la comunidad chhipa. La técnicas tradicionales de decoración con cera y de impresión por estampado tiene en la actualidad la competencia de la serigrafía, que permite una producción en gran escala, mientras que los pigmentos naturales se dejan a un lado en beneficio de los colorantes químicos. En cambio, los múltiples remojos destinados a fijar el color y el secado de los tejidos al sol, como aquí en Jaipur, capital del Estado, se practican todavía. Las mujeres chippa que realizan este trabajo forman parte del 32% de mujeres de la población activa india, y esta participación de las mujeres en la actividad económica se incrementa. Si desde hace unos años presenciamos un mejor reconocimiento de los derechos y las aspiraciones de las mujeres a través del mundo, queda mucho por recorrer para numerosos países donde las desigualdades entre hombres y mujeres siguen siendo escandalosas...

COTTON FABRICS DRYING IN THE SUN IN JAIPUR, RAJASTHAN, INDIA.

An important center for textile production, the state of Rajasthan, in northwest India, has been reputed for centuries for its handicraft work of dyeing and printing on cotton and silk, practised by the Chhipa community. The traditional techniques of wax decoration and pad printing compete today with silk-screen printing, which makes large-scale production possible, while natural pigments are being progressively abandoned in favor of chemical dyes. On the other hand, the practice of soaking many times in order to fix the color and of drying the cloth in the sun, as seen here in Jaipur, the state capital, is still continued. Chhipas women who do this work form part of the 32% of women involved in the Indian labor force, and this participation of women in economic activity is on the increase. Although the rights and aspirations of women have been increasingly recognized throughout the world in the last few decades, there still is room for improvement in several countries where flagrant inequalities between men and women continue...

COTONNADES SÉCHANT AU SOLEIL À JAIPUR, RAJASTHAN, INDE.

Important centre de production textile, l'État du Rajasthan, au nord-ouest de l'Inde, est réputé depuis des siècles pour son artisanat de teinture et d'impression sur coton et sur soie, pratiqué par la communauté Chhipa. Les techniques traditionnelles de décoration à la cire et d'impression au tampon sont aujourd'hui concurrencées par la sérigraphie qui permet une production à grande échelle, tandis que les pigments naturels sont progressivement délaissés au profit de colorants chimiques. En revanche, les multiples trempages destinés à fixer la couleur et le séchage des tissus au soleil, comme ici à Jaipur, capitale de l'État, sont toujours pratiqués. Les femmes Chhipa qui exécutent ce travail font partie des 32 % de femmes de la population active indienne, et cette participation des femmes à l'activité économique s'accroît. Si depuis quelques décennies on assiste à une meilleure reconnaissance des droits et des aspirations des femmes à travers le monde, du chemin reste à parcourir pour nombre de pays où les inégalités entre hommes et femmes demeurent criantes...

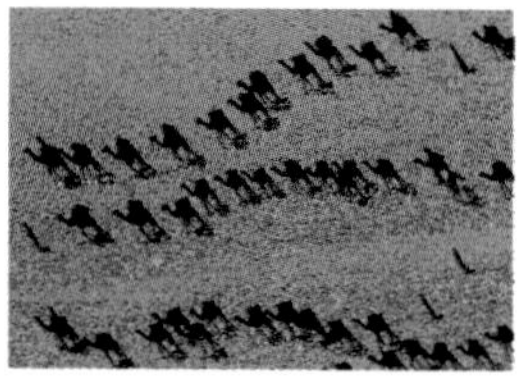

N 18°14' E 11°40'

CARAVANAS DE DROMEDARIOS CERCA DE FACHI, DESIERTO DE TENERÉ, NIGERIA.

Desde hace decenios, los tuaregs recorren regularmente con sus caravanas de dromedarios los 610 km que separan la ciudad de Agadez de las salinas de Bilma practicando el comercio tradicional de la sal, producto raro en este país encerrado. Atados unos detrás de otros y guiados por un hombre experimentado a la cabeza, los dromedarios circulan en convoy al ritmo de 40 km diarios, a pesar de las temperaturas que alcanzan los 46° C a la sombra y de cargas de cerca de 100 kg por animal. En la pista de los Azalai (caravanas de sal), Fachi, única localidad importante, constituye un alto indispensable para sostenerse y descargar una parte de la mercancía. Las caravanas, que contaban antes hasta 20 000 bestias, apenas rebasan hoy el centenar de animales; poco a poco son suplantados por el camión que, con respecto al transporte de mercancías equivale por sí solo a 250 dromedarios. El número de vehículos de motor aumenta rápidamente en todas las regiones del globo: se ha multiplicado por dos en el curso de los treinta últimos años en Europa occidental. El sector de los transportes, que absorbe actualmente un cuarto de la energía que se consume y cerca de la mitad de la producción mundial de petróleo, es uno de los que más contribuyen a las emisiones de gas con efecto invernadero, y consecuentemente al calentamiento global del planeta.

DROMEDARY CARAVANS CLOSE TO FACHI, TÉNÉRÉ DESERT, NIGER.

For decades, the Tuareg have regularly roamed the 610 km (380 mi.) separating the city of Agadez from the salt marshes in Bilma, practicing the traditional salt trade, a rare commodity in this land-locked country. Tied together in single file and led by a man, dromedaries travel in convoy at a pace of 40 km (25 mi.) per day, in spite of temperatures reaching 46°C (115°F) in the shade and loads weighing 100 kg (220 lb) per animal. On the piste des Azalaï (salt caravans), Fachi is the only important locality and offers an essential halt to take on provisions and unload part of the cargo. The caravans, once counting up to 20,000 animals, seldom comprise more than a hundred today : they are gradually being replaced by trucks, which, for transporting goods, equal to about 250 dromedaries each. The number of motor vehicles is rapidly increasing in all regions of the planet : it has doubled over the last thirty years in Western Europe. The transport sector today, which absorbs one-quarter of the energy consumed worldwide and nearly half of the world oil production, is among those contributing the most to greenhouse gas emissions, and thus to global warming.

CARAVANES DE DROMADAIRES PRÈS DE FACHI, DÉSERT DU TÉNÉRÉ, NIGER.

Depuis des décennies, les Touareg parcourent régulièrement avec leurs caravanes de dromadaires les 610 km qui séparent la ville d'Agadez des salines de Bilma, pratiquant le commerce traditionnel du sel, denrée rare dans ce pays enclavé. Attachés les uns derrière les autres et guidés par un homme de tête, les dromadaires circulent en convoi au rythme de 40 km par jour, malgré des températures atteignant 46 °C à l'ombre et des charges de près de 100 kg par animal. Sur la piste des Azalaï (caravanes de sel), Fachi, seule localité importante, constitue une halte indispensable pour se sustenter et décharger une partie de la cargaison. Les caravanes, qui comptaient autrefois jusqu'à 20000 bêtes, ne dépassent guère aujourd'hui la centaine d'animaux ; peu à peu elles sont supplantées par le camion qui, pour le transport de marchandises, équivaut à lui seul à 250 dromadaires. Le nombre de véhicules à moteur s'accroît rapidement dans toutes les régions du globe : il a été multiplié par deux au cours des trente dernières années en Europe occidentale. Le secteur des transports, qui absorbe aujourd'hui un quart de l'énergie consommée et près de la moitié de la production mondiale de pétrole, est l'un de ceux qui contribuent le plus aux émissions de gaz à effet de serre, et par conséquent au réchauffement global de la planète.

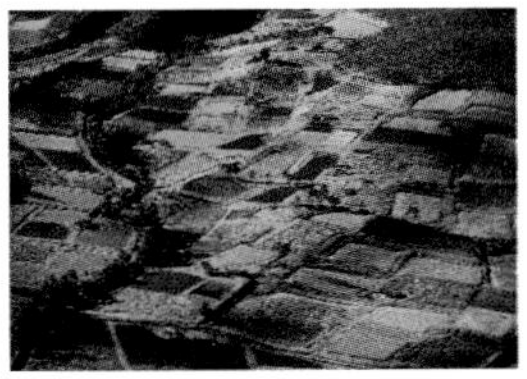

N 0°17' W 78°41'

CAMPOS CERCA DE QUITO, REGIÓN DE LA SIERRA, ECUADOR.

Entre las cordilleras occidental y real, las mesetas de la región de Quito se benefician del clima húmedo y templado de la sierra que permite la práctica de cultivos de cereales (maíz, trigo, cebada) y de papas. Aunque mayoritariamente alimenticia y destinada al mercado interior, la agricultura sigue siendo importante en la economía, al emplear 3.5 millones de personas y representar el 12% del PNB. Modela igualmente el paisaje: un tercio de la superficie de Ecuador está en efecto cubierta de tierras arables, de terrenos cultivados y de pastizales. La expansión incesante de superficie agrícola que, en ciertas regiones se ha más que duplicado en el curso del último decenio, se hace en detrimento de la cubierta forestal que representa actualmente cerca de la mitad del territorio nacional. Las tres quintas partes de los bosques tropicales húmedos del mundo se localizan además en Latinoamérica. Amenazados por el desarrollo agrícola y la sobreexplotación, los bosques tropicales desaparecen en todas partes del mundo al ritmo de 1% anual.

FIELDS CLOSE TO QUITO, SIERRA REGION, ECUADOR.

Between the Cordillera Occidental and Cordillera Real, the plateaus in the region of Quito enjoy the humid, mild climate of the Sierra that makes it possible to grow cereal (corn, wheat, barley) and potatoes. Agriculture represents 12% of the GNP and is practiced by 3.5 million people. Although it mostly produces food crops intended for the domestic market, it still remains important for the economy. Furthermore, agriculture shapes the landscape with one-third of Ecuador's surface area covered by arable lands, farming lands and pastures. The constant expansion of the agricultural area, which in some regions has more than doubled over the last decade, requires the removal of forests, which represent close to half of the national territory today. Three-fifths of the tropical rainforests in the world are located in Latin America. Threatened by agricultural development and overexploitation, the tropical forests are disappearing everywhere in the world at the rate of 1% per year.

CHAMPS PRÈS DE QUITO, RÉGION DE LA SIERRA, ÉQUATEUR.

Entre les cordillères Occidentale et Royale, les plateaux de la région de Quito bénéficient du climat humide et doux de la sierra qui permet la pratique de cultures de céréales (maïs, blé, orge) et de pommes de terre. Bien que majoritairement vivrière et destinée au marché intérieur, l'agriculture reste importante dans l'économie, employant 3,5 millions de personnes et représentant 12 % du PNB. Elle modèle également le paysage : un tiers de la superficie de l'Équateur est en effet couvert de terres arables, de terrains cultivés et de pâturages. L'expansion incessante de la surface agricole qui, dans certaines régions, a plus que doublé au cours de la dernière décennie, se fait au détriment du couvert forestier qui représente actuellement près de la moitié du territoire national. Les trois cinquièmes des forêts tropicales humides du monde sont d'ailleurs localisés en Amérique latine. Menacées par le développement agricole et la surexploitation, les forêts tropicales disparaissent partout dans le monde au rythme de 1 % par an.

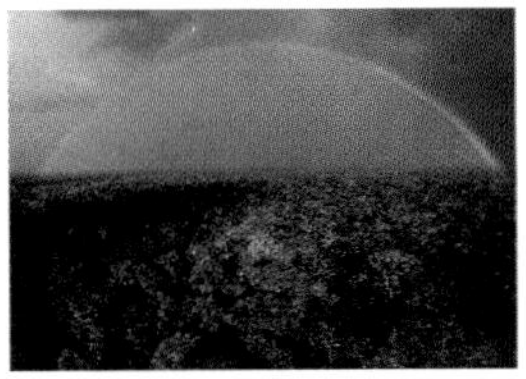

S 3°32' W 64°53'

TORMENTA EN LA SELVA AMAZÓNICA CERCA DE TEFÉ, ESTADO DE AMAZONAS, BRASIL.

La selva amazónica cubre el 63% de la superficie de Brasil. La Amazonia es el ecosistema de bosque tropical más vasto del mundo con 3.7 millones de km^2, y representa un tercio de los bosques tropicales del planeta. Estos bosques, que cubren el 8% de las tierras emergidas, guardan cerca del 90% del patrimonio biológico, lo que hace de ellos los medios más ricos del globo. La Amazonia alberga, por sí sola, el 10% de los 1.7 millones de especies vivas catalogadas al día de hoy. El inventario de las formas de vida animales y vegetales del planeta está no obstante lejos de terminarse, sobre todo en las regiones tropicales: se estima en 12.5 millones el número de especies que faltan por descubrir. La industria farmacéutica se interesa especialmente en estas investigaciones; en efecto, más de la mitad de los medicamentos que se utilizan actualmente tienen como principio activo una sustancia natural extraída de plantas o animales. Cerca de 200 km^2 de selva desaparecen irremediablemente cada día de la superficie del globo, y con ellos un número inestimable de especies que se llevan para siempre sus secretos.

STORM OVER THE AMAZON RAINFOREST CLOSE TO TEFÉ, AMAZONAS, BRAZIL.

The Amazon rainforest covers 63% of Brazil. Amazonia is the most extensive tropical rainforest ecosystem in the world with an area of 3.7 million sq. km. (1.4 million sq. mi.). Representing one-third of the tropical rainforests on the planet, these forests cover 8% of emerged land and harbor close to 90% of the planet's biological heritage, making it the richest environment on the globe. Amazonia harbors 10% of the 1.7 million living species listed to date alone. However, the inventory animal and plant life forms on the planet is far from being completed, especially in the tropical regions: the number of species yet to be discovered is estimated at 12.5 million. This research is of particular interest to the pharmaceutical industry. In fact, more than half the medicine currently being used has an active principle that is a natural substance extracted from plants or animals. Nearly 200 sq. km. (40 sq. mi.) of forest are disappearing irretrievably each day from the surface of the globe, and with them an inestimable number of species that are taking their secrets with them forever.

ORAGE SUR LA FORÊT AMAZONIENNE PRÈS DE TÉFÉ, ÉTAT D'AMAZONAS, BRÉSIL.

La forêt amazonienne couvre 63 % de la superficie du Brésil. L'Amazonie est le plus vaste écosystème forestier tropical du monde avec 3,7 millions de km^2, et représente le tiers des forêts tropicales de la planète. Ces forêts, couvrant 8 % des terres émergées, abritent près de 90 % du patrimoine biologique, ce qui en fait les milieux les plus riches du globe. L'Amazonie héberge, à elle seule, 10 % des 1,7 million d'espèces vivantes répertoriées à ce jour. L'inventaire des formes de vie animales et végétales de la planète est cependant loin d'être achevé, surtout dans les régions tropicales : on estime à 12,5 millions le nombre d'espèces restant à découvrir. Ces recherches intéressent notamment l'industrie pharmaceutique ; en effet, plus de la moitié des médicaments actuellement utilisés ont pour principe actif une substance naturelle extraite de plantes ou d'animaux. Près de 200 km^2 de forêt disparaissent irrémédiablement chaque jour de la surface du globe, et avec eux un nombre inestimable d'espèces qui emportent à jamais leurs secrets.

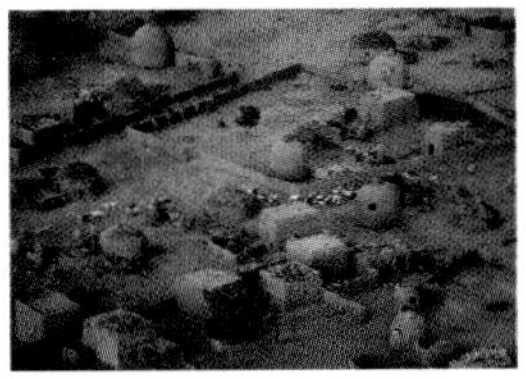

N 15°03' E 5°12'

DETALLE DE UN PUEBLO EN LOS ALREDEDORES DE TAHOUA, NIGERIA.

Este pueblo cerca de Tahoua, al suroeste del Níger, presenta una arquitectura hausa característica, con sus casas cúbicas hechas de banco (mezcla de tierra y de fibras vegetales) asociadas a imponentes graneros con formas ovoides. Mayoritaria en el país (53% de la población), el pueblo hausa está constituido esencialmente por agricultores sedentarios. No obstante, debe sobre todo su reputación a la calidad de su artesanía y a su sentido del negocio, por lo que las ciudades-estados hausa instaladas al norte de Nigeria impusieron su poderío comercial a numerosos países de África durante varios siglos. En la actualidad, la región de Tahoua está atravesada por un eje carretero que conduce al norte y al que comúnmente se lo llama "la ruta del uranio": un yacimiento, descubierto en 1965 en el subsuelo del macizo del Aïr, hizo nacer las minas de Arlit. Extraen cada año más de 3 000 toneladas de uranio, es decir, cerca del 10% de la producción mundial, lo que coloca a Nigeria en el cuarto lugar de los productores mundiales.

DETAIL OF A VILLAGE IN THE VICINITY OF TAHOUA, NIGER.

This village close to Tahoua, in southwestern Niger, is built according to typical Hausa architecture with its cube-shaped mud houses (made of a mixture of earth and plant fibers) joined to imposing, egg-shaped granaries. A majority in the country (53% of the population), the Hausa people are essentially made up of sedentary farmers. However, they are especially known for the quality of their handicraft and for their business sense. The Hausa City-states installed in northern Nigeria have indeed imposed their commercial strength in many African countries over a period of several centuries. Today, the region of Tahoua is divided by a road that leads northwards and is commonly called the "uranium route": the discovery of a deposit in 1965, in the sub-soil of the Air massif gave rise to the mines of Arlit. They extract more then 3,000 metric tons (3,300 tons) of uranium every year, or close to 10% of world production, making Niger the fourth largest world producer.

DÉTAIL D'UN VILLAGE AUX ENVIRONS DE TAHOUA, NIGER.

Ce village près de Tahoua, au sud-ouest du Niger, présente une architecture haoussa caractéristique avec ses maisons cubiques en banco (mélange de terre et de fibres végétales) associées à d'imposants greniers à grain aux formes ovoïdes. Majoritaire dans le pays (53 % de la population), le peuple haoussa est essentiellement constitué d'agriculteurs sédentaires. Cependant, il doit surtout sa réputation à la qualité de son artisanat et à son sens du négoce, les Cités-États haoussa installées au nord du Nigeria ayant imposé leur puissance commerciale à de nombreux pays d'Afrique pendant plusieurs siècles. Aujourd'hui, la région de Tahoua est traversée par un axe routier qui mène vers le nord et qui est communément appelé la « route de l'uranium » : un gisement, découvert en 1965 dans le sous-sol du massif de l'Aïr, fit naître les mines d'Arlit. Elles extraient chaque année plus de 3 000 tonnes d'uranium, soit près de 10 % de la production mondiale, plaçant le Niger au quatrième rang des producteurs mondiaux.

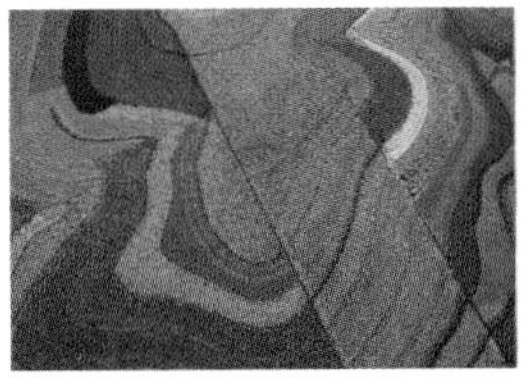

S 27°24' W 54°24'

CULTIVOS EN LOS BORDES DEL RÍO URUGUAY, PROVINCIA DE MISIONES, ARGENTINA.

Al noreste de Argentina, esta provincia que debe su nombre a las misiones jesuitas instaladas en la región del siglo XVI al XVIII estaba en su origen mayoritariamente cubierta de bosque tropical. El paisaje, no obstante, ha sido modelado por los colonos de origen europeo que desforestaron una parte importante del territorio con el fin de explotar la tierra roja, rica en óxido de hierro y muy fértil. Labrando a lo largo de las curvas de nivel dejando las banda herbosas entre los surcos para atenuar la erosión, han desarrollado diversos cultivos como el algodón, el tabaco, el té, el mate, el girasol, el arroz y los cítricos. Los agricultores han sabido aprovechar la vasta red hidrográfica que riega esta región enclavada entre los ríos Paraná y Uruguay, juiciosamente llamada Mesopotamia, término que significa "entre los ríos" en griego.

CROPS ON THE BANKS OF THE RIO URUGUAY, MISIONES PROVINCE, ARGENTINA.

Located in northeastern Argentina, this province, which owes its name to the Jesuit missions built in the region during the 16th and 17th centuries, was originally principally covered by tropical rainforest. For nearly a century, however, the landscape has been shaped by settlers of European origin, who deforested a large part of the territory in order to exploit the very fertile red earth, rich in iron oxide. Ploughing along contour lines, and leaving grassy strips between the furrows to decrease erosion, they have developed several crops such as cotton, tobacco, tea, maté, sunflowers, rice and citrus fruits. The farmers have been able to take advantage of the huge river system that waters this region enclosed between the Paraná and Uruguay Rivers, aptly called Mesopotamia, a term meaning "between rivers" in Greek.

CULTURES SUR LES BORDS DU RIO URUGUAY, PROVINCE DE MISIONES, ARGENTINE.

Au nord-est de l'Argentine, cette province qui doit son nom aux missions jésuites installées dans la région du XVIe au XVIIIe siècle était à l'origine majoritairement couverte de forêt tropicale. Le paysage a cependant été modelé depuis près d'un siècle par les colons d'origine européenne qui ont déboisé une partie importante du territoire afin d'exploiter la terre rouge, riche en oxyde de fer et très fertile. Labourant le long des courbes de niveau en laissant des bandes herbeuses entre les sillons pour atténuer l'érosion, ils ont développé diverses cultures comme le coton, le tabac, le thé, le maté, le tournesol, le riz et les agrumes. Les agriculteurs ont su tirer profit du vaste réseau hydrographique qui arrose cette région enclavée entre les fleuves Paraná et Uruguay, judicieusement appelée Mésopotamie, terme signifiant « entre les fleuves » en grec.

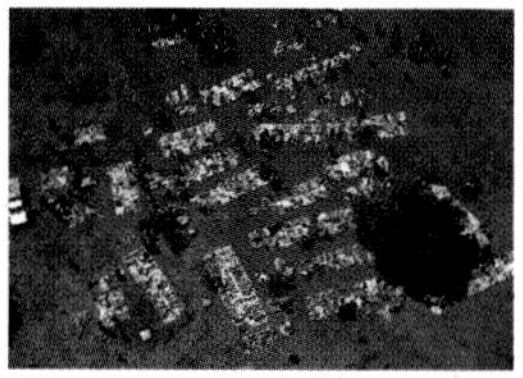

S 1°14' E 34°48'

MERCADO CERCA DE LA RESERVA NACIONAL DE MASAI MARA, KENYA.

Entre la reserva nacional de Masai Mara y el Lago Victoria, en Kenya, se improvisa regularmente un mercadito rural en las proximidades del pueblo de Lolgorien. Pueblerino sedentarios y nómadas masai de la región no dudan en recorrer varios kilómetros para ir allá. Presentadas en esteras colocadas en el suelo, las mercancías que se ofrecen en este mercado son en su mayoría vestimentas de ocasión provenientes de asociaciones caritativas así como productos de cestería, cerámica o joyas que salen de una artesanía local exclusivamente femenina. Estos mercados, que se organizan casi siempre espontáneamente en las orillas o en la intersección de pistas, son importantes lugares de aprovisionamiento para los kenyanos. En efecto, en este país de alrededor de 582 640 km² que cuenta con pocas aglomeraciones grandes, el 70% de la población vive en el medio rural, en el seno de pueblitos o de campamentos diseminados en el conjunto del territorio.

MARKET CLOSE TO MASAI MARA NATIONAL PARK, KENYA.

Between Masai Mara National Park and Lake Victoria, Kenya, a small rural market is regularly set up close to the village of Lolgorien. Sedentary villagers and Masai nomads in the region do not hesitate to travel several miles to attend it. Set out on mats placed directly on the ground, goods offered in this market are mostly second-hand clothing from charity associations as well as local, exclusively women's handicrafts of basketwork, pottery or jewelry. These markets, which are usually organized spontaneously by the side or at the intersection of paths, are important places to stock up on supplies. In fact this country has few urban areas, and is nearly 582,640 sq. km. (225,000 sq. mi.) wide. 70% of the population lives in a rural environment, in small villages or in camps scattered around the entire territory.

MARCHÉ PRÈS DE LA RÉSERVE NATIONALE DE MASAI MARA, KENYA.

Entre la réserve nationale de Masai Mara et le lac Victoria, au Kenya, s'improvise régulièrement un petit marché rural à proximité du village de Lolgorien. Villageois sédentaires et nomades Masai de la région n'hésitent pas à parcourir plusieurs kilomètres pour s'y rendre. Présentées sur des nattes posées à même le sol, les marchandises proposées sur ce marché sont en majorité des vêtements d'occasion provenant d'associations caritatives ainsi que des produits de vannerie, poteries ou bijoux émanant d'un artisanat local exclusivement féminin. Ces marchés, qui s'organisent le plus souvent spontanément en bordure ou à l'intersection de pistes, sont d'importants lieux d'approvisionnement pour les Kenyans. En effet, dans ce pays d'environ 582 640 km² qui compte peu de grandes agglomérations, 70 % de la population vit en milieu rural, au sein de petits villages ou de campements disséminés sur l'ensemble du territoire.

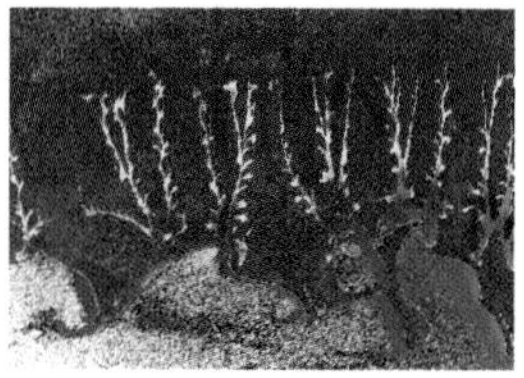

S 18°50' E 15°32'

ORILLA DE UN LAGO EN EL PARQUE NACIONAL DE ETOSHA, NAMIBIA.

Vistos desde el cielo, los depósitos de sal acumulados en las anfractuosidades de las orillas de este lago del Parque Nacional de Etosha, en Namibia, dibujan formas sorprendentes de plantas o de animales quiméricos. Este parque, el espacio protegido más vasto de África, con 22 270 km², está situado alrededor de una hondonada de 6 000 km² cubierta de sal (Etosha pan) que se transforma en lago en la estación de las lluvias, de noviembre a abril. Su agua salobre repele a los mamíferos, pero permite el desarrollo de un alga azul verdosa, que atrae decenas de miles de flamencos. Desecada, la hondonada se cubre de gramíneas con las que se alimentan los grandes herbívoros del parque. Namibia cuenta con 20 parques nacionales (13% del territorio nacional), que son el testimonio de un proceso activo en materia de conservación del medio ambiente. Este objetivo figura además entre los principales inscritos en la Constitución nacional. Actualmente, existen en el mundo alrededor de 13 000 áreas protegidas, que totalizan más de 13.2 millones de km² (8.8% de las tierras emergidas del globo), y esta superficie se ha casi triplicado en el curso de los treinta últimos años. Algunos no son, sin embargo, sino teóricos y no se salvan de las degradaciones: la agricultura estaría presente en cerca de la mitad de ellos.

LAKESHORE IN ETOSHA NATIONAL PARK, NAMIBIA.

Salt deposits that have accumulated in crevices on the shores of this lake in Etosha National Park, Namibia, reveal astonishing shapes of plants or animals from above, reminiscent of fairytales. This park is the largest protected area in Africa, representing 22,270 sq. km. (8,600 sq. mi.). It is established around a 6,000 sq. km. (2,300 sq. mi.) pan covered by salt (Etosha Pan) that turns into a lake during the rainy season from November to April. Its brackish water is unpalatable to mammals but enables the development of a type of blue-green alga that attracts close to tens of thousands of rose-colored (greater) flamingos. When it dries up, the pan is covered by grass, which large herbivores in the park feed upon. Namibia has 20 national parks (13% of the national territory), which testify to the steps being taken to conserve the environment. This objective is also one of the most important points inscribed in the national Constitution. There are about 13,000 protected areas in the world today, totaling over 13.2 million sq. km. (5.1 million sq. mi.) - 8.8% of the emerged land on the globe. This surface has nearly tripled over the last thirty years. However, some are simply theoretical, and are subject to degradation, as farming is believed to be practiced on close to half of them.

RIVE D'UN LAC DANS LE PARC NATIONAL D'ETOSHA, NAMIBIE.

Vus du ciel, les dépôts de sel accumulés dans les anfractuosités des rives de ce lac du parc national d'Etosha, en Namibie, dessinent des formes étonnantes de plantes ou d'animaux chimériques. Ce parc, le plus vaste espace protégé d'Afrique avec 22 270 km², est établi autour d'une cuvette de 6 000 km² couverte de sel (Etosha pan) qui se transforme en lac lors de la saison des pluies, de novembre à avril. Son eau saumâtre rebute les mammifères mais permet le développement d'une algue bleu-vert, qui attire des dizaines de milliers de flamants roses. Desséchée, la cuvette se recouvre de graminées dont se nourrissent les grands herbivores du parc. La Namibie compte 20 parcs nationaux (13 % du territoire national), qui témoignent d'une démarche active en matière de conservation de l'environnement. Cet objectif figure d'ailleurs parmi les principaux inscrits dans la Constitution nationale. Aujourd'hui, il existe dans le monde environ 13 000 aires protégées, totalisant plus de 13,2 millions de km² (8,8 % des terres émergées du globe), et cette surface a presque triplé au cours des trente dernières années. Certaines ne sont cependant que théoriques et n'échappent pas aux dégradations : l'agriculture serait présente dans près de la moitié d'entre elles.

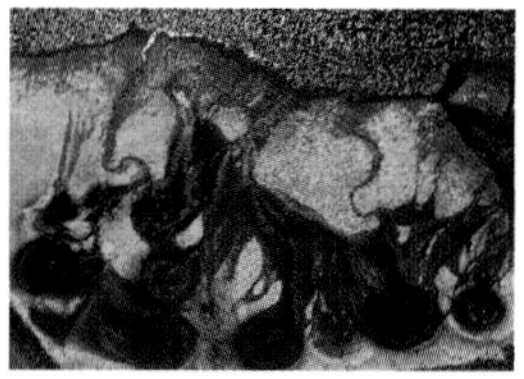

S 12°41' E 132°53'

MINA DE URANIO EN EL PARQUE NACIONAL DE KAKADU, TERRITORIO DEL NORTE, AUSTRALIA.

El Parque Nacional de Kakadu, en Australia, dispone de importantes recursos de uranio (10% de las reservas mundiales) repartidos en tres parcelas: Ranger, Jabiluka y Koongarra, que, aunque situadas en el recinto de un espacio protegido, y figurando desde 1981 en la Lista del Patrimonio Mundial de la UNESCO, están estatutariamente excluidas. Sólo Ranger se beneficia de una autorización de extracción y está explotada por compañías mineras que depositan una parte de sus beneficios a los propietarios. La explotación de los otros sitios suscita una controversia en cuanto a los riesgos de contaminación, y los aborígenes de Mirrar, propietarios tradicionales de las tierras, se oponen vigorosamente al desarrollo de minas en su territorio. En esta zona de rechazos de residuos, anchos aspersores riegan las orillas del pantano, con el fin de aumentar la evaporación y reducir los riesgos de propagación en polvo, dejando depósitos de sales de sulfato. Con otros dos grandes yacimientos en su territorio, Australia posee un cuarto de las reservas del globo y produjo en 1999 cerca del 20% de las 37 000 toneladas de uranio que se extrajeron en el mundo. El uranio abastece de combustible al parque nuclear mundial, repartido principalmente entre Estados Unidos, Francia y Japón.

URANIUM MINE IN KAKADU NATIONAL PARK, NORTHERN TERRITORY, AUSTRALIA.

Kakadu National Park in Australia has important uranium resources (10% of the world's reserves) distributed over three parcels: Ranger, Jabiluka and Koongarra, which are statutorily excluded from the protected area inscribed on the UNESCO World Heritage List since 1981 which they belong to. Extraction is authorized in Ranger only, which is exploited by mining companies who pay part of their profits to the owners. Exploitation of the other sites has caused a controversy in regards to the risks of pollution, and the Mirrar Aborigines, traditional owners of the land, are vigorously opposed to the development of mines on their territory. In this area of waste disposal, large sprinklers water the edges of the swamp in order to increase evaporation and reduce risks of dust spreading, leaving sulfate salt deposits. With two other large deposits on its territory, Australia possesses one-quarter of the globe's reserves, and in 1999 produced close to 20% of the 37,000 metric tons (40,700 tons) of uranium extracted all over the world. Uranium supplies the world's nuclear power plants, distributed mainly between the United States, France and Japan.

MINE D'URANIUM DANS LE PARC NATIONAL DE KAKADU, TERRITOIRE DU NORD, AUSTRALIE.

Le parc national de Kakadu, en Australie, dispose d'importantes ressources en uranium (10 % des réserves mondiales) réparties sur trois parcelles : Ranger, Jabiluka et Koongarra, qui, bien que situées dans l'enceinte d'un espace protégé, figurant depuis 1981 sur la Liste du patrimoine mondial de l'Unesco, en sont statutairement exclues. Seul Ranger bénéficie d'une autorisation d'extraction et est exploité par des compagnies minières qui versent une part de leurs bénéfices aux propriétaires. L'exploitation des autres sites suscite une controverse quant aux risques de pollution, et les aborigènes Mirrar, propriétaires traditionnels des terres, s'opposent vigoureusement au développement de mines sur leur territoire. Dans cette zone de rejets de déchets, de larges asperseurs arrosent les berges du marais, afin d'augmenter l'évaporation et de réduire les risques de propagation en poussière, laissant des dépôts de sels de sulfate. Avec deux autres grands gisements sur son territoire, l'Australie possède un quart des réserves du globe et a produit en 1999 près de 20 % des 37 000 tonnes d'uranium extraites dans le monde. L'uranium approvisionne en combustible le parc nucléaire mondial, réparti principalement entre les Etats-Unis, la France et le Japon.

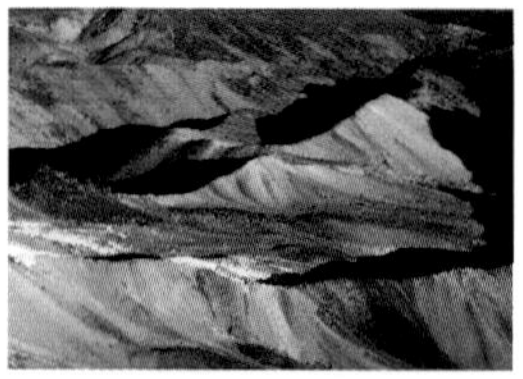

S 15°14' W 71°48'

LA CORDILLERA DE LOS ANDES ENTRE CUZCO Y AREQUIPA, PERÚ.

La Cordillera de los Andes y sus estribaciones cubren un tercio del territorio peruano. Al sur del país, entre Cuzco y Arequipa, las montañas que culminan a más de 6 000 m de altitud dejan progresivamente el lugar a la región de los altiplanos andinos encaramados entre 3 500 y 4 500 m de altitud, llamada Puna. Ésta alberga a las únicas poblaciones sedentarias del mundo que, con los tibetanos, viven en altitudes semejantes. La Cordillera de los Andes es una formación joven nacida hace veinte millones de años como consecuencia de levantamientos de la corteza terrestre y de la acumulación de depósitos de arenisca y de granito. Se extiende a lo largo de los 7 500 km de la costa del Pacífico de América del Sur, atravesando siete países desde el Mar Caribe hasta el Cabo de Hornos. Es la única cadena montañosa que mantiene sin ruptura una altitud elevada en una distancia tan larga.

CORDILLERA OF THE ANDES BETWEEN CUZCO AND AREQUIPA, PERU.

One-third of Peru is covered by the Cordillera of the Andes and its foothills. In the southern part of the country between Cuzco and Arequipa, mountains reaching an altitude of over 6,000 m (20,000 ft.) at their highest point progressively give way to Puna, the Andean Altiplano perched between 3,500 m (11,500 ft.) and 4,500 m (14, 760 ft.) above sea level. This area shelters the only sedentary populations in the world who live at such altitudes, aside from Tibetans. The Cordillera de los Andes is a young formation, born twenty million years ago following upheavals of the Earth's crust and the accumulation of sandstone and granite deposits. It extends 7,500 km (4,660 mi.) along the Pacific coast of South America, crossing seven countries from the Caribbean Sea to Cape Horn. It is the only mountain chain that maintains an unbroken high altitude over such a long distance.

LA CORDILLÈRE DES ANDES ENTRE CUZCO ET AREQUIPA, PÉROU.

La Cordillère des Andes et ses contreforts couvrent le tiers du territoire péruvien. Au sud du pays, entre Cuzco et Arequipa, les montagnes qui culminent à plus de 6 000 m d'altitude laissent progressivement la place à la région des hauts plateaux andins perchés entre 3 500 m et 4 500 m d'altitude, appelée Puna. Celle-ci abrite les seules populations sédentaires au monde qui, avec les Tibétains, vivent à de telles altitudes. La Cordillère des Andes est une formation jeune née il y a vingt millions d'années à la suite de soulèvements de la croûte terrestre et de l'accumulation de dépôts de grès et de granit. Elle s'étire sur 7 500 km le long de la côte Pacifique d'Amérique du sud, traversant sept pays depuis la mer des Caraïbes jusqu'au Cap Horn. Elle est la seule chaîne montagneuse qui maintient sans rupture une altitude élevée sur une aussi longue distance.

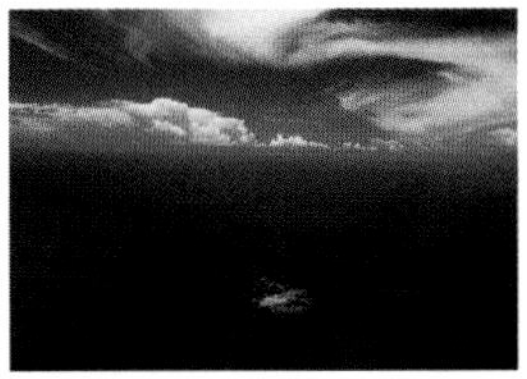

N 6°05' E 120°54'

ISLOTE EN EL ARCHIPIÉLAGO DE SULÚ, FILIPINAS.

Más de 6 000 de las 7 100 islas con que cuenta Filipinas no están habitadas y más de la mitad no tienen nombre alguno. Es el caso de este islote del Archipiélago de Sulú, conjunto de 500 islas que forma al sur del país una frontera natural entre el Mar de las Célebes y el Mar de Sulú. Según la leyenda, estas tierras diseminadas serían perlas desparramadas por una pareja de gigantes después de un pleito. Más prosaicamente, las islas son de origen volcánico y coralino, y su poblamiento en flora y fauna se efectuó progresivamente, como en la mayor parte de los sistemas insulares, gracias a los aportes de las corrientes marinas, los vientos, las aves migratorias y, a veces, del hombre. Perdido en la inmensidad azul, este islote nos recuerda además que cerca del 70% de la superficie de la tierra está cubierta de agua, pero que los recursos de agua dulce del "planeta azul" se debilitan: las reservas mundiales por habitante bajaron más de un tercio desde 1970, y el consumo mundial se multiplicó por 6 en el siglo pasado, mientras que la población no hacía sino triplicarse. En la escala mundial, el 70% del agua captada en el suelo o en los ríos se utiliza para la irrigación y el 20% para la industria (en Europa, estas proporciones se invierten). Los usos domésticos representan el 10%.

ISLET IN THE SULU ARCHIPELAGO, PHILIPPINES.

More than 6,000 of the 7,100 islands in the Philippines are uninhabited, and over half of them are unnamed, including this islet in the Sulu Archipelago, a group of 500 islands that form a natural border in the southern part of the country between the Celebes and Sulu Seas. According to legend, these dispersed lands are said to be pearls scattered by a couple of giants after a quarrel. More prosaically, the islands are of volcanic and coral origin, and they were gradually populated by flora and fauna, as were most of the island systems, because of the contributions of sea currents, winds, migratory birds and sometimes, man. Lost in the blue vastness, this islet reminds us that close to 70% of the earth's surface is covered by water, but that fresh water resources of the "blue" planet are dwindling: the world's reserves per inhabitant have dropped over a third since 1970, and world consumption has increased by a factor of 6 in the last century, while the population has only tripled. At the world level, 70% of all water taken from the soil or from rivers is used for irrigation and 20% for the industry (in Europe, these proportions are reversed). Domestic use represents 10%.

ILOT DANS L'ARCHIPEL DE SULU, PHILIPPINES.

Plus de 6 000 des 7 100 îles que comptent les Philippines sont inhabitées et plus de la moitié ne portent aucun nom. C'est le cas de cet îlot de l'archipel de Sulu, ensemble de 500 îles qui forme au sud du pays une frontière naturelle entre la mer des Célèbes et la mer de Sulu. Selon la légende, ces terres disséminées seraient des perles éparpillées par un couple de géants après une querelle. Plus prosaïquement, les îles sont d'origine volcanique et corallienne, et leur peuplement en flore et faune s'est effectué progressivement, comme dans la plupart des systèmes insulaires, grâce aux apports des courants marins, des vents, des oiseaux migrateurs et, parfois, de l'homme. Perdu dans l'immensité bleue, cet îlot nous rappelle en outre que près de 70 % de la surface de la terre sont recouverts d'eau, mais que les ressources en eau douce de la « planète bleue » s'amenuisent : les réserves mondiales par habitant ont baissé de plus d'un tiers depuis 1970, et la consommation mondiale a été multipliée par 6 au siècle dernier, tandis que la population ne faisait que tripler. A l'échelle mondiale, 70 % de l'eau captée dans le sol ou dans les fleuves est utilisée pour l'irrigation et 20 % pour l'industrie (en Europe, ces proportions sont inversées). Les usages domestiques représentent 10 %.

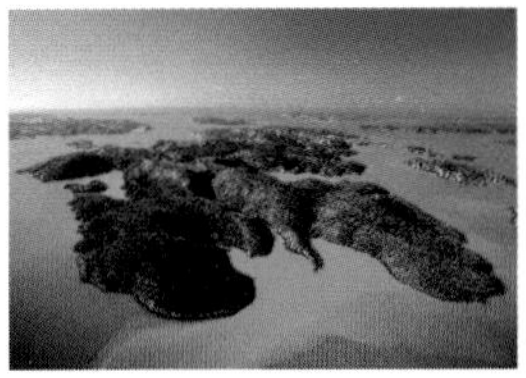

N 63°50' W 19°12'

ARCHIPIÉLAGO DE LOS BUCANEROS, WEST KIMBERLEY AUSTRALIA.

A lo largo de las costas muy recortadas y erosionadas del noroeste de Australia emergen miles de islotes que aún se encuentran en estado salvaje, como los del Archipiélago de los Bucaneros. Las actividades agrícolas e industriales tienen poco presencia en el litoral, el agua del Mar de Timor, que se insinúa entre las islas, se ha salvado relativamente de la contaminación, lo que permite a especies frágiles, como la de las ostras Pinctada máxima desarrollarse en las mejores condiciones. Recogidas en su medio natural, en los fondos marinos, estos moluscos se explotan para la elaboración de perlas cultivadas. Las perlas australianas, que representan el 70% de la producción de los Mares del Sur, son dos veces más gruesas (12 mm de diámetro en promedio) y también según los expertos, más bellas que las de Japón, país pionero, sin embargo, en la actividad (desde principios del siglo xx) y primer productor mundial.

BUCCANEER ARCHIPELAGO, WEST KIMBERLEY, AUSTRALIA.

Off the very jagged, eroded coasts of northwestern Australia, thousand of islets that have remained wild emerge, including those of the Buccaneer Archipelago. Since agricultural and industrial activities are scarce along the coastline, the water of the Timor Sea, which flows among the islands, is relatively free of pollution, allowing fragile species such as the Pinctada maxima oysters, to develop in optimal conditions. Caught in their natural habitat on the seafloor, these mollusks are exploited for their pearls. Australian pearls represent 70% of the South Seas' production. They are two times thicker (12 mm (0.5 in.) in diameter, on average) and more beautiful (according to experts), than those from Japan, a country that is nevertheless a pioneer in this activity (since the beginning of the century) and the leading producer in the world.

ARCHIPEL DES BOUCANIERS, WEST KIMBERLEY, AUSTRALIE.

Au large des côtes très découpées et érodées du Nord-Ouest de l'Australie émergent des milliers d'îlots restés sauvages, comme ceux de l'archipel des Boucaniers. Les activités agricoles et industrielles étant peu présentes sur le littoral, l'eau de la mer de Timor, qui s'insinue entre les îles, est relativement épargnée par la pollution, ce qui permet à des espèces fragiles, comme celle des huîtres Pinctada maxima, de se développer dans les meilleures conditions. Prélevés dans leur milieu naturel, sur les fonds marins, ces mollusques sont exploités pour l'élaboration de perles de culture. Les perles australiennes, qui représentent 70 % de la production des mers du Sud, sont deux fois plus grosses (12 mm de diamètre, en moyenne) et aussi d'après les experts, plus belles que celles du Japon, pays pourtant pionnier de l'activité (depuis le début du siècle) et premier producteur mondial.

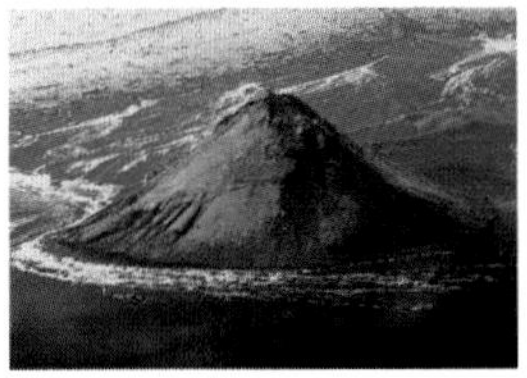

N 63°50' W 19°12'

EL MAELIFELL EN EL BORDE DEL GLACIAR MYRDALSJÖKULL, ISLANDIA.

Nacido en una de las numerosas erupciones ocurridas en el casquete del glaciar Myrdalsjökull, en el sur de Islandia, el Maelifell es una toba volcánica, es decir, un cono constituido por una acumulación de cenizas y otras proyecciones volcánicas solidificadas. Poco a poco, este montículo se ha cubierto de grimmia, un musgo que prolifera en las lavas que se han enfriado y cuyo color varía del gris plata al verde luminoso según el índice de humedad del suelo. Este musgo forma parte de la raras plantas que han podido desarrollarse en el territorio islandés, país que se caracteriza por cierta pobreza botánica, con menos de 400 especies vegetales catalogadas y solamente el 25% de las tierras cubiertas de vegetación permanente. Muy joven geológicamente, con 23 millones de años de existencia, Islandia, cuyo nombre significa literalmente "tierra de hielo" cuenta con más de 200 volcanes activos y numerosos glaciares que ocupan cerca de un octavo de la superficie de la isla.

MAELIFELL ON THE EDGE OF THE MYRDALSJÖKULL GLACIER, ICELAND.

Born out of one of the many eruptions produced under the cap of the Myrdalsjökull glacier in southern Iceland, the Maelifell is a volcanic tuff - a cone formed by the accumulation of ash and other volcanic projections that have solidified. This mound is covered by grimmia, a moss that proliferates on cooled lava and whose color varies from silver-grey to luminous green according to the level of humidity in the soil. This moss is among the few plants that have been able to grow in Icelandic territory, a country that is characterized by a certain botanical poverty, with fewer than 400 plant species listed and only 25% of the land covered with permanent vegetation. In existence for 23 million years and geologically very young, Iceland, literally meaning "land of ice", has over 200 active volcanoes and many glaciers that occupy close to one-eighth of the island's surface.

LE MAELIFELL EN BORDURE DU GLACIER MYRDALSJÖKULL, ISLANDE.

Né de l'une des nombreuses éruptions survenues sous la calotte du glacier Myrdalsjökull, au sud de l'Islande, le Maelifell est un tuf volcanique, c'est-à-dire un cône constitué d'une accumulation de cendres et autres projections volcaniques solidifiées. Peu à peu, cette butte s'est recouverte de grimmia, une mousse qui prolifère sur les laves refroidies et dont la couleur varie du gris argent au vert lumineux selon le taux d'humidité du sol. Cette mousse fait partie des rares plantes qui ont pu se développer sur le territoire islandais, pays qui se caractérise par une certaine pauvreté botanique, avec moins de 400 espèces végétales répertoriées et seulement 25 % des terres couvertes de végétation permanente. Géologiquement très jeune, avec 23 millions d'années d'existence, l'Islande, dont le nom signifie littéralement « terre de glace », compte plus de 200 volcans actifs et de nombreux glaciers qui occupent près du huitième de la superficie de l'île.

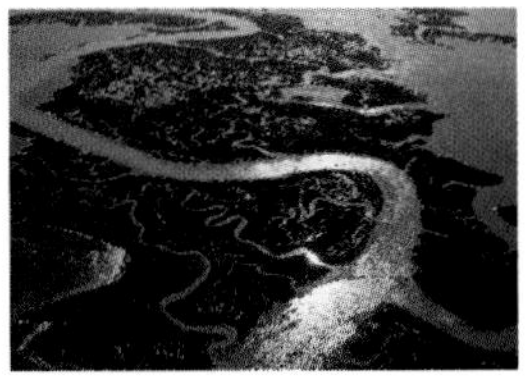

N 29°43' E 31°17'

LA LAGUNA DE VENECIA, VENETO, ITALIA.

La laguna de Venecia, que se extiende sobre 500 km² entre las costas italianas y el Mar Adriático, es la mayor zona húmeda de Italia. Lugar de encuentro de aguas dulces y saladas, este pantano de limo, de arcilla y de arena es particularmente rico en elementos nutritivos que permiten el desarrollo de una multitud de especies acuáticas y que atraen numerosas aves. La laguna está actualmente amenazada por las contaminaciones urbanas e industriales, principalmente los hidrocarburos y los metales pesados. También presenta una gran concentración de fosfatos y nitratos resultado de la agricultura, que favorecen la proliferación de un alga verde, la Ulva rigida. Ésta da lugar a un fenómeno de eutrofización, es decir una disminución del contenido de oxígeno en las aguas, que es fatal para los peces. En los países industrializados, la concentración de nitratos de las aguas continentales se ha duplicado, incluso quintuplicado en algunos países, en el curso de los últimos treinta años.

VENICE LAGOON, VENETO, ITALY.

Venice Lagoon, spreading over 500 sq. km. (200 sq. mi.) between the Italian coasts and the Adriatic sea, is the most extensive wetland in Italy. A meeting-place for fresh and salt water, this marsh of silt, clay and sand is particularly rich in nutrients making the development of a multitude of aquatic species possible and attracting many birds. The lagoon is threatened today by urban and industrial pollution, particularly hydrocarbons and heavy metals. It also presents a high concentration of phosphates and nitrates produced by farming, that encourage the proliferation of a type of green alga called Ulva rigida. This generates a phenomenon of eutrophication: a reduction in the oxygen content of water that is fatal for fish. In the industrialized countries, the concentration of nitrates in continental water has doubled, or even quintupled for certain countries, over the last thirty years.

LA LAGUNE DE VENISE, VÉNÉTIE, ITALIE.

La lagune de Venise, qui s'étend sur 500 km² entre les côtes italiennes et la mer Adriatique, est la plus vaste zone humide d'Italie. Lieu de rencontre d'eaux douces et salées, ce marécage de limon, d'argile et de sable est particulièrement riche en éléments nutritifs qui permettent le développement d'une multitude d'espèces aquatiques et attirent de nombreux oiseaux. La lagune est aujourd'hui menacée par les pollutions urbaines et industrielles notamment les hydrocarbures et les métaux lourds. Elle présente aussi une concentration importante en phosphates et nitrates issus de l'agriculture qui favorisent la prolifération d'une algue verte, l'Ulva rigida. Celle-ci engendre un phénomène d'eutrophisation, c'est-à-dire une diminution de la teneur en oxygène des eaux fatale pour les poissons. Dans les pays industrialisés, la concentration en nitrates des eaux continentales a doublé, voire quintuplé pour certains pays, au cours des trente dernières années.

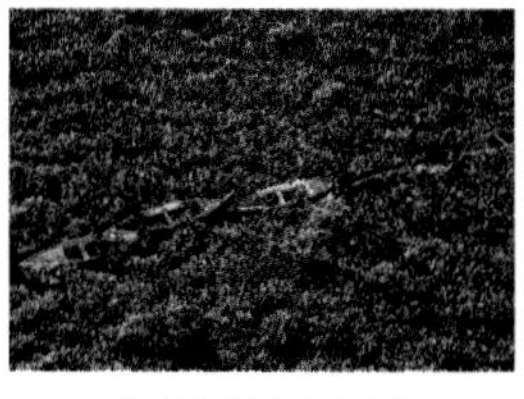

N 29°43' E 31°17'

BARCAS ATRAPADAS EN LOS CAMALOTES DEL NILO, EGIPTO.

Señalado por primera vez a principios del siglo xx en el delta del Nilo, en Egipto, y en la provincia de Natal, en Sudáfrica, el camalote (*Eichhornia crassipes*) es un vegetal acuático invasor. Originario de Brasil, donde se desarrolla moderadamente en su hábitat natural, fue introducido en el continente africano como planta ornamental, y ha formado colonias en menos de cien años en más de 50 países del mundo. Obstáculo para la navegación, obstruye los canales de irrigación agrícolas y las turbinas de las presas hidroeléctricas. La gruesa alfombra vegetal que constituye, y cuya superficie puede duplicarse en 12 días, crea un fenómeno de eutrofización, es decir, una disminución del contenido de oxígeno de las aguas profundas, que conlleva la desaparición por asfixia de la vida acuática. Todavía no se ha encontrado ninguna medida eficaz para erradicar a este invasor, pero medidas de lucha biológica permiten limitar su proliferación. Solamente el 1% de las especies introducidas provoca importantes pérdidas ecológicas y económicas, pero su presencia sigue siendo la segunda causa, después de la destrucción de los hábitats naturales, de la desaparición de especies en el mundo.

BOATS STUCK IN WATER HYACINTHS ON THE NILE, EGYPT.

Noticed for the first time at the beginning of the 20th century in the Nile Delta, Egypt, and in the province of Natal, South Africa, the water hyacinth (*Eichhornia crassipes*) is an invasive aquatic plant. Originally from Brazil, where it grows moderately in its natural habitat, it was brought to the African continent as an ornamental plant, and in less than one hundred years, settled in more than 50 countries throughout the world. It obstructs the agricultural irrigation channels and hydroelectric dam turbines, and is a hindrance to navigation. Forming a thick natural carpet whose surface can double in 12 days, it generates a phenomenon of eutrophication, which reduces the oxygen content in deep waters and kills aquatic life by asphyxia. No efficient way to eradicate this invader has yet been found, but there are some forms of biological control that make it possible to limit its proliferation. Only 1% of all species introduced bring about important ecological and economic losses, but their presence is still the second main cause, after the destruction of natural habitat, for the disappearance of species in the world.

BARQUES PRISES DANS LES JACINTHES D'EAU SUR LE NIL, ÉGYPTE.

Signalée pour la première fois au début du siècle dans le delta du Nil, en Égypte, et dans la province du Natal, en Afrique du Sud, la jacinthe d'eau (*Eichhornia crassipes*) est un végétal aquatique envahissant. Originaire du Brésil, où elle se développe modérément dans son habitat naturel, elle a été introduite sur le continent africain comme plante ornementale, et a colonisé en moins de cent ans plus de 50 pays dans le monde. Entrave à la navigation, elle obstrue les canaux d'irrigation agricoles et les turbines des barrages hydroélectriques. L'épais tapis végétal qu'elle constitue, et dont la surface peut doubler en 12 jours, engendre un phénomène d'eutrophisation, c'est-à-dire une diminution de la teneur en oxygène des eaux profondes, entraînant par asphyxie la disparition de la vie aquatique. Aucun moyen efficace d'éradiquer cet envahisseur n'a encore été trouvé, mais des moyens de lutte biologique permettent de limiter sa prolifération. Seulement 1% des espèces introduites provoque d'importantes pertes écologiques et économiques, mais leur présence reste la deuxième cause, après la destruction des habitats naturels, de la disparition des espèces dans le monde.

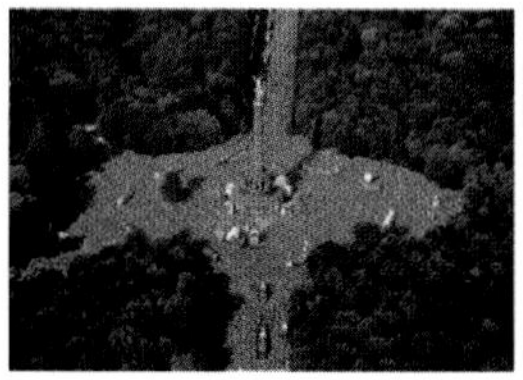

N 52°31' E 13°25'

EL "LOVE PARADE" EN EL PARQUE TIERGARTEN, BERLÍN, ALEMANIA.

En 1989, un "disc jockey" berlinés reunía a 150 amantes de la música electrónica alrededor de una modesta fiesta. Trece años más tarde, el "Desfile del Amor", un neocarnaval desmesurado que reúne a 1 millón de jóvenes y que está a punto de volverse un acontecimiento comercial, es su descendencia. Dos cortejos parten simultáneamente de la Ernst Reuter Platz y de la Puerta de Brandenburgo, inundando la avenida del 17 de junio con una multitud extravagante que baila al ritmo de la música "tecno", y se reúnen al pie de la Columna de la Victoria en el centro del Parque Tiergarten. Estas reuniones experimentan un éxito creciente: en París, Zurich, Ginebra o Newcastle, el "Love Parade" berlinés ya tiene sus émulos. Incluso se lo esperaba en las calles de Moscú en 2001, si el ayuntamiento no se hubiera opuesto a ello. Para algunos, este rechazo habría resultado de una confusión, común, con la Marcha del Orgullo Lésbico-Gay. Ésta vio la luz en 1997, creada por un movimiento homosexual que reivindicaba el derecho a la diferencia. Si bien la tolerancia progresa, especialmente gracias a estas movilizaciones, en numerosos países esta diferencia sigue siendo fuente de discriminaciones y a veces de violencia.

"LOVE PARADE" IN THE TIERGARTEN PARK, BERLIN, GERMANY.

In 1989, a Berlin "disc jockey" gathered 150 electronic music amateurs around a modest party. Thirteen years later, its descendant the "Love Parade", an extravagant "neo-carnival" attracting 1 million young people, has come close to becoming a commercial event. Two corteges leave simultaneously from Ernst Reuter Platz and the Brandenburg Gate, flooding June 17th Avenue with an outlandish crowd that dances to the rhythm of "techno" music, to then reassemble at the foot of the Victory Column in the middle of Tiergarten Park. These gatherings have met an increasing success: in Paris, Zurich, Geneva or Newcastle, the Berlin "Love Parade" already has imitators. Had City Hall not opposed it, it was even expected in the streets of Moscow in 2001. According to some, this refusal was the result of a common confusion with "Lesbian & Gay Pride", which came into existence in 1997, created by a homosexual movement claiming the right to be different. Tolerance is progressing, especially thanks to these get-togethers, although this difference remains a source of discrimination, and sometimes violence, in many countries.

LA « LOVE PARADE » DANS LE PARC TIERGARTEN, BERLIN, ALLEMAGNE.

En 1989, un « disc jockey » Berlinois réunissait 150 amateurs de musiques électroniques pour une modeste fête. Treize ans plus tard, la « Love Parade », un néo-carnaval démesuré rassemblant 1 million de jeunes, en passe de devenir un événement commercial, en est la descendance. Deux cortèges partent simultanément de l'Ernst Reuter Platz et de la Porte de Brandebourg, inondant l'avenue du 17 juin d'une foule extravagante dansant au rythme de la musique « techno », et se rejoignent au pied de la Colonne de la Victoire au centre du parc Tiergarten. Ces rassemblements connaissent un succès grandissant : à Paris, Zurich, Genève ou Newcastle, la « Love Parade » Berlinoise a déjà fait des émules. Elle était même attendue dans les rues de Moscou en 2001, si la mairie ne s'y était opposée. Pour certains, ce refus résulterait d'une confusion – courante – avec la « Lesbian & Gay Pride ». Celle-ci a vu le jour en 1997, créée par un mouvement homosexuel revendiquant le droit à la différence. Si, notamment grâce à ces mobilisations, la tolérance progresse, dans de nombreux pays, cette différence reste source de discriminations, parfois de violences.

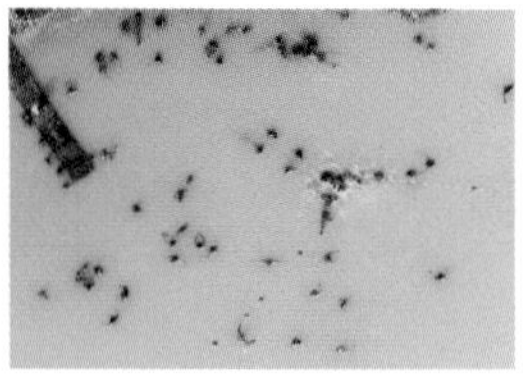

N 63°54' W 22°25'

LAGUNA AZUL, CERCA DE GRINDAVIK, PENÍNSULA DE REYKJANES, ISLANDIA.

Región volcánica, la península de Reykjanes, en Islandia, cuenta numerosas fuentes calientes naturales. La Laguna Azul (o Blá Lónidh) es un lago artificial alimentado por el excedente de las aguas extraídas de la central geotérmica de Svartsengi. Captada a 2000 m bajo tierra, el agua, llevada a 240° C por el magma en fusión, alcanza la superficie a 70° C, donde se utiliza para calentar las ciudades vecinas. El color azul lechoso de laguna resulta de la mezcla mineral de silicio y caliza de la cuenca combinado con la presencia de algas en descomposición. Rica en sales minerales y materias orgánicas, las aguas calientes (alrededor de 40°) de la Laguna Azul son especialmente renombradas por sus propiedades curativas (enfermedades de la piel). Fuente de energía renovable relativamente reciente, propia y poco costosa, la geotermia se explota cada vez más. En Islandia, en 1960, menos de un cuarto de la población se beneficiaba de esta fuente de calor, mientras que actualmente cubre las necesidades del 85% de los islandeses, y sirve para el calentamiento de las piscinas y de los invernaderos.

BLUE LAGOON, CLOSE TO GRINDAVIK, NEAR THE ISLAND OF REYKJANES, ICELAND.

The volcanic peninsula of Reykjanes, Iceland, has many natural hot springs. Blue Lagoon (or Blaá Lónidh) is an artificial lake fed by the surplus of waters drawn by the geothermal power plant in Svartsengi. Brought to the surface from a depth of 2000 m (6,600 ft), the water, heated to a temperature of 240°C (464°F) by molten magma, reaches the surface at a temperature of 70°C (160°F), where it is used to warm the neighboring cities. The blue, milky color of the lagoon is a result of the mineral mixture of silica and limestone in the basin combined with the presence of decomposing algae. Rich in mineral salts and organic matter, the Blue Lagoon's warm waters (about 40°C (100°F)) are especially known for their curative properties (in skin diseases). A source of relatively recent renewable energy, clean and inexpensive, geothermics is being increasingly exploited. In Iceland, less than a quarter of the population in 1960 used this source of heat, while today it covers the needs of 85% of all Icelanders, and is used to heat swimming pools and greenhouses.

BLUE LAGOON, PRÈS DE GRINDAVIK, PRESQU'ÎLE DE REYKJANES, ISLANDE.

Région volcanique, la péninsule de Reykjanes, en Islande, compte de nombreuses sources chaudes naturelles. Le Blue Lagoon (ou Blaá Lónidh) est un lac artificiel alimenté par le surplus des eaux puisées par la centrale géothermique de Svartsengi. Captée à 2000 m sous terre, l'eau, portée à 240 °C par le magma en fusion, atteint la surface à 70 °C, où elle est utilisée pour chauffer les villes voisines. La couleur bleu laiteux du lagon résulte du mélange minéral de silice et de calcaire du bassin combiné avec la présence d'algues en décomposition. Riche en sels minéraux et matières organiques, les eaux chaudes (environ 40°) du Blue Lagoon sont notamment réputées pour leurs propriétés curatives (maladies de peau). Source d'énergie renouvelable relativement récente, propre et peu coûteuse, la géothermie est de plus en plus exploitée. En Islande, en 1960, moins d'un quart de la population bénéficiait de cette source de chaleur, alors qu'elle couvre aujourd'hui les besoins de 85 % des Islandais, et sert au chauffage des piscines et des serres.

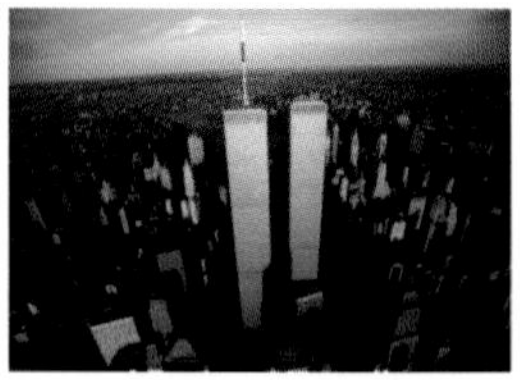

N 40°45' W 73°59'

EL WORLD TRADE CENTER, NUEVA YORK, NY.

Más de un mes después de los atentados terroristas del 11 de septiembre de 2001 contra el Centro Mundial del Comercio, la ceniza y el polvo siguen cubriendo el Lower Manhattan, el barrio de los negocios de Nueva York. Pero, a pesar de las heridas, la ciudad no aspira sino a resurgir después de la catástrofe. Ya sea Chicago o San Francisco, ambas destruidas por las llamas a lo largo de su historia, o de nueva cuenta Nueva York, que vivió dos terribles incendios, uno en 1776 y el otro en 1835, cada una de estas ciudades ha visto el corazón de su barrio de negocios aniquilado por las llamas. Estos espacios se reconstruyeron, así como se reconstruirá el Distrito Financiero de Manhattan. Ya se están llevando a cabo debates respecto de una próxima rehabilitación, un futuro reordenamiento del sitio devastado sobre el que se levantaba el Centro Mundial del Comercio, sin que por ello se haya llegado a un consenso inmediato. Autoridades municipales, arquitectos, urbanistas e historiadores están poniéndose de acuerdo para discutir sobre el porvenir de este barrio. Su reconstrucción es segura, no solo con objeto de rehabilitar esta parte de la ciudad, sino sobre todo para rendir homenaje a los miles de estadounidenses y de ciudadanos de otras nacionalidades que ahí perecieron. Hoy se trata de un lugar sagrado.

THE WORLD TRADE CENTER, NEW YORK, UNITED STATES.

More than a month after the September 11th terrorist attacks that wiped out the World Trade Center, ashes and dust still cover Lower Manhattan, New York city's business and financial district. Nevertheless, in spite of its wounds, the city aims to rebound after the catastrophe. Chicago and San Francisco, both destroyed by flames throughout their history, as well as New York city who lived through two terrible fires in 1776 and in 1835, witnessed the heart of their business districts engulfed by flames. Nevertheless, these areas were rebuilt, as will one day be Manhattan's Financial District. Shortly after the attack, a discussion reuniting architects, urbanists, historians and municipal authorities began. Its outcome, still undetermined, will decide upon the new face of this devastated area where the World Trade Center once stood. Reconstruction is certain, not only to rehabilitate this part of the city but mainly to honor the thousands of Americans and other citizens of different nationalities who perished. It is today a sacred site.

LE WORLD TRADE CENTER, NEW YORK, ETATS-UNIS.

Plus d'un mois après les attentats terroristes du 11 septembre 2001 qui ont anéanti le World Trade Center, cendres et poussière recouvrent toujours le Lower Manhattan, le quartier des affaires de New York. Mais, malgré les blessures, la ville n'aspire qu'à rebondir après la catastrophe. Chicago et San Francisco, toutes deux détruites par les flammes au cours de leur histoire, ou encore New York qui connut deux terribles incendies en 1776 puis en 1835, virent chacune le cœur de leur quartier d'affaires disparaître dans les flammes. Chaque fois, ces espaces furent reconstruits, tout comme le sera le Financial District de Manhattan. Peu après l'événement, une concertation, réunissant architectes, urbanistes et historiens aux côtés des autorités municipales, s'est engagée. Son issue, encore indéterminée, devra décider du nouveau visage du site dévasté sur lequel s'élevait le World Trade Center. Mais la reconstruction est certaine, non seulement pour réhabiliter cette partie de la ville, mais surtout pour rendre hommage aux milliers d'Américains et de ressortissants d'autres nationalités qui ont péri sur place. C'est aujourd'hui un lieu sacré.

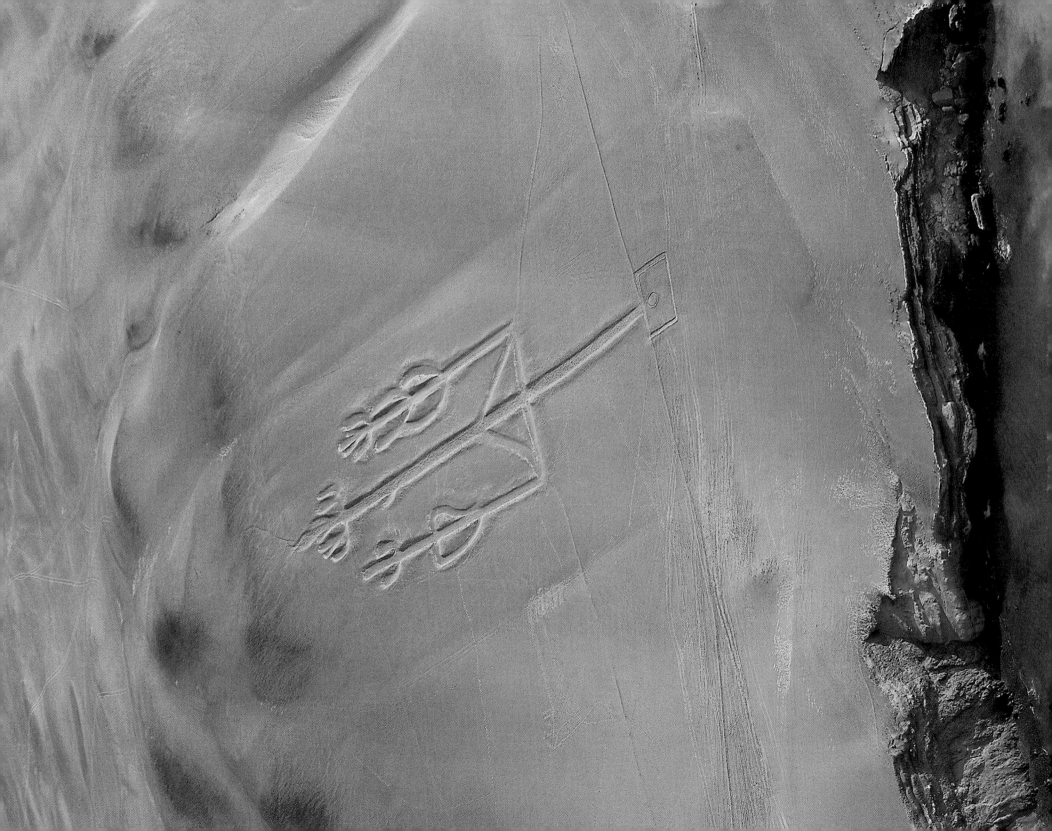

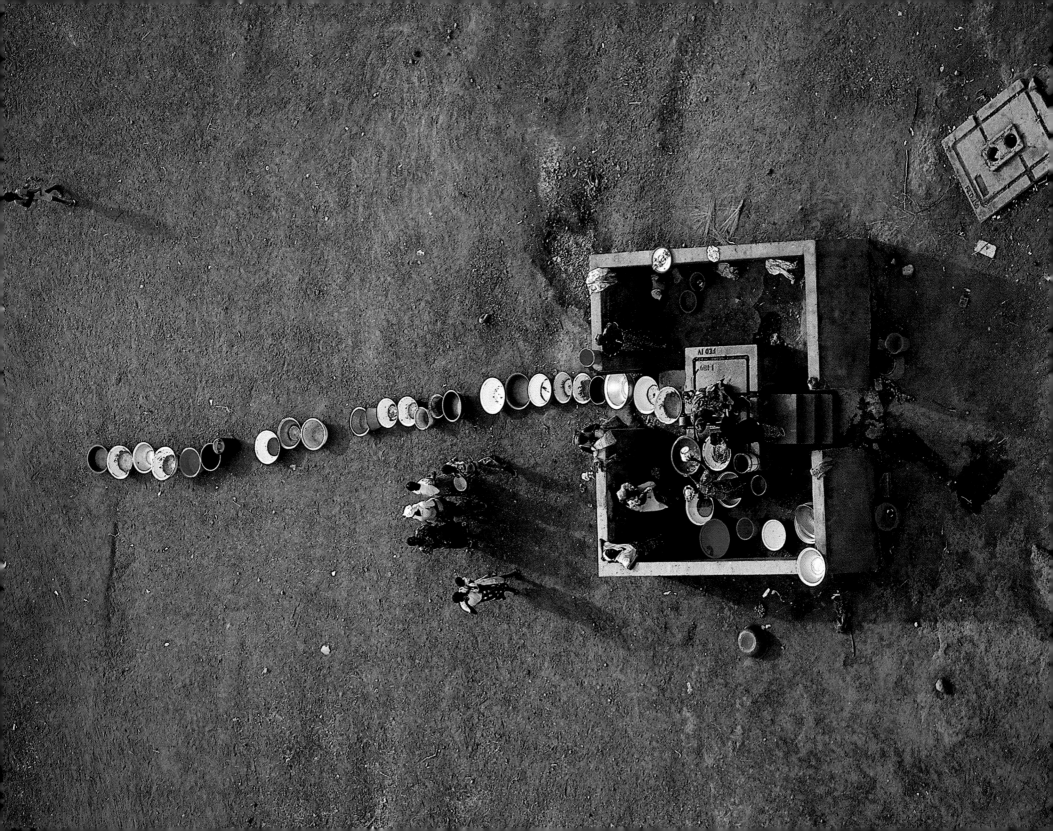

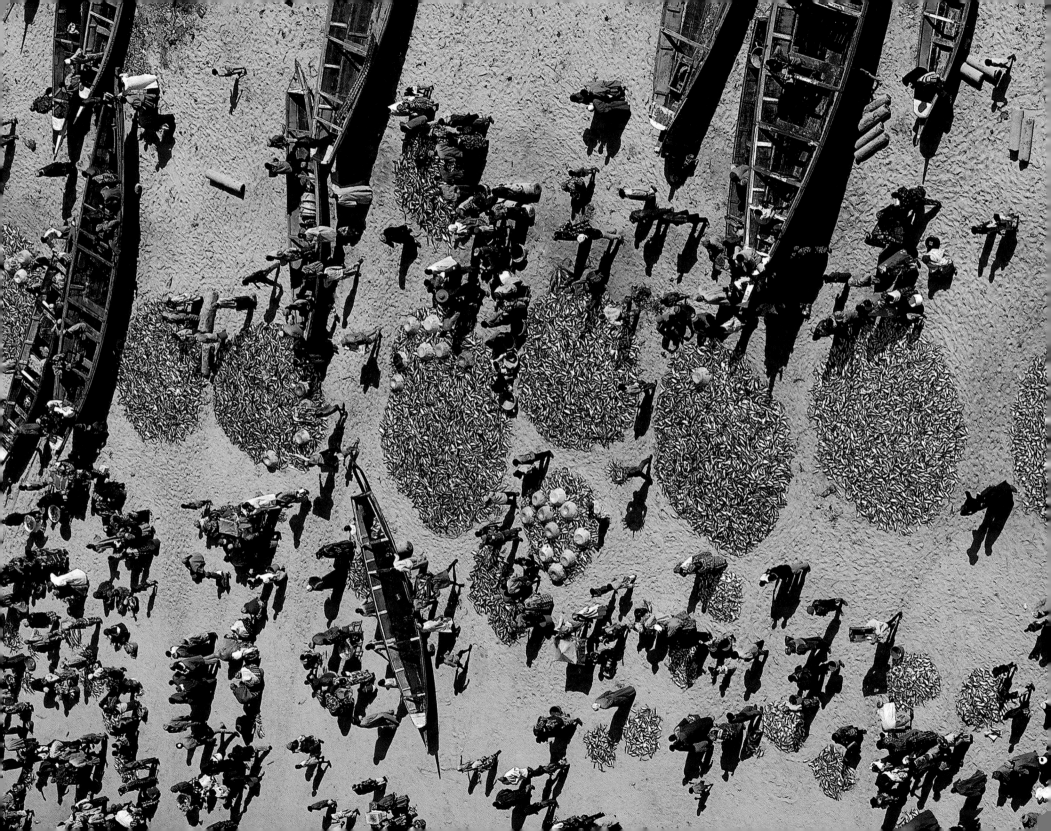

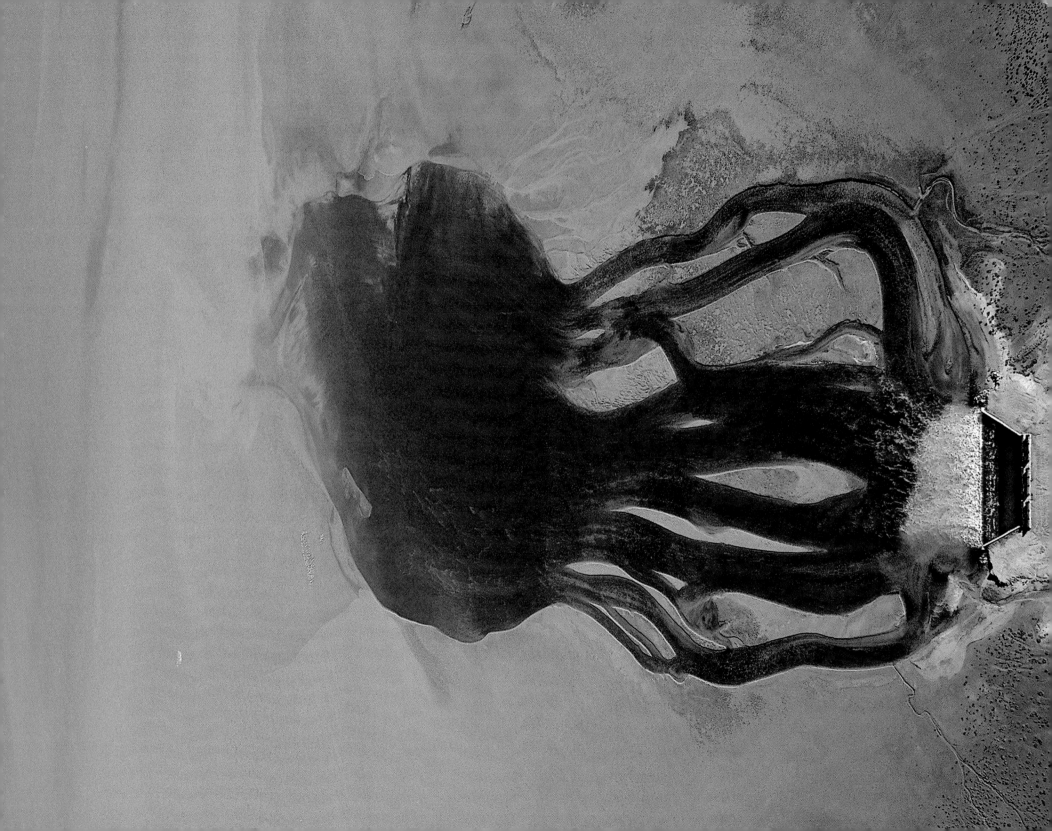

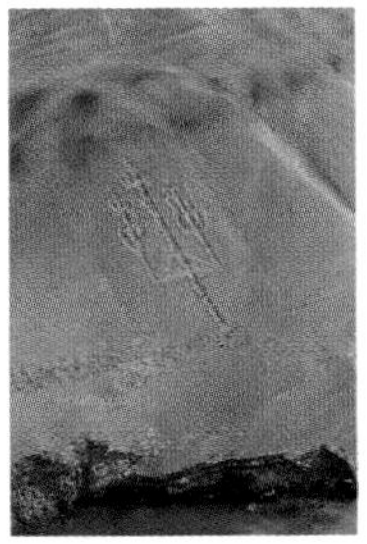

S 13°48' W 76°24'

EL CANDELABRO DE LA PENÍNSULA DE PARACAS, PERÚ.

Comúnmente llamado "el candelabro", este dibujo de 200 m de alto por 60 m de ancho grabado en el acantilado de la península de Paracas en la costa peruana, sería, según los especialistas, la representación de un cactus o de la constelación de la Cruz del Sur. Si presenta similitudes con los célebres trazos de Nazca, a alrededor de 200 km al sureste, es cambio obra de una civilización anterior, los paracas, de los cuales se encontró en la región una necrópolis de 429 cuerpos momificados, o fardos funerarios. Afamados por sus tejidos, bordados y cerámica, los paracas, cuya civilización floreció hacia 650 a. c., eran sobre todo un pueblo de pescadores. Visible desde muy lejos en el mar, "el candelabro" constituía ciertamente un punto de referencia para la navegación, como lo es todavía en la actualidad para los marinos que cruzan de largo.

THE "CANDELABRA" ON THE PARACAS PENINSULA, PERU.

Commonly called the "Candelabra", this drawing 200 m (660 ft) high by 60 m (200 ft) wide, sculpted in the cliff of the Paracas Peninsula on the coast of Peru, represents either a cactus or the constellation of the Southern Cross according to specialists. Although similar to the famous Nazca lines located 200 km to the southeast, it is actually the work of the Paracas, a previous civilization whose necropolis of 429 mummified bodies, or funeral "fardos", was found in the region. Mostly fishermen, the Paracas, whose civilization flourished around 650 B.C., were also known for their cloths, embroideries and ceramic. Visible from far out at sea, the "Candelabra" certainly made a landmark for navigation, as it still does today for sailors crossing the high seas.

LE CHANDELIER DE LA PÉNINSULE DE PARACAS, PÉROU.

Communément appelé « le chandelier », ce dessin de 200 m de haut sur 60 m de large gravé dans la falaise de la péninsule de Paracas sur la côte péruvienne, serait selon les spécialistes la représentation d'un cactus ou de la constellation de la Croix du sud. S'il présente des similitudes avec les célèbres tracés de Nazca, à environ 200 km au sud-est, il est en revanche l'œuvre d'une civilisation antérieure, les Paracas, dont on a retrouvé dans la région une nécropole de 429 corps momifiés, ou fardos funéraires. Réputés pour leurs tissus, broderies et céramiques, les Paracas, dont la civilisation s'est épanouie vers 650 av. J.-C., étaient surtout un peuple de pêcheurs. Visible de très loin en mer, « le chandelier » constituait certainement un point de repère pour la navigation, comme il l'est encore aujourd'hui pour les marins qui croisent au large.

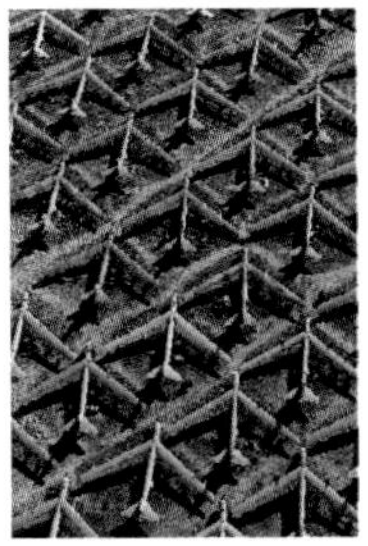

N 32°11' W 110°53'

B-52 EN LA BASE AÉREA DAVIS MONTHAN CERCA DE TUCSON, ARIZONA, ESTADOS UNIDOS.

Varios cientos de bombarderos norteamericanos B-52 Stratofortress, conservados como reservas de piezas sueltas, están almacenados en la Base Aérea Davis Montan, en el corazón del Desierto de Arizona. Después de su primer vuelo de prueba en 1952 en Seattle, este avión se utilizó intensamente cuando la Guerra de Vietnam (1954-1975), después, en una nueva versión modernizada, durante la Guerra del Golfo (1991). Los últimos modelos alcanzaron a participar, en 1999, en los bombardeos de los Balcanes, y en 2001, de Afghanistan. Este avión de guerra simboliza el poderío del ejército más fuerte del mundo, que marcó la entrada en el siglo XXI de su incontestable dominio en el terreno militar. Desde la Guerra del Golfo, el papel de Estados Unidos en los conflictos se ha vuelto de capital importancia, y su influencia en las instituciones internacionales como la OTAN resulta preponderante. No obstante, el poderío militar no es sino una de las numerosas facetas del modelo norteamericano que, del comercio a la cultura, se extiende actualmente por todo el planeta.

B-52S ON DAVIS-MONTHAN AIR BASE, CLOSE TO TUCSON, ARIZONA, UNITED STATES.

Several hundreds of American B-52 Stratofortress bombers are kept for their spare parts on Davis-Monthan Air Base, in the heart of the Arizona Desert. After its first test flight in 1952 in Seattle, this plane was extensively used during the Vietnam war (1954-1975), and then in a new modernized version during the Gulf War (1991). In 1999, the latest models were used to bomb the Balkans, and in 2001, Afghanistan. This warplane symbolizes the power of the world's strongest army, which entered the 21st century as the indisputable leader in the military field. The United States have been playing a major role in conflicts since the Gulf War, and their influence over international institutions such as NATO is becoming predominant. However, military power is only one of the numerous facets of the American model, spreading today in all fields around the planet, from business to culture.

B-52 SUR LA BASE AÉRIENNE DAVIS MONTHAN PRÈS DE TUCSON, ARIZONA, ÉTATS-UNIS.

Plusieurs centaines de bombardiers américains B-52 Stratofortress, conservés comme réserves de pièces détachées, sont entreposés sur la base aérienne Davis Monthan, au cœur du désert de l'Arizona. Après son premier vol d'essai en 1952 à Seattle, cet avion a été intensément utilisé lors de la guerre du Vietnam (1954-1975), puis, dans une nouvelle version modernisée, pendant la guerre du Golfe (1991). Les derniers modèles ont encore participé, en 1999, à des bombardements dans les Balkans, et en 2001, en Afghanistan. Cet avion de guerre symbolise la puissance de la plus forte armée du monde, qui a marqué l'entrée dans le 21e siècle de son incontestable domination dans le domaine militaire. Depuis la Guerre du Golfe, le rôle des Etats-Unis dans les conflits est devenu majeur, et leur influence dans les institutions internationales comme l'OTAN se fait prépondérante. Cependant, la puissance militaire n'est qu'une des nombreuses facettes du modèle américain qui, du commerce à la culture, s'étend aujourd'hui sur toute la planète.

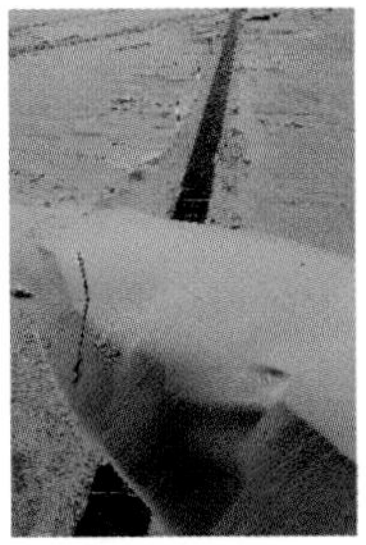

N 25°24' E 30°26'

CARRETERA CORTADA POR UNA DUNA, VALLE DEL NILO, EGIPTO.

Provenientes de antiguos aluviones fluviales o lacustres acumulados en depresiones, y expurgados por miles de años de vientos, los granos de arena se acumulan frente al menor obstáculo y crean dunas. Éstas cubren cerca de 1/3 del Sahara y las más altas, de forma lineal, pueden alcanzar 300 m. Algunas, llamadas barkhanes, con forma de cuerno, son móviles: se desplazan en el sentido del viento dominante, a un ritmo que puede alcanzar 10 m por año, y llegan a cubrir a veces las infraestructuras, como esta carretera en el Valle del Nilo. Los desiertos han existido siempre en la historia del planeta y evolucionan constantemente desde hace cientos de millones de años, en respuesta a los cambios climáticos y a la deriva de los continentes. Bosques y praderas cubrían así, hace 20 000 años, las montañas del centro del Sahara, donde también se han descubierto pinturas rupestres que representan elefantes, rinocerontes y jirafas, que dan testimonio de su presencia en esta zona, hace alrededor de 8 000 años. En la actualidad, las actividades humanas, especialmente la sobre explotación de la vegetación de las tierras semiáridas en los bordes de los desiertos, desempeñan igualmente un papel en la desertización.

ROAD CUT OFF BY A DUNE, NILE VALLEY, EGYPT.

Grains of sand accumulating around the smallest obstacles originate from ancient fluvial or lacustrine alluvium accumulated in depressions and sifted through by thousands of years of winds, thus creating dunes. They cover nearly 1/3rd of the Sahara and the highest, which are linear, can reach 300 m. Others called barkhanes, are crescent-shaped and mobile. They move in the direction of the dominant wind, at a rate that can reach 10 m (33 ft.) per year, sometimes covering infrastructures, such as this road in the Nile Valley. Deserts have always existed in the history of the planet, constantly evolving in response to climatic changes and continental drift for hundreds of millions of years. Thus 20,000 years ago, forests and plains used to cover the mountains in the central Sahara, where cave paintings were also discovered representing elephants, rhinoceroses and giraffes, testifying to their presence in this area about 8,000 years ago. Today, human activities, especially the overexploitation of the semi-arid earth vegetation on the edge of the deserts, also play a role in desertification.

ROUTE COUPÉE PAR UNE DUNE, VALLÉE DU NIL, EGYPTE.

Issus d'anciennes alluvions fluviales ou lacustres accumulées dans des dépressions, et triés par des milliers d'années de vents, les grains de sable s'accumulent devant le moindre obstacle et créent des dunes. Celles-ci couvrent près d'1/3 du Sahara et les plus hautes, de forme linéaire, peuvent atteindre 300 m. Certaines, appelées barkhanes, en forme de croissant, sont mobiles : elles se déplacent dans le sens du vent dominant, à un rythme pouvant atteindre 10 m par an, allant parfois jusqu'à recouvrir des infrastructures, comme cette route dans la vallée du Nil. Les déserts ont toujours existé dans l'histoire de la planète, évoluant constamment, depuis des centaines de millions d'années, en réponse aux changements climatiques et à la dérive des continents. Forêts et prairies couvraient ainsi, il y a 20 000 ans, les montagnes du centre du Sahara, où l'on a aussi découvert des peintures rupestres représentant éléphants, rhinocéros et girafes, qui attestent de leur présence dans cette zone, il y aurait environ 8 000 ans. Aujourd'hui, les activités humaines, notamment la surexploitation de la végétation des terres semi-arides en bordure des déserts, jouent également un rôle dans la désertification.

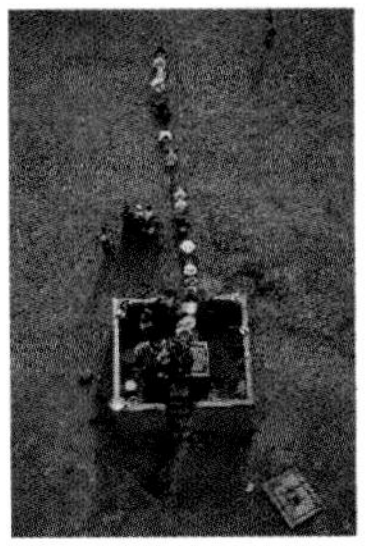

N 9°47' W 3°19'

PERFORACIÓN HIDRÁULICA PUEBLERINA CERCA DE DOROPO, REGIÓN DE BOUNA, COSTA DE MARFIL.

Por todas partes en África, la colecta del agua es un papel habitualmente reservado a las mujeres, como aquí, cerca de Doropo al norte de Costa de Marfil. Las perforaciones hidráulicas, equipadas con bombas generalmente manuales, reemplazan poco a poco a los pozos tradicionales de los pueblos y los recipientes de material plástico, metal esmaltado o aluminio, suplantan a los canarios (grandes jarras de barro cocido) y calabacinos para transportar el precioso recurso. Extraída de los mantos freáticos, el agua de estas perforaciones presenta menos riesgos sanitarios que la de los pozos tradicionales que, en más del 70% de los casos no es propia para el consumo. En el año 2000, el 20% de la población mundial no dispone de agua potable. En África, esto representa 2 de cada 5 personas en promedio, pero más de la mitad de la población de la zona rural no tiene acceso a un agua salubre. Las enfermedades debidas a la insalubridad del agua constituye la primera causa de mortalidad infantil de los países en desarrollo: la diarrea le arrebata así, cada año, la vida a 2.2 millones de niños antes de haber cumplido cinco años. En África y en Asia, el mejoramiento del acceso al agua potable se presenta como uno de los desafíos mayores de los decenios futuros, frente al incremento esperado de la población.

HYDRAULIC DRILLING IN A VILLAGE CLOSE TO DOROPO, NEAR BOUNA, CÔTE-D'IVOIRE.

Everywhere in Africa, collecting water is usually a woman's responsibility, as seen here close to Doropo, in northern Côte-d'Ivoire. Hydraulic drilling, generally equipped with manual pumps, is progressively replacing traditional village wells, while plastic, enameled metal or aluminum containers are gradually replacing the canaris (large earthenware jars) and calabashes used in transporting this precious resource. The water coming from these drillings, drawn from ground waters, presents fewer health risks than the one from traditional wells, which in over 70% of all cases, is unsuitable for human consumption. In the year 2000, 20% of the world population lacked available drinking water. In Africa, this means 2 out of 5 people on average, but more than half the population in rural areas do not have access to clean water. Illnesses due to unclean water constitute the first reason for infant mortality in developing countries: thus diarrhea is responsible, every year, for the death of 2.2 million children under five years of age. In Africa and Asia, considering the expected population increase, improved access to drinking water is becoming one of the major challenges in the decades to come.

FORAGE HYDRAULIQUE VILLAGEOIS PRÈS DE DOROPO, RÉGION DE BOUNA, CÔTE-D'IVOIRE.

Partout en Afrique, la collecte de l'eau est un rôle habituellement dévolu aux femmes, comme ici près de Doropo, au nord de la Côte-d'Ivoire. Les forages hydrauliques, équipés de pompes généralement manuelles, remplacent peu à peu les puits traditionnels des villages et les récipients en matière plastique, métal émaillé ou aluminium, supplantent les canaris (grandes jarres en terre cuite) et calebasses pour transporter la précieuse ressource. Puisée dans les nappes phréatiques, l'eau de ces forages présente moins de risques sanitaires que celle des puits traditionnels qui, dans plus de 70 % des cas, est impropre à la consommation. En l'an 2000, 20 % de la population mondiale ne dispose pas d'eau potable. En Afrique, cela représente 2 personnes sur 5 en moyenne, mais plus de la moitié de la population en zone rurale n'a pas accès à une eau salubre. Les maladies dues à l'insalubrité de l'eau constituent la première cause de mortalité infantile des pays en développement : la diarrhée emporte ainsi, chaque année, la vie de 2,2 millions d'enfants avant leurs cinq ans. En Afrique et en Asie, l'amélioration de l'accès à l'eau potable se présente comme un des défis majeurs des décennies à venir, face à l'accroissement attendu de la population.

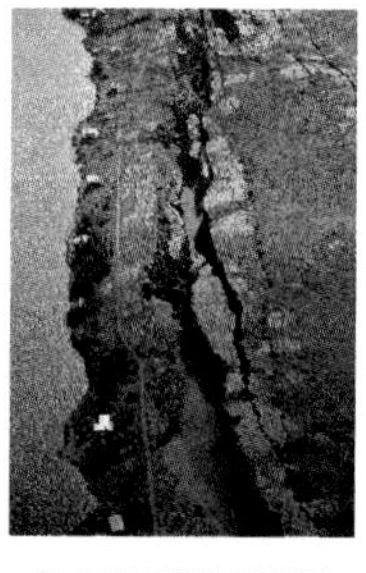

N 64°18' W 21°08'

FALLA DE PINGVELLIR AL ESTE DE REYKJAVIK, ISLANDIA.

La peña quebrada por enormes tensiones debería enseñar a los ribereños que la separación proseguirá por mucho más tiempo que la duración de la vida de diez generaciones. Islandia está situada en el punto donde emerge la dorsal submarina medioatlántica, y se encuentra así en la unión de dos placas tectónicas. La isla se extiende a merced de la actividad volcánica de este rift que, por la producción de magma, separa a Europa de Norteamérica a un ritmo promedio de 2 cm por año. Nuestra Tierra está hecha de tal modo que la escala de sus movimientos es fundamentalmente diferente de la de las acciones humanas. La pequeña carretera que roza las resquebrajaduras, igual que las casas en la orilla del agua, revela una audacia habitual en las sociedades humanas y, paradójicamente, su confianza en la naturaleza. Cada noche de sueño tranquilo es el resultado de una apuesta ganada a las resquebrajaduras siniestras, hasta el día en que...

PINGVELLIR FAULT EAST OF REYKJAVIK, ICELAND.

Residents should be aware that rock splitting is going to continue much longer than the life span of ten generations, as suggests this rock broken by enormous tensions. Iceland is located on the emerged part of the underwater Mid-Atlantic Ridge, and thus at the junction of two tectonic plates. The island stretches at the mercy of this rift's volcanic activity, which is separating Europe from North America at an average rate of 2 cm (nearly 1 in.) per year by producing magma. Our Earth is such that the scale of its movements is fundamentally different from that of human actions. The small road that lines the cracks, as well as the houses on the water's edge, reveal both a daring customary to human societies and paradoxically, confidence they have in nature. Every night of quiet sleep is a bet won against the threats coming from these sinister cracks...

FAILLE DE PINGVELLIR À L'EST DE REYKJAVIK, ISLANDE.

La roche brisée par d'énormes tensions devrait apprendre aux riverains que l'écartement va se poursuivre bien plus longtemps que la durée de vie de dix générations. L'Islande est située sur l'émergence de la dorsale sous-marine médio-atlantique, et se trouve ainsi à la jonction de deux plaques tectoniques. L'île s'étire au gré de l'activité volcanique de ce rift, qui, par production de magma, écarte l'Europe de l'Amérique du Nord au rythme moyen de 2 cm par an. Notre Terre est ainsi faite que l'échelle de ses mouvements est fondamentalement différente de celle des actions humaines. La petite route qui frôle les craquelures, tout comme les maisons au bord de l'eau, révèle une hardiesse dont les sociétés humaines sont coutumières et, paradoxalement, leur confiance dans la nature. Chaque nuit de sommeil tranquille est le résultat d'un pari gagné contre les craquements sinistres, jusqu'au jour où...

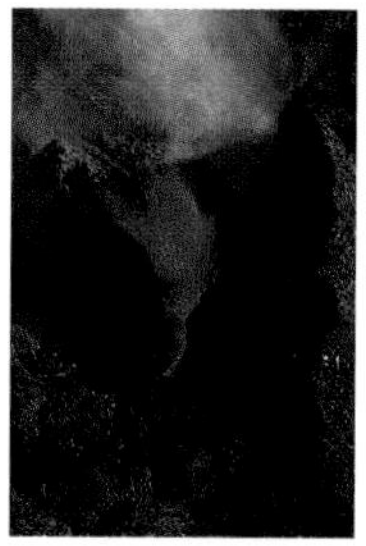

S 21°14' E 55°43'

CONO ERUPTIVO DEL PICO DE LA FOURNAISE, ISLA DE LA REUNIÓN, FRANCIA.

El pico de La Fournaise, que culmina a 2 631 m al sureste de la Isla de la Reunión, es el volcán más activo del planeta después del Kilauea en Hawai. En actividad desde hace 400 000 años, entra en erupción en promedio cada 14 meses; no obstante, en la gran mayoría de los casos, las proyecciones de magma no rebasan las tres zonas de depresiones, o caldeiras, que lo rodean. Excepcionalmente, como en 1997 y 1986, sobrevienen erupciones en el curso de las cuales corrientes de lava devastadoras invaden las pendientes boscosas y las zonas habitadas de la isla. En la actualidad, de los 500 volcanes activos del planeta, situados por encima del nivel del mar, 140 se supervisan permanentemente; es el caso del pico de La Fournaise que, desde la instalación de un observatorio volcánico en 1979, es ciertamente uno de los más controlados del mundo.

CINDER CONE OF THE PITON DE LA FOURNAISE, RÉUNION ISLAND, FRANCE.

The Piton de la Fournaise, which reaches a height of 2,631 m (8,630 ft.) in the southeastern part of Réunion Island, is the most active volcano on the planet after Kilauea in Hawaii. Active for the last 400,000 years, it erupts on average every 14 months. In most cases, the magma projections do not go beyond the three zones of depressions, or calderas, that surround it. In exceptional cases, such as in 1977 and 1986, more violent eruptions occured, during which the devastating lava flows invaded the wooded slopes and inhabited zones of the island. Today, out of the 500 active volcanoes on the planet situated above sea level, 140 are permanently monitored; this is the case of the Piton de la Fournaise which certainly is one of the best monitored in the world, since a volcanic observatory was installed in 1979.

CÔNE ÉRUPTIF DU PITON DE LA FOURNAISE, ÎLE DE LA RÉUNION, FRANCE.

Le piton de la Fournaise, qui culmine à 2 631 m au sud-est de l'île de la Réunion, est le volcan le plus actif de la planète après le Kilauea à Hawaï. En activité depuis 400 000 ans, il entre en éruption en moyenne tous les 14 mois ; cependant, dans la grande majorité des cas, les projections de magma ne dépassent pas les trois zones de dépressions, ou caldeiras, qui l'entourent. Exceptionnellement, comme en 1977 et 1986, surviennent des éruptions plus violentes au cours desquelles des coulées de lave dévastatrices envahissent les pentes boisées et les zones habitées de l'île. Aujourd'hui, sur les 500 volcans actifs de la planète situés au-dessus du niveau de la mer, 140 sont surveillés en permanence ; c'est le cas du piton de la Fournaise qui, depuis l'installation d'un observatoire volcanique en 1979, est certainement l'un des plus contrôlés au monde.

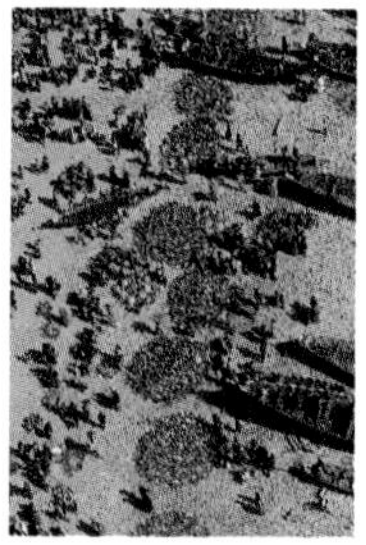

N 14°43' W 17°26'

MERCADO DE PESCADO EN LOS ALREDEDORES DE DAKAR, SENEGAL.

Beneficiándose de una alternancia estacional de corrientes frías ricas en materias minerales que vienen de las Islas Canarias y de corrientes cálidas ecuatoriales, los 700 km del litoral senegalés son favorables al desarrollo de una fauna marina rica y variada. En esta costa se ha desarrollado una explotación intensa de recursos pesqueros, con una producción anual de cerca de 400 000 toneladas. Artesanal en un 80%, la pesca en el mar se practica a bordo de piraguas de madera de baobab o de ceiba, por medio de cañas o de redes. El producto de esta pesca, primer recurso económico de Senegal, alimenta principalmente el mercado local; atunes, sardinas y merluzas se venden, en cuanto a los esencial, en la playa misma, en los lugares donde desembarcan las piraguas. Los senegaleses, como mil millones de personas en los países en desarrollo, dependen del pescado, que proporciona el 40% de las proteínas que consume la población.

FISH MARKET IN THE VICINITY OF DAKAR, SENEGAL.

Enjoying a seasonal alternation of cold currents rich in mineral matter coming from the Canary Islands, as well as warm equatorial currents, the 700 km (430 mi.) of the Senegalese coastline encourages the development of a rich, varied marine fauna. On this coast a heavy exploitation of fish resources has developed, producing close to 400,000 metric tons (440,000 tons) yearly. 80% traditional, deep-sea fishing is practiced in pirogues made of baobab or ceiba wood, using lines or nets. Catch from this fishing, Senegal's most important economic resource, mainly feeds the local market; tuna, sardine and hake are for the most part, sold directly on the beach, where the pirogues unload. The Senegalese depend on fish, which provides 40% of all proteins consumed by the population, as do a billion other people in developing countries.

MARCHÉ DE POISSON AUX ENVIRONS DE DAKAR, SÉNÉGAL.

Bénéficiant d'une alternance saisonnière de courants froids riches en matières minérales venant des îles Canaries et de courants chauds équatoriaux, les 700 km du littoral sénégalais sont favorables au développement d'une faune marine riche et variée. Sur cette côte s'est développée une exploitation intense des ressources en poisson, avec une production annuelle de près de 400 000 tonnes. À 80 % artisanale, la pêche en mer se pratique à bord de pirogues en bois de baobab ou de fromager, au moyen de lignes ou de filets. Le produit de cette pêche, première ressource économique du Sénégal, alimente principalement le marché local ; thons, sardines et merlus sont, pour l'essentiel, vendus à même la plage, sur les lieux de débarquement des pirogues. Les Sénégalais, comme un milliard de personnes dans les pays en développement, dépendent du poisson qui fournit 40 % des protéines consommées par la population.

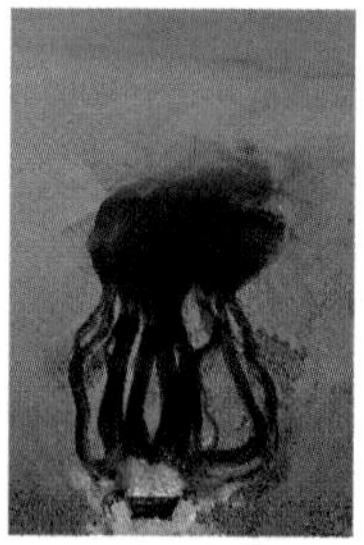

N 29°21' E 47°48'

DESECHOS DE UNA FÁBRICA DE DESALINIZACIÓN DE AGUA DE MAR DE AL-DOHA, REGIÓN DE AL-JAHRA, KUWAIT.

Las dos fábricas desalinización de agua de mar de Al-Doha en Kuwait producen respectivamente 1 200 y 6 000 m³ al día de agua dulce según la técnica de destilación térmica instantánea (sistema "flash"). Después del tratamiento, el agua no apta para el consumo se vuelve a echar al mar donde, dibujando la imagen de un monstruo tentacular, se mezcla a la del Golfo Pérsico. Tributarias por largo tiempo de pozos artesanales y de importaciones provenientes de Iraq para abastecerse de agua potable, Kuwait dispone en la actualidad de varias fábricas que producen más de 400 millones de litros de agua desalinizada al año, con lo que se cubre el 75% de las necesidades del país. Fuertes consumidoras de energía, las estaciones de desalinización sólo son accesibles para los estados que disponen de recursos importantes, especialmente petroleros, como los de la Península de Arabia que, con unas cuarenta fábricas, producen más de la mitad del agua desalinizada del mundo. En el momento en que el abastecimiento de agua dulce se vuelve una preocupación para un número creciente de países, en Europa se consumen de 150 a 250 litros de agua diariamente por persona (una simple descarga representa 10 litros de agua). De esta cantidad, tratada para que sea potable, menos del 1% se bebe efectivamente.

DUMPING FROM A SEAWATER DESALINATION PLANT AT AL DOHA, REGION OF AL JAHRA, KUWAIT.

The two factories for desalinating seawater at Al Doha, Kuwait, produce 1,200 and 6,000 cu. m. (315,600 and 1,578,000 gal.) of fresh water respectively per day using the technique of instantaneous thermal distillation (the "flash" system). After being treated, the water unfit for human consumption is dumped into the sea where, taking on the shape of a tentacled monster, it mixes with the waters of the Persian Gulf. Long dependent on traditional wells and on imports from Iraq for its supplies of drinking water, Kuwait today has several factories that produce more than 400 million liters (100 million gal.) of desalinated water per year, meeting 75% of the country's needs. Heavy consumers of energy, desalination stations are only accessible to states with major resources - especially oil, such as those of the Arabian Peninsula, which produce more than half the desalinated water in the world with nearly forty factories. At a time when supplies of fresh water are becoming a problem for an increasing number of countries, 150 to 250 liters (40 to 65 gal.) of water are consumed per day per person in Europe (a single flush of water represents 10 liters (2.6 gal) of water). Although totally treated for drinking water, less than 1% is actually drunk.

REJETS D'UNE USINE DE DESSALEMENT D'EAU DE MER D'AL-DOHA, RÉGION DE JAHRA, KOWEÏT.

Les deux usines de dessalement d'eau de mer d'Al-Doha au Koweït produisent respectivement 1 200 et 6 000 m³ par jour d'eau douce selon la technique de distillation thermique instantanée (système « flash »). Après traitement, l'eau impropre à la consommation est rejetée en mer où, dessinant l'image d'un monstre tentaculaire, elle se mêle à celle du golfe Persique. Longtemps tributaire de puits artisanaux et d'importations en provenance d'Irak pour s'approvisionner en eau potable, le Koweït dispose aujourd'hui de plusieurs usines qui produisent plus de 400 millions de litres d'eau dessalée par an, couvrant 75 % des besoins du pays. Grosses consommatrices d'énergie, les stations de dessalement ne sont accessibles qu'aux États disposant d'importantes ressources, notamment pétrolières, comme ceux de la péninsule Arabique qui, avec une quarantaine d'usines, produisent plus de la moitié de l'eau dessalée du monde. À l'heure où l'approvisionnement en eau douce devient une préoccupation pour un nombre croissant de pays, on consomme, en Europe, 150 à 250 litres d'eau par jour et par personne (une simple chasse d'eau représente 10 litres d'eau). Sur cette quantité, traitée pour être potable, moins de 1 % est effectivement bue.

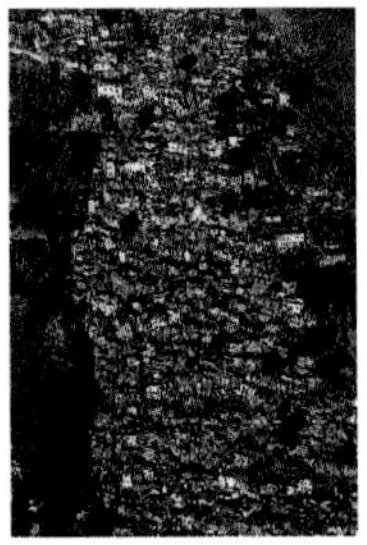

S 22°55' W 43°15'

FAVELAS EN RÍO DE JANEIRO, BRASIL.

Cerca de un cuarto de los 10 millones de cariocas, habitantes de Río de Janeiro, en Brasil, vive en las 500 ciudades perdidas de la aglomeración, o favelas, que han tenido una expansión creciente desde principios de siglo y se han convertido en la cuna de una importante delincuencia. Colgados en su mayoría en los flancos de las colinas, estos barrios pobres y subequipados son víctimas regularmente de deslizamientos de tierra asesinos en el la temporada de lluvias fuertes. Paralelamente, bajando de las favelas, las clases medias y acomodadas de la ciudad (18% de los cariocas) ocupan los barrios residenciales que bordean el malecón. Este contraste social es la imagen del conjunto de Brasil, donde el 10% de la población controla la mayor parte de las riquezas del país, mientras que cerca de la mitad vive por debajo del umbral de pobreza. Consecuencia del crecimiento urbano, alrededor de 25 millones de personas en Brasil, y 600 millones en el mundo, viven en las ciudades perdidas de las grandes aglomeraciones, donde la sobrepoblación y la insalubridad amenazan su salud y su vida.

FAVELAS IN RIO DE JANEIRO, BRAZIL.

Close to a quarter of the 10 million Cariocas - inhabitants of Rio de Janeiro, Brazil, live in the 500 shantytowns or favelas in the metropolitan area that have increasingly been expanding since the beginning of the century, and have become the breeding-ground for criminality. With most of them clinging to the hillsides, these poor, underserviced districts are regularly victims of murderous landslides during heavy rains. At the same time, downstream from the favelas, the middle and upper classes of the city (18% of the Cariocas) occupy residential districts that border the seafront. This social contrast is representative of Brazil itself, where 10% of the population controls the greater part of the country's wealth while close to half live below the poverty line. As a consequence of urban growth, about 25 million people in Brazil and 600 million in the world, live in shantytowns in large urban centers, where overcrowding and unsanitary conditions threaten their health and their lives.

FAVELAS À RIO DE JANEIRO, BRÉSIL.

Près d'un quart des 10 millions de Cariocas, habitants de Rio de Janeiro au Brésil, vit dans les 500 bidonvilles de l'agglomération, ou favelas, qui ont connu une expansion croissante depuis le début du siècle et sont devenus le berceau d'une forte délinquance. Pour la plupart accrochés aux flancs des collines, ces quartiers pauvres et sous-équipés sont régulièrement victimes de glissements de terrain meurtriers lors des fortes pluies. Parallèlement, en aval des favelas, les classes moyennes et aisées de la ville (18 % des Cariocas) occupent les quartiers résidentiels qui bordent le front de mer. Ce contraste social est à l'image de l'ensemble du Brésil où 10 % de la population contrôlent la majeure partie des richesses du pays alors que près de la moitié vit au-dessous du seuil de pauvreté. Conséquence de la croissance urbaine, environ 25 millions de personnes au Brésil, et 600 millions dans le monde, habitent dans les bidonvilles des grandes agglomérations, où le surpeuplement et l'insalubrité menacent leur santé et leur vie.

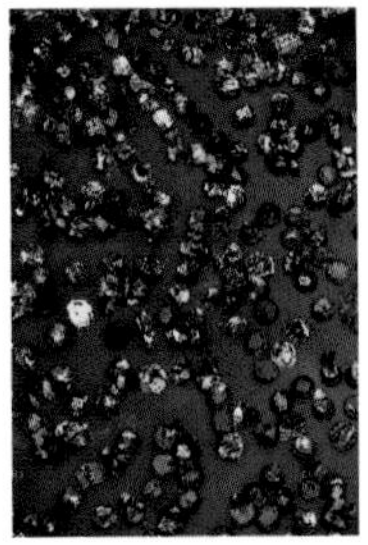

N 5°19' W 4°02'

LAVADO EN UNA MARISMA BARRIO DE ADJAMÉ EN ABIDJÁN, COSTA DE MARFIL.

En el barrio de Adjamé, al norte de Abidján, centenares de lavadores de ropa profesionales, los fanicos, lavan ropa todos los días en la marisma situada en la entrada del bosque tropical de Banco (clasificado como parque nacional en 1953). Utilizando las rocas y llantas llenas de arena para tallar y exprimir la ropa, lavan a mano los miles de vestidos que les encargan. Barrio popular con algunas zonas carentes de agua corriente y electricidad, Adjamé, que hace poco era un pueblito de pescadores, quedó englobado poco a poco en la aglomeración abidjanesa. En esta ciudad de 3.5 millones de habitantes, que experimentó uno de los crecimientos urbanos más fuertes de África del Oeste (se multiplicó por 30 en 40 años), se desarrollaron decenas de pequeños oficios del sector informal, como estos fanicos, que constituyen el único medio de subsistencia de las capas menos favorecidas de la población.

WASHING IN A CREEK, ADJAMÉ DISTRICT IN ABIDJAN, CÔTE-D'IVOIRE.

In the Adjamé district in northern Abidjan, hundreds of professional laundry washers, or fanicos, wash every day in the backwater located at the entrance to Banco tropical rainforest (classified as a National Park in 1953). Using rocks and tires full of sand to rub and wring the laundry, they hand-wash thousands of clothes that are left with them. A working-class district in which some areas lack running water and electricity, Adjamé, which not long ago was a small fishing village, has progressively merged into the greater Abidjan area. In this city of 3.5 million inhabitants, which has undergone one of the greatest urban growths in West Africa (increasing by a factor of 30 in 40 years), dozens of small businesses in the informal sector have sprung up, such as these fanicos, constituting the only means of subsistence for the most underprivileged strata of the population.

LESSIVE DANS UN MARIGOT, QUARTIER D'ADJAMÉ À ABIDJAN, CÔTE-D'IVOIRE.

Dans le quartier d'Adjamé, au nord d'Abidjan, des centaines de laveurs de linge professionnels, les fanicos, font chaque jour la lessive dans le marigot situé à l'entrée de la forêt tropicale du Banco (classée parc national en 1953). Utilisant les rochers et des pneus remplis de sable pour frotter et essorer le linge, ils lavent à la main les milliers de vêtements qui leur sont confiés. Quartier populaire dont certaines zones sont dépourvues d'eau courante et d'électricité, Adjamé, qui était naguère un petit village de pêcheurs, a été englobé peu à peu dans l'agglomération abidjanaise. Dans cette ville de 3,5 millions d'habitants, qui a connu une des plus fortes croissances urbaines d'Afrique de l'Ouest (elle a été multipliée par 30 en 40 ans), se sont développés des dizaines de petits métiers du secteur informel, comme ces fanicos, qui constituent l'unique moyen de subsistance des couches les moins favorisées de la population.

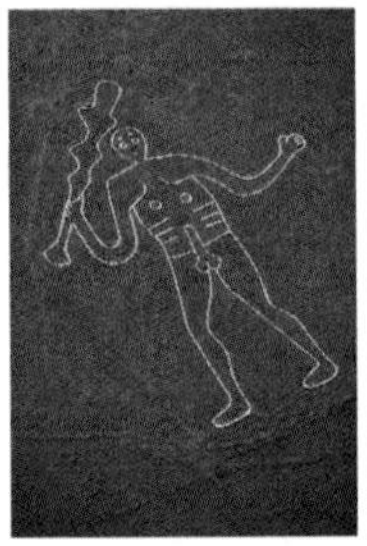

N 50°49' W 2°29'

GIGANTE DE CERNE ABBAS, DORSET, INGLATERRA.

Este gigante armado con un mazo rompecabezas y con 55 m de largo, parece muy moderno, con sus ojos redondos, sus cejas, su boca y su ausencia de nariz, los cinco dedos de la mano bien alineados, sus senos marcados como sus costillas, su estuche peniano detenido con un cordel y sus pantorrillas moldeadas. Podría tratarse también de un hermafrodita en erección. Su imagen se publicó por primera vez en 1746 y se atribuyó maliciosamente a los papistas. Otras interpretaciones ven en él ya sea un dios de la fecundidad anterior a nuestra era, ya sea un Hércules mitad romano, mitad celta de principios de nuestra era. Este dibujo testimonia el deseo de representación del guerrero. Es igualmente una incitación a potencias exteriores, según un esquema mental que continúa marcando la mente de un buen número de seres humanos.

CERNE ABBAS GIANT, DORSET, ENGLAND.

This 55 m (180 ft.) giant, holding a bludgeon, appears quite modern with his round eyes, eyebrows, mouth and missing nose, five well aligned fingers, marked breasts and ribs, penis sheath held by a string and well-shaped calves. This could also be a hermaphrodite with an erection. His image was published for the first time in 1764 and was mischievously attributed to the papists. Other interpretations see in him either a fertility god from before our era, or a half-Roman, half-Celtic Hercules from the beginning of our era. This drawing testifies the desire to represent warriors, and according to a mental scheme that continues to leave its imprint on the minds of many human beings, is also an invitation addressed to powers beyond.

GÉANT DE CERNE ABBAS, DORSET, ANGLETERRE.

Ce géant armé d'une massue casse-tête et long de 55 m paraît bien moderne, avec ses yeux ronds, ses sourcils, sa bouche et son absence de nez, les cinq doigts de ses mains bien alignés, ses seins marqués comme ses côtes, son étui pénien retenu par une ficelle et ses mollets galbés. Il pourrait aussi s'agir d'un hermaphrodite en érection. Son image fut publiée pour la première fois en 1764 et attribuée malicieusement aux papistes. D'autres interprétations voient en lui soit un dieu de la fécondité antérieur à notre ère, soit un Hercule mi-romain, mi-celtique du début de notre ère. Ce dessin témoigne du désir de représentation du guerrier. C'est également une invite adressée à des puissances extérieures, selon un schéma mental qui continue de marquer l'esprit de bon nombre d'êtres humains.

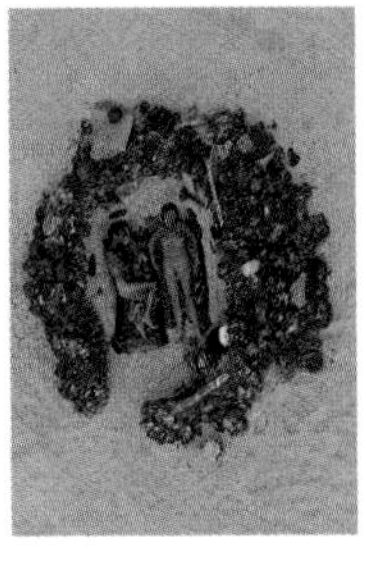

N 28°43' W 13°52'

TURISTAS EN UNA PLAYA DE FUERTEVENTURA, CERCA DE CORRALEJO, ISLAS CANARIAS, ESPAÑA.

Fuerteventura, la segunda de las Islas Canarias por su tamaño, alberga las playas más vastas del archipiélago. Pensando aprovechar la intimidad de una de las numerosas calas aisladas, estos turistas se entregan a los goces del naturismo. Inspirados tal vez por las prácticas agrícolas locales, edificaron un murito de piedras volcánicas con el fin de protegerse de los vientos provenientes del Sahara que barren constantemente la costa. Fuerteventura se previó para la construcción del mayor complejo hotelero del mundo, pero la escasez de agua dulce en la isla, problema que también afecta a más del 20% de la población del archipiélago, condujo rápidamente al abandono de este ambicioso proyecto. El turismo sigue siendo no obstante el polo económico principal de las Canarias, que acogen a 4 millones de visitantes al año, de los cuales el 97% es de origen germánico. España, tercero destino turístico mundial después de Francia y de los Estados Unidos, se involucró desde 1955 en la vía del turismo "sustentable", mejor integrado a la economía local, y menos perjudicial para el medio ambiente.

TOURISTS ON A BEACH IN FUERTEVENTURA, CLOSE TO CORRALEJO, CANARY ISLANDS, SPAIN.

Fuerteventura, the second largest island of the Canaries, harbors the most extensive beaches in the archipelago. Intending to take advantage of the intimacy of one of the numerous isolated creeks, these tourists abandon themselves to the joys of nudism. Certainly inspired by local agricultural practices, they have built a wall of volcanic stone in order to protect themselves from winds blowing off the Sahara that constantly sweep the coast. Fuerteventura was to undergo the construction of the biggest hotel complex in the world, but the shortage of fresh water on the island, a problem affecting more than 20% of the population on the archipelago, quickly led to abandoning this ambitious project. However, tourism is still the economic mainstay of the Canaries, who welcome 4 million visitors per year, 97% of whom are of German origin. Spain, the third favorite tourist destination worldwide after France and the United States, committed in 1995 to "sustainable" tourism, which is better integrated into local economy and less damaging to the environment.

TOURISTES SUR UNE PLAGE DE FUERTEVENTURA, PRÈS DE CORRALEJO, ÎLES CANARIES, ESPAGNE.

Fuerteventura, deuxième plus grande île des Canaries, abrite les plages les plus vastes de l'archipel. Pensant profiter de l'intimité d'une des nombreuses criques isolées, ces touristes s'adonnent aux joies du naturisme. Sans doute inspirés par les pratiques agricoles locales, ils ont édifié un muret de pierres volcaniques, afin de se protéger des vents venant du Sahara qui balaient constamment la côte. Fuerteventura était pressentie pour la construction du plus grand complexe hôtelier du monde, mais la pénurie d'eau douce sur l'île, problème qui touche d'ailleurs plus de 20 % de la population de l'archipel, a rapidement conduit à l'abandon de cet ambitieux projet. Le tourisme reste cependant le pôle économique majeur des Canaries, qui accueillent 4 millions de visiteurs par an, dont 97 % d'origine germanique. L'Espagne, troisième destination touristique mondiale après la France et les Etats-Unis, s'est engagée, depuis 1995, sur la voie d'un tourisme « durable », mieux intégré à l'économie locale, et moins dommageable pour l'environnement.

CIFRAS PARA LA TIERRA

Nuestra aparente riqueza se basa en el crecimiento económico, cuyos indicadores no toman en cuenta el estado de los recursos naturales. Por lo tanto, la deforestación de un país se considera como creación de valor.

Riqueza mundial	1990	1999
PIB mundial	21 billones de dólares	30 billones de dólares

Deforestación anual entre 1990 y 1995 : 101 724 km², o sea 20 % de la superficie de Francia.

Ahora bien, desde los años 1970, la riqueza natural de la Tierra ha disminuido 1/3 bajo la presión del Hombre.

Población mundial	1980	1999
Población urbana	40 %	46 %
Tasa de mortalidad de los menores de cinco años	123 %	75 % (1998)
Población entre 15 y 64 años	2 billones 5 mil millones	3 billones 761 mil millones (1990)
Población activa	2 billones 35 mil millones	2 billones 892 mil millones
Porcentaje de mujeres de la población activa	39 %	41 %
Porcentaje de niños entre 10 y 14 años de la población activa	20 %	12 %

Éducación en el mundo	1980	1997
Gasto público en educación	3,9 % del PNB	4,8 % del PNB
Analfabetismo en hombres de más de quince años	18 %	32 %

4 900 millones (80%) de la población vive en países en vías de desarrollo.

- 40% de la población mundial no tiene electricidad, o sea aproximadamente 2 500 millones de personas.
- 47% de la población mundial vive con menos de 15 francos diarios.
- La participación de los 50 países más pobres en el comercio mundial pasó de 4% a 2% durante los últimos diez años (hasta 2000).
- 33% de los niños menores de 5 años sufren de desnutrición.
- De 4 adultos en el mundo, uno es iletrado (o nunca aprendió a leer - analfabeta -, o ya lo olvidó).
- De 5 personas en el mundo, una no tiene acceso a servicios de salud modernos.
- 95% de las personas infectadas por el SIDA viven en países en vías de desarrollo.
- La deuda externa de los países en vías de desarrollo se ha multiplicado por más de 6 desde 1970, y ha alcanzado los 2 billones 800 mil millones de dólares en 1999.

1 200 millones (20 %) de la población vive en los países desarrollados.

- Los países desarrollados representan el 86% de los gastos privados de consumo.

- Los países de la OCDE se reparten el 67% del comercio mundial (7 billones de dólares).
- La suma de la riqueza de las 200 personas más ricas alcanza el valor de 1 billón 140 mil millones de dólares.
- El desempleo se encuentra a su nivel histórico más bajo, alrededor del 4%. Se invirtió un dólar de cada 10 en "Fondos Éticos" en los Estados Unidos en 2000, o sea un 13% del dinero invertido.

Una cosa es evidente: la vida es posible gracias al aire, a la tierra y al agua. Se ha confirmado otra: están en peligro, por lo tanto, todos estamos amenazados:

Por asfixia. Actualmente, la atmósfera absorbe 1/3 del gas carbónico que producimos cada año. Los 2/3 restantes se acumulan y provocan, por el efecto de invernadero, un desequilibrio climatológico que genera catástrofes naturales (inundaciones, tempestades, sequías, incendios).

- El consumo de combustibles fósiles se ha cuadruplicado en 50 años. El consumo de petróleo, en particular, se ha multiplicado por 7 (actualmente, en un mes y medio se consume la misma cantidad de petróleo que se consumía en un año en 1950).
- Emisiones de gas carbónico: en 1990: 3.3 toneladas/habitante en 1996: 4.0 toneladas/habitante.
- Consumo de electricidad en 1990: 1 928 Mwh/habitante en 1999: 2 053 Mwh/habitante
- La producción de energía eólica se multiplicó por 10 entre 1990 y 2000, y alcanzó el 1% de la energía mundial producida en 1999.

Por crisis alimentarias. Las tierras cultivables son un recurso limitado. Existen cada vez menos tierras para un número cada vez mayor de habitantes (cada año, el equivalente a 10 departamentos franceses es convertido en desiertos). Como consecuencia, la superficie para el cultivo de cereales por habitante se ha dividido entre dos en 50 años. Los medios destinados a la agricultura en los países pobres son demasiado débiles para compensar esta evolución, lo que provoca hambrunas (en 1000, 1/3 de los niños de menos de 5 años sufrían de desnutrición).

Evolución de las tierras en el mundo	1980	1996
Tierras en cultivos permanentes	0.9 %	1.0 % (1997)
Tierras irrigadas	17.8 %	19.2 %
Tierras arables	0.24 ha/hab	0.24 ha/hab
Número de tractores por miles de trabajadores agrícolas	18	20
Carreteras asfaltadas	39 % du total	43.1 % du total (1998)

Un francés produce 350 kg de desechos domésticos al año (o sea 1 kg al día) Un norteamericano produce 700 kg de desechos domésticos al año (o sea 2 kg al día). Cerca de la mitad de las 17 000 reservas naturales en el mundo se utilizan actualmente con fines agrícolas.

Por guerras por el agua. La cantidad de agua disponible por habitante ha disminuido más de un 30% desde 1970. Hoy en día, cerca de diez conflictos mundiales están relacionados con el agua: en Turquía, en India, en Egipto, en Israel. El número de personas que no tienen acceso al agua potable se ha cuadruplicado durante los últimos diez años, y ha alcanzado la cifra de mil millones de personas en 2000.

Reparto del consumo de agua en el mundo
- Un francés consume entre 150 y 250 litros de agua al día, de los cuales solo 2 litros son para beber. Así pues, menos del 0.5% del agua tratada para beber en efecto se consume.
- Un keniano promedio dispone, por su parte, de 4 litros de agua al día.
- Un neoyorkino consume 680 litros al día.

Evolución del consumo de agua en el mundo
Se ha multiplicado por 7 desde 1990 y por 5 desde 1940 (mientras que la población se duplicó).
Recursos mundiales de agua dulce en 1990: 8 000 m³ por habitante.
Mínimo requerido por habitante: 1 000 m³/año.
Menos del 10% de la ciudades del mundo cuentan con una estación de purificación (tratamiento de aguas usadas).

Empleo del agua dulce en el mundo
- 70% para la agricultura (irrigación, de los cuales 3/4 se evaporan).
- 22% para la industria.
- 8% para uso doméstico (del cual 50% se pierde por fugas en las redes).

Reparto de la disponibilidad de agua en el mundo
Regiones más irrigadas: lluvias de 20 metros de agua al año.
Regiones menos irrigadas: lluvias de 50 a 200 mililitros de agua al año.

¿Por qué tanta diferencia?
Por una parte, porque la mayoría de las degradaciones de estos 30 últimos años se localizan en los países del Sur, que nos parecen lejanos aunque las consecuencias nos afectarán directamente. Por otra parte, porque nuestra manera de abordar el medio ambiente se sigue sustentando en una visión heredada de la época en la que los recursos del planeta parecían inagotables. Finalmente, porque tenemos la impresión, errónea, de ser impotentes ante la magnitud del problema. Sin embargo, todos podemos actuar: reduciendo nuestros consumos superfluos y presionando a las empresas y a los gobiernos para que se imponga un desarrollo sustentable, que responda a las necesidades de todos en el presente sin sacrificar a las generaciones futuras. Por lo tanto, la primera solución es concientizar, y como el medio ambiente no va a la gente, hay que llevárselo.

Ese es el procedimiento adoptado por Yann Arthus-Bertrand. Es un despertar necesario - por momentos maravilloso, por momentos preocupante - si esperamos poder transmitir a nuestros hijos una cierta calidad de vida, y asegurarnos un desarrollo sustentable.

Maximilien Rouer

Nota: cada cifra que se menciona está documentada (fuentes: Banco Mundial, PNUD, PNUE, UNESCO, WWF, UICN, WorldWatch Institute, OCDE, FAO, INSEE, World Health Organization, UNICEF, Global Water Supply, UN, GIEC (grupo de expertos intergubernamental sobre la evolución del clima), Organización Mundial de Meteorología, ADEME). Cuando dos cifras relacionadas con el mismo tema eran diferentes, se tomó la cifra más moderada.

THE EARTH IN NUMBERS

Our apparent wealth is measured by economic growth, which doesn't take into account the state of natural resources. The deforestation of a country is therefore considered to create value.

Worldwide wealth	1990	1999
Worldwide GDP	21 trillion dollars (U.S.)	30 trillion dollars (U.S.)
Annual deforestation between 1990 and 1995: 101 724 km² or 20% of France		

However, since the 1970s, the natural wealth of the Earth has been reduced by one third because of man.

Worldwide population	1980	1999
Urban population	40%	46%
Death rate of children younger than 5	123%	75%
Population of 15–64 year olds	2,595 billion	3,761 billion (1990)
Active population	2,035 billion	2,892 billion
Women as % of the active population	39%	41%
Children between 10-14 years as % of the active population	20%	12%

Education in the world	1980	1997
Public spending on education	3.9% of GDP	4.8% of GDP
Illiteracy among men older than 15	18%	32%

4.9 billion, or 80% of the population lives in a developing country

- 40% of the world's population does not have electricity - that totals about 2.5 billion people.
- 47% of the world's population lives on less than two U.S. dollars per day.
- The share of the 50 poorest countries in world trade has gone from 4% to 2% over the last decade (until 2000).
- 33% of children under the age of 5 suffer from malnutrition.
- One out of four adults is illiterate in the world.
- One out of five people in the world does not have access to modern healthcare.
- 95% of the people infected with AIDS live in developing countries.
- The foreign debt of developing countries has grown more than 6 times its amount since 1970, totaling 2.8 trillion dollars in 1999.

1.2 billion, or 20% of the population lives in an industrialized country

- Developed countries represent 86% of private expenditure consumption
- OECD countries share 67% of worldwide trade (7 trillion dollars).
- The total wealth of the 200 richest people is 1.14 trillion dollars.
- The unemployment rate is at an historic low, around 4%.

One out of ten U.S. dollars was invested into ethical funds in the United States in 2000, that is 13% of invested money.

Fact: life is possible because of air, land and water. Note: they are in danger, therefore we are threatened.

By Suffocation. Today, the atmosphere absorbs one third of the carbonic gases that we produce every year. The two thirds that remain build up and result in, through the greenhouse effect, an off-balance climate that generates natural disasters (floods, storms, droughts, fires, etc.)

- The use of fossil fuels has multiplied by 5 in 50 years. Oil consumption has multiplied by 8 (today we use in 1.5 months the amount of oil that we used in 1 year in 1950).
- Carbonic gas emissions in 1990: 3.3 tons/inhabitant in 1996 : 4.0 tons/inhabitant
- Consumption of electricity in 1990: 1,928 Mwh/inhabitant in 1999: 2,053 Mwh/habitant
- The production of wind energy multiplied by ten between 1990 and 2000, becoming 1% of the energy produced in the world in 1999.

By food shortage. Land suitable for cultivation is a limited resource. There is less and less land for more and more inhabitants (every year, the equivalent of 10 French departments turn into desert). As a result, growing land per inhabitant has been cut in two in 50 years. The resources allocated to agriculture in poor countries is too little to compensate for this evolution, which causes famines (in 2000, one third of the world's children younger than 5 suffered from malnutrition).

Evolution of land in the world	1980	1996
Lands permanently being farmed	0.9%	1.0%
Irrigated land	17.8%	19.2%
Arable land	0.24 ha/hab	0.24 ha/hab
Number of tractors for a thousand agricultural workers	18	20
Paved roads	39% of total	43.1% of total

One person in France produces 350 kg of household waste in one year (that is, 1 kg per day).
One person in the United States produces 700 kg of household waste in one year (that is, 2 kg per day).
Almost half of the 17,000 natural reserves in the world are currently being used for agricultural purposes.

By water wars. The quantity of water available per inhabitant has gone down more than 30% since 1970. Today, more than ten conflicts in the world are linked to water: in Turkey, India, Egypt, Israel, and other countries. The number of people that do not have access to drinkable water has multiplied by four over the past decade, totaling 1 billion people in 2000.

Distribution of water consumption in the world

- One person in France consumes between 150 and 250 liters of water per day. Only 2 liters of this is used for drinking. Therefore, less than 0.5% of the water treated for drinking is in fact drunk.
- The average Kenyan uses 4 liters of water per day.
- One person in New York consumes 680 liters per day.

Evolution of water consumption in the world

Multiplied by 7 since 1900 and by 5 since 1940 (while the population doubled).
Worldwide resources for non-saltwater in 1990: 8,000 m³ per inhabitant.
Minimum necessary per inhabitant: 1,000 m³/year.
Less than 10% of the world's cities have purification facilities (used water treatment).

Use of non-saltwater in the world

- 70% for agriculture (irrigation, three quarters of which evaporates).
- 22% for industry.
- 8% for household use (50% of which is lost in pipe leaks).

Distribution of the availability of water in the world

Wettest areas: rainfall totaling 20 meters of water per year.
Driest areas: rainfall totaling 50 to 200 millimeters of water per year.

Why is there so much indifference?

One, because most of the deterioration over the last 30 years has occurred in southern countries, which seem far away to us - even if the consequences will affect us directly.

Two, because our way of approaching the environment still stems from a vision inherited from a time when the world's resources seemed endless.

Finally, because we are under the impression - unjustly - that we are helpless in the face of such a large problem. And yet, we can all take action: by reducing our unnecessary consumption and by putting pressure on companies and governments in order to develop a long-lasting system, one that meets the needs we have now, without sacrificing future generations.

The first solution is therefore to make people aware, and, because the environment doesn't come to people, to bring the environment to them.

This is Yann Arthus-Bertrand's approach. If we want our children to have a certain quality of life, and if we want to guarantee long-lasting development for ourselves, there will need to be an awakening - sometimes wonderful, sometimes worrisome.

Maximilien Rouer

Founder of BeCitizen.com, website for Développement Durable [Durable Development].

Note: each statistic has a source (sources: World Bank, PNUD [UNDP], PNUE [UNEP], UNESCO, WWF, UICN [IUCN], WorldWatch Institute, OECD, FAO, INSEE, World Health Organization, Unicef, Global Water Supply, UN, GIEC (Intergovernmental group of experts on the evolution of the climate), Worldwide organization of meteorology, ADEME). When two statistics about the same subject differed, the more moderate statistic was used.

DES CHIFFRES POUR LA TERRE

Notre richesse apparente repose sur la croissance économique, dont les indicateurs ne tiennent pas compte de l'état des ressources naturelles. Par exemple, déforester un pays est donc comptabilisé comme de la création de valeur.

Richesse mondiale	1990	1999
PIB mondial	21 millions de dollars (US)	30 millions de dollars (US)

Déboisement annuel entre 1990 et 1995 : 101 724 km², soit 20 % de la surface de la France

Or, depuis les années 1970, la richesse naturelle de la Terre a diminué d'un tiers sous la pression de l'homme.

Population mondiale	1980	1999
Population urbaine	40 %	46 %
Taux de mortalité des moins de 5 ans	123 %	75 % (1998)
Population des 15-64 ans	2,595 milliards	3,761 milliards (1990)
Population active	2,035 milliards	2,892 milliards
Femmes en % de la population active	39 %	41 %
Enfants de 10-14 ans en % de la population active	20 %	12 %

Éducation dans le monde	1980	1997
Dépenses publiques d'éducation	3,9 % du PNB	4,8 % du PNB

4,9 milliards, soit 80 % de la population habitent dans les pays en voie de développement

- 40 % de la population mondiale n'a pas l'électricité – soit environ 2,5 milliards de personnes.
- 47 % de la population mondiale vit avec moins de 15 francs par jour.
- La part des 50 pays les plus pauvres dans le commerce mondial est passée de 4 % à 2 % ces 10 dernières années (jusqu'en 2000).
- 33 % des enfants de moins de 5 ans souffrent de malnutrition.
- Un adulte sur 4 est illettré dans le monde (soit il n'a jamais appris à lire – analphabète – soit il a oublié).
- Une personne sur cinq dans le monde n'a pas accès à des services de soins modernes.
- 95 % des personnes infectées par le sida vivent dans les pays en voie de développement.
- La dette extérieure des pays en voie de développement a été multipliée par plus de 6 depuis 1970, atteignant 2,8 mille milliards de dollars en 1999.

1,2 milliard, soit 20 % de la population habite dans les pays développés

- Les pays développés représentent 86 % des dépenses privées de consommation.
- Les pays de l'OCDE se partagent 67 % du commerce mondial (7 mille milliards de dollars).
- La richesse additionnée des 200 personnes les plus riches atteint la valeur de 1,14 mille milliards de dollars.
- Le chômage est à son taux historique le plus bas, autour de 4 %.

Un dollar sur dix a été investi dans des Fonds éthiques aux États-Unis en 2000, soit 13 % de l'argent investi.

Une évidence : la vie est possible grâce à l'air, à la terre et à l'eau.

Un constat : ils sont en danger, donc nous sommes menacés :

Par manque d'air. Aujourd'hui, l'atmosphère absorbe un tiers du gaz carbonique que nous produisons chaque année. Les deux tiers restants s'accumulent et entraînent, par le biais de l'effet de serre, un déséquilibre climatique qui génère des catastrophes naturelles (inondations, tempêtes, sécheresses, incendies…).

- La consommation de combustibles fossiles a été multipliée par 4 en 50 ans. En particulier la consommation de pétrole a été multipliée par 7 (on consomme aujourd'hui en 6 semaines le pétrole que l'on consommait en 1 an en 1950).
- Émissions de gaz carbonique en 1990 : 3,3 tonnes/habitant en 1996 : 4 tonnes/habitant
- Consommation d'électricité en 1990 : 1,928 Mwh/habitant en 1999 : 2,053 Mwh/habitant
- La production d'énergie éolienne a été multipliée par dix entre 1990 et 2000, atteignant 1 % de l'énergie mondiale produite en 1999.

Par des crises alimentaires. Les terres cultivables sont une ressource limitée. Il y a de moins en moins de terres pour de plus en plus d'habitants (chaque année, l'équivalent de 10 départements français est transformé en désert). En conséquence, la surface céréalière par habitant a été divisée par deux en 50 ans. Les moyens consacrés à l'agriculture des pays pauvres sont trop faibles pour compenser cette évolution, ce qui déclenche des famines (en 2000, dans le monde, un tiers des enfants de moins de 5 ans souffraient de malnutrition).

Evolution des terres dans le monde	1980	1996
Terres sous cultures permanentes	0.9 %	1.0 % (1997)
Terres irriguées	17.8 %	19.2 %
Terres arables	0.24 ha/hab	0.24 ha/hab
Nombre de tracteurs par milliers de travailleurs agricoles	18	20
Routes revêtues	39 % du total	43.1 % du total (1998)

Le Français produit 350 kg de déchets ménagers par an (ou 1 kg par jour). L'Américain produit 700 kg de déchets ménagers par an (ou 2 kg par jour). Près de la moitié des 17 000 réserves naturelles dans le monde sont actuellement utilisées pour faire de l'agriculture.

Par des guerres de l'eau. La quantité d'eau disponible par habitant a baissé de plus de 30 % depuis 1970. Aujourd'hui, une dizaine de conflits sont liés à l'eau dans le monde : en Turquie, en Inde, en Égypte, en Israël… Le nombre de personnes n'ayant pas accès à l'eau potable a été multiplié par quatre ces dix dernières années, atteignant 1 milliard d'individus en 2000.

Répartition de la consommation de l'eau dans le monde
- Le Français consomme de 150 à 250 litres d'eau par jour, dont seulement 2 litres sont bus. Ainsi, moins de 0,5 % de l'eau traitée pour être potable est effectivement bue.
- Le Kenyan dispose quant à lui de 4 litres d'eau par jour.

- Le New-Yorkais consomme 680 litres par jour.

Évolution de la consommation d'eau dans le monde
Multipliée par 7 depuis 1900 et par 5 depuis 1940 (pendant que la population doublait).
Ressources mondiales en eau douce en 1990 : 8 000 m³ par habitant.
Minimum nécessaire par habitant : 1 000 m³/an.
Moins de 10 % des villes du monde possèdent une station d'épuration (traitement des eaux usées).

Utilisation de l'eau douce dans le monde
- 70 % pour l'agriculture (irrigation, dont les trois quarts s'évaporent).
- 22 % pour l'industrie.
- 8 % pour les usages domestiques (dont 50 % perdus en fuites dans les réseaux).

Répartition de la disponibilité de l'eau dans le monde
Régions les plus arrosées : 20 mètres d'eau de pluie par an.
Régions les moins arrosées : 50 à 200 millimètres d'eau de pluie par an.

Pourquoi tant d'indifférence ?
D'une part, parce que la majorité des dégradations de ces 30 dernières années sont localisées dans les pays du Sud, qui nous paraissent loin – même si les conséquences vont nous toucher directement. D'autre part, parce que notre façon d'aborder l'environnement repose encore sur une vision héritée de la période où les ressources de la planète paraissaient inépuisables. Enfin, parce que nous avons l'impression, à tort, d'être impuissants face à l'ampleur du problème. Pourtant, nous pouvons tous agir : en réduisant nos consommations superflues, et en faisant pression sur les entreprises et les gouvernements pour que s'impose un développement durable, qui réponde aux besoins de tous au présent sans sacrifier les générations futures. La première solution est donc de sensibiliser, et, puisque l'environnement n'atteint pas les gens, de faire venir l'environnement à eux.

C'est la démarche retenue par Yann Arthus-Bertrand. Il s'agit d'un éveil nécessaire - parfois merveilleux, parfois inquiétant - si nous voulons espérer transmettre à nos enfants une certaine qualité de vie, et nous assurer un développement durable.

Maximilien Rouer

Fondateur de becitizen.com, site internet au service du Développement Durable.

Note : chaque chiffre cité est documenté (sources : Banque Mondiale, PNUD, PNUE, UNESCO, WWF, UICN, WorldWatch Institute, OCDE, FAO, INSEE, World Health Organization, Unicef, Global Water Supply, UN, GIEC (groupe d'experts intergouvernemental sur l'évolution du climat), Organisation mondiale de météorologie, ADEME). Dans le cas où deux chiffres portant sur le même sujet étaient différents, la valeur la plus modérée a été retenue.

Toutes les légendes de ce catalogue sont extraites du livre « La Terre vue du ciel » paru aux Editions de la Martinière,
et ont été réactualisées par Anne Jankeliowitch du bureau de coordination de La Terre vue du ciel.
La traduction des légendes et des textes a été rendue possible grâce à la collaboration de Jacqueline André, Marta Gegúndez, Erika Gil, Valérie Juquois,
Christel Kopp et Arturo Vázquez Barrón, membres du Professional Translation and Research Centre (CPTI) au CCC-IFAL.

Les photographies aériennes de Yann Arthus-Bertrand sont diffusées par l'agence Altitude,
Tél. +33 (0)1 48 42 18 00 - Fax +33 (0)1 48 42 08 00
e-mail : altitude@club-internet.fr
www.yannarthusbertrand.com
Photos p.2 et p.208 : © Raphaël Gaillarde / Gamma - rabat : Antoine Verdet

F-GTGB